The Frankfurt School, Jewish I

The history of the Frankfurt School cannot be fully told without examining the relationships of Critical Theorists to their Jewish family backgrounds. Jewish matters had significant effects on key figures in the Frankfurt School, including Max Horkheimer, Theodor W. Adorno, Erich Fromm, Leo Lowenthal, and Herbert Marcuse. At some points, their Jewish family backgrounds clarify their life paths; at others, these backgrounds help to explain why the leaders of the School stressed the significance of antisemitism. In the post–Second World War era, the differing relationships of Critical Theorists to their Jewish origins illuminate their distinctive stances toward Israel. This book investigates how the Jewish backgrounds of major Critical Theorists, and the ways in which they related to their origins, affected their work, the history of the Frankfurt School, and differences that emerged among them over time.

Jack Jacobs is a professor of political science at John Jay College and the Graduate Center, City University of New York. He is the author of *On Socialists and "the Jewish Question" after Marx* (1992) and *Bundist Counterculture in Interwar Poland* (2009), and the editor of *Jewish Politics in Eastern Europe: The Bund at 100* (2001). Professor Jacobs was a Fulbright Scholar at Tel Aviv University in 1996–1997, and was also a Fulbright Scholar at the Vilnius Yiddish Institute in 2009. Dr. Jacobs's work has been translated into French, German, Hebrew, Italian, Japanese, Polish, Russian, and Yiddish.

The Frankfurt School, Jewish Lives, and Antisemitism

JACK JACOBS
*John Jay College and the Graduate Center
City University of New York*

CAMBRIDGE
UNIVERSITY PRESS

32 Avenue of the Americas, New York NY 10013-2473, USA

Cambridge University Press is part of the University of Cambridge.

It furthers the University's mission by disseminating knowledge in the pursuit of education, learning and research at the highest international levels of excellence.

www.cambridge.org
Information on this title: www.cambridge.org/9780521730273

© Jack Jacobs 2015

This publication is in copyright. Subject to statutory exception and to the provisions of relevant collective licensing agreements, no reproduction of any part may take place without the written permission of Cambridge University Press.

First published 2015
First paperback edition 2015

A catalogue record for this publication is available from the British Library

Library of Congress Cataloguing in Publication data
Jacobs, Jack, author.
The Frankfurt School, Jewish Lives, and Antisemitism / Jack Jacobs.
pages cm
ISBN 978-0-521-51375-3 (Hardback)
1. Institut für Sozialforschung (Frankfurt am Main, Germany) 2. Frankfurt School of sociology–History–20th century. 3. Jewish sociologists–Germany–Biography.
4. Sociology–Germany–History–20th century. 5. Antisemitism–Germany–20th century.
I. Title.
HM467.J33 2014
301.01–dc23   2014021016

ISBN 978-0-521-51375-3 Hardback
ISBN 978-0-521-73027-3 Paperback

Cambridge University Press has no responsibility for the persistence or accuracy of URLs for external or third-party internet websites referred to in this publication, and does not guarantee that any content on such websites is, or will remain, accurate or appropriate.

Contents

Acknowledgments		*page* vi
Introduction		1
1	Jewish Life Paths and the Institute of Social Research in the Weimar Republic	7
2	The Significance of Antisemitism: The Exile Years	43
3	Critical Theorists and the State of Israel	111
Conclusion		149
Notes		152
Bibliography		231
Index		258

Acknowledgments

I have received information, feedback, and good advice from many people in the years during which I have worked on this book. I am particularly grateful to Steven E. Aschheim, Shlomo Avineri, Marshall Berman, Monika Boll, Stephen Eric Bronner, Dan Diner, Lars Fischer, Peter-Erwin Jansen, Douglas Kellner, David Kettler, Richard King, Michael Lerner, Michael Löwy, Peter Marcuse, Yeshi Neumann, Yoav Peled, Uri Ram, Lars Rensmann, Zvi Rosen, Thomas Wheatland, Richard Wolin, and Eva-Maria Ziege, all of whom took the time to answer questions I posed or to comment on my ideas. I am also grateful to those, including Evelyn Adunka, Reinard Blomert, Jeremy Brown, Christian Fleck, Harvey Goldberg, Rachel Heuberger, Martin Jay, Rick Kuhn, Dafna Mach, Guy Miron, Elliot A. Ratzman, and Liliane Weissberg, who informed me of relevant source material, helped me to obtain such material, or provided me with copies of their own works prior to publication. My thanks to Patrizia Nobbe and Martin Riedl, who transcribed handwritten letters for me; to Asaf Shamis, who translated articles; and to Jason Schulman, who served, at one time, as my research assistant. Past and present staff members of the archives and libraries in Austria, Germany, Israel, and the United States where I conducted my research were consistently helpful. I remember with particular gratitude the trust placed in me by Gunzelin Schmid Noerr in the years during which he worked in the Stadt- und Universitätsbibliothek in Frankfurt am Main, and the friendly way in which I was received in Frankfurt, in later periods, by Mathias Jehn, Stephen Roeper, Jochen Stollberg, and others. Tobe Levin and her family served as my hosts in Frankfurt on several occasions. Their hospitality greatly facilitated my work. I also remember the hospitality of Rainer Funk, who welcomed me into his home while I was conducting research in the Erich-Fromm-Archiv in Tübingen, and who shared his insights on Fromm's life and thought with me. Toni Simon, similarly, invited me into her home, in Jerusalem, discussed with me matters pertaining to Erich Fromm, Leo Lowenthal, Ernst Simon, and others, and allowed me to make use of documents and letters in her possession. I thank Rainer Funk, Fromm's literary executor, for granting me permission to quote from unpublished letters written by Erich Fromm, and add here that all quotations from the letters of Erich Fromm in this work are used with the written permission of Dr. Funk. Similarly, my heartfelt thanks go to both Peter-Erwin Jansen and Susanne Löwenthal for granting me permission to make use of the Leo-Löwenthal-Archiv, which is located in the Archivzentrum of the Stadt- und Universitätsbibliothek in Frankfurt am Main, and for the permission they have granted me to cite and quote from specific materials by Leo Lowenthal.[1] I am equally thankful to Peter Marcuse for permission to quote from unpublished correspondence and other pieces by Herbert Marcuse. The permission of Peter Marcuse, executor of the Literary Estate of Herbert Marcuse, is required for any further publication of the letters and pieces from which I have quoted. As a condition for quoting from the Marcuse materials, I gladly add that supplementary material from previously unpublished work of Herbert Marcuse, now stored in the Stadt- und Universitätsbibliothek in Frankfurt, is being published by Routledge Publishers in a six-volume series edited by Douglas Kellner, and in a German series edited by Peter-Erwin Jansen published by zu Klampen Verlag, Germany, and that all rights to further publication are retained by the Estate. David Kettler generously granted permission for me to reprint, in Chapter 2, material by me that first appeared in a volume that David co-edited with Gerhard Lauer: *Exile, Science, and Bildung. The Contested Legacies of German Émigré Intellectuals* (New York: Palgrave Macmillan, 2005). I have tested my ideas before both academic and popular audiences in Australia, England, Germany, Israel, Lithuania, Scotland, South Africa, and the United States, and have benefitted from the comments and questions I received. I conducted some of the early research for this book while serving as a Fulbright Fellow in the Institute for German History at Tel Aviv University, and am grateful for the material support that my fellowship provided (as well as for the help of all those who worked for the Institute). I also received material support for portions of this project from the German Academic Exchange Service, the Lucius N. Littauer Foundation, the John Jay College Research Assistance

Fund, and the University Committee on Research Awards of the City University of New York. Their support made my research possible. Beatrice Rehl's confidence in my work enabled me to complete it. Anastasia Graf provided an enormous amount of editorial guidance. My partner, Susan Milamed, and our son, Mikhl Jacobs, indulged my insistence on tracking down source material far from our home. I owe them more than I can say.

Introduction

There is already a very large – and impressive – literature focused on the Frankfurt School, the Institute of Social Research (the institutional framework within which the Frankfurt School developed), or on particular members of the Institute. Key figures associated with the Frankfurt School, such as Theodor W. Adorno, Erich Fromm, Max Horkheimer, and Herbert Marcuse, have been the subject of any number of full-scale monographs.[1] Groundbreaking histories of the Frankfurt School, including books by Helmut Dubiel, Martin Jay, Rolf Wiggershaus, and Thomas Wheatland, have described and analyzed the School's genesis and development.[2] There is a significant body of scholarly literature centered not on the history of the Institute or on the lives of its members but on the sources, content, and importance of the Western Marxist–influenced approach that they created and embraced, which has come to be known as Critical Theory.[3] Why, then, write yet another work on these thinkers and their thought?

It is the intent of this book to demonstrate that the Jewish origins of key members of the Frankfurt School, and the differing ways in which the Critical Theorists related to their origins, shed light on the development of the School, on specific works written by its leading figures, and even on differences that emerged among these figures over time. It is manifestly the case that Critical Theory has multiple roots. I vigorously reject any attempt to explain Critical Theory per se solely, or even primarily, via biography. And yet, it is my contention that the history of the Frankfurt School – in the Weimar Republic, in exile, and in the decades following the Holocaust – cannot be fully told unless due attention is paid to the relationships of Critical Theorists in all three of these periods to their (Jewish) family backgrounds.

The Institute of Social Research was, of course, never an explicitly Jewish institution. Created in the city of Frankfurt am Main in 1923 by a decree issued by the Prussian Ministry of Culture, the Institute initially concerned itself primarily with such subjects as the labor movement, socialism, and economic history.[4] In the period beginning in 1931 during which Horkheimer served as the Institute's director – the era during which Critical Theory crystallized – the Institute was characterized first and foremost by a desire to promote interdisciplinary research on major questions. "Today...," Horkheimer proclaimed in his inaugural address, "all depends on organizing research around current philosophical problematics which, in turn, philosophers, sociologists, political economists, historians, and psychologists engage by joining enduring research groups in order to ... pursue their philosophical questions directed at the big picture with the finest scientific methods, to transform and to make more precise these questions as the work progresses, to find new methods, and yet never lose sight of the whole."[5] Hardly any of the articles published in the Institute's most important periodical, *Zeitschrift für Sozialforschung*, which first appeared in 1932, touched on explicitly Jewish subjects. While those who launched the Institute mentioned antisemitism[6] as an example of the kind of issue to which an institution dedicated to social research could devote itself when they conducted their initial negotiations with Hermann Weil (who was Jewish and who provided the Institute's endowment) and with the University of Frankfurt (with which the Institute was formally affiliated when it was created), these allusions to the need for studies of antisemitism seem to have been lures and disguises – designed, on the one hand, to attract funds, and, on the other hand, to deflect political criticism – rather than actual indications of the core interests of the Institute's founders.[7] The Institute per se did not devote sustained attention either to Jewish matters or to antisemitism during the Weimar years.

Nevertheless, the backgrounds of those affiliated with the Institute, and certain elements of the theory developed by the Institute's members, have led a number of commentators to inquire as to whether there may have been a connection between Jewish identity and affinity for the work of the Institute of Social Research.[8] Among those who were – in whole or part – of Jewish origin and who were formally associated with the Institute before its core members went into exile in 1932–1933 were Erich Fromm, Henryk Grossmann, Carl Grünberg (the Institute's first director), Julian Gumperz, Max Horkheimer, Leo Lowenthal, Friedrich Pollock, and Feliks J. Weil.[9] These men formed the overwhelming majority of those formally associated with the Institute in the Weimar Republic. There were, to be sure, individuals who were of non-Jewish origin affiliated, in a variety of ways, with the Institute before the Nazi *Machtergreifung*, such as Karl August Wittfogel[10] (a full-time research associate at the Institute beginning in 1925) and Paul Massing[11] (who began his dissertation, under Grünberg and at the Institute, in 1927). The number of such individuals, however, was rather small. Moreover, Massing, for one, eventually came to feel that his non-Jewish background was a factor preventing him from being fully accepted by what ultimately became the inner circle of Institute members.[12]

The preponderance of men of Jewish origin in the Institute of Social Research became particularly noticeable after 1930. Lowenthal was promoted to the rank of chief assistant in that year, alongside Grossmann, who held the same rank.[13] This was also the period during which Fromm became a member of the teaching staff of the Institute. While members of the Institute were definitely not chosen on the basis of their family backgrounds, all of the full members of the Institute in residence in Frankfurt and actively involved in its affairs in the period immediately preceding the Institute's relocation out of Germany – Horkheimer, Pollock, Grossmann, Fromm, and Lowenthal – were Jews.[14] The Leftist Jewish intellectuals attracted to the Institute had an elective affinity for others like themselves.

The ancestries and early lives of the most significant Critical Theorists have certainly been explored in the past. The studies of antisemitism written by members of the Institute of Social Research in the post-Weimar periods have also been repeatedly analyzed and critiqued.[15] I have benefitted enormously from my reading of works on this latter theme by sterling scholars, including Dan Diner, Martin Jay, Anson Rabinbach, and Lars Rensmann. However, I know of no work which grapples adequately with the variety of ways in which Jewishness and antisemitism impacted on the careers and thought of the first generation of Critical Theorists over the course of their lives. It is my intent to fill this gap.

Chapter 1 will focus on describing the backgrounds of the major members of the Institute of Social Research in the years immediately before the Nazi seizure of power, and the importance of these backgrounds. The differences in the families of Horkheimer, Pollock, Grossmann, Fromm, and Lowenthal notwithstanding, all five of these men had Jewish life paths. It is not my intent to demonstrate that the backgrounds of these five figures provide keys to explaining the works that they created in the Weimar years, nor is it my intent to demonstrate that the works of these writers which were produced in pre-Nazi Germany were infused with Jewish ideas. It *is* my intent to explore *how* these men arrived at the Institute, and to explain why I contend that all of them did so via recognizably Jewish roads.

In Chapter 2, I will demonstrate that a growing awareness of the importance of antisemitism in the period during which the members of the Frankfurt School were living in exile in the United States had a profound impact on the work of the School, and even, to some degree, on the development of Critical Theory itself. Both *Dialectic of Enlightenment* and *The Authoritarian Personality* – arguably the most important works associated with the Critical Theorists and written while they were in America – are deeply colored by the desire to elucidate and confront hatred of Jews. Indeed, neither of these two classic works can be understood without an understanding of how and why Horkheimer and Adorno (who was only partially of Jewish origin, and who had not been a full member of the Institute during the Weimar years) came to believe that explaining antisemitism was a crucial task. A growing fear that anti-Jewish sentiment was both dangerously strong in the United States and might grow stronger, and a dawning comprehension of the nature and implications of Nazi antisemitism – both of which were affected by their family backgrounds and their experiences – shaped the views of Horkheimer and Adorno during this period, and led to major alterations in their ideas. In addition, Adorno, who had not been involved in Jewish life while living in Germany, seems to have come, eventually, to think of himself as a Holocaust survivor, and even, to some extent, as a Jew. Though raised without a positive Jewish identity, Adorno's Jewish roots ultimately impacted his sense of himself and his analysis of the world in which he lived.

The final portion of this book will focus on the years following Horkheimer's return to Germany in 1950. The Institute of Social Research was re-established in Frankfurt after the defeat of the Nazis, and Horkheimer served as Director of the Institute in the early years of the Federal Republic of Germany. Pollock and Adorno, the latter of whom succeeded Horkheimer as Director of the Institute in 1958, also returned to Frankfurt after the Second World War, and maintained warm relationships with Horkheimer throughout this era. However, a substantial portion of those who had been closely associated with the Institute during the Weimar and/or exile periods – including individuals who had, at various points, been part of Horkheimer's inner circle, and who had played major roles in the creation of Critical Theory per se – did not maintain comparable ties with Horkheimer in the post-war decades. Fromm, Lowenthal, and Herbert Marcuse (who, like Adorno, had not been a member of the Institute during the years of the Weimar Republic, but who, like Adorno, became closely tied to the Institute during the Nazi years) each developed his own grievances with Horkheimer. These grievances were of very different kinds. The issues that ultimately separated Fromm, who parted ways with the Institute in 1939, Lowenthal, and Marcuse from Horkheimer had nothing to do with Jewish matters. But it is precisely by examining the attitudes of one-time members of the Horkheimer circle towards the State of Israel – an issue that had emotional resonance for key members of the Frankfurt School – that I hope to shed new light on the range of opinion that emerged among the Critical Theorists over time. Horkheimer, Fromm, Lowenthal, and Marcuse ultimately arrived at their own, individual, attitudes towards Israel. These attitudes were intimately related to the (differing) relationships of these men to Jewishness and Judaism. Thus, by exploring the attitudes of these four one-time colleagues towards Israel, I hope to clarify how their relationships to their Jewish origins continued to have an impact on their thought and on the history of the Frankfurt School, not only early in their careers but also in their later years.

The "Jewish question" had markedly different content in Weimar Germany, in the years of the Third Reich, and in the decades following the end of the Second World War. For the Critical Theorists, history is marked by rupture, not by continuities.[16] And yet, in all three of these very different eras, Jewish matters had a significant effect, directly or indirectly, on key individuals who were, or had been, members of the Institute of Social Research. At some points, the Jewish family backgrounds of leading members of the Frankfurt School clarify their life paths. At other points, these backgrounds help us to understand the issues on which the leaders of the School chose to focus, and the content of some of their ideas. In the decades following the Second World War, the differing relationships of Critical Theorists to their Jewish origins help to explain their stances towards Israel, and the distinctive natures of their modes of analysis of that topic.

I hasten to ensure that my readers understand that I write not from the perspective of philosophy, but rather from that of the history of ideas. I do not intend either to explain or to critique Critical Theory as a whole. These tasks have been performed by superb scholars. I stand on the shoulders of giants, and see no need to rehearse their insights.

I do not believe that Critical Theory is a Jewish theory, any more than psychoanalysis is a "Jewish science." The latter assertion was a Nazi calumny. The former is deeply suspect. And yet, I intend to argue that the lives of key members of the Frankfurt School's founding generation are illuminated by situating these men in multiple contexts – including that of Jewish history.

Chapter 1

Jewish Life Paths and the Institute of Social Research in the Weimar Republic

In an introduction to a series of articles on prominent intellectuals of Jewish origin, Leo Lowenthal – who was associated with the Institute of Social Research beginning in 1926 – once commented:

> It is of no fundamental significance whether or not these persons were members of their religious communities or congregations. Nor is it decisive whether or not the topics to which these Jews devoted themselves were substantively Jewish. The great Jewish names of our epoch – Maimon and Heine, Börne and Moses Hess, Marx and Lassalle, Einstein and Freud, Landauer and Trotsky – are essentially not associated with specifically Jewish topics. It is for this reason that questions of biography take over the place of the evolution of questions within Judaism, so that this very substitution becomes one of the important problems of Jewish history.[1]

The better part of a century after the establishment of the Institute of Social Research, it is apparent that the Institute's key members, including Lowenthal, ought to be considered precisely as Lowenthal dealt with those in his pantheon. The pre-history of the Horkheimer circle is considerably clarified by examining its members' lives through a Jewish lens. Study of the biographies of the five full-time members of the Institute who were actually in residence in Frankfurt in the years immediately following Horkheimer's accession to the position of Director – Horkheimer, Pollock, Lowenthal, Fromm and Grossmann – demonstrates that each and every one of these men had distinctively Jewish life paths, and that these paths help to explain how and why they came to be associated with the Institute.

*

Max Horkheimer, who eventually became the single most powerful figure in the Institute,[2] was cognizant of and affected by his Jewish background. Born near Stuttgart in 1895, Horkheimer was raised in a somewhat observant household. Horkheimer's parents were members of Stuttgart's Jewish Community, and were described by Horkheimer as having been "strongly attached" to that Community.[3] The family abided by Jewish dietary laws when Horkheimer was a young child. However, the dietary laws ceased to be observed in the Horkheimer household not because of a growing secularization or assimilation on the part of the Horkheimer family, but because of a suggestion from Max's physician, when Max was around seven years old, that a change in Max's diet would improve his somewhat fragile health. Upon receiving instructions from Max's doctor to feed her son non-kosher food, tellingly, Max's mother, Babette Horkheimer, née Lauchheimer, contacted the family's rabbi – who told her to follow the doctor's advice.[4]

Max's father, Moses [Moritz] Horkheimer, who owned textile factories and who was a prominent businessman, attended synagogue services on the Sabbath.[5] Max reminisced, during a later period in his life, about the times when he had gone to such services together with his father.[6] Moses Horkheimer was also a "devoted member" of B'nai B'rith [Sons of the Covenant], a Jewish service organization, and participated in its events. Max once asserted that his father's affiliation with B'nai B'rith had been a "contributing determinant" of Max's youth.[7]

Horkheimer had a Bar Mitzvah in a synagogue in Stuttgart, and, it can be safely presumed, received at least as much of a Jewish education as would make possible his participation in that coming of age ceremony.[8] In general, the Horkheimer family continued to practice Judaism during Max's childhood years, though not in a strictly Orthodox manner. According to Max, his family had been "neither Orthodox nor Liberal," but rather somewhere in between the two in its religious practices.[9] The provisions of Jewish law were adhered to "as far as possible," Horkheimer has noted, though not as "pedantically" as was the case in Orthodox circles. Like most Jews in Germany of his generation, Moses Horkheimer could aptly be described as a patriotic German citizen of the Jewish faith. Max, in turn, was raised to think of himself as Jewish by religious affiliation, and to think of Germany as his homeland.[10]

When he was sixteen years old, Max met Friedrich Pollock, who became a life-long friend. Pollock, who was born in Freiburg in 1894, was closely tied to the Institute from the time of its foundation in Frankfurt in 1923, and wrote primarily on economic issues in the Weimar years.

Like Horkheimer, Pollock was of Jewish origin, was the son of a businessman, and was initially expected by his father to eventually take over the family business. Friedrich Pollock's parents, however, were far more acculturated than were Horkheimer's. Indeed, according to Horkheimer, Pollock's father "belonged to those assimilated Jews, who transformed their unease [with Jewishness] into a certain negative attitude towards Jews."[11] As a result, Pollock, unlike Horkheimer, was not raised with a Jewish consciousness. Indeed, Pollock was raised to disdain Judaism.

Pollock's attitude towards Jewish matters was known to Horkheimer as early as 1911, which was the year during which Horkheimer and Pollock first became friends. In the fall of that year, Horkheimer invited Pollock to participate in a dance class for young members of the Jewish community. Pollock declined the invitation, on the grounds that he suspected "cliques" of all sorts, whatever the basis for their formation[12] – a response, it is worth noting, which apparently surprised Horkheimer. While Pollock ultimately acceded to Horkheimer's repeated requests that he give the class a chance, Pollock attended only once, and never returned.

Pollock's indifference to Judaism and Jewish life apparently made an impression on the young Horkheimer. The latter's eventual rebellion against his parents, seemingly encouraged by Pollock, included, at one point, rebellion against his family's observance of (specific) Jewish rituals.

Horkheimer's rebellion also manifested itself, from 1916 onwards, in Horkheimer's romantic involvement with a non-Jewish woman, Rose Christine Riekher. While Riekher's background and economic status – she was the daughter of a bankrupt, one-time hotel proprietor and worked as a private secretary to Moses Horkheimer when Max first came to know her – seems to have predisposed Moses against his son's girlfriend, the fact that Riekher was not Jewish particularly distressed Max's mother.[13] Max Horkheimer's relationship with Riekher led to years of estrangement between Max and his parents. "It was apparently much harder," Martin Jay concludes, "for his parents to get used to the idea that Horkheimer was marrying a gentile than that he was becoming a revolutionary."[14]

Horkheimer's serious involvement with a non-Jewish woman, and the tension that this involvement caused between Horkheimer and his parents, however, should not be taken as indicating that Horkheimer ceased to worry about matters affecting the Jewish community after 1916. He was, for example, as Zvi Rosen has demonstrated, concerned with antisemitism even in his earliest writings, which date from the period of the First World War.[15] I do not mean to suggest that Horkheimer's concern with antisemitism was the result of his having been scarred by this phenomenon in his childhood. He reports that the existence of antisemitism was mentioned in his parents' household and that rude youngsters sometimes shouted "Jew" at him as he walked home from school, or, somewhat more rarely, when he was in class. But Horkheimer insisted that these incidents did not leave any "great wounds."[16] "He did not recall any of his teachers being anti-Semitic, and the occasional prejudiced remarks he heard from his schoolmates he dismissed as a sign of their envy."[17] Why then did Horkheimer manifest concern about antisemitism in his First World War writings? Abromeit suggests that "Horkheimer was probably confronted with overt anti-Semitism during his period of military service," which took place in the course of that war, and cites, in support of this idea, a letter by Horkheimer written in August 1917 in which Horkheimer, while describing his return to military service following a leave, notes "I was regarded with spiteful apprehension because I am Jewish."[18]

Horkheimer's experiences in the German military do in fact help to explain his apparent concern with antisemitism in the era in question – a concern which is evident in several pieces. In July 1917, for example, Horkheimer wrote a sketch entitled "Jochai," which revolves around a young Jew who had been ordered to execute the daughter of a general, and which contains a prescient passage in which a mob, while screaming "Vengeance! Vengeance!" sets on fire "the house of wealthy Jews," and in which, despite the "pale corpses" that result from its actions, the mob is not satiated.[19] Horkheimer returned to the theme of antisemitism several months later, at the beginning of November 1917, in his short story "Gregor." In one scene, a street agitator, addressing a vast crowd, rhetorically asks for whom those in the crowd and their families have sacrificed in the course of the war, and replies to his own question by underscoring that those responsible were "Not even people of our own clan, not even people of our own faith, not Germans, not Christians: *Jews* are responsible for everything; *Jews* pocket the profit from our wounds; the same villains that struck our Lord on the cross – Down with the Jews!"[20] Horkheimer, in these passages, is clearly worried about antisemitism. Julius Carlebach's conclusion, apparently resting not on "Jochai" or "Gregor" but rather on altogether different, and somewhat later, work, that Horkheimer's "early writings on the Jews" reflect a feeling on Horkheimer's part that his "Jewish origins were an embarrassment and a handicap," therefore, is not supported by the currently available evidence.[21]

Horkheimer's concern with antisemitism did not disappear during the Weimar years. Moreover, though Horkheimer's Marxism colored his analysis during much of that period, Martin Jay's description of Horkheimer's position, in a piece first published by Jay in 1979, as characterized by a "facile dismissal of specifically Jewish problems" is overly harsh.[22] Jay's appraisal of Horkheimer's position is based primarily on a passage in Horkheimer's *Dämmerung* (which was written before 1931, but which first appeared in print in 1934). The passage reads:

> Jewish capitalists become terribly excited about anti-Semitism. They say that what they hold most sacred is under attack. But I believe that their unspeakable annoyance merely comes from the fact that something about them is being threatened which yields no profit, yet cannot possibly be changed. If present-day anti-Semitism were directed against religious belief and not 'the blood,' a great many of those who now show the most profound indignation about it would renounce this thing they 'hold most sacred' 'with a heavy heart.' As the material base of ghetto life was left behind, the willingness to sacrifice life and property to one's religious belief also became a thing of the past. Among bourgeois Jews, the hierarchy of goods is neither Jewish nor Christian but bourgeois. The Jewish capitalist brings sacrifices to power, just like his Aryan class colleague. He first sacrifices his own superstition, then the lives of others, and finally his capital. The Jewish revolutionary in Germany is not different from his 'Aryan' comrade. He commits his life to the liberation of man.[23]

Horkheimer does not dismiss Jewish problems in this passage. He does harshly criticize the hypocrisy of [certain] bourgeois Jews. There were in fact many individuals of Jewish descent in the German *Kulturbereich* who had, in earlier eras, sloughed off their Judaism in the hope that this would make it possible for them to succeed in German society. Baptism, as Heine put it, was seen as "the entrance ticket to European culture." Grünberg, the Institute's first director, for example, had formally converted to Roman Catholicism in 1892, apparently in order to advance his career. However, the rise of racial antisemitism had foreclosed this option, and made it necessary for Jews who may otherwise have converted, and had no intrinsic interest in Jewish affairs, to protest against antisemitism. The passage from *Dämmerung* cited by Jay was meant by Horkheimer to stress that the tears of certain German Jewish capitalists were crocodile tears. It was not meant to suggest that Jewish fears were altogether unfounded.

Horkheimer himself later asserted that he was already aware that antisemitism was a threat that needed to be addressed, and attempted to act on that awareness, in the year during which he became Director of the Institute. "As early as 1930 when I still was in Frankf[u]rt," Horkheimer wrote in 1944, "I became aware of the gravity of the problem of anti-Semitism, which even then was a real menace in Germany and in the rest of the world. At that time, I tried to convince outstanding leaders of community life in Germany, in France, and in other countries of its seriousness."[24] In later years – that is to say, after Horkheimer had gone into exile in the United States – Horkheimer's sense that antisemitism was a very serious problem that needed to be addressed increased markedly, and led him to devote substantial portions of the Institute's resources to that issue. Significantly, Horkheimer's analysis of antisemitism during his American years – which I'll discuss in the next chapter – which suggested that the phenomenon had irrational, political, and religious roots, echoed themes already apparent in his early works of fiction cited above.

His upbringing notwithstanding, Horkheimer was by no means a practicing Jew in the brief period between his accession to the Directorship of the Institute of Social Research and his flight from Germany. In all likelihood, the Horkheimer of 1930 would have heatedly rejected as wholly unwarranted the suggestion that there were similarities between his ideas at that time and those of Judaism (and, in that pre-Critical Theory period, there were precious few if any such similarities). But no less a commentator than Leo Lowenthal has stressed that "in his thinking [Max Horkheimer] was always very conscious of the Jewish heritage."[25] That is to say, Horkheimer did not consciously make use of Jewish religious ideas as, in the 1930s, he brought into being the program which resulted in the emergence of the Frankfurt School. He was, on the other hand, fully aware of his Jewish family background, and of the rise of antisemitism, even during that period.

*

Lowenthal, born in Frankfurt in 1900, who ultimately was best known for his work on sociology of literature, was far more intimately involved with Jewish affairs in the period immediately preceding his initial involvement with the Institute in 1926 than Horkheimer had ever been. Lowenthal's paternal grandfather, Mendel (1830–1904), lived a strictly Orthodox lifestyle, and taught at the *Realschule* of the Israelitische Religionsgesellschaft [Jewish Religious Community] of Frankfurt, a neo-Orthodox grouping molded by Rabbi Samson Raphael Hirsch.[26] Leo's father, Victor Löwenthal (1864–1942), attended the school in which Mendel taught, and lived in accord with Orthodox Jewish law throughout his childhood years. Victor remained Orthodox during his first years in a non-Jewish *Gymnasium*, continued to study Hebrew during those years, and was a member of a club made up of Orthodox youth who were pupils in the *Gymnasium*.[27] As a university student, Victor moved away from Orthodox practice, but continued to observe the laws of kashrut.[28] Ultimately, however, Victor came to feel that the Jewish rules and regulations which he had been taught to live by were of no meaning to him. He completely rejected not only Jewish dietary laws but also all other manifestations of Orthodoxy, and indeed of Jewish religious tradition. Victor, a doctor, believed in science, and in materialism.[29] Like a number of other German citizens of Jewish origin living in the late nineteenth and early twentieth centuries, he apparently came to see Judaism per se as relevant to the past, not the future, and seems to have been eager to assimilate himself and his family into the larger non-Jewish society in which he lived. He raised Leo in a secular, and anti-religious, manner.

To be sure, Leo lived, as a child, in circles made up mostly of Jews. Indeed, the social circle of Leo's parents was limited, by and large, to Jews.[30] This latter fact is of some consequence, and suggests that Victor – like other German Jews of his class and generation – was not quite as integrated into German society as he yearned to be. Gershom Scholem reports, on the basis of his own experience and that of his friends, that many German Jews of Victor's era found that they had little or no social contact with non-Jews.[31] Hannah Arendt comments, writing about the intellectuals among the Central European Jews of that time, that "their own Jewishness, which played hardly any role in their spiritual household, determined their social life to an extraordinary degree and therefore presented itself to them as a moral question of the first order."[32] Leo himself notes simply that "many of my classmates and most of my friends were Jews."[33] In fact, in the first two decades of the twentieth century, between twenty and thirty per cent of the pupils in the Wöhlerschule, a school in Frankfurt's Westend neighborhood attended not only by Leo Lowenthal but also by Erich Fromm and Felix Weil, were Jewish.[34] If most of Lowenthal's childhood friends were Jewish, his friends were members of a very specific subset of the pupils with whom he came into contact on a day-to-day basis.

But Lowenthal was apparently unaware of the *meaning* of his Jewish family background in the years during which he attended school. "I hardly knew anything about Judaism" as a child, Leo once noted "…I still remember when they divided us up for 'obligatory' religious instruction in sixth grade. When the teacher told the Protestants to gather in one part of the classroom, the Catholics in another, and the Jews in a third, I remained seated – I really didn't know what religion I belonged to!"[35] Though he knew enough to know that simply walking on Frankfurt's Kiesstraße, which was very close to where he lived as a child, could well subject him to antisemitic taunts, he didn't take the matter very seriously. Lowenthal's experience with antisemitism in Frankfurt in his childhood years was quite similar to that of Horkheimer.

But Lowenthal's sense of his own Jewishness, like Horkheimer's sense of the extent of antisemitism, may well have been fanned by his service in the German military during the First World War. Upon graduation from *Gymnasium* in 1918, Lowenthal was drafted. Unlike others of his social class, who, through discreet bribes and other means, succeeded in minimizing many of the inconveniences of army life, Lowenthal simply reported to a railway regiment made up overwhelmingly of men of peasant and working class origin. Lowenthal did not fit in, and "experienced the potential anti-Semitism and anti-intellectualism of the German proletariat and peasants."[36] Lowenthal was mocked constantly. His experience was so grim that he volunteered for the front in a desperate attempt to escape his tormentors. In a revealing phrase, Lowenthal, decades later (and after the Nazi years), described this period of his life as "a kind of anticipatory concentration-camp experience."[37]

Ernst Simon, who, like Lowenthal, came from a highly acculturated milieu, who, like Lowenthal, had not been exposed to or involved with Jewish life as a child, and who, alongside Lowenthal, became actively involved in Jewish cultural and religious life after World War I, directly links the change of orientation that he underwent during that war to his experiences in the German army. "The massive antisemitism in the army of the Kaiser made it clear to me that I was not a German."[38]

Whether or not Lowenthal's consciousness of himself as a Jew (like that of his good friend Simon)[39] was raised by exposure to German antisemitism, the ideas of Hermann Cohen definitely had an impact on him.[40] Cohen was a leading neo-Kantian philosopher, and head of the Marburg school. While not accepting historical materialism, he praised the Social Democratic party, and influenced attempts – by Paul Natorp and others – to link Kantian and socialist ideas. He also wrote on Jewish themes, and taught regularly at the Berlin-based Lehranstalt für die Wissenschaft des Judentums [School for Judaic Studies] after he retired from Marburg.[41] Cohen believed that there was a close relationship between Jewish and German (i.e. Kantian) ideas, and asserted that Jews had a specific mission: "to prepare mankind for the reception of a new social spirit springing from Judaism's belief in monotheism."[42] In the summer semester of 1919, Lowenthal went to Giessen, where he was influenced by the approach of Walter Kinkel, a professor of philosophy at the University of Giessen who ultimately published a book on Cohen's work.[43] By the time that Lowenthal began to study at the University of Heidelberg, in 1920, he was "committed to the Marburg neo-Kantian school of Hermann Cohen and Paul Natorp."[44]

Lowenthal was, as a young man, strongly attracted not only to Cohen's thought but also to oppositional movements. In the period from 1879 to 1914, a majority of German Jews supported left-liberal political parties, not radical or socialist movements.[45] This stance was rooted in the antisemitism of parties on the right, such as the Conservatives, the confessionalism of the Center Party,[46] and the sense among German Jews (many of whom were businessmen) that their economic interests would be hurt by socialist proposals put forth by the Social Democratic Party [SPD]. In the years immediately following the First World War, though the left-liberal parties were in decline in Germany, most German Jews were still firmly committed to liberal, democratic, political movements. Lowenthal, on the other hand, became, in 1919, a member of the Independent Social Democratic Party [USPD] (which had broken away from the SPD because of the latter's pro-war policy, and which, on the critically important issue of the day, thus stood further to the Left than did the SPD).

The USPD was, initially, substantially smaller than was the SPD. At the time of the German Revolution in November 1918 (which was opposed by the SPD and enthusiastically supported by the party with which Lowenthal had affiliated), the former had some 250,000 members countrywide, and the latter 100,000.[47] To be sure, the USPD attracted a substantial number of workers immediately thereafter, in part, it would appear, because of its advocacy of more radical positions, but it remained a smaller party than was the SPD throughout its (short) life. Indeed, in Frankfurt am Main, the USPD was a rather small entity, with some 800 members when the Revolution began.[48] Lowenthal, when choosing a political affiliation, chose the minority tendency.

Lowenthal chose, during this era, to affiliate with minority perspectives not only in political terms, but also within the Jewish world. Cohen rejected Zionism. Initially, so too did Lowenthal. Writing to his parents from Heidelberg in June 1920, Lowenthal commented on the recent deaths of Kurt Eisner, Gustav Landauer and Max Weber – who he described as "two Jews and ... a great philo-Semite."[49] These deaths led him to consider the roles which Eisner, Landauer, and other Jews had played, and on their fate: "Jews as intellectuals, as revolutionaries, as pioneers, all murdered!" If, Lowenthal reflected, referring to the Jewish population, it is our calling to be pioneers, announcers of a new spirit, trailblazers through revolution, than the thought arises as to whether our task would be better accomplished though a close-knit community. One can, he added, respond that this role would be even better accomplished through creation of "a new communal home" [eine neue gemeinschaftliche Heimat]. Is it, Lowenthal asked, no more than a coincidence that Landauer, Albert Einstein, and Martin Buber, among others, are Zionists? But, Lowenthal concluded "I am not – perhaps not yet – a Zionist. I am a seeker, a problematic person. I am not satisfied, and never satisfied, with a formula."

Only months thereafter, however, Lowenthal joined a Zionist student organization – the Kartell jüdischer Verbindungen [Federation of Jewish Fraternities], widely known as the KJV. At the time of its formation, in 1914, the KJV had described its purpose by proclaiming: "The K.J.V. strives to educate its members as men who will be conscious of the national unity of the Jewish people and are resolved to stand up for a renewal in Erez-Israel which will be worthy of its history."[50]

The number of German Zionists was growing in the period during which Lowenthal became affiliated with the Zionist students' movement. There were only 9,000 individuals in the Zionistische Vereinigung für Deutschland [Zionist Federation of Germany] in 1914, 20,000 members in 1920–1921, and approximately 30,000 in 1922–1923.[51] This increase in membership appears to have been due, at least in part, to the emergence of a new generation during the period in question. German Jews raised in the latter part of the nineteenth century had fiercely embraced their Germanness. Hermann Cohen proclaimed "We love our Germanness..., not only because we love our homeland as a bird loves its nest, [but because]... we have drawn our intellectual culture... from the treasures and mines of the German spirit... we German Jews feel ourselves integrated as Jews and as Germans..."[52] But German Jews of the younger generation were more likely to question the ideology of assimilation than were their parents. Direct experience with antisemitism in the ranks of the German military by younger Jews who served during the First World War (like that experienced by Lowenthal and Simon), a more widespread rise of antisemitism during that war, and a decline in the power of non-Jewish German liberalism, may have contributed to this phenomenon, and, in some cases, helps to explain new-found interest in Zionism.

But there can be no doubt that Zionism remained very much a minority tendency among German Jewry in the early 1920s, and that it was sharply opposed by the largest German Jewish organizations. Just as Lowenthal was taking an oppositionist stance by affiliating with the

Independent Social Democratic Party, so too was he flaunting his oppositionism by becoming a member of the KJV. Gershom Scholem reports that the growing sympathy for Zionism on the part of certain younger German Jews led to bitter disputes in many families. "The reason," Scholem explains, "was clear. To question the German identity of German Jews – and this was exactly what my generation was doing between 1910 and 1920 – was not regarded as purely theoretical dialectics but as a personal provocation and a destructive attack against something held taboo."[53] Whereas men like Victor Lowenthal – and most German Jews of his day – were likely to embrace Germanness, and likely to consider their Germanness as an essential element of their being, Zionists were putting in question the extent to which Jews in Germany were actually German. Most German Jews, whether Orthodox or Liberal, thought that being Jewish was a matter of religious affiliation. Zionists, on the other hand, suggested that Jews were not merely a religious group but a nation. As a result, in or around 1920, identifying with Zionism was seen by many of the most powerful leaders of German Jewry – and by the bulk of German Jewry – as undermining the acculturation at which they aimed.

By joining the KJV, therefore, Lowenthal was placing himself outside the German Jewish mainstream, which yearned to be thought of as German by the non-Jewish German population. The major organization of German Jewish university students at that time was the Kartell-Convent der Verbindungen deutscher Studenten jüdischen Glaubens [Federation of Fraternities of German Students of the Jewish Faith], which was ideologically sympathetic to the Centralverein deutscher Staatsbürger jüdischen Glaubens [Central Association of German Citizens of the Jewish Faith], (the strongest German Jewish organization), known as the CV.[54] The CV was assimilationist, liberal, and non-Zionist in its orientation, and bourgeois in its composition. From Lowenthal's perspective, it was also a fellow traveler of German nationalism.

Lowenthal wrestled with the decision as to whether or not to join the KJV over a period of weeks, and definitively decided to do so in September 1920. He reported to Simon at that time on his thought process, asking, rhetorically, "Is the fact that I am not altogether convinced that to be a Zionist means to want Palestine an objection? No! To be a Zionist means to be a Jew..." It means, Lowenthal continued, becoming aware of the problem created by discord between "blood- and state- affiliation ... awareness of this tragedy and striving for a solution. It is not the solution but the task that makes the Zionist. In that sense

I am a Zionist. If I am also a Zionist in another sense: on that point I am not altogether clear. But this much I see clearly: my Zionism is a step to the overcoming of the 'metaphysical cowardliness' of our times." In addition, Lowenthal added that his acceptance of Zionism was linked to a "will that longs for the transcendent Messianic Community" and was thus "the first step to God" – noting that in order to understand just what he meant, Simon would have to wait until they were both at home and able to talk about the matter face to face.[55] The "constellation of political radicalism, messianism, and Judaism" that Lowenthal once described as "characteristic of [Walter] Benjamin" was, for a period of years following 1920, just as characteristic of Lowenthal himself.[56] Late in life, Lowenthal provided another explanation for his 1920 attachment to Zionist ideas that he had at the time that that attachment had occurred. In an interview published in 1989, Lowenthal proclaimed "[my] engagement with Zionism – and precisely with a socialist version of Zionism – was connected to the fact that I was a radical, and that I wanted to marry my communistic-revolutionary way of thinking with a messianic and in that sense probably Zionist way of thinking...."[57]

A statement signed by Lowenthal, Simon, Fromm, and two other like-minded young Zionists and published in the *Jüdische Rundschau*, the most important German Zionist newspaper, reveals Lowenthal's orientation and concerns during his Zionist period.[58] The statement was written in the context of discussions between the KJV and a Jewish youth movement, the Jüdischer Wanderbund Blau-Weiss [Jewish Hiking Association Blue-White], which, as its name suggested, devoted itself to activities such as hiking, not to higher education. Blau-Weiss was, in other words, a German Jewish version of the (non-Jewish) German Wandervögel [Ramblers] movement.[59] A convention of KJV members assembled in Berlin at the end of December 1922, and endorsed a fusion between their organization and Blau-Weiss.[60] But not all those in the KJV were in favor of this step – and many of the adherents of the KJV in Frankfurt were opposed.[61] The Frankfurt opposition argued that the members of Blau-Weiss were incapable of infusing their movement with "Jewish content".

The statement of which Lowenthal was a signatory reflects misgivings about the youth movement. It began by asserting that the Zionist youth movement in Germany had, since its beginnings, been characterized by complete intellectual anarchy, and had, therefore, repeatedly shifted from one perspective to the next. This, the authors proclaimed, had been caused by lack of knowledge of the essence of the Jewish people. The Zionist idea had come into being among assimilated Jews, who had forgotten about the Diaspora. These assimilated Jews failed to realize that the Jewish nation was constructed in an altogether different manner than was the European nation, and denied thereby the sense of all Jewish history up until that point in time. The Prophets, the masters of the Kabbalah, and the leaders of Chassidism had been made into strangers among their own people. The national Jewish youth movement had made a fundamental error: It had destroyed the bridges between generations. Return to a national community, the authors insisted, is only possible if the Jewish youth as a whole strive to learn the Bible, and the Jewish nation's language, literature, form and song. "We will ... have to speak about how we will once again move the Sabbath, which was always in the center of the life of our people, back into the center of our communal life."[62] The statement culminates with the following declaration: "Only a unified people can live. The rip that today goes through the Jewish people, such that two manifestations of the Jewish soul, the Chalutz [Zionist pioneer] and the Chassidic Rebbe, no longer understand each other, must disappear."[63] Thus, by 1922, Lowenthal's Zionism was one which was infused with commitment to Jewish learning and tradition.

Leo Lowenthal does not explicitly report on the response by his father to his having become a Zionist. It is highly likely, however, that Victor objected to Leo's affiliation. "For the [German] Jews of" Leo's generation, Arendt notes "the available forms of rebellion were Zionism and Communism, and it is noteworthy that their fathers often condemned the Zionist rebellion more bitterly than the Communist. Both were escape routes from illusion into reality, from mendacity and self-deception to an honest existence."[64] Moreover, whatever Victor may have thought of his son's support for Zionism, it is clear that Leo Lowenthal despised the mainstream CV, and was attracted to the Zionist students whom he encountered, at least in part, because of their oppositional position vis-à-vis the CV.

Indeed, the common thread uniting the diverse aspects of Lowenthal's political, cultural, and personal stance during the 1920s was that each of these aspects was oppositional. Lowenthal was attracted throughout this period to everything his father, and those like his father, would be likely to oppose: "My parents' home symbolized, so to speak, everything I didn't want – bad liberalism, bad enlightenment, and two-sided morality."[65] Thus, like many well-born German Jewish intellectual males of his generation, Lowenthal identified with that which his father opposed.

In some cases, conflict by young German Jewish men with their fathers manifested itself in Jewish self-hatred.[66] In others, including that of Horkheimer, it was apparent in the embrace of radical political ideas by the sons of successful Jewish businessmen.[67] In Lowenthal's case, however, as in those of Franz Rosenzweig and Gershom Scholem, generational conflict was underscored partially by enthusiastic endorsement by the younger generation of precisely those elements of Jewish identity that their bourgeois, assimilated fathers rejected. "The natural route of modern German Jewry, as it appeared to Georg Rosenzweig and Arthur Scholem, was a path that led away from Judaism (without officially renouncing it) and straight into German society."[68] Victor Löwenthal, I suspect, shared their sense of the direction in which German Jewry was moving, and approved of this direction.

But just as Victor had earlier broken from the Orthodoxy of his father Mendel, so Leo, in turn, broke from Victor's assimilationist and liberal views not merely by becoming a left socialist, and not merely by becoming a Zionist, but also by enthusiastically embracing the Orthodoxy that his father had cast off. In so doing, Leo was part and parcel of a pattern quite evident among certain young German Jews of his time and place. While Victor manifested his disdain for Jewish religious tradition by ensuring that the Löwenthal family had a "particularly good dinner at home" on Yom Kippur[69] – a fast day, and the holiest day of the Jewish year – Leo expressed his new-found Jewish identity, which included an attraction to messianic and other religious ideas,[70] by becoming involved with the Frankfurt-based circle revolving around Rabbi Nehemiah Anton Nobel.

Nobel, who struck Erich Fromm as a charismatic "mystic in the Habad style,"[71] was born into a rabbinic family in Hungary in 1871, and was raised in Halberstadt.[72] After completing his studies in the Orthodox rabbinical seminary run by Esriel Hildesheimer in Berlin, he wrote a dissertation on Schopenhauer, and, somewhat later, also studied in Marburg with Hermann Cohen (with whom he became close friends). It may, in fact, well have been Nobel's ties to Cohen that explain Lowenthal's initial attraction to Nobel.

In certain respects, Lowenthal was likely to have been even more sympathetic to Nobel's ideas than he was to the ideas of Cohen. Unlike Cohen, Nobel was a Zionist. Indeed, Nobel was a founding member of the Mizrachi, a party within the Zionist movement made up of religiously observant Jews. There were very few Orthodox rabbis in Germany who publicly identified themselves as Zionists. On this matter, Nobel differed quite markedly from most of his peers.

After serving as a rabbi of a "secessionist" congregation in Leipzig, and as a communal rabbi in Hamburg, Nobel moved to Frankfurt in 1910 in order to take a position as rabbi of the Börneplatz synagogue. Nobel was strictly observant during his Frankfurt years (although he was uncomfortable with the label "Orthodox").[73] He was, however, also tolerant of others, and, while serving in Frankfurt, was strongly committed to preserving Jewish unity. This stance differentiated Nobel from the Orthodox secessionists with whom he had earlier been identified in Leipzig. However, his commitment to Torah-true Judaism also differentiated Nobel from the Reform Jews of Frankfurt. On some issues, therefore, Nobel stood outside (or between) these two wings of German Jewry.

Nobel is known to have reached out to Jews from a broad range of backgrounds. His open approach helps to explain why, after the First World War, Nobel attracted a significant number of Jewish intellectuals, including not only Lowenthal, but also Fromm, Ernst Simon, Martin Buber, Franz Rosenzweig, and Siegfried Kracauer.[74] Simon, for example, (characterized by Gershom Scholem as Nobel's "favorite student"),[75] is known to have studied with Nobel every morning from 8 to 10 at one point in his life.

Frankfurt am Main was (only) the second largest Jewish community in Germany, according to the census of 1925, and had a Jewish population far smaller in size than Berlin. While Berlin had a Jewish population of approximately 173,000 in the mid-1920s (the only post-First World War point for which reliable population figures are available), Frankfurt was home to fewer than 30,000 Jews. However, the proportion of the total population that was Jewish was somewhat higher in Frankfurt than in Berlin.[76] It was, moreover, Frankfurt and not Berlin that was the center of the neo-Orthodox movement, and Frankfurt that was the cradle of the German Jewish renaissance. Indeed, Nobel, who was characterized by "an unusual combination of talmudic learning, mystical leanings, and love for Goethe,"[77] was one of those who helped give rise to this renaissance.

Leo Lowenthal, reflecting late in his life on the circle around Nobel, once described it as something like a "cult community." Nobel, Lowenthal concluded, "represented a curious mixture of mystical religiosity, philosophical rigor, and quite likely also a more or less repressed homosexual love for young men."[78] When, in 1921, Lowenthal became seriously ill – he was diagnosed as having tuberculosis – Rabbi Nobel provided considerable spiritual and material support. Nobel wrote to Lowenthal regularly throughout the period of Leo's sickness and recuperation, during a substantial portion of which Lowenthal was in St. Blasien, in the Black Forest.[79] Immediately before Rosh Hashanah [the Jewish

New Year], in September 1921, at which time Nobel clearly wanted to bolster Lowenthal's spirits, Nobel told Lowenthal that he would be missed during the holiday, and that Nobel hoped to see him back in Frankfurt by Yom Kippur.[80] Ten days later, Nobel wrote that he greeted Lowenthal "with paternal feelings."[81] As an indication of how warmly he felt towards Leo, Nobel began one postcard to Leo from this period with the salutation "Mein Leochen!" – that is, with an affectionate diminutive version of Leo's name of the kind which a parent might use with a young child.[82]

In honor of Nobel's fiftieth birthday [November 8, 1921], his friends and students decided to issue a *Festschrift* – to which Lowenthal contributed an article (originally written for a seminar taught by Karl Jaspers in Heidelberg in 1920) entitled "The Demonic. Outline of a Negative Philosophy of History."[83] The piece, Lowenthal's first publication, argued that we live in a space "between paradise and the Messiah," a space, as Michael Löwy has put it, which is "without God and without redemption, a cold world handed over to despair."[84] But Lowenthal's piece ends with a reference to the downfall of demonology, and to beaming messianic light, and thus also indicates his yearning to end the condition in which the world found itself. In retrospect, Lowenthal recognized that his contribution was "a mix of Marxist theory, phenomenology, psychoanalysis, and religious-mystic-Jewish themes." From his perspective at that time, however, it "all seemed to go very well together."[85]

Nobel's death on January 24, 1922, was a great blow for Lowenthal.[86] He described the intensity of this blow in a piece published in *Der jüdische Student*, a periodical issued by the KJV. Lowenthal began his article with a quote from the Baal Shem Tov, the founder of Hasidic Judaism. He continued by noting that he was not prepared for Nobel's death: "This death struck me with the fury and suddenness of a huge cosmic event. No, like the collapse of the entire cosmos."[87] He compared Nobel to Goethe – very high praise indeed coming from a German Jew! – and described Nobel as a great Rabbi, a great Jew, and a great person.[88]

But Lowenthal's involvement with Jewish affairs was not ended by the death of Rabbi Nobel. It was, in fact, strengthened in the period immediately following that loss by Lowenthal's marriage, at the end of 1923, to Golde Ginsburg. Ginsburg, who was from Königsberg, had been raised in a "relatively orthodox" Jewish family and was a Zionist.[89] She had, at one time, been engaged to Erich Fromm.[90] Significantly, Lowenthal's father was none too pleased by Leo's choice, clearly fearing that Ginsburg was too Jewish, and would exert a bad influence on his son.

Upon hearing of Leo's engagement, Victor Löwenthal replied: "You're crazy! Königsberg, that's practically in Russia!" and point blank refused to attend his son's wedding ceremony.[91] Leo responded in turn by actualizing his father's worst fears: at the beginning of their marriage, Leo and Golde lived an Orthodox lifestyle, maintained a kosher kitchen, attended synagogue, and observed Jewish holidays.[92] To Leo's father, this "positive attitude toward Judaism" was "quite dreadful."[93] Leo reports that when he and Golde began to observe Jewish dietary laws in their home, his father "broke out in tears of anger."[94]

Lowenthal's romantic relationship with Ginsburg, which began in 1922, and his conscious or semi-conscious desire to act contrary to his father's wishes in any number of different ways, may help to explain his first job choice. In 1923, upon completion of his Ph.D. dissertation – which dealt with the social philosophy of Franz von Baader (1766–1841), a conservative Roman Catholic theologian and philosopher, to whom Lowenthal was attracted because of Baader's "radical critique of liberal society"[95] – Lowenthal accepted a position as "Syndic" of the Beratungsstelle für ostjüdische Flüchtlinge [Advisory Board for East European Jewish Refugees].[96] The Board, which was affiliated with the Berlin-based Arbeiterfürsorgeamt der jüdischen Organisationen Deutschlands [Workers' Welfare Agency of the Jewish Organizations of Germany],[97] attempted to help find work for some *ostjüdische* refugees, and provided material support to others. Lowenthal was responsible for "political affairs," including the "legal, political, and humanitarian" defense of those East European Jews who were in Germany, and for relations with relevant officials.[98] His office also served as an employment agency, helping to locate positions for East European Jews which would enable them to support themselves, and to create new positions where needed and where possible. In some cases, finally, Lowenthal located apprenticeships for those in need of training prior to employment.

For many German Jews of that era, including Leo's father, East European Jews were an embarrassment. Bourgeois German Jews of the generation of Lowenthal's parents were far more likely to put psychological distance between themselves and their East European counterparts than to identify themselves with them.[99] Referring to the Jews of Germany's capital city, Peter Gay once wrote "To distance themselves from the *Ostjuden* ... was, for Berlin's German Jews, an appeal to fellow-Germans for full acceptance, on the time-honored principle that two who despise the same outsider will not despise each other."[100] The same attitude was doubtless evident among bourgeois liberal Jews in Frankfurt am Main. Oscar Wiesengrund, the father of Theodor Adorno, when informed that Lowenthal had taken a position with the Advisory Board, pointedly stressed that "Lowenthal was not welcome in his house as long as he had something to do with Eastern European Jews."[101] Victor Löwenthal was also put off by the fact that his son's job brought him into contact with *Ostjuden*.[102] Here as elsewhere, Leo seems to have pointedly rejected the attitude of people like Oscar Wiesengrund, and, we can presume, his own father.

To be sure, Leo expressed a desire to leave his job shortly after beginning to work for the Advisory Board, but there is no evidence that this desire had anything at all to do with the views of Oscar Wiesengrund or of Victor Löwenthal.[103] He remained employed by the Advisory Board – albeit with a two month break in service at one point – until mid-1924.[104]

Lowenthal's social circle while he was working for the Advisory Board included a number of people affiliated with the Freie Jüdische Lehrhaus [Free Jewish House of Learning].[105] The Lehrhaus, animated by Franz Rosenzweig in 1920, fostered Jewish identity through adult education. The rise of the Lehrhaus was yet another manifestation of a turn among (some) German Jews away from assimilationism as an ideology. Most of those who taught in the Lehrhaus were not Zionists, but liberal German Jews.[106] But these individuals seem to have recognized that there were hard limits to the extent to which Jews had become integrated into German society, and, as a result, sought to create a community for themselves. Here as elsewhere, Lowenthal's attraction to a positive Jewish institution was a result of his need to distinguish himself from his father.[107]

Rosenzweig pithily described the orientation of the Lehrhaus as "non-specialist, non-rabbinical, non-polemical, non-apologetic, universalist in content and spirit."[108] He deliberately encouraged intellectual Jews who had grown up in acculturated surroundings but who were interested in exploring Jewish issues – such as Ernst Simon and Lowenthal – to teach at the Lehrhaus, and was extremely successful in attracting both teachers and students. At its height, during its fourth year of operation, the Lehrhaus enrolled eleven hundred students (the equivalent of four percent of the Jews living in Frankfurt at that time).[109] Most of those in Nobel's circle cooperated with the Lehrhaus, and many members of that circle taught in the Lehrhaus at one time or another. In addition to studying at the Lehrhaus (in a group led by Gershom Scholem), Fromm, for example, taught on Karaism in 1922–1923, and gave an advanced course centered on Rashi's commentary on Exodus in the summer of 1923.[110] Lowenthal gave a course entitled "On the Periphery of Jewish History" during the academic year 1925–1926.[111] When Jews in the city of Wiesbaden, imitating those in Frankfurt, created a Lehrhaus of their own, Lowenthal also participated in its activities, delivering a lecture on Buddha in January 1928 as part of a series devoted to major religious figures (including Moses, Jesus, Mohammed, and Luther).[112]

In the early 1920s Lowenthal had had good relations with Rosenzweig and had been "a frequent visitor" to Rosenzweig's home.[113] However, a dispute between Franz Rosenzweig and Lowenthal's close friend Siegfried Kracauer (1889–1966), who had not only been an admirer of Rabbi Nobel, but who had also been involved in the Lehrhaus,[114] created a rift between Lowenthal and Rosenzweig that was only patched up near the end of Rosenzweig's life. The dispute in question arose in the wake of the publication of a translation of Genesis directly from Hebrew into German that had been prepared by Martin Buber and Rosenzweig.

Both the context in which this translation was prepared and the deeper meaning of the controversy raised by this project have been expertly discussed by Martin Jay.[115] We have already noted that German Jews of Victor Löwenthal's generation had often embraced acculturation, that the largest organization of Jews in Germany at the beginning of the twentieth century had had a liberal, assimilationist, orientation, and that the non-Jewish German liberal movement declined markedly in the wake of the First World War. As it declined, some German Jews began to search for alternatives. The Buber/Rosenzweig translation was a major manifestation of this search. Whereas Jews like Victor Löwenthal seemingly believed and hoped that the future would bring a full and complete assimilation of Jews into German society, Buber and Rosenzweig stood firmly for the continued existence of Jewry, and hoped to foster knowledge of Judaism and Jewish-related matters.

The Buber/Rosenzweig translation appeared late in 1925, under the title *Das Buch im Anfang*, and was characterized by its attempt to provide both as literal a translation of the original text as possible and one which would preserve the rhythm and sounds of the Hebrew language.[116] In so doing, the translators made use of a Hebraized German, and deliberately avoided commentary. The distinctive language used by Buber and Rosenzweig was apparently intended to foster a growing sense among German Jews that they were culturally distinct.[117]

In April 1926, Kracauer published a sharply critical review of the Buber/Rosenzweig translation in the *Frankfurter Zeitung*, the newspaper by which he was employed, and for which he regularly wrote on cultural matters (and sometimes on matters related to Jews).[118] Kracauer asserted that thanks to the historical context in which Luther had produced his Bible, "the revolutionary protest against church abuses (which were also socioeconomic abuses) found precise expression" in Luther's work. Luther's translation of the Bible "was a weapon meant to impede the 'papist' employment of the vulgate."[119] On the other hand, the Buber/Rosenzweig translation "lacks topical relevance," and had privatizing and reactionary implications.[120] It did not address the actual situation of contemporary Jews, but was merely "a flight into an ideological pseudo-alternative."[121] The language of the Buber/Rosenzweig Bible was reactionary. It gave off "[t]he stench of runes of a Wagnerian sort."[122] Indeed, Kracauer pronounced, "The potential consequences (including the political ones) of" Buber and Rosenzweig's "retreat emerge from the nationalist intonation of some of the neobiblical manifestations."[123] "Today," he concluded, "access to truth is by way of the profane" – not by way of religious renewal.[124]

Buber and Rosenzweig rebutted Kracauer's allegations and his critique, insisting that "the reviewer's objections to our translation are all in fact objections to the Hebrew text" and that it was "the reviewer's lively imagination" and not their work that had led him to take "flight for Bayreuth."[125] Lowenthal, in turn, who was very loyal to Kracauer,[126] and who found the tone of the rebuttal distasteful,[127] wrote a strongly-worded letter to Rosenzweig, seemingly intended as a counter-rebuttal. Rosenzweig returned Lowenthal's letter to him without commenting on it in any way.[128] Outraged and humiliated, Lowenthal broke off all further contact with Rosenzweig.[129]

Lowenthal asserted in 1988 that he had "completely shared the gist of the critique" that Kracauer had made of the Buber/Rosenzweig translation, and that he had also agreed with Kracauer's "deep distrust of Buber as a self-stylized charismatic character and saint."[130] From Lowenthal's perspective, the alliance between Buber and Rosenzweig had been "a tragic mistake."[131] In 1925–1926, Lowenthal had stood with Buber and Rosenzweig in rejecting the complete absorption of German Jewry into the German people. Like them, he had been seeking an alternative to ideological assimilationism. But Kracauer had pointed to the nationalistic, politically reactionary, implications of the Buber/Rosenzweig translation – and Lowenthal, who, as we have seen, had become a left-wing political radical, agreed with his friend's critique. Lowenthal was opposed to liberalism. However, he was opposed to it from a socialist perspective, not from a privatizing one. The controversy over the Buber/Rosenzweig translation revealed that there were very deep – and widening – divisions *among* those German Jews who rejected the views of the German Jewish assimilationists – with some rejecting such views from the right and others from the left – and not only between those who were proud members of the CV and those who were opposed to it.

Lowenthal was involved much more closely with two other Jewish institutions – a periodical, the *Jüdisches Wochenblatt*, and a Jewish sanatorium initiated by Frieda Reichmann – than he was with the Lehrhaus. The *Jüdisches Wochenblatt*, which first appeared in 1924, was founded as the official organ of Achduth [Unity] – an organization of Orthodox Jews in Germany – and was initially edited by Rabbi Harry Levy.[132] The paper moved its base of operations to Frankfurt around the beginning of 1925, however, and was co-edited after that point by Ernst Simon and Lowenthal.[133] In an interview conducted decades after the *Wochenblatt* had ceased publishing, Helmut Dubiel asked Lowenthal whether the weekly was a "Zionist newspaper."[134] Lowenthal replied affirmatively. Simon, on the other hand, insisted, in 1925, that the editorial line of the periodical was Torah-true but anti-separatist, and was neutral vis-à-vis Zionism.[135] Golde Lowenthal, Leo's spouse, published a number of stories for children in its pages.[136] Leo Lowenthal contributed book, film, and theater reviews,[137] and short pieces on Polish Jewish affairs that were sympathetic to the plight of his co-religionists.[138]

Not long after he commenced co-editing the *Wochenblatt*, Lowenthal began to have even greater doubts about Zionist policies than he had had when he first became a university student, and, in a piece published under the pseudonym Haereticus, alluded to these misgivings in the pages of his publication.[139] Lowenthal's article, entitled "Die Lehren von China," declared that the most important political lesson of the preceding ten years had been that the legitimate criterion for a revolution was the fraternization of the intelligentsia and of the proletariat. In Russia, Lowenthal claimed, fraternization of this kind had led to a successful revolution by the majority against the Czarist regime, and a comparable fraternization was taking place at that time between Chinese students with European education and "Coolies" [unskilled laborers]. "In this sense," Lowenthal concluded, "China now has its legitimate revolution, the revolution of the national majority" against the foreigners (who had dominated in China). He then posed the question: What are the lessons for Palestine of events in China? Lowenthal replied to his rhetorical question by noting that "[i]f, especially in earlier years, one looked at

Zionism's ideological products, it would be easy to remark ironically on what bloody laughter it would cause in the world if, for instance, a remnant of Celts scattered on a remote island were to travel to France today and claim its territory as a national property belonging to them by historical right. Zionism's dangerous vice, its ethnocentric naïveté in historical matters, found in Jewish history a fertile field."[140] Arab youth were already studying in European universities, Lowenthal continued, and in Palestine as well as in China a national majority was crying out for its rights. Lowenthal ended his article by proclaiming "We are not so politically naïve as to suggest ... a favorable prognosis" for Zionist settlement in Palestine.

In a letter to Buber written just before Lowenthal released "Die Lehren von China," Simon wrote that Lowenthal would have to be let go from his position at the *Wochenblatt* because the newspaper could not support two editors. Lowenthal's political positions were not so much as mentioned.[141] He published in the *Wochenblatt's* pages until late in January 1926, but never identified himself in print as a Zionist at any point after the appearance of "Die Lehren von China."[142]

Just as Lowenthal evolved from an initially non-Zionist stance first to a position in which he was affiliated with a Zionist student movement and later to a rejection of Zionism, so too did he move from a non-Orthodox family background, through a period in which he embraced Orthodoxy, and, down the line, back to a decidedly non-observant lifestyle. Gershom Scholem has suggested that psychoanalytic treatment conducted by Frieda Reichmann played a significant role in the latter of these shifts.

Frieda Reichmann, born into an Orthodox household in Karlsruhe in 1889, was far more Jewishly rooted than was Lowenthal.[143] Her father, Adolf Reichmann, had served as a member of the board of directors of the Orthodox, secessionist, synagogue in Königsberg of which Nobel was briefly Rabbi in 1900, and Reichmann herself was strictly observant during her student years.

Like Golde Ginsburg – who had been friends with Reichmann since their days in Königsberg, and who introduced both Lowenthal and Fromm to Reichmann – Reichmann was not only a practicing Jew in the early 1920s, but also a Zionist. The psychoanalytically oriented sanatorium Reichmann created in Heidelberg was intended to help individual patients with emotional difficulties. It was also intended to do something "for the Jewish people."[144] As Reichmann put it "We thought we would first analyze the people, and second, make them aware of their tradition and live in this tradition, not because the Lord has said so, but because that meant becoming aware of our past..."[145]

Once Reichmann established her institution, Leo and Golde Lowenthal moved to Heidelberg. Golde did housework in her friend's new sanatorium, and also helped care for the children staying in it.[146] Golde Lowenthal, Leo Lowenthal, Simon, and Fromm were among those analyzed by Reichmann.[147]

Ernst Simon – who was analyzed in 1924[148] – notes that during that period Reichmann remained strongly Torah-true in her practice of Judaism, but was not dogmatically Orthodox.[149] He describes the sanatorium in the following terms:

The Jewish 'rhythm of life' was an integral part of the intellectual atmosphere of the community, which was purely Jewish. At meals, there were prayers and readings from traditional Jewish scriptures. The Sabbath and Jewish holidays were carefully observed.[150]

Lowenthal confirms Simon's account:

The sanatorium was a kind of Jewish-psychoanalytic boarding school and hotel. An almost cultlike atmosphere prevailed there... The sanatorium adhered to Jewish religious laws: the meals were kosher, and all religious holidays were observed. The Judeo-religious atmosphere intermingled with the interest in psychoanalysis. Somehow, in my recollection I sometimes link this syncretic coupling of the Jewish and the psychoanalytic traditions with our later 'marriage' of Marxist theory and psychoanalysis in the Institute, which was to play such a great role in my intellectual life.[151]

Thus, Lowenthal moved from the "cult community" around Nobel to the "cultlike" sanatorium. Lowenthal's pithy summary of the sanatorium's orientation and significance is a revealing one: "[T]he sanatorium was a somewhat utopian experiment to combine a Jewish lifestyle with a healing institution – an experimental attempt in the search for utopia which was quite symptomatic for the first years after the breakdown of Germany and the increasing disillusionment about the revolution."

Reichmann's "Torah-peuticum" – a label later made famous by Gershom Scholem but disliked by Lowenthal – in which, according to Scholem, "the Torah and therapy were cultivated on a Freudian foundation" lasted only for a few years.[152] Over time, Reichmann and Fromm began to distance themselves from Jewish religious practice (and became romantically involved with one another). Scholem suggests that psychoanalysis led to their secularization. Referring to "[s]ome of my best students and acquaintances from Zionist youth groups, such as Simon,

Fromm, and Leo Löwenthal" Scholem comments: "With the exception of one person" – Ernst Simon, who remained observant and who immigrated to Palestine in 1928 – "they all had their Orthodox Judaism analyzed away."[153] Reichmann's sanatorium closed in the same year in which Simon left Germany.[154]

But Lowenthal did not accept Scholem's analysis of the process by which he came to reject Orthodox practice: "The speculation of Scholem about the dissolution of adherence to Jewishness by the climate of the Heidelberg institution," Lowenthal wrote sixty years after the sanatorium had shuttered its doors, "are in my opinion sheer nonsense. The move away from Jewish conservatism to which Fromm, of course, was more dedicated than I, occurred gradually in the early twenties, and speaking for myself but perhaps also for Fromm was motivated politically much more than by inner religious psychological considerations."[155]

Lowenthal once asserted that Kracauer's advice also had a significant impact on his further development. On April 24, 1924, Kracauer wrote to Lowenthal "I would find it regrettable if you always remained distant from things that you can approach more closely, and establish yourself as a pure Hebraist disdainful of European philosophy. You are just as much a hybrid as I, and the glow of the actual is not the halo that suits you. Precisely the fact that you are capable of philosophizing like Buber, or even like Scholem, is the danger to you as I see it, or perhaps a threatening temptation. But please believe me: the positive word is not ours ... At bottom you yourself have an aversion to the rosy religiosity of Buber."[156] Lowenthal commented that this "was a very decisive letter in my own development."

Whether Lowenthal's break from Orthodox Judaism was a result of psychoanalysis, of Kracauer's influence, or of a change in political orientation, it is quite evident that this break did not entail a rift with all aspects of Jewish life. He wrote for Jewish organs – primarily on intellectuals of Jewish origin such as Moses Mendelssohn, Salomon Maimon, Ferdinand Lassalle, Hermann Cohen, and Sigmund Freud – throughout the remainder of the 1920s, and well into the year 1932.[157]

Lowenthal's generally sympathetic portraits of these figures in articles written for Jewish audiences provide additional evidence as to his own position on Jewish questions during the period under discussion. Karl Marx is described as "the genuine continuation of the rationalization of Judaism that culminated in Maimonides" and as "a true heir of the noblest rabbinical tradition."[158] Lowenthal also describes Freud's position vis-à-vis Judaism in a congenial manner, and comments:

Those who are living positively religious lives will not be eager to regard as sensible the circumstances that, for [Freud], religion becomes an illusion, capable, perhaps, of offering people consolation for the misery of their social and psychological situation, but incapable, to be sure, of changing decisively the conditions responsible for it. And yet the best defenders of religion, including the Jewish religion, will not close themselves to Freud's fundamental conviction.[159]

Antisemitism did not play a major role in Lowenthal's consciousness for most of the 1920s. Though he experienced antisemitism from time to time, he "didn't take all that seriously," and believed that German Jews had achieved "an apparently completely successful emancipation."[160] According to Lowenthal, it made no difference whether or not one was Jewish in everyday life. Pollock and Feliks J. Weil (who initiated the effort that culminated in the foundation of the Institute of Social Research), among many others, shared Lowenthal's perspective on this issue. Weil, for example, who commented on the matter decades after the end of the Second World War, believed that "discrimination against Jews had retreated completely to the 'social club level'" in Weimar Germany.[161] Was this attitude, as Gershom Scholem has charged, an example of an "astounding lack of critical insight" by German Jews into the reality of their lives?[162] Probably. It was, however, similar to the attitude held by most of the leading lights of German Jewry living in Germany in the first decade of the Weimar era. If Lowenthal (and Weil and Pollock) were myopic in the 1920s, they were suffering from an unusually widespread malady.[163]

Lowenthal was introduced to Horkheimer by Kracauer, and, as a result of this introduction, became affiliated with the Institute of Social Research. He began working for the Institute, in a part-time capacity, in 1926. Thus, his involvement with Jewish affairs continued for years after he began to work with the Institute. Lowenthal, however, accepted a full-time post at the Institute in 1930. It seems likely that it was the pressures associated with a new, demanding, full-time position – including, beginning in September of 1930, preparation for the Institute's eventual emigration, and his work for the Institute's newly founded *Zeitschrift für Sozialforschung* – rather than an ideological shift on his part that explain why Lowenthal did not remain active in Jewish affairs in the final years of the Weimar Republic. His new responsibilities at the Institute may well have precluded him from taking on additional, outside obligations. In fact, given the nature of these responsibilities, it is striking that Lowenthal continued to be published in the *Bayerische Israelitische Gemeindezeitung* – which was published by the Bavarian Union of Jewish Communities, and edited by Ludwig Feuchtwanger – in 1931 and 1932, as he had been in earlier years.[164] Lowenthal remained perfectly willing to be publicly identified with an explicitly Jewish organ even at the very end of the Weimar Republic.

What was it that attracted Lowenthal to the Institute, and to Horkheimer? Is it mere coincidence that Lowenthal, who had earlier felt comfortable taking subordinate positions in circles dominated by strong leaders (like Nobel and Rosenzweig), also felt comfortable working in such a capacity at the Institute, in which there was a principled commitment to the notion of the "dictatorship of the director"?[165] Lowenthal's years in the institutions of the Jewish cultural renaissance, it would appear, prefigured his years in the Frankfurt School.

Was the Horkheimer circle, moreover, comfortable and familiar to Lowenthal not only in its structure, but also, in other significant ways? "However much I once tried to convince Martin Jay that there were no Jewish motifs among us at the Institute," Lowenthal acknowledged in 1979, without explicitly specifying the period of the Institute's history to which he was referring but apparently thinking about the Weimar era, "now, years later and after mature consideration, I must admit to a certain influence of Jewish tradition, which was codeterminative" in the development of Critical Theory.[166] Lowenthal apparently came to believe that Jewish motifs had had a key role in the development of Critical Theory even if the members of the Frankfurt School had not been conscious of that role as the Frankfurt School was brought into being.

*

Erich Fromm – a psychologist and psychoanalyst who, after leaving Europe, became world renowned through his many books, including *Escape from Freedom*, *The Sane Society*, and *The Art of Loving* – was even more deeply involved in Jewish life before he became associated with the Institute of Social Research than was Lowenthal.[167] Unlike Lowenthal, who was raised in a non-religious environment, Fromm, born in Frankfurt in 1900, was raised in an observant household.[168] Fromm, like Lowenthal, became closely associated with the institutions of the Jewish cultural renaissance in Germany in the early 1920s. But where Lowenthal had become engaged in these institutions precisely because he rejected the manner in which he had been raised, Fromm became engaged with them as a result of having grown up in an Orthodox family.

Fromm was influenced, as a young man, by the ideas of Hermann Cohen, and was part of the Nobel circle.[169] He was active in Zionist organizations. He was a co-founder (in 1919) with Rabbi Georg

Salzberger, of the Gesellschaft für jüdische Volksbildung in Frankfurt am Main (Frankfurt's Society for Jewish Adult Education),[170] Fromm and Salzberger jointly came up with the idea of inviting Rosenzweig to Frankfurt during the summer of the following year – a move that resulted in the formation of the Lehrhaus.[171] At several points – presumably after Rosenzweig became too ill to continue to lead – it was suggested that Fromm might be a suitable director for the Lehrhaus.[172] Similarly, Fromm played an even more significant role in Reichmann's sanatorium than did Lowenthal. Indeed, Fromm's engagement with Judaism and Jewish institutions was of a longer duration than was Lowenthal's, and had deeper roots.

Both Fromm's mother and his father were descended from rabbinic families. His great grandfather, Seligmann Bär Bamberger, known as the Würzburger Rav, was a Talmudist and a leader of the Jewish Orthodox world in southern Germany. Fromm seems to have grown up hearing about his ancestor. Fromm's grandfather, Seligmann Pinchas Fromm, son-in-law of the Würzburger Rav, served for many years as a rabbi in Bad Homburg, and later as personal rabbi to a member of the Rothschild family. To be sure, Erich's father, Naphtali Fromm, was a businessman, and not a rabbi – but Naphtali was very active in Jewish affairs and certainly did not reject the Jewish religious tradition. He always closed his business on Jewish holidays, conducted commercial transactions in accord with Jewish law, and represented the Jewish Community of Frankfurt in the Prussia-wide association of Jewish communities.[173] He also maintained ties with his extended family. Half a century after the event, Fromm reported that "I still remember having visited, as a boy of 16, with my father, his uncle, the Sennheimer Rav when he was in a hospital in Würzburg ... I still remember the glow on his face; it is the closest I ever saw to a saintly man."[174] Erich Fromm's early interest in and involvement with Judaism, unlike Lowenthal's, did not stem from, or cause, generational conflict. He became a member of a grouping of young people at the synagogue in Frankfurt of which Nobel was rabbi when he was about sixteen years old.[175]

Fromm was a member of the KJV quite some time before Lowenthal joined that organization. He was already involved with the Frankfurt-based "Saronia" affiliate of the KJV in 1918, and, in that year, urged his fellow KJV members not to battle against Agudas-Jisroel [Union of Israel], an Orthodox Jewish youth movement, but rather to leave relations with the latter in the hands of those Zionists (including Fromm) who were strictly observant.[176] Fromm became a leader of the Achduth [Unity] chapter of the KJV in Frankfurt in the spring of 1919, at the time of that chapter's formation, and, later in 1919, apparently served as a delegate from the Heidelberg KJV chapter to a KJV country-wide conference.[177] In the summer of 1920, he led a seminar meant as an introduction to the prayer book under the auspices of that chapter.[178] During the following year (and, in all likelihood, at earlier points in his youth) Fromm was also active in Blau-Weiss.[179]

Fromm completed his dissertation at the University of Heidelberg in 1922.[180] The dissertation, which was on the sociological function of Jewish law for Jewry, had sections devoted, among other matters, to the Karaites, depicted by Fromm as having arisen primarily due to economic causes,[181] to Reform Jewry (which was characterized in a critical manner, and which was also traced back to the economic context in which it arose), and Chasidism (which Fromm described sympathetically). The Reform movement was criticized as having an "anti-national tendency" and as adapting the Judaism of its German Jewish adherents to the dominant Christian religion.[182] The neo-Orthodox German Jewish separatists associated with Samson Hirsch were also criticized, since, as Fromm saw it, Jewish law lost its soul among those in this religious tendency.[183] Fromm's dissertation, in other words, was clearly written by a young man deeply committed to (non-separatist) Orthodox Judaism and to Zionism.

Rosenzweig thought highly of Fromm.[184] Fromm, in turn, clearly respected Rosenzweig. In 1922 and 1923, Fromm helped to lead services in conjunction with the Jewish High Holidays in Rosenzweig's home in Frankfurt.[185]

Lowenthal's disavowal of Scholem's sense of the impact that the "Torah-peuticum" had on him notwithstanding, there is no question that Fromm underwent a process of secularization in the period during which Reichmann's sanatorium was open. Though he remained an observant Jew in 1925, Fromm was strongly critical of trends within the world of German Jewry's Orthodox wing by that point in time. "I am of the opinion," he wrote to Simon, who was considering enrolling in the Orthodox Rabbinical Seminary in Berlin, "that the Orthodox are becoming ever more fanatical, hostile to science, and reactionary..."[186] To be sure, Reichmann and Fromm had a traditional Jewish wedding in Königsberg in June of 1926, in which all elements of Jewish law were observed. But Reichmann has noted, in her recollections of the sanatorium, that she and Fromm eventually "became more interested in the Leftist view of things," and describes an incident in which they both went to a park in Heidelberg during Passover (when observant Jews abstain from eating bread) and deliberately ate bread in violation of Jewish law.[187] Not long thereafter, they announced their break from Orthodox practice via articles in a German psychoanalytic journal, *Imago*.[188] Fromm's article dealt with observance of the Sabbath from an analytic perspective, and argued that "The Sabbath originally served as a reminder of the killing of the father and the winning of the mother; the commandment not to work served as a penance for original sin and for its repetition through regression to the pre-genital stage."[189] Fromm had published short pieces in Jewish periodicals before he wrote the article that appeared in *Imago*. The article on the Sabbath, however, was Fromm's first published work written from a psychoanalytic perspective. The beginning of his long career as a writer influenced by psychoanalytic ideas, in other words, was intimately linked with Fromm's public renunciation of Orthodoxy.

Frankfurt's Institute of Psychoanalysis, with which Fromm was associated, was housed in the same building as was the Institute of Social Research. Thus, Fromm, though actually in Berlin rather than Frankfurt much of the time, had contact with the latter institute even in the late 1920s. Fromm did not, however, become a full member of the Institute of Social Research in the formal sense of that term until 1930 – some four years or so after he had given up the practice of Judaism. But it is worthy of note that Fromm was brought into contact with the Institute of Social Research, at least in part, by Lowenthal, with whom he had become friends via Jewish circles, and with whom he had shared the experiences of having been in the Nobel circle, the KJV, the Lehrhaus, and the "Torah-peuticum."[190] It is of even greater import that the men with whom Fromm learned about Judaism in his childhood, youth, and young adult years had an explicit impact upon him throughout the remainder of his life.

Fromm studied Talmud, at an early age, with Jakob Horovitz, son of the Orthodox rabbi Markus Horovitz, and, somewhat later, with his mother's uncle, Ludwig Krause. Krause, who was from Posen, was a well-known Talmudist[191] and a *dayan* (a member of a Rabbinic court). He was already over seventy when Fromm studied with him.[192] According to Fromm, Krause, who was both Orthodox and humanistic, was "a traditionalist, little touched by modern thought."[193] Krause's impact on Fromm is evident from the fact that Fromm dreamed of following in his great-uncle's footsteps – that is, of becoming a Talmudist and moving to Posen. After the First World War, both Fromm and Simon were part of a small circle which regularly studied *gemore* (the portion of the Talmud made up of commentaries on the *mishne*) with Krause.[194]

From approximately 1919 or 1920 until 1924 or 1925,[195] Fromm studied almost daily with Salman Baruch Rabinkow in Heidelberg.[196] Though the bulk of their time together was devoted to the Talmud, Fromm also studied Maimonides, Tanya, Jewish history, and sociological questions with his teacher.

Rabinkow, who was Russian born, came from a Chassidic family, but reportedly studied in the non-Chassidic Telshe Yeshiva. He was brought to Heidelberg by the Steinberg family after the Revolution of 1905 in order to teach Isaac Nachman Steinberg, a Russian Jew who was both religiously observant and a leftist, and who had had to leave Russia after having been arrested for political reasons. Despite his training in Telshe, Rabinkow was near in spirit to the *khabad* movement (which was closely associated with Lubavitcher Chassidim). Like Steinberg, he was also sympathetic to socialism.[197] Rabinkow exuded joy, had a good sense of humor, and loved to sing chassidic tunes. Decades later, Fromm particularly remembered Rabinkow's "aliveness... kindness... humanity and his thorough honesty."[198] Fromm also characterized Rabinkow as "essentially a mystic in his religious attitude."[199] Rabinkow's students report that he lived very simply, devoted his time to his studies of Torah and Talmud, slept little, and would not accept any fee from most of those who came to study with him.[200] Unlike Nobel, who attracted students from acculturated backgrounds, Rabinkow attracted primarily those from a more traditional milieu, and those who had had prior training in Talmud before beginning their studies with him.[201] Fritz Gumpertz, a student of Rabinkow's, notes that "Rabinkow was for his disciples what a 'Rebbe' is for a Hasid."[202] "All his influence," Fromm writes "was his being, his example, although he was the last man to want to present an example. He was just himself."[203] Fromm explicitly notes that Rabinkow took "great interest" in Fromm's dissertation, and was "very helpful" to Fromm while Fromm was working on it.[204] More than forty-five years after last seeing Rabinkow, Fromm concluded that "Rabinkow influenced my life more than any other man, perhaps, and although in different forms and concepts, his ideas have remained alive in me."[205]

Long after he had ceased to observe Jewish religious law, Fromm continued to be deeply affected by his teachers. In *You Shall be as Gods*, published in 1966, Fromm, referring explicitly to Kraus, Nobel, and Rabinkow, notes: "Not being a practicing or a 'believing' Jew, I am, of course, in a very different position from theirs, and least of all would I dare to make them responsible for the views expressed in this book. Yet my views have grown out of their teaching, and it is my conviction that at no point has the continuity between their teaching and my own views been interrupted."[206]

*

Henryk Grossmann, who had first been brought to the Institute by Horkheimer's predecessor, Carl Grünberg, in 1925, was interested in political economy, and, in 1929, published an important book, under the auspices of the Institute, on the law of accumulation and the breakdown of the capitalist system. He remained a formal member of the Institute for decades after Horkheimer became its director. Judith Marcus and Zoltán Tar, writing on Judaic elements in the teachings of the Frankfurt School, once asserted that Grossmann ought to be categorized as a person on whom there was " 'no' or 'minimal' Jewish influence."[207] In truth, Grossmann, like Lowenthal and Fromm, had been deeply involved in Jewish affairs as a young man. Unlike the most prominent of the Institute's figures, however, Grossmann came to the Institute via the world of Yiddish-speaking, East European, Jewry, not via that of its German Jewish counterpart.

Grossmann, whose legal given name was originally Chaskel, was born in 1881 (and who was, therefore, significantly older than Horkheimer, Pollock, Lowenthal or Fromm) in Cracow, was circumcised, and was registered by his parents as a member of the Jewish community.[208] His family was relatively prosperous, and socially assimilated. This is evidenced, for example, by the fact that he is known to have attended the Sw. Jacka (St. James) Gymnasium (in which Polish was the language of instruction). After graduation from this institution, Grossmann continued his studies at the Jagiellonian University, and also studied under Carl Grünberg at the University of Vienna.

Grossmann became involved in radical politics at an early age, initially in the context of the Polish Social Democratic Party (often known by its Polish initials, PPSD). He learned Yiddish in order to be able to work among Jewish workers, manifested concern about antisemitism early on, and, in late 1902, formed a Jewish workers' association, Postęp (Progress), which was affiliated with the PPSD.[209] Grossmann served as secretary of this group, and succeeded in attracting 130 adherents by 1903. However, in 1904–1905, he became very critical of the PPSD, which he came to believe neglected the needs of Jewish workers, and eventually left it in order to help organize the Jewish Social Democratic Party in Galicia (most commonly known as the ŻPSD, its initials in Polish). Thus, just as Lowenthal turned away from the assimilatory course taken by his father and embraced Judaism and Zionism, at one point in his life, so did Grossmann turn away from the Polonized, linguistically acculturated, lifestyle of his family, and become closely tied to the Yiddish-speaking workers of Galicia. Grossmann never manifested any interest in Judaism per se. The Jewish cultural renaissance in which Lowenthal, Fromm, Kracauer, Simon and others participated in the Weimar years was a German-Jewish phenomenon, with no direct counterpart among the East European, primarily Yiddish-speaking, Jews living in the far reaches of the Austro-Hungarian Empire at the beginning of the twentieth century. But Grossmann's embrace of the ŻPSD was every bit as much a turn away from the road of his father as was that of Lowenthal. Moreover, the path taken by Grossmann and the path taken by Lowenthal were parallel to one another in a second sense as well. In Germany, Jews like Lowenthal and Simon who wanted to differentiate themselves from the established leadership of German Jewry (dominated by ideological assimilationists) while remaining involved with the Jewish world (sometimes) did so by engaging intensively with Judaism. In Galicia, Jews who were alienated from the Jewish establishment (which was often made up of strictly observant Jews) but who did not want to move altogether outside of the Jewish orbit were more likely to become political radicals than to become fervently observant. Grossmann's engagement with the ŻPSD was oppositional, a reaction to the Jewish mainstream of his time and place, in much the same way as was Lowenthal's engagement with the Nobel circle.

The ŻPSD had a political perspective similar to that of the General Jewish Workers' Bund, which operated not in Austria-Hungary but rather in the Czarist Empire. The Bund ultimately argued that the Jews of the Russian Empire ought to be granted national rights, and that the Bund ought to be recognized both as an autonomous component of the Russian Social Democratic Workers' Party and as the sole representative in the Party of the Russian Empire's Jewish proletariat. The ŻPSD made a similar case on behalf of the Yiddish-speaking Jews of Galicia (and, in a later period, of Bukovina), arguing that the ŻPSD ought to be admitted into the Austrian Social Democratic Workers' Party as a federal component.[210]

Grossmann was deeply involved in the formation of the ŻPSD. He was, for example, one of the eight signatories of a letter to the executive committee of the Austrian Social Democratic Workers' Party informing the executive of a plan to form a Jewish socialist group, and inviting the members of the executive to attend the new group's founding congress.[211] When the Social Democratic Party reacted negatively to this initiative, Grossmann – who was elected Secretary of the ŻPSD at its founding congress – wrote directly to Victor Adler (the preeminent leader of Austrian Socialism) to express his dismay.[212] Works by Grossmann appeared in Yiddish during this period, both in pamphlet form and in the ŻPSD's party organ, *Der sotsial-demokrat*, including a long piece on Bundism in Galicia issued in conjunction with the tenth anniversary of the founding of the Bund in the Russian Empire.[213]

Rick Kuhn points out that in the years immediately following the formation of the ŻPSD "Grossman[n] was fully and intensely involved in the socialist workers' movement as a political leader, though he, like the rest of the [ŻPSD] leadership, received no salary from the Party. The [ŻPSD's] first four congresses reelected Grossman[n] to the Party Executive. He represented his Party at the Bund's 7th Congress in September 1906. His history of the early Jewish socialist movement in Galicia, 'Der [b]undizm in [g]alitsyen', published in 1907, was a reaffirmation of the rationale of the [ŻPSD's] existence on the basis of historical research and theoretical argument."[214]

During the course of 1908, Grossmann moved to Vienna, where he initially maintained contact with his Jewish socialist comrades. In 1910, for example, he apparently agreed to deliver a lecture on the economic history of Galician Jews sponsored by the Ferdinand Lassalle Verein (a small grouping of friends and sympathizers of the ŻPSD based in the Austrian capital that engaged primarily in cultural and educational work).[215] As late as October of 1910, Grossmann was reelected to the executive committee of the ŻPSD. He seems to have drifted away from the Jewish socialist world, however, at some time thereafter.

To say that Grossmann ultimately distanced himself from the ŻPSD is not to say that he ceased identifying himself as a Jew. When, in December of 1908, Grossmann married, his wedding ceremony was conducted in the Vienna City Synagogue, and duly registered with the Israelitische Kultusgemeinde [the Jewish Community of Vienna].[216] Similarly, the birth of his son Stanislaus Eugen Grossmann in May 1914 was also reported to the Kultusgemeinde.[217] While manifestly not religiously observant, Grossmann continued his formal affiliation with the Jewish community for many years thereafter.[218]

Grossmann served in the Austro-Hungarian army during the First World War, worked in Warsaw in the post-war years, and was named a Professor of Political Economy in that city in 1922. Politically, Grossmann was to the left of the Polish Bund during the 1920s, and was sympathetic to the Polish Communist Party. He is not known to have had any Jewish ties during that period of his life. It ought to be noted, however, that a large number of those Marxists of Jewish origin that had earlier been in the Bund were radicalized by the Bolshevik revolution. Grossmann followed a well-trod path in his transformation from Bundist to Communist.

In 1925, at the invitation of his onetime teacher Carl Grünberg, Grossmann moved to Frankfurt and accepted a position as an *Assistent* in the Institute of Social Research.[219] He retained an affiliation with the Institute until after World War II.

*

Not all of the Institute's members during the Weimar era that were of Jewish origin had been involved in Jewish affairs in their younger years. Friedrich Pollock, whose background we have already described, kept Jewish affairs of all kinds at arm's length throughout the period of the Republic. Yet Pollock's life path is as Jewish as is that of his colleagues, albeit in a different sense. For Pollock's assimilatory perspective was *more* typical for German Jews than were the explicitly Jewish stances taken early on by Fromm or Lowenthal. A significant proportion of German Jews of Pollock's generation were highly acculturated, uninvolved in Jewish affairs, and not particularly interested in Judaism, Zionism, or related matters.

Most German Jews were not leftists. A plurality of German Jews in the Weimar Republic tended to vote for middle-of-the-road liberal political parties for so long as such parties continued to be viable. Nevertheless, Pollock's involvement in German (non-Jewish) leftist intellectual life is similar to and parallels the involvement of countless of his German Jewish counterparts in a range of left-wing political and cultural movements. Acculturated German Jews played visible roles among intellectuals in the Social Democratic party and (in its earliest years) in the Communist party,[220] in such periodicals as the *Weltbühne*,[221] and in left-wing cultural circles. The young German Jews involved in these institutions may well have had no interest in Judaism or Jewishness, but spent much of their time in a milieu in which Jews were present in far greater numbers than their presence in the general population could explain. Unlike Horkheimer, Fromm, Lowenthal, and Grossmann (all of whom, as we have seen, were associated, at various points in their early years, with Jewish institutions) Pollock was a "non-Jewish Jew." But non-Jewish Jews, by definition, are also Jewish.[222]

Jewish identity was not important to Pollock. There can be no doubt, however, that the larger, non-Jewish, world tended to relate to Pollock and to other individuals of Jewish origin active on the left or in German cultural life as Jews. The Jewish origins of the active members of the Institute meant that much of the population of the country in which they were born and raised perceived these men as separate from Germans and Germanness.[223] Jewishness, Istvan Deak reminds us, "was a publicly imposed condition" in Weimar Germany: "A significant minority of those whom the German public considered Jews were not aware of their Jewishness or, rather, denied this awareness."[224] The career choices of German Jews remained circumscribed in the 1920s and early 1930s not only by their own abilities and inclinations, but also by continuing anti-Jewish prejudice.

*

German Jews of a somewhat older generation than that of Fromm and Lowenthal had embraced *Bildung* – perhaps best (though still not altogether satisfactorily) rendered in English as self-cultivation – as their ideal. The men with whom I have been concerned in this chapter were manifestly deeply influenced by this process. In the words of George Mosse, "Whatever their individual concerns were, the Frankfurt school as a whole is a part of the German-Jewish tradition of *Bildung* ... the roots of [their] unorthodox socialism lie in large measure within the peculiar nature and evolution of a German-Jewish identity."[225] Lowenthal, for one, ultimately found this analysis to be insightful.[226]

Of course Jewishness was only one star in the large constellation of forces that help to explain and to illuminate members of the Institute of Social Research – and, as many of those who have written on the Frankfurt School have convincingly demonstrated, Marxism was a far brighter star in that constellation during the Institute's Weimar period.[227] Neither Georg Lukács nor Karl Korsch was a member of the Institute, but there is no doubt that the members of the Frankfurt School were highly attentive to certain of the ideas with which these two writers were associated in the 1920s. The Frankfurt School was a constituent component of the Western Marxist tradition.

Jewishness was, moreover, a star hidden by ideological clouds at some points, and thus a star the very existence of which was denied by many of those subject to its magnetic pulls and pushes. No less an authority than Feliks Weil insisted throughout his life that Jewishness – however defined – had no influence whatsoever on the development of the ideas of the Institute's members.[228]

But Weil to the contrary notwithstanding, the Jewish origins of the bulk of the members of the Institute sheds light on their lives, careers, and even, at some points, on their thought. "Origins," Horkheimer wrote in an afterword to a work entitled *Portraits of German Jewish Intellectual History*, "shine through the thoughts and feelings of the adult human being."[229] The pre-history of the Horkheimer circle is illuminated not only by examining its development in the crucible of the history of Marxism – as has been ably done in the past by others – but also by familiarity with the history of Central European Jewry.

None of the members of the Institute of Social Research were practicing members of the Jewish religion in the late 1920s or in the 1930s. Indeed, the movement away from an earlier practice of Judaism on the part of some of those whom I have discussed was part of what made the Institute attractive to them. However, "[t]he Jewish heretic who transcends Jewry belongs to a Jewish tradition."[230] Gershom Scholem, who was not only an internationally renowned expert on Judaism but who was also personally acquainted with leading members of the Institute of Social Research, once quipped that the Institute, in the era during which it was headed by Max Horkheimer, was one of "the three most remarkable 'Jewish sects' that German Jewry produced."[231] He also recognized that certain members of the Institute would by no means appreciate this designation. But whether (like Lowenthal, Fromm, and Horkheimer), the members of the Horkheimer circle eventually admitted the impact of their Jewish origins on their life paths and thought, or whether (like Weil), they strenuously denied it throughout their lives, Scholem's quip appears to have been on target.

In the brief period between Horkheimer's installation as the Institute's Director and the emigration from Germany of most of those associated with the Institute, all of the individuals formally and closely involved with the Institute of Social Research on a full-time basis – Horkheimer, Lowenthal, Grossmann, Fromm, and Pollock – were Jewish.[232] The members of the Institute of Social Research, to be sure, arrived at the Institute via somewhat different paths. Fromm and Lowenthal arrived via intense involvement with Judaism and Zionism. Grossmann arrived via Bundism. Horkheimer and Pollock arrived via rebellion against the lives, aspirations, and values of their wealthy, Jewish fathers. But however different the paths that led all of these men to the Institute, it remains true that they all traveled to it down recognizably Jewish roads.

Chapter 2

The Significance of Antisemitism: The Exile Years

Max Horkheimer took steps to counter the dangers to the Institute posed by the rise of the Nazis at a point when a considerable portion of German Jewry, and many German leftists, underestimated the Nazi threat. Many of those in Germany who opposed the Nazis believed, in 1931–1932, that it would be possible to "muddle through."[1] Horkheimer, on the other hand, signaled that he was not so sure that that was the case by proposing the creation of a branch of the Institute in Geneva, by approving transfer of the Institute's endowment to the Netherlands in 1931, and by spending much of the following year in Switzerland. At some point, he also chose to stay in a hotel room in Frankfurt located near the central railroad station rather than in the suburban home in which he had resided up until that time when his work made it necessary for him to be in Germany – thus facilitating the possibility of a quick get away if need be. By the time, in March 1933, that the Nazi regime closed the Frankfurt Institute and confiscated its property, Horkheimer had quietly returned to Geneva.[2]

Those most closely associated with Horkheimer, including Lowenthal and Pollock, joined him there. Herbert Marcuse – who, like Horkheimer, Lowenthal, and Pollock, was of Jewish origin, and who, like them, had been born and raised in Germany – first began working for the Institute in 1933, moved to Switzerland, and was employed on a full-time basis in the Geneva office.[3] But a sense that fascism might well overtake not only Germany but also Switzerland, and complications caused by the fact that Horkheimer was the only member of his inner circle who had a Swiss residency permit, contributed to the feeling among the members of the Frankfurt School that Switzerland was not likely to remain a refuge for them over the long haul.[4] The Jewish family backgrounds of those members of the Frankfurt School who moved to Switzerland played a role in their dawning awareness that they would need to move on. Lowenthal reports that after the key members of the Institute had relocated to Geneva, "We often found that Jewish emigrants were scrutinized closely, and in their cases regulations were enforced most strictly."[5] It was, first and foremost, the political perspective of the Critical Theorists – their Western Marxist understanding of society ["an alert historical-political sense and relevant research"][6] – that led them to conclude that they ought to leave the country in which they were born. But, as evidenced by the quote from Lowenthal, their Jewish origins ultimately played a part in their decision to leave Europe altogether. In 1934, Horkheimer traveled to the United States. Lowenthal, Pollock, Marcuse, and Fromm also left Europe for the United States during the course of that year.[7]

When Max Horkheimer arrived in the United States he was (still) highly influenced by Marxism, albeit of a very specific kind.[8] By the time that he returned to Frankfurt am Main, several years after the end of the Second World War, Horkheimer had distanced himself far more from Marxist traditions than had earlier been the case.[9] This general tendency in Horkheimer's work was particularly evident in his writings on antisemitism.[10] It was, moreover, also clear in the work on that subject done during the exile years by many of Horkheimer's closest collaborators in the Institute of Social Research. The reassessment of the nature and significance of antisemitism made by the Critical Theorists while in exile contributed to the overarching alteration of Critical Theory itself. The changes in Horkheimer's approach to antisemitism, however, were linked not so much to the experiences of American exile as to the growing influence of Adorno and to Horkheimer's confrontation with events in Europe.

As late as 1938–1939, Horkheimer could still write an article on antisemitism that analyzed that phenomenon from a bluntly Marxist perspective.[11] This article, though published under the title "Die Juden und Europa" ["The Jews and Europe"], actually had relatively little to say about Jews, and was focused on the nature and origins of fascism.[12] "Whoever wants to explain anti-Semitism," Horkheimer famously proclaims in the opening lines of his essay, "must speak of National Socialism ... The new anti-Semitism is the emissary of the totalitarian order, which has developed from the liberal one. One must thus go back to consider the tendencies within capitalism."[13] Horkheimer's piece was published in the *Zeitschrift für Sozialforschung*, which Horkheimer edited, and appeared only in German – significant in light of the fact that another substantive article in that same issue of the *Zeitschrift* and also written by an Institute member was published only in English.[14] Though Horkheimer was living in New York when his article appeared in print, his piece was not directed at American readers. Horkheimer was manifestly interested in attracting the attention of those Germans who had become refugees or exiles.[15] Horkheimer was not, moreover, interested in the Jews as such when he wrote "The Jews and Europe." He was, on the other hand, deeply concerned about the ways in which, as he saw it, bourgeois society had been transformed as a result of direct control by the state over a capitalist economy.[16]

As noted above, Horkheimer, had, at at least one point in the Weimar years, been exceptionally critical of "Jewish capitalists," and suspicious of their motivations.[17] Horkheimer's critique of German refugees in "The Jews and Europe" is similar in tone to that earlier remark. He was well aware that many of his fellow refugees had retained their long-term commitments to liberal as distinguished from Marxist ideas, and was censorious of those who fell into that category (implicitly including that very considerable portion of the German refugee population which was of Jewish origin), bitingly noting that "it is as if the refugee intellectuals have been robbed not only of their citizenship, but also of their minds."[18] He also censures refugees from Germany for having been too gentle, before Hitler came to power, in their critiques of "the flaws of bourgeois democracy" and for their "flirtation with the forces of reaction"[19] – alluding, perhaps, in the latter case, to those who, like Dr. Max Naumann, a leader of the League of National German Jews, had argued, as late as 1932, that the Nazis could perform great services, and who, in March 1933, endorsed the German Nationalist People's Party (which had formed an alliance with the Nazis).[20] Naumann represented only a small segment of German Jewry. However, there were also prominent German Zionists who, in 1931–1932, courted reactionary forces in German political life by underscoring that Zionists, who had a Jewish national consciousness, and who respected the validity of a nationalist perspective, could find ways to cooperate with German nationalists, who had a parallel point of view.[21] On this one point, if not necessarily on others, Horkheimer's critique of (some) German refugees was on target.

Horkheimer asserts that in an earlier era "the sphere of circulation" had provided both a way for Jews to make a living (as merchants), and had also provided a material foundation for democracy.[22] Changes in the economic structure of society – the emergence of what Pollock would later call state capitalism – however, had reduced the significance of the market, for the state takes control of distribution in fascist societies.[23] Horkheimer suggests that this economic tendency, which had already undermined the role of Jews in society, would continue, and that, therefore, "As agents of circulation the Jews have no future. They will not be able to live as human beings until human beings finally put an end to prehistory"[24] – alluding to the notion, rooted in Marx, that it was only after the elimination of the existing, capitalist, relations of production that the prehistory of human society would come to an end. Horkheimer's wording is noteworthy. Before Auschwitz, Dan Diner has pointed out, it was still possible for Horkheimer to write about "the Jews" rather than about actually existing individual Jews.[25]

"The Jews and Europe" was among the most despairing of Horkheimer's works.[26] In his concluding paragraph Horkheimer proclaimed quite definitively both that the progressive forces had been defeated and that fascism "can last indefinitely."[27] If, however, his general prognosis was bleak, his prediction as to the future of antisemitism in Germany was not quite as dark. For Horkheimer also noted, in the final portion of "The Jews and Europe," that "the hatred of Jews belongs to the ascendant phase of fascism" thereby hinting that he anticipated (naively) that antisemitism would diminish in Nazi Germany after that country had passed through the stage in which it found itself in the late 1930s – though he also commented that by that point it was possible that only a few Jews might remain.[28]

Horkheimer was not affiliated with any political party, and was not actively engaged in political affairs in the United States. He was quietly sympathetic to Western Marxism, not to the Marxism–Leninism of the Communist International. But Horkheimer's analysis of antisemitism on the eve of the Second World War was reminiscent of that which had been propounded by orthodox Marxists, including an analysis made by the German Communist Otto Heller, who, in a book on "the downfall of Jewry" published in 1931, had also linked modern antisemitism to changes in the economic position occupied by Jews in contemporary society.[29] This is particularly striking in light of the fact that "The Jews and Europe" – Horkheimer's first piece to directly tackle the nature of fascism – hints at analogies between Soviet and fascist societies. To be sure, Horkheimer ultimately removed from an early draft of his article a passage that had made these analogies more explicit.[30] Yet a close reading of "The Jews and Europe" as published in the *Zeitschrift* reveals that even this version describes fascism in terms of "domination by a minority on the basis of actual possession of the tools of production" and depicts "modern society" as a system in which the bureaucracy decides on matters of life and death, both of which were true in the Soviet Union as well as in Nazi Germany.[31] In addition, Horkheimer made use, when explaining the nature of National Socialism in "The Jews and Europe," of the notion of social character (which had been used by Fromm in his psychoanalytically influenced works published under the auspices of the Institute in the 1930s). At the time that he wrote "The Jews and Europe," in other words, Horkheimer's understanding of fascism was already one that contained seeds of an approach, influenced by psychoanalysis, leading well beyond that of the orthodox Marxists of his day.[32] Moreover, as early as 1937, Horkheimer's *private* ruminations on antisemitism already made use of psychological insights: "Structurally... hatred [of thinking] is very similar to anti-Semitism, as it is, of course, similarly dependent on the mechanism of concurrence and, in terms of its psychological core, represents sexual envy and resentment of a pleasurable attitude toward life of which one doesn't feel oneself capable. Hatred of the Jews has always been hatred of thinking, and naturally the Jews themselves are also in large measure animated by this."[33] But Horkheimer's *public* analysis of antisemitism, on the other hand, showed little trace of such seeds even in the late 1930s. Bahr describes "The Jews and Europe" as "the first document to reveal the failure of Critical Theory..."[34] Doesn't it actually reveal that Horkheimer's ideas were in transition when "The Jews and Europe" was formulated, and that Horkheimer was groping his way towards a more sophisticated and complex understanding of fascism – if not yet consciously working towards a comparable analysis of hatred of Jews?

Horkheimer's essay was, naturally, read closely by those with ties to the Horkheimer circle who were still in Europe when the essay was published. Horkheimer's friend Katharina von Hirsch (born 1902), who had been married to Felix Weil from 1921 to 1929, and who had participated, in 1923, in the "Marxistische Arbeitswoche" [Marxist Work Week], at which a number of individuals who went on to play roles in the Institute of Social Research or in the development of Western Marxism gathered to discuss their ideas, wrote to Horkheimer from London immediately after having read his piece, and noted that she had been strongly impressed by it.[35] She described its analysis of fascism as "splendid," the essay itself as "wonderful," and proclaimed that "the Jewish question" could only be grasped as Horkheimer had grasped it in his essay. To be sure, she also noted that she was not in agreement with all of the essay's details, and expressed doubts as to whether Jewish entities would react favorably to it, but predicted that the essay would make a strong impression not only on her but also on others.[36] Hans Mayer (born 1907), a jurist who went into exile in 1933, and who received material support from the Institute between 1936 and 1941,[37] writing to Horkheimer from Geneva, found "The Jews and Europe," which he described as an article on "the deeper origins of racism," to be "alarmingly ... true and correct."[38] At this time, Mayer informed Horkheimer, he could scarcely think of anyone else who "would say what needs to be said." Another of those who were linked to the Institute but who were in Europe when Horkheimer wrote his article, Andries Sternheim (1890–1944), who had served as director of the Institute's Geneva branch in 1931,[39] was more critical of Horkheimer's view than was Mayer, noting that, in his opinion, Horkheimer wrote as if antisemitism was an outgrowth of National Socialism, when, in truth, antisemitism had actually existed in other, pre-Nazi eras, such as the Middle Ages. Sternheim also questioned whether the fact that the sphere of circulation was losing its importance in economic terms really could explain why antisemitism was increasing.[40] Somewhat later, Siegfried Kracauer, describing to Horkheimer the impression that "The Jews and Europe" had initially made on him when he had read it in France, noted that "it appeared to me at that time, that one had to commit suicide, if that so depressing essay was correct."[41]

Olga Lang, who had been married to Karl Wittfogel from 1933 to 1939, writing not from Europe but rather from Cambridge, Massachusetts, told Horkheimer that she found the essay to be "extraordinarily smart and bold." She had reached this conclusion, she pointed out, because "the polemic is directed not only against the Jews but against the entire wing of the emigration that stands on the ground of capitalism and that hopes for the return of liberalism."[42]

Walter Benjamin also responded very positively, albeit briefly, to Horkheimer's article. Despite its brevity, this response warrants a more extensive analysis. Benjamin had had contact with both Horkheimer and Adorno as early as the 1920s, but had not been formally affiliated with the Institute in the era of the Weimar Republic or in the short period during which it was based in Geneva. However, Benjamin published an article in the *Zeitschrift* in 1934, became an Institute member in 1935, and received a regular – and gradually increased – stipend from the Institute after that point in time. Benjamin had left Germany for France in 1933, and was living in Paris when the Second World War began. Though he produced a significant number of pieces between 1933 and

1940, he had a great deal of difficulty in finding outlets for his work, and often received very modest fees from those periodicals that were willing to publish him:[43] "There is scarcely a letter in Benjamin's voluminous exile correspondence in which he does not complain about the precariousness of his financial situation."[44] Benjamin was, in addition, lonely and isolated in his exile years. The material and moral support Benjamin received from the Institute beginning with 1935 was, therefore, important to him. Given the significance of this support, one can well imagine Benjamin's feelings when he received a letter from Horkheimer, dated February 23, 1939, in which Horkheimer noted that the Institute found itself in a very serious economic situation, and that, therefore, "not withstanding our efforts, in the not too distant future the day may come on which we will have to inform you, that we, with the best of wills, are not in a position to continue your research stipend."[45] He replied to Horkheimer that he had read this letter "with horror" and informed Scholem that he understood Horkheimer's letter as "preparing me for the end of the financial stipend that has been my sole subsistence..."[46]

Benjamin was told by Adorno about Horkheimer's article on the Jews and Europe not long thereafter, and before the piece had appeared in print. Adorno also explicitly informed Benjamin that he had played a notable role in shaping the article. Describing an upcoming number of the *Zeitschrift*, Adorno wrote to Benjamin, in mid-July 1939, "this issue will ... contain an extremely important essay by Max which I have intensely collaborated on myself – the piece is provisionally entitled 'Europe and the Jews', but it essentially presents the first outline of a theory of fascism."[47] Having been tipped off in advance, Benjamin went out of his way to read Horkheimer's piece as soon as possible, requesting galley proofs of "The Jews and Europe" from a representative of the *Zeitschrift*'s publisher, Librairie Félix Alcan, which was based in Paris.[48]

Benjamin was interested in Judaism, and influenced by Jewish ideas. He discussed messianism, Jewish mysticism, Zionism, and the nature of his Jewishness, among other topics, at different points in his life.[49] However, he did not devote sustained study to antisemitism per se.

Upon reading Horkheimer's essay, however, Benjamin gushingly reported back to its author that "[t]here has been no political analysis in years that has so impressed me. This is the word we have been waiting for.... The entire time I was reading this essay, I had the feeling of coming upon truths."[50] In a letter to Gretel Adorno [Theodor Adorno's spouse], Benjamin adds that he had had "quite a few conversations about" Horkheimer's article, "all stressing how solid it is," and that it had occurred to him that "The question addressed in the article should be expanded by dealing with the way in which the anti-Semitic movement either depends on or stands in opposition to medieval anti-Semitism. This is exactly what Teddie [Adorno] pointed out regarding Wagner..."[51]

We'll turn shortly to Adorno's work on Wagner (in which Adorno made use of notions derived from Benjamin) and the importance of that work for understanding Adorno's role in the evolution of Critical Theory's approach to the study of antisemitism. For the moment, however, we'll focus on an altogether different question: Should Benjamin's comments to Horkheimer (and to Gretel Adorno) concerning "The Jews and Europe" be taken at face value?

Gershom Scholem, a close friend of Benjamin's, may be read as suggesting that Benjamin's enthusiastic comments on "The Jews and Europe" were intimately linked to Benjamin's more general relationship to the Institute itself. To be sure, Scholem's comments on Benjamin's reaction to "The Jews and Europe" may well themselves have been colored by Scholem's own distaste for that piece (and for Horkheimer). It is significant in this regard that when Benjamin, having already read Horkheimer's essay, explicitly asked Scholem what the latter thought of "The Jews and Europe,"[52] Scholem, (who was a committed Zionist, and had moved from Germany to Palestine in 1923) replied at length, and in both strong and highly negative terms.

Scholem, who had visited New York in 1938, had met with Horkheimer in the course of his trip, and had already informed Benjamin, in early November of that year, that he and Horkheimer had not hit it off. Horkheimer, Scholem proclaimed to his friend, "is not a pleasant fellow."[53] Moreover, "[i]t proved impossible to conduct even a single sensible conversation in his presence without having his infinitely and vividly bored expression make the words die in your (or rather my) mouth." Scholem attributed his inability to establish a warmer personal relationship with Horkheimer to "mutual antipathy." In addition, he wrote to Benjamin, "the personal impression I have of the man reinforces my opinion that, perhaps precisely *because* he feels he has to admire you, such a man can of necessity have only an inscrutable relationship to you, heavily burdened by a sense of embitterment... I wouldn't be surprised in the least if he turned out to be a scoundrel someday."[54] In this same letter, and immediately thereafter, Scholem alludes to the financial relationship between the Institute and Benjamin, and notes that he had made certain not to share his true feelings about Horkheimer with Adorno: "I thought it right not to say anything that could have

The Significance of Antisemitism: The Exile Years

tempered [Adorno's] enthusiasm to obtain, someday soon and the sooner the better, as decent a living for you as possible, by way of said H[orkheimer]."[55]

The poor impression that Horkheimer had made on Scholem in 1938 formed the backdrop for Scholem's reaction to the contents of "The Jews and Europe," which Scholem describes, when writing to Benjamin in February, 1940, as "an entirely useless product about which, astonishingly enough, nothing beneficial and new can be discovered."[56] Scholem flatly declares that Horkheimer did not have either any knowledge of the Jewish problem or any interest in it. He further suggests that in these ways Horkheimer's position is comparable to that of Marx in what Scholem describes as Marx's "repulsive" essay "On the Jewish Question," and that "The Jews and Europe" reads as if Horkheimer wanted to rewrite Marx's essay for the contemporary era. "[T]he Jews interest him not as Jews but only from the standpoint of the fate of the economic category that they represent for him ... he has no answer of any kind to give to the Jews." Beyond his feelings about this piece, Scholem admits, "The style of Horkheimer's writings has always been repugnant to me because of a certain brash impudence of instrumentation..."[57]

When, in the fall of 1939, the Second World War began, Benjamin was, like other German refugees living in France, incarcerated by the French government. Though he was released at the end of November 1939, Benjamin was even more in need of the Institute's support in the wake of his detention than had earlier been the case. For in the wake of his incarceration and release, Benjamin seems to have understood better than he had prior to those events how urgent it had become that he leave Europe for the United States[58] (though he remained ambivalent about emigrating) and also understood – correctly – that he would need substantial help from the Institute in order to do so.

A year earlier, Benjamin had sent to New York a manuscript on Baudelaire, anticipating that the Institute would publish it. Adorno, however, who was, in general, one of Benjamin's most enthusiastic supporters, had responded by informing Benjamin that he was disappointed by Benjamin's treatise, and by urging Benjamin to rewrite it. "The impression which your entire study conveys – and not only to me ... – is that you have here done violence upon yourself. Your solidarity with the Institute, which pleases no one more than myself, has led you to the kind of tributes to Marxism which are appropriate neither to Marxism nor to yourself."[59] This was by no means the first time that Adorno and Benjamin had disagreed sharply about intellectual matters.[60] Moreover, Adorno's treatment of Benjamin's typescript was no different than the way that the members of the Frankfurt School were likely to have treated any submission to the *Zeitschrift*. But Benjamin began his long response to Adorno's critique of his piece on Baudelaire by noting that Adorno's letter "came as quite a blow to me."[61]

Hannah Arendt – personally acquainted with both Benjamin and Adorno – famously charged, at a later point, that Benjamin perceived a "threat" that the Institute "would desert him."[62] Whether or not Benjamin felt such a "threat" (he never did say, one way or the other) and whether or not those associated with the Institute understood, in 1938–1940, that its actions vis-à-vis Benjamin could be perceived by some as resulting from a power dynamic – Leo Lowenthal, for one, compellingly exonerated the Institute, in later years, from having engaged in the course of action suggested by Arendt's wording[63] – it is beyond doubt that Benjamin's relationships with Adorno and with Horkheimer were essential to him, and complex. To be sure, when, in 1968, George Lichtheim repeated the allegation that Adorno's relationship with Benjamin was colored by financial considerations, and did so "without the slightest justification,"[64] Scholem slammed Lichtheim. On another occasion, Scholem insisted that "the accusations that have been made against Adorno and his critique" [of Benjamin] "are ludicrous."[65] Adorno did not threaten Benjamin, and the Institute did not make use of its financial position in order to coax Benjamin into reassessing vitally important matters. Nevertheless: it is not out of the question that Benjamin, in the late 30s and in early 1940, was "wooing" Horkheimer "because of financial concern."[66] Moreover, while Scholem rejected Arendt's "gloomy speculations about the Institute's conduct toward Benjamin, which far exceeded" Scholem's "own reservations,"[67] Scholem himself once described Benjamin's high praise for "The Jews and Europe" in December of 1939 as indicative of "[t]he extent of Benjamin's accommodation to the Institute, even in the case of a subject that by no means placed him under any pressure...."[68]

Scholem by no means altered his critical attitude towards Horkheimer's essay after he wrote the letter to Benjamin in which he comments directly on that piece. He made similar points in a letter to Theodor W. Adorno written in April 1940 arguing once again that Horkheimer's work took its tone from Marx's "On the Jewish Question," and that it therefore did not suffice.[69] Yet another letter to Adorno, dating from 1943, demonstrates that time did not change Scholem's opinion.[70]

The Significance of Antisemitism: The Exile Years

*

Adorno, like Scholem, was critical of Marx's piece on the Jewish question (at least implicitly).[71] On the other hand: Adorno voiced no reservations about the published version of Horkheimer's essay.[72] And yet, it was ultimately Adorno who led Horkheimer to revise his understanding of the persecution of the Jews, and to analyze antisemitism in a manner more consistent with Horkheimer's emerging approach to fascism and other issues.

In a prescient letter written by Adorno to Horkheimer on February 15, 1938 – that is, on the day before Adorno left Europe for the United States – Adorno predicted that there would be no country that would admit Jews who remained in Germany, and that those Jews would, therefore, be extirpated [*ausgerottet*].[73] This, it must be underscored, was not only before the extermination of European Jewry had actually begun, but also before most people – including most Jews in Germany – believed that such an extirpation would take place. Adorno's prediction is noteworthy not only for its contents, but also because his sense of things differed so markedly from that of others. "[U]ntil November 1938 [when the so-called *Kristallnacht* took place] the majority of [German] Jews attempted to adjust ... they clung to mixed signals from the government as well as from non-Jewish friends and strangers – a lull in antisemitic boycotts here, a friendly greeting there."[74] The timing of Adorno's premonition is significant, for it demonstrates that Adorno was thinking about antisemitism in a dramatic manner on the eve of his arrival in the United States, and that Adorno thought that antisemitism was a vital issue to raise with Horkheimer. Adorno continued to concern himself with the fate of the Jews, and the significance of this fate, for years to come.

How did Adorno explain antisemitism on the eve of World War II? A piece by Adorno on Wagner written between the fall of 1937 and the spring of 1938 and published in volume eight of the *Zeitschrift für Sozialforschung* – the volume in which "The Jews and Europe" was also published – comments that Wagner's "idiosyncratic hatred" of Jews can be clarified by keeping in mind Benjamin's definition of disgust as the fear of being thought to be the same "as that which is found disgusting" and notes parallels between Wagner's personal appearance, his loquacity, and his habit of gesticulating extravagantly while speaking, on the one hand, and a description of a Wagnerian character who is himself a caricature of a Jew on the other.[75] Adorno also notes that "[t]he realm of idiosyncrasy, usually conceived as the individual sphere par excellence, is in Wagner's case the realm also of the social and universal" and describes racist theories such as those of Wagner as situated "between idiosyncrasy and paranoia."[76] Wagner's idiosyncrasy is not merely a personal issue, but at the same time indicative of his social setting. Adorno ends his discussion of this topic by asserting that the final section of an essay by Wagner on Jews contains a passage "reminiscent of another tract on the Jewish Question" – by which Adorno clearly meant Marx's essay "Zur Judenfrage." "Without any attempt at differentiation we find intertwined here emancipation of the Jews as the emancipation of society from the profit-motive of which they are the symbolic representatives, and the ideas of the destruction of the Jews themselves."[77] Where Horkheimer, in the late 1930s, wraps himself in the Marxist understanding of "the Jewish question," Adorno links Wagner's views, of which he is very critical, with those of Marx.

Adorno's piece on Wagner strongly suggests the impact that Adorno's analysis of antisemitism would ultimately have on Horkheimer, for it presages the understanding of antisemitism published under the names of both men in *Dialectic of Enlightenment*, an understanding quite different from that evident in "The Jews and Europe." The differences between the explanation of antisemitism in "The Jews and Europe" on the one hand and in *Dialectic of Enlightenment* on the other are due in large part to the increasing influence of Adorno on Horkheimer during the Second World War.[78]

Neither Adorno's premonition of 1938, nor his increasing conviction of the importance of antisemitism, can be attributed to Jewish identity. Though Oscar Wiesengrund, Theodor Adorno's father, had been born a Jew, he converted to Protestantism in 1910, when Adorno was seven years old.[79] Oscar was reportedly an agnostic, and inclined to sympathize with the political left.[80] Theodor's mother, Maria, was a Catholic of Catholic origin (though she was initially, altogether erroneously, listed on Theodor's birth certificate as Jewish), and Theodor was baptized in the faith of the maternal half of his family.[81] In 1924, Theodor, who had, under the influence of a Protestant teacher, been confirmed in a Protestant church[82] considered converting to Catholicism "which" he declared "lay close enough to me as the son of a very Catholic mother."[83]

Adorno became acquainted with Siegfried Kracauer as the First World War was coming to an end, and soon began to meet with him regularly, on Saturday afternoons, in order to study Kant.[84] Their study sessions, Adorno reports, continued for years. Adorno, therefore, had ongoing contact with Kracauer when the latter first met Anton Nobel, Martin Buber and Franz Rosenzweig.[85] He would certainly have been aware that

The Significance of Antisemitism: The Exile Years 55

Kracauer taught at the Freie Jüdische Lehrhaus in 1921–1922[86] and that Kracauer contributed to a *Festschrift* for Rabbi Nobel during this same period. Kracauer, in fact, read Leo Lowenthal's contribution to the Nobel *Festschrift* together with Adorno.[87]

However, Adorno is not known to have evinced any interest in Jewish affairs during the 1920s, was not attracted to the theoreticians of the Jewish cultural renaissance, and was not involved with any explicitly Jewish organizations. As a very young man, he had shared the prejudices of many Germans – and German Jews – against East European Jews.[88] When Kracauer told Adorno about Rosenzweig's *Star of Redemption*, Adorno quipped, in a letter to Lowenthal, that "These are linguistic philosophemes I would not understand even if I understood them" – but added immediately thereafter that he nevertheless meant to read Rosenzweig's book because it dealt with matters of the greatest importance.[89] Several years later, when Lowenthal and Fromm (both of whom, as we have seen, had taught at the Lehrhaus, and both of whom had been intimately involved with Judaism and with Jewish organizations prior to their affiliation with the Institute of Social Research) became members of the Institute, Adorno referred to them as professional Jews ["*Berufsjuden*"], a term dripping with disdain.[90] Adorno, manifestly, had no problem socializing with Jews. Margarete [Gretel] Karplus, who he met in 1923 and married in 1937, was of Jewish origin.[91] But Adorno did not engage with Judaism, did not have a positive Jewish identity, and displayed precious little understanding for why some of his friends and colleagues thought differently about these matters than he did.

There is little evidence that Adorno (who was known as Wiesengrund or Wiesengrund-Adorno in pre-Nazi Germany, and who, therefore, would have been presumed to have had Jewish family roots by those with whom he came into contact) was deeply scarred by antisemitism as a boy or young man. Episodes of taunting and bullying by his classmates contain more than a whiff of anti-Jewish prejudice. An incident that took place while Adorno was a school boy, in the course of which five children jumped out from a hiding place while Adorno was on his way to school and shouted "Greetings to Father Abraham!", hints at how the young Adorno was perceived by his fellow students.[92] Adorno, however, later claimed that antisemitism had been "quite unusual in the commercial city of Frankfurt," the city in which he had been born and raised.[93]

One could argue that Adorno underestimated the depth of pre-Nazi antisemitism in his native city. But there was no question, even for Adorno, that the success of the Nazi movement dramatically altered

Frankfurt's atmosphere. In September 1933, Adorno lost his official permission to teach because he was a "non-Aryan."[94] He initially responded to this change not by publicly condemning antisemitism (which would likely have attracted harsh punishment), but rather by "hibernating."[95] When, later in 1933, the composer Alban Berg complained to his one-time student Adorno that not a single note of his was being played in Germany, the fact that he was not a Jew notwithstanding, while purported "martyrs" such as the violinist Bronisław Huberman, who was Jewish, were lauded in Vienna,[96] Adorno replied "[I]f I were you, I would send a letter to the Musikerkammer ... and clarify the fact that, contrary to certain claims that keep being made in Germany, you are of pure Aryan descent. For if one is celebrating the likes of Hubermann ... in Vienna while forgetting you, then I do not see why you should still show solidarity with a Jewry to which you do not even belong, that certainly shows you none, and about which you should, after all, have no more illusions than about other matters. In this context, it might interest you that the 'Jüdischer Kulturbund' ... forbade my co-operation in Frankfurt on the grounds of being of Christian confession and only half-Jewish by race."[97] Adorno had one piece accepted through the efforts of a non-Jewish editor of the *Stuttgarter Neues Tagesblatt*, who had known Adorno as a school boy, and described the decision to publish his piece as one of the very few examples of independence and of solidarity from which he benefitted in the first years of Hitler's regime. "One never forgets something like this" he wrote forty-four years after the event had taken place.[98] In 1934 (when, because of his partially "non-Aryan" origins, few journals in Germany would publish Adorno's work, and some might say there were, therefore, given his need to make a living, extenuating circumstances) Adorno went so far as to write a review for a periodical that had become ever more sympathetic to Nazi views, and that eventually became an organ of the *Reichsjugend*, a right-wing youth movement eventually absorbed into the Hitler Youth.[99] "I looked for a way to remain in Germany regardless of cost..." Adorno wrote in that year to the composer Ernst Krenek.[100] In a letter to his parents written when he was already in New York, Adorno explained his decision to stay in Germany by pointing out that the conditions for the rise of antisemitism were "at least as present" in the United States "as in Germany" and adds "I am convinced that one is hopelessly trapped, regardless of where one may be. And it was this conviction that was the root of my resistance against emigration – first my own and then yours. If one is definitely going to be struck dead, I thought, then at least in the place where one belongs most, according to one's whole nature and the character of one's insights."[101] It was, he explained to Krenek, only when one possibility after another, even the most modest, was taken away from him that he decided to leave. He added at that time that he had had no political objection to remaining in Germany after the Nazis came to power.[102] Even if Adorno's contribution to a pro-Nazi periodical can be rationalized and his self-proclaimed lack of political objection to remaining in Germany dismissed as hyperbole, they seem to corroborate the sense that Adorno did not think of himself as Jewish during the Weimar years or at the beginning of the Nazi era, and that his self-understanding was linked to German culture far, far more than to his father's Jewish roots. Yet, as Benjamin was to point out to Adorno after the Second World War had begun, "The very fact that Proust was only half Jewish allowed him insight into the highly precarious structure of assimilation; an insight which was then externally confirmed by the Dreyfus Affair."[103] Much the same can be said about the source of Adorno's insights into antisemitism, later confirmed by the Holocaust. It was, it would appear, precisely the fact that Adorno was only partially of Jewish origin that enabled him to understand the significance of totalitarian antisemitism (even) before his closest (altogether Jewish) colleagues in the Frankfurt School came to comparable realizations.

Adorno had not been employed as an official, full-time, member of the Institute of Social Research during the Weimar era. When he first arrived in the United States in 1938, having spent much of the preceding four years in Oxford, moreover, Adorno worked on a half-time basis for the Princeton Radio Research Project.[104] Adorno moved to the United States at the explicit urging of Horkheimer. But he did not begin to occupy a full line at the Institute until 1940 ... and it was not until this long-hoped for position finally materialized that Adorno and Horkheimer could devote themselves, as Adorno had hoped for quite some time, to the project of co-writing a major work.[105]

The precise topics around which this joint work would revolve were, for an extended period, still very much up in the air. Horkheimer was busy attempting to acquire funding for any number of different research projects, on any number of different themes – including a project on antisemitism, first proposed in 1939. This was, as we have already noted, not a theme to which the Institute had devoted sustained attention in the works that it published during the Weimar era or, for that matter, during its earliest years in the United States. On the eve of the Second World War, however, the long-term financial situation of the Institute did not look good, and Horkheimer decided on a scattershot strategy for pursuing funds. At one point, Horkheimer was shepherding proposals for nine projects simultaneously. Horkheimer's willingness to propose a project on antisemitism was linked to Horkheimer's sense that Jewish organizations in the United States would be most likely to provide material support to the Institute if they could be convinced that the Institute was conducting research on a topic close to their hearts. The antisemitism project, however, was not merely a gambit, but rather a proposed undertaking that Horkheimer explicitly declared he was particularly invested in: "I put more libido into" this proposal, he wrote to his friend Katharina von Hirsch, "than in others."[106]

It was Horkheimer rather than Adorno who first proposed that the Institute pursue funds for a project on antisemitism.[107] When, however, in the spring of 1939, Horkheimer first began to distribute copies of the project proposal, he characterized it as having been drafted by Adorno and himself.[108] It is also noteworthy that it was Adorno who was charged with drafting a second version of the project proposal – a task that he completed, with the aid of his wife, at the end of July 1940.[109]

Days after completing this draft, Adorno described the proposed project to a prominent American who was sympathetic to the Institute – Professor Charles E. Merriam of the University of Chicago, who had agreed to serve on the Institute's Advisory Committee, and to allow his name to appear on the Institute's letterhead – as "concerned with the problem of Anti-Semitism, especially with such questions as the historic origin of Anti-Semitism and the influence of economic developments on anti-semitic psychology and with the different types of present day anti-semitism." "We intend," Adorno continued, "to include an extensive experimental psychological section. At present we are trying to supplement this project with research into antisemitic theory and practice in National Socialist Germany, as well as its international repercussions."[110]

In a draft of this letter, Adorno had noted that Horkheimer's essay "The Jews and Europe" would provide the theoretical foundation for the proposed project.[111] The fact that no such passage appears in the letter as ultimately sent may suggest that Adorno and Horkheimer were moving beyond "The Jews and Europe" by the summer of 1940 (or that they did not want to reveal the contents of that piece to an important American contact).

Adorno explained his ideas about antisemitism, and his view of his place in the world, in a private letter to his parents: "Fascism in Germany, which is inseparable from anti-Semitism, is no psychological anomaly of the German national character. It is a universal tendency and has an economic basis... namely the dying out of the sphere of circulation, i.e. the increasing superfluity of trade in the widest sense, in the age of monopoly capitalism. The conditions for it – and I mean *all of them*, not only the economic but also the *mass psychological* ones – are at least as present here as in Germany... and the barbaric semi-civilization of this country will spawn forms no less terrible than those in Germany ... I consider the solution dreamt of by..." Oscar Wiesengrund, "namely that the Jews could still mingle with the others, out of the question. It is too late; the business has taken on the character of catastrophe."[112] Both Adorno's continuing agreement with a key portion of the Marxist-influenced essay "The Jews and Europe," and his interest in psychological explanations of sociological phenomena, are evident here. In addition, Adorno states here for the first time his explicit rejection of the viability of assimilationism, the classic program of liberal, bourgeois, German Jews of his father's generation.

Not all the members of the Institute of Social Research agreed with Adorno's understanding of Jew-hatred as expressed in the revised draft of the proposal for a project on antisemitism. Franz Neumann – who was explicitly asked by Horkheimer to comment on Adorno's ideas[113] – wrote to Adorno, for example, that he read Adorno as indicating that antisemitism was necessary to an understanding of Nazism, but that in fact National Socialism could be presented without allocating a central role to the Jewish problem. Antisemitism, Neumann asserted, no longer played a major role in the foreign policies of the Nazi regime. Moreover, "I consider the contention that what happens to the Jews happens in truth to all to be fundamentally false."[114] Neumann also underscored in his commentary on Adorno's proposal that members of the Institute ought to be careful, even in drafting project proposals, not to abandon "our theoretical standpoint," and that Adorno's wording, which, Neumann believed, had been adopted for tactical reasons, overestimated the significance of antisemitism.[115]

But Adorno's wording was not merely the result of a tactical maneuver, and revealed a genuine distinction between his analysis and that of Neumann. Adorno devoted a considerable amount of thought to the "Jewish question" in the summer of 1940, after he had prepared the second draft of the Institute's project proposal. In a letter to Horkheimer written on August 5 of that year Adorno writes: "I am beginning to feel, particularly under the influence of the latest news from Germany, that I cannot stop thinking about the fate of the Jews any more. It often seems to me that everything that we used to see from the point of view of the proletariat has been concentrated today with frightful force upon the Jews. No matter what happens to the project, I ask myself whether we should not say what we want to say in connection with the Jews, who are now at the opposite pole to the concentration of power."[116] "These lines," Rolf Tiedemann has correctly stressed, "provide us with a key to Adorno's thinking from 1940 on."[117] Whereas Horkheimer had, in the 1930s, seen the world "from the point of view of the proletariat" – that is, from a Western Marxist-influenced perspective – Adorno now believed that that perspective no longer sufficed. "It is plain that class struggles of the past had been succeeded by something worse," Tiedemann glosses, "by the 'concentration of power,' domination as such, a completely rationalized system of manipulation. Human beings, far from organizing themselves as a proletariat into the subject of history, were being definitively degraded in the camps to mere objects of the most brutal oppression."[118]

The Institute published its proposed plan for a full-scale study of antisemitism in 1941, and proclaimed at that time that antisemitism was neither an anachronism nor an aberration but rather "one of the dangers inherent in all more recent culture."[119] As had Horkheimer's "The Jews and Europe," the Institute's project proposal also contended that "the foreign rather than the German masses are the spectators for whom German pogroms are arranged" and suggested how Nazism and liberalism were linked: "National Socialism has more in common with the French Revolution than is generally assumed."[120] In light of the Institute's long-term commitment to interdisciplinary study of large social issues, it should come as no surprise that the Institute explicitly stated that it intended to "combine historical, psychological, and economic research."[121] In 1941 (unlike in Horkheimer's article) the Institute insisted that an economic interpretation of antisemitism, while partially correct, had to be "supplemented by an analysis of ... psychological mechanisms."[122] Through the use of experimental films and other techniques, the Institute proposed both to measure antisemitism in various strata of the American population and to develop a typology of antisemites.[123] The proposed antisemitism project, in sum, echoed some of the ideas suggested by Horkheimer in "The Jews and Europe." It went beyond the approach that had been used by Horkheimer by placing much greater emphasis than he had on non-Marxist approaches to the issue at hand and by proposing to add empirical analysis to Horkheimer's theoretical explanation.[124] The growing influence of Adorno on Horkheimer may well help to explain this shift – at least in part.

In the course of a first rate analysis of the construction of antisemitism in *Dialectic of Enlightenment* Anson Rabinbach once suggested (following, as he has noted, Wiggershaus) that it may have been the death of Walter Benjamin, and the arrival, in June 1941, of Benjamin's testament, "Theses on the Philosophy of History," which provided Horkheimer and Adorno with a " 'guiding star' around which the constellation of themes – the fate of the exile, the fate of the Jews, and the catastrophe of civilization – that ultimately make up 'Dialectic of Enlightenment' could be organized."[125] It is manifestly the case that Benjamin displayed interest in Judaism over a period of decades, and that this interest (encouraged by Gershom Scholem) had a dramatic impact on his thought and writings.[126] It is also universally acknowledged that Benjamin's thought, in turn, had a profound effect on Adorno. In this sense, it may well be true that Benjamin, and worry as to Benjamin's fate, increased Adorno's concern with antisemitism. But I would add that Adorno's letter to Horkheimer of August 5, 1940, demonstrates that Adorno suggested a theoretical project that would revolve around antisemitism before the suicide of Adorno's old friend, and before Adorno's reading of Benjamin's last major piece.

Moreover, Rabinbach, whose work is otherwise exceptionally reliable and accurate, slipped up, at one time, by attributing to Horkheimer a crucial letter, dating from October 1941, which discusses the book that Horkheimer and Adorno were planning to co-write, and thus contributed to a misunderstanding as to why Horkheimer became so keen to write a serious, theoretical, piece on antisemitism.[127] It was Adorno – not Horkheimer – who writes: "How would it be if the book ... were to crystallize around anti-Semitism? This would bring with it the concretization and limitation that we have been looking for. It would also be possible for the topic to motivate most of the Institute's associates..."[128] Adorno's continuing desire to write on antisemitism was sparked not by Benjamin's death per se, but by a deeper sense that, as he put it in this letter, antisemitism had become the contemporary world's "central injustice," and that it was the task of Critical Theory to "attend to the world where it shows its face at its most gruesome."[129] Horkheimer found Adorno's reasoning compelling, and became convinced that he should devote sustained attention to antisemitism, and [co]-write a theoretical piece grappling with that topic. But considerably different factors explain Horkheimer's interest in having the Institute (as distinguished from himself) also devote attention to hatred of Jews.

Horkheimer's desire that the Institute conduct a research project on antisemitism was fed by a number of streams.[130] Horkheimer's Jewish family background, which led him to identify himself as Jewish when speaking to American audiences in the 1940s, was among these streams, and ultimately sensitized him to the general issue of Jew hatred. In a speech on antisemitism delivered on April 16, 1943, Horkheimer told his audience that "[o]ur interest as Jews which leads us to engage in such a work is identical with our task as laborers for the future of mankind."[131] It is altogether possible that Horkheimer was inclined to make such statements by his belief that he would be telling American Jews what they wanted to hear, and thus increasing the level of support he could obtain from American Jewish organizations. However, there were more heartfelt reasons for Horkheimer to make declarations of this kind.

The extent of antisemitism in the United States made the Horkheimer circle more aware of the issue than they had previously been. Antisemitism had become increasingly troublesome in the United States during the 1920s, and accelerated its growth in the 1930s and early 1940s. In the 1920s, specific colleges and universities in the United States introduced quotas designed to decrease or limit the proportion of Jewish students who were enrolled in these institutions. These quotas became more rigid in the following decade.[132] Jews found it ever harder to be admitted into professional schools: "From 1920 to 1940" that is to say in a period during a portion of which members of the Horkheimer circle were living in New York, and during which the Institute was affiliated with Columbia University, "the percentage of Jews in Columbia University's College of Physicians and Surgeons fell from 46.94 to 6.45; the percentage of City College of New York graduates admitted to any medical school dropped from 58 to 15; and not one graduate of either Hunter or Brooklyn College in New York City entered an American medical school... A similar decline occurred in law schools..."[133] Jews in the United States also encountered discrimination in employment in the period between the two world wars: "Few manufacturing companies, corporate law firms, private hospitals, or such governmental bureaucracies as the State Department welcomed Jews as businessmen, lawyers, doctors, or career diplomats. This pattern of exclusion, begun in college and extended to business and professional life, did not change significantly until after World War II."[134] Discrimination against Jews was common in social clubs and in country clubs across the United States.[135] "Restricted covenants" prevented Jews from living in particular neighborhoods or buildings. During the years of the Great Depression, antisemitic organizations, such as the Silver Legion, Defenders of the Christian Faith, the Knights of the White Camelia, the James True Associates, the American Nationalist Confederation and the National

Union for Social Justice, were established. By 1939, according to one source, there were over five hundred such groups in the United States[136] These organizations disseminated antisemitic ideas, which resonated beyond the ranks of their own memberships. Father Charles Coughlin, a priest based in Detroit with a particularly wide following among Irish Catholics living in urban areas, substantially broadened the constituency of organized antisemitism beyond its Protestant base. Three and a half million people listened regularly to Father Coughlin's weekly radio addresses in 1938. Fifteen million more had tuned in to hear him at least once. During that same year, Father Coughlin called for a unified Christian Front. At rallies of the organization thereby brought into being, members were exhorted to "liquidate the Jews in America."[137] A rally organized by the German American Bund in 1939 demanding that "Jewish domination of Christian America" be stopped attracted 19,000 people to Madison Square Garden in New York. Pollsters found, on the eve of American entry into the Second World War, that ever higher proportions of the American population replied affirmatively to the question, "Do you think Jews have too much power in the United States?" Forty one percent of those polled responded affirmatively to this question in March 1938. Forty three percent responded positively in April 1940. The proportion rose to 45 percent in February 1941, and to 48 percent in October 1941.[138] Leo Lowenthal later noted that it was not until he and his colleagues had come to the United States that they "suddenly discovered that something like a real everyday antisemitism did exist here and that as a Jew one couldn't freely take part in all social spheres. That hotels and clubs, even whole professions, were simply closed to Jews – that didn't yet exist in Germany to such an extent" in the formative years of the members of the Institute.[139] There is no doubt whatsoever that the members of the Frankfurt School also became aware, at some point during their American years, of figures like Father Coughlin.

The Institute's pressing financial needs – mentioned above – certainly played a major role in Horkheimer's decision to have his associates seek large-scale grants for a series of projects related to antisemitism.[140] However, it was not, in the last analysis, the need for funds that best explains why Horkheimer himself chose to write on antisemitism, but rather Adorno's premonition of the destruction of European Jewry, Adorno's repeated suggestions that he and Horkheimer write on antisemitism, and a growing sense on the part of both Horkheimer and Adorno of the significance of continuing Jew hatred.[141] By 1941, Horkheimer – unlike, it can be safely assumed, Neumann – had come to believe, as he wrote in a letter to Harold Laski, that "society itself can be properly understood only through Antisemitism."[142]

It ought to be noted that not only Neumann but also certain other members of the Institute were not immediately convinced. Lowenthal was inclined, during this period, to be heavily influenced by views expressed by Horkheimer, the Institute's director. However, as late as the fall of 1942, Lowenthal (who, as we have seen, continued to publish works in Jewish organs at the end of the Weimar era, but who, on the other hand, was not actively involved with Jewish institutions after he became a full-time member of the Institute in 1930) frankly admitted to Horkheimer "so far I have not developed a genuine affinity towards the problem itself"[143] and implored Horkheimer to explain to him "the esoteric significance of the whole enterprise."[144] Horkheimer replied by assuring Lowenthal that he would write about the project's importance when the project's funding had been assured and the work on it had actually begun.[145] At a later date, he wrote to Lowenthal: "These days are days of sadness. The extermination of the Jewish people has reached dimensions greater than at any time in history. I think that the night after these events will be very long and may devour humanity."[146]

In April 1943, by which point the Institute's antisemitism project was in progress (and by which point Horkheimer was living in Los Angeles), Horkheimer explained his motivations in an important letter to Herbert Marcuse, who had become part of Horkheimer's inner circle, and who was clearly respected by the Institute's director:

I more than share your pessimism concerning the general situation. That is one of the reasons why I finally conceded our accepting the cooperation with the [American Jewish] Committee [discussed below – JJ]. Though I am most skeptical about the chances for an expansion of the project after the first year, I still think I have not the right to ignore Pollock's conviction that it would be unwise to decline the offering of a connection which is one of the very few which holds certain potentialities for after the war. But more important than the practical point of view seemed to me the theoretical one... [Y]ou will remember that in the beginning of our stay here you and I tried to find a topic which would fulfill the two requirements of first, encountering a somewhat broader interest than our ideas in their abstract form and second, offering an opportunity to develop some of those ideas in a more concrete material. I wanted to have an occasion for expressing our theoretical thoughts and at the same time presenting ourselves as experts in particular social problems.... [M]y wish not to stay too distant from pertinent questions was so strong that Teddie [Adorno] and I had ... written part of the new memorandum on German Chauvinism which we had thought should have become a book. Instead of the book on Germany we shall now write on Anti-Semitism and instead of devoting half of our time we shall devote most of it to that purpose.[147]

Members of the Institute who distrusted the development of Critical Theory beyond Marxism had far greater misgivings about the direction endorsed by Horkheimer than those initially expressed by Lowenthal. Lowenthal reported in 1943, for example, that Henryk Grossmann's "opinions about our research project and about the political situation are as stupid as they always were."[148]

Differences of opinion within the Institute as to how to assess antisemitism were also apparent in a dispute that arose over a memo written by Lowenthal in 1944 on the prevention of antisemitism in post-War Germany. Paul Massing, who left Germany in 1934 (after a period of incarceration in a concentration camp), and who became a research associate at the Institute in New York in 1941, and Arkady Gurland (1904–1979), a left social democrat born in Russia and educated in Germany who had been driven into exile by the rise of the Nazis and who had become affiliated with the Institute after he arrived in the United States in 1940,[149] vigorously attacked Lowenthal's memo, arguing that the position taken by Lowenthal "is a complete reversal of the position up to now maintained by the Institute" and informing Horkheimer that "we cannot imagine that it expresses your thought on the issues involved."[150] According to Massing and Gurland, antisemitism was "a phenomenon of our class culture" and "the integration of Nazi Germany was furthered by the use of antisemitism only as far as clearly defined groups and classes were concerned; ... the larger part of the German population rejected it."[151] They had any number of issues with Lowenthal's memo, and asserted that considerations such as these had purportedly not even entered into the thinking evident in Lowenthal's piece. But Horkheimer sympathized with Lowenthal – not with Massing and Gurland – in this dispute, and so did Adorno and Pollock.[152] Lowenthal underscored some of the differences between his perspective and that of his opponents in the following terms: "If they had really understood that the image as well as the fate of the Jew is the living, or better, the dying witness of nefarious imitation and of all attempts to destroy it, they would realize the shock-like effect which can emerge by focusing theoretical and practical endeavors around the Jewish problem."[153]

Unlike Grossmann, and certain other affiliates of the Institute, Adorno, Horkheimer, and Pollock had become committed to the attempt to explain antisemitic behavior, and Lowenthal was willing to follow Horkheimer's lead. Adorno underscored as early as September 1940[154] that a theoretical explanation of Jew-hatred would have to depend on a primeval history, and that this history could not be grounded *simply* in psychological factors, as Freud had attempted, but also had to be rooted in archaic social movements. In a very preliminary attempt to present to Horkheimer some thoughts as to the origins of antisemitism and the reasons for its persistence – an attempt that must be quoted at length – Adorno writes:

> The survival of nomadism among the Jews might provide not only an explanation for the nature of the Jew himself, but even more an explanation for anti-Semitism. The abandonment of nomadism was apparently one of the most difficult sacrifices demanded in human history. The Western concept of work, and all of the instinctual repression it involves, may coincide exactly with the development of settled habitation. The image of the Jews is one of a condition of humanity in which work is unknown, and all of the later attacks on the parasitic, miserly character of the Jews are mere rationalizations. The Jews are the ones who have not allowed themselves to be 'civilized' and subjected to the priority of work. This has not been forgiven them, and that is why they are a bone of contention in class society. They have not allowed themselves, one might say, to be driven out of Paradise, or at least only reluctantly. In addition, the description that Moses gives of the land flowing with milk and honey is a description of Paradise. This holding firm to the most ancient image of happiness is the Jewish utopia. It does not matter whether the nomadic condition was in fact a happy one or not.... But the more the world of settled habitation – a world of work – produced repression, the more the earlier condition must have seemed to be a form of happiness which could not be permitted, the very idea of which must be banned. This ban is the origin of anti-Semitism, the expulsions of the Jews, and the attempt to complete or imitate the expulsion from Paradise.[155]

*

The Institute's proposal for a research project on antisemitism was pitched to a number of potential sponsors, including the American Jewish Committee [AJC].[156] The AJC was founded in New York in 1906 by wealthy, and acculturated, American Jews of German-speaking origin. It had long been concerned about antisemitism in America, but it had not, in the 1920s, taken proactive and public steps to counter it. The AJC, for example, did not officially take "part in opposing the college quota system" and "developed no positive program to combat the creeping discrimination" in the business world, preferring, instead to engage in quiet diplomacy, often involving individual leaders of the AJC but not the organization per se.[157]

The Institute's proposal did not, at first, attract interest from the AJC[158] – and it is not surprising that the AJC didn't rush to support the Institute's initiative. The AJC and the Institute were by no means natural allies. Despite the portion of the proposal devoted to empirical matters, the Institute's leading figures were primarily interested in theoretical investigations. The AJC, on the other hand, was concerned first and foremost with matters having direct policy implications. The Institute had a Marxist past, and was made up, on the eve of the Second World War, of men with (varying kinds and degrees of) left-wing sympathies. AJC was dominated by bourgeois figures closely associated with major, established, financial and business institutions who were wholly opposed to communism. The Critical Theorists were deeply European both in their style and in their inclinations. The AJC was proudly American. Years later, Lowenthal noted yet another source of strain between those in the Institute and those in the AJC: the long-standing tensions between German-speaking Jews and Jews of East European origin.[159] Virtually all of the members of the Institute – including all of the Critical Theorists – fell firmly into the first of these categories. Though the AJC had been founded by German Jews, some of those in or working for the AJC in the 1940s were in the second. Nevertheless, the AJC ultimately agreed to fund the Institute's proposed antisemitism project.

Its decision to do so was linked to the marked rise in antisemitism in the United States. In 1931, an entity that was technically independent of the AJC but that was fostered by AJC leaders, the Information and Service Associates, began investigating antisemitic organizations operating in the United States. Five years later, the work of that grouping was handed over to the Survey Committee, which was officially subject to the AJC, and which undertook a more vigorous program of education and investigation.[160] However, polls both right before and immediately after the beginning of the Second World War indicated that despite these efforts antisemitism was nevertheless increasing in the United States, and the AJC apparently became receptive to new initiatives.

It was, to be sure, unimpressed by the Institute's first draft for a research project on antisemitism. But Franz Neumann, encouraged by Horkheimer, revised the Institute's proposal late in 1941.[161] This new version of the Institute's proposal was far better, from the AJC's perspective, than its predecessor. It argued that there was a "new anti-Semitism" which was "totalitarian" and which aimed "not only at exterminating the Jews but also at annihilating liberty and democracy. It has become the spearhead of the totalitarian order, and the aims and functions of this order can be vastly clarified by a study of anti-Semitism."[162] Similarly, at a later point, the revised proposal claimed that "the attacks on the Jews are not primarily aimed at the Jews but at large sections of modern society, especially the free middle classes, which appear as an obstacle to the establishment of totalitarianism. Anti-Semitism is a kind of rehearsal; when the results of the rehearsal are satisfactory, the real performance – the attack on the middle classes – takes place."[163] Here and elsewhere the Institute's revised proposal was fully in accord with statements that had long been made by those associated with the AJC. When, for example, the Survey Committee had stated its goals it proclaimed that "Our program is based upon the belief that the civil and religious rights of the Jews in the United States are dependent upon the maintenance of our democratic form of government ... we can best help maintain ... rights by fortifying adherence to the fundamental principles of democracy ... We wish to appeal to the spirit of democracy...."[164] The AJC came to believe, over time, that the best way to deal with antisemitism in America was "to expose its true character as a miserable anti-democratic and anti-American manifestation."[165] To be sure, the Institute's revised proposal repeated a number of the same arguments as had been made in its predecessor, such as the contention that many antisemitic trends were based on psychological drives, and that the most appropriate way to study antisemitism was by cutting across disciplines and making use of insights from history, sociology, psychology and other fields. On the other hand, the revised proposal was more compelling than had been its predecessor – as evidenced by the fact that it accomplished its task of attracting funds.

In the summer of 1942, Franz Neumann and Isacque Graeber (an American sociologist who had experience interacting with Jewish organizations, who had written on questions dealing with antisemitism, and who was engaged by the Institute to help obtain funding for the antisemitism project)[166] met with David Rosenblum, Chairman of the Public Relations Committee of the AJC, in order to discuss the Institute's proposed project on antisemitism with him. By sheer coincidence, this meeting took place on the day that the *Contemporary Jewish Record*, the AJC's organ, published a very favorable review of Neumann's newly released book, *Behemoth*. *Contemporary Jewish Record* had also published a favorable review of a book by Graeber several months earlier. These two reviews had a great and highly positive impact on Rosenblum, who left Neumann with the distinct impression that the AJC would be likely to provide the Institute with a grant of $10,000 for the Institute's antisemitism project.[167]

The account given by Neumann of his meeting with Rosenblum led the Institute's inner circle to make additional efforts to secure a grant from the AJC. In the fall of 1942, for example, the Institute prepared yet another memorandum for a proposed research project on antisemitism, and solicited the input of prominent Americans, such as Robert Lynd, a professor of sociology at Columbia University who was sympathetic to the Institute, in the preparation of this memo. This version of the Institute's project proposal emphasized that the defeat of Nazi Germany would by no means eliminate the threat posed by antisemitism and that there were circumstances under which a strong demand for antisemitic policies might emerge in post-war society. Lynd was worried that such a project might turn the Institute into an entity for the study of antisemitism.[168] He nevertheless agreed to support the Institute's efforts, and contributed his name, ideas, and advice to the Institute's initiative.[169]

Whatever the misgivings of Lynd, Horkheimer came to accept Neumann's spearhead understanding of the issue at hand. He repeatedly argued during this period – just as did Neumann – that antisemitism was a spearhead, that is, that it was "not alone a menace to the Jews, but a symptom of the crisis facing democratic civilization."[170] "Hatred of the Jew," Horkheimer insisted, "is hatred of democracy..."[171] Thus, "an organized investigation into the psychology of antisemitism is in no way a matter concerning Jews exclusively, but it is of the greatest importance for all who are interested in the fate of democratic civilization."[172]

Even within his inner circle, however, Horkheimer did not find unanimity with this approach. Herbert Marcuse, for one, wrote to Horkheimer in July 1943 that he found the spearhead theory increasingly inadequate. The function of fascist antisemitism, Marcuse claimed

is apparently more and more the perpetuation of an already established pattern of domination in the character of men ... in ... German propaganda, the Jew has now become an 'internal' being, which lives in Gentiles as well as Jews, and which is not conquered even with the annihilation of the 'real' Jews. If we look at the character traits and qualities which the Nazis designate as the Jewish elements in the Gentiles, we do not find the so-called typical Jewish traits (or at least not primarily) but traits which are regarded as definitively Christian and 'humane'. They are furthermore the traits which stand most decidedly against repression in all its forms... Der Jude ist von dieser Welt, and diese Welt is the one which fascism has to subject to the totalitarian terror."[173]

Horkheimer responded sympathetically to Marcuse.[174] But he did not abandon the spearhead theory – and apparently had the support of Adorno on this issue.[175]

Just what was it that made the antisemitism project attractive for Rosenblum? According to Pollock, Rosenblum was taken with the notion that "a blending of European and American methods in the field of the study of anti-Semitism" might well lead to concrete results, and accepted the Institute's suggestion that "a strong social demand for antisemitism in this country" might outlive the war against Nazi Germany.[176]

More generally, the palpable increase in antisemitism in America in the late 1930s and early 1940s led those in the AJC to believe that counter measures of some kind ought to be taken. The relationship between the AJC and the Institute had its roots in the AJC's growing sense that more needed to be done.

A formal document setting forth an understanding between the AJC and the Institute dated March 3, 1943, and sent to Pollock notes that it had been agreed that there would be two groups working on the project simultaneously. One group, based in New York, would be headed by Pollock and by Professor Robert M. MacIver (who, like Lynd, was a member of the Department of Sociology of Columbia University), and would also involve the collaboration of a number of individuals directly affiliated with the Institute in various capacities, such as Franz Neumann, Arkady Gurland, Leo Lowenthal, and Paul Massing. The second group, based in California, would work under the direction of Horkheimer, who, the agreement explicitly states, "will have as his assistant Dr. Theodor Adorno who will devote full time to it."[177]

The Institute promptly went to work, and, in a document dated March 15, 1943, spelled out the methodological principles and the assumptions that would form the basis of its project. This document makes a sharp differentiation between pre-totalitarian and totalitarian antisemitism, emphasizing that the former is directed against the Jews per se, while the latter "is an offensive instrument designed to change the structure of society."[178] Whereas non-totalitarian antisemitism distinguishes between purportedly good and purportedly bad Jews, and allows for the integration of the former, totalitarian antisemitism does not. The "scope and techniques of totalitarian anti-Semitism are directly determined by the political functions the totalitarian system of government requires it to perform. In consequence, totalitarian anti-Semitism is always manipulated." Thus certain groups that had been antisemitic in the pre-totalitarian era might become allied with Jews in the struggle against totalitarianism.

Horkheimer, however, had misgivings about this distinction, arguing that "Antisemitism has always been totalitarian, it was the incarnation of totalitarianism a thousand years before it took shape in Nazism."[179] The Institute responded to Horkheimer's critique by modifying its language, referring, at one point, to "political" antisemitism where it had earlier used the term "totalitarian."[180]

By mid-1943, the Institute's research project on antisemitism was well underway and joint meetings of the AJC and the Institute were arranged at which preliminary results were presented. Gurland, for example, presented a paper at one such meeting in which he argued that emancipation had failed in Germany, that German Jews had "felt much to[o] secure" and, that they had not understood their own situation prior to the rise of the Nazis.[181] The implications for American Jewry were manifest to those present. Paul Massing – the only long-term non-Jewish research associate of the Institute involved with the antisemitism project on a full-time basis – presented a paper at the same joint session, arguing that antisemitism has, in the final analysis, "no relation to whatever the Jews might" [or might not] do, because "there is no causal relationship between A[nti]-S[emitism] and its victims."[182] He also pointed out, however, that this should not be taken to mean that antisemitism is irrational. From Massing's perspective, antisemitism was "highly rational insofar as it is based on existing aggressive trends."[183]

On a later occasion, in July 1943, Pollock discussed the conditions that might give rise to the emergence of "political" antisemitism in the United States. He discussed a hypothetical scenario in which the continued existence of the free enterprise system in the United States in the postwar era would lead first to a boom lasting a number of years, and then to an economic depression of hitherto unknown dimensions. In the context of such a depression, he hypothesized, "[t]here will be a pressing social demand not only for a scapegoat but even more for a group against which all the resentment, aggressiveness, frustration, craving for vengeance, disappointment, fears for the future and all the other disintegrating passions can be channelled."[184] The Jews, he suggested, could well be that scapegoat – and the political antisemites who would come to the fore might also usher in a totalitarian government. According to Pollock "There is no better known means to usher in totalitarianism than violent political Antisemitism."[185] Though Pollock was careful to throw in the caveat that the scenario he had sketched out was by no means written into the course of history, and might not be actualized, he noted that the situation he described "might arise if its preparatory stages will not be stopped."[186]

Otto Kirchheimer (1905–1965) – a German Jew and German Social Democrat who fled Germany in 1933 and who later became a research associate of the Institute in New York[187] – also conducted research on antisemitism with material support derived from the AJC grant. Kirchheimer concentrated on the attitudes of American Catholics towards Jews, and conducted field research in an Irish Catholic neighborhood in Brooklyn. In a preliminary summary of his findings as of mid-September 1943, Kirchheimer is reported to have found that the Catholic Church in the United States did not have a consistent attitude towards antisemitism, but used it when it believed that it would benefit the Church to do so.[188]

Adorno presented a summary of findings based on studies of specific American agitators (which had been conducted by Lowenthal, Massing and himself as components of the antisemitism project) at a psychiatric symposium on antisemitism held in San Francisco (in June, 1944) and organized by Ernst Simmel.[189] In the published version of the talk he delivered at that conference, Adorno explained that the studies on which he based his remarks had analyzed radio addresses made by American fascist agitators and other sources. He underscored that the radio addresses that had been examined did not present arguments but rather attempted to win people over by making use of unconscious mechanisms. "[C]oncrete political ideas," Adorno stressed, "play but a minor role compared with the psychological stimuli applied to the audience."[190] Adorno went on to describe specific techniques used by fascist propagandists in the United States, including their tendencies to spend a great deal of time discussing themselves or their audiences, to spend very little time describing their goals, and to act as if they were informing their audiences about important matters that had been previously hidden from these audiences. American fascist propagandists, Adorno continued, had not attacked real, live Jews so much as they had created an image of the Jew and attacked that image. Making a point similar to that which had already been made by Massing, Adorno stressed that this was not irrational, but rather consciously planned. It was "a kind of psychotechnics reminiscent of the calculated effect conspicuous in most presentations of today's mass culture, such as in movies and broadcasts.... Conditions prevailing in our society tend to transform neurosis and even mild lunacy into a commodity which the afflicted can easily sell, once he has discovered that many others have an affinity for his own illness."[191] Thus, even if American fascist agitators were paranoid, these agitators could "sell" their approach because those to whom they were pitching their ideas had specific psychological issues similar to those of the agitators. The agitators put on a good show "reminiscent of the theater, of sport, and of so-called religious revivals,"[192] and the listeners, gratified, responded by buying the agitators' product just as they bought the products advertised during their favorite soap operas. There is, Adorno notes, a ritual that occurs in the address of every fascist agitator studied – "the temporary abandonment of responsible, self-contained seriousness."[193] "A comprehensive theory of fascist propaganda," he concludes, "would be tantamount to a psychoanalytic deciphering" of this ritual – a deciphering that Adorno was able to hint at, but not explore in depth, in the context of his paper.[194]

Horkheimer too spoke on antisemitism at the conference in San Francisco. Horkheimer emphasized the psychological roots of the problem of Jew-hatred, noting that "anti-Semitism and the susceptibility to anti-Semitic propaganda spring from the unconscious."[195] He also claimed (incorrectly) that "At present the only country where there does not seem to be any kind of anti-Semitism is Russia," and explained that that was (allegedly) the case because there were laws prohibiting antisemitism in the Soviet Union, and those laws were enforced.[196] Horkheimer further claimed that though there were obvious differences between the United States and Nazi Germany "The basic features of destructive hatred are identical everywhere."[197]

The initial grant given by the AJC to the Institute covered a year-long period ending in March 1944. At the conclusion of this period, the Institute presented the AJC with the studies it had conducted, including not only the papers written by Massing, Pollock, Gurland, and Kirchheimer mentioned above but also a large number of other specific works on various aspects of antisemitism. These individual studies, totaling some 1200 typewritten pages, were delivered to the AJC in four thick volumes.

Somewhat belatedly, the Institute presented to the AJC a final report on its grant. In comments on a draft of this final report, Adorno set forth a number of basic ideas in broad strokes. Adorno writes, for example, "We should stress that the so-called psychology of antisemitism does not operate in an empty space, but is essentially and intrinsically related to social situations, nay, that it is part and parcel of this psychology to lead to different behaviors under different conditions..."[198] Significantly, in this same set of comments, Adorno also tentatively suggests that it might be appropriate "at least to hint at some of the easier points of the 'Elemente des Antisemitismus.'"[199] Adorno, in other words, explicitly underscored the fact that the work done by members of the Institute with the support of funds from the AJC was intertwined with the theoretical work being conducted by the Institute's inner circle during this same period of time.

The final report as submitted to the AJC points out that the authors had come to believe that "[A]ntisemitism appears as an expression of hostility which is an inherent trait of our particular civilization. Hostility aims at the 'stranger', the 'alien' – and it is an elementary lesson of history that the Jew was considered an 'alien' in all societies in which he has lived under the Diaspora...".[200] "The image of the Jew in contemporary society – still an image of 'otherness' and 'foreignness' – has evolved," the final report proclaims, "from the Jewish group's peculiar proximity to and rivalry with the non-Jewish middle classes. It is connected – through psychological projection mechanisms – with the social and economic functions which the Jews performed in the development of capitalism... The psychological study of this 'image of the Jew' is thus intimately interconnected with the analysis of the specific position of the Jewish group in modern society."[201]

Economic changes in Europe that had battered the middle classes had also made the Jews "economically more vulnerable and increasingly isolated"[202] and led the non-Jewish middle classes to blame their economic defeat on the Jews. The "frustrations of the subjugated were turned by a process of projection from the real forces of oppression to the Jews."[203] Much of this language will no doubt sound hauntingly familiar to those who have studied *Dialectic of Enlightenment*, and tends to corroborate the claim made by Horkheimer and Adorno that "Elements of Anti-Semitism," that book's final chapter, was "directly related to empirical research by the Institute of Social Research."[204]

*

In *Dialectic of Enlightenment*, Horkheimer and Adorno describe the development of Western civilization as involving both the rational domination of nature and a reversion from enlightenment to mythology.[205] They were determined to explain how and why these processes had led to disaster, such that humanity "instead of entering into a truly human state, is sinking into renewed barbarism."[206] The rise of fascist antisemitism was, from the perspective of the Critical Theorists, in itself a manifest indicator of contemporary barbarism – and, as Horkheimer put it late in 1944, "we can read the positive ideologies of history even better in the idiosyncrasies, injustices and crimes than in their positive expressions."[207] The phenomenon of fascist antisemitism, Adorno and Horkheimer argue in the "Elements of Anti-Semitism" chapter of *Dialectic*, helps to elucidate the dialectic of enlightenment itself. Modern antisemitism explains and is explained by the history of civilization.

Ideas suggested by Adorno in his memo of September 1940 planted the seeds for the approach taken by Horkheimer and Adorno in "Elements of Anti-Semitism."[208] But most of "Elements" was written jointly by Horkheimer and Adorno in 1943,[209] after much of what eventually became *Dialectic of Enlightenment* had already been drafted.[210] Five theses were written that year. Some ideas reflected in the first three theses were contributed by Leo Lowenthal.[211]

The theses in "Elements" are meant to permeate each other, not to stand alone. And yet it remains useful to delineate each of the original five theses in turn. The first of the theses presents two alternative understandings of contemporary antisemitism, one put forth by fascists, and a second supported by liberals, and is intended to explicate the flaws in both. Fascists assert that the happiness of the world depends on the extermination of the Jews. The Nazis label the Jews as absolutely evil. But in the image of the Jew that the racial nationalists hold up before the world these nationalists "express their own essence."[212]

Liberals – including many "successfully adapted" Jews within their ranks – believe in the unity of humanity, and believe it "to have been already realized in principle" in liberal societies.[213] They further believe that "only anti-Semitism disfigured" the harmonious society that liberalism advocated, and suggest that antisemitism could be eliminated by and through liberalism. For Horkheimer and Adorno, however, "the liberal thesis serves as an apology for the existing order." The Critical Theorists asserted that fascism emerged from liberalism and that liberals fail to acknowledge that antisemitism cannot be expunged from such a society.

There are shards of truth, the authors tell us, in both the fascist and the liberal approaches to hatred of the Jews. The fascist approach is true insofar as the fascists had succeeded in making the Jews into what they had long claimed them to be. As Horkheimer put it in a letter written in 1944 and meant for public consumption, "the Jews have been made what the Nazis always pretended that they were – the focal point of world history."[214] The liberal, alternative, approach is true insofar as it provides an image of a society "in which rage would no longer reproduce itself."[215] But it is crystal clear that, nevertheless, for the Critical Theorists liberalism, fascism, and how each comprehended Jews and antisemitism, are all deeply flawed.

A second thesis suggests that antisemitism cannot be understood *solely* by making use of rational explanations, and cannot be successfully combated via rational counterarguments. Like the fascist and liberal approaches described in the first thesis, "plausibly rational, economic, and political explanations" of antisemitism may well be partially correct. Nevertheless, they cannot cure the malady "since rationality itself, through its link to power, is submerged in the same malady."[216] Horkheimer spelled out his understanding of the emergence of instrumental or subjective reason – a rationality that "is essentially concerned with means and ends, with the adequacy of procedures for purposes more or less taken for granted and supposedly self-explanatory," as distinguished from objective reason in which "the emphasis was on ends rather than on means" and in which "reason is a principle inherent in reality" – not so much in the original theses of "Elements of Anti-Semitism" as in marginally later work such as *Eclipse of Reason*.[217] It was in this latter work, based on lectures Horkheimer delivered at Columbia University early in 1944, that Horkheimer explored how reason had become "completely harnessed to the social process".[218] However, "Elements" already suggests that an alteration in the nature of reason itself makes understandings of antisemitism rooted altogether in, for example, changes in the significance of the sphere of circulation – in other words, the kind of explanation that Horkheimer had himself offered in "The Jews and Europe" – less compelling than they had appeared to be at an earlier point.

Alternatively, Horkheimer indicates, one may explain the appeal of antisemitism by exploring how it provides a form of release: "Rage is vented on those who are both conspicuous and unprotected. And just as, depending on the constellation, the victims are interchangeable: Negroes, Mexican wrestling clubs, vagrants, Jews, Protestants, Catholics, so each of them can replace the murderer, in the same blind lust for killing, as soon as he feels the power of repressing the norm. There is no authentic anti-Semitism, and certainly no born anti-Semite."[219] In other words, far from explaining Nazi antisemitism by reference to, let's say, German national character or German history, Horkheimer and Adorno believed antisemitism to be an example of a pattern that had been seen innumerable times before, in altogether different contexts, and that had a psychological component.

In the specific case at hand, liberalism had promised happiness to all. But the masses were not happy – and indeed could not become happy for so long as classes continued to exist. The anger of the masses is taken out on Jews, who appear to have attained the happy life. Both "lascivious Jewish bankers" and Jewish intellectuals who "enjoy in thought what the others deny themselves" and who are "spared the sweat of toil" are pointed to by antisemites as examples of why they hate Jews – and, having pointed to these examples, the antisemites proceed to victimize all Jews within reach. Antisemitism is a release valve in which Jews are the targets of mass, deeply rooted, anger for matters over which they have no power.

The third thesis – which is in fact reminiscent of the position propounded by Horkheimer in "The Jews and Europe" – is designed to explain the "objective" roots of antisemitism: "Bourgeois anti-Semitism has a specific economic purpose: to conceal domination in production."[220] Those who own and control the means of production exploit the proletariat.

"That the circulation sphere is responsible for exploitation is a socially necessary illusion" – necessary, that is to say, to the bourgeoisie, in order to deflect attention from the role played by others.[221] Jews were not the only ones who worked as merchants in Europe, but some Jews did in fact serve in such capacities at earlier points in European history and "[a]s bearers of capitalist modes of existence from country to country they earned the hatred of those who suffered under that system."[222] In present day society, as the roles that Jews played have been eliminated, Jews "have been flung to the margins of a class." This explanation of anti-Jewish attitudes was manifestly of Marxist descent. But unlike "The Jews of Europe," which offered solely a Marxist understanding of antisemitism, "Elements" subsumes a Marxist component into a multi-dimensional approach.[223]

Thesis four, for example, approaches a component of Jew hatred from an altogether different perspective, by exploring the religious origin of antisemitism, and, in so doing, indicates that Christians ["[t]he adherents of the religion of the Son"] have hated Jews ["the supporters of the religion of the Father"] as "one hates those who know better" – an explanation clearly informed by psychoanalysis.[224] Nazi antisemites claim that the distinctions between Germans and Jews are racial and national, rather than first and foremost religious in their nature. "But the religious hostility which motivated the persecution of the Jews for two millennia is far from completely extinguished.... Religion has been incorporated as cultural heritage, not abolished.[225] Unlike Arendt, who underscored how modern antisemitism was sharply different from the religiously rooted anti-Jewishness of earlier eras, the Critical Theorists proclaimed in "Elements" that religious hostility towards Jews had actually been *aufgehoben*.[226]

The last of the theses written in 1943 describes the relationship of mimesis to contemporary antisemitism. The notion of mimesis is first used in *Dialectic of Enlightenment* in the work's opening chapter. Mimesis for Adorno and Horkheimer, Simon Jarvis explains, "is not just the attempt to make a copy of nature but the attempt to become like nature in order to ward off what is feared."[227] Mimesis entails affinity. In archaic times, humans had mimetic relationships with nature. But, following Freud, Horkheimer and Adorno note in "Elements" that "[u]ncontrolled" mimesis is eventually "proscribed"[228] – and the [Jewish] prohibition against graven images is the first significant manner in which the check on mimesis is enforced. The Jews "have not so much eradicated the adaptation to nature as elevated it to the pure duties of ritual."[229] The major point of the fifth thesis of "Elements" is that contemporary antisemitism entails, as Rabinbach has taught us, "the return of the archaic impulse to mimesis, which in its paranoid fear, imitates and therefore liquidates the Jews all the more consequently..."[230] Jews are pronounced by antisemites to be guilty of what the Jews were the first to subdue in themselves – "the susceptibility to the lure of base instincts ... the worship of images."[231] But the antisemite who pronounces the Jews guilty feels "an instinctive urge to ape what he takes to be Jewishness." "The same mimetic codes are constantly used..." by antisemitic leaders.[232] The murderous antisemitism of the Nazis, which makes ritualized use of mimetic behaviors, is a revenge directed against the ur-source of the proscription against mimesis – Jews, who prohibited graven images – and the question of whether real, individual, Jews living today actually have the traits that contemporary antisemites ascribe to them becomes irrelevant.[233]

Jonathan Judaken concludes that Horkheimer and Adorno "blame the Jewish victim for having become the target of fascist domination" and "reinforce" the image of the Jew "by repeating the negative construction of Jews that facilitated their destruction."[234] True enough. Both Horkheimer and Adorno, products of a time and place, were influenced by antisemitic stereotypes. And yet, in "Elements" the Critical Theorists, despite their failings, illuminate the causes of antisemitism and underscore the significance of the phenomenon in a new and compelling manner. "Elements," a sub-set of fragments in a collection of philosophic fragments, Nietzschean in format, does not present a complete theory of antisemitism – and, in Adorno's case, if not in Horkheimer's – was never intended to do so.[235] Like the works of Freud, Horkheimer and Adorno's "Elements" is characterized by flashes of brilliance, and sheds light in ways that contemporary social science does not, even if its insights are unverifiable.

*

The claim made by Horkheimer and Adorno in a preface of *Dialectic of Enlightenment* as to the relationship between their theoretical work on antisemitism, as expressed in "Elements," and the empirical projects on that theme undertaken by the Institute was intended to emphasize not only the links between the work conducted with the aid of the AJC and the ideas that ultimately appeared in the final chapter of *Dialectic*, but also the links between the qualitative work of the Institute's leading theorists and empirical research done by Institute associates with the financial support of the Jewish Labor Committee [JLC]. There were, however, substantial differences in this regard between the

AJC-sponsored antisemitism study and the labor study financed in part by the JLC. Work on the theses, which ultimately appeared in "Elements," began in earnest in mid-1943 – that is while the AJC-supported antisemitism project was in progress. The labor study, on the other hand, was conducted *after* the bulk of these theses had been formulated, and *reflects* the theorizing that had been done by Horkheimer, Adorno, and Lowenthal prior to the labor study's initiation. Indeed, the labor study is closer in spirit to "Elements of Anti-Semitism" than is *The Authoritarian Personality* (which grew out of the AJC-sponsored work, but a considerable portion of which was written by individuals unaffiliated with the Institute).[236]

A brief history of the labor study is in order. In December 1943 Arkady Gurland met in New York with Charles B. Sherman, the Field Director of the JLC, and discussed with him the Institute's interest in conducting research on antisemitism among American workers.[237]

The JLC, which had been founded in New York in February 1934, was supported by organizations working among East European Jewish immigrants living in the United States. Its founding meeting was attended by representatives from the trade union movement, the Workmen's Circle (a fraternal organization strongest, at that time, among Yiddish-speakers), the Forward Association (publisher of a major, social democratic, Yiddish language daily newspaper, the *Forverts*), the Left Poalei Zion (a socialist Zionist organization), and the Jewish Socialist Farband (which, like the *Forverts*, had a social democratic orientation). In ideological terms, the JLC was made up of Jewish organizations that were left of center, but non-Communist. While its core constituency was made up of Jewish workers in New York and other American cities who were of East European origin, it was exceptionally supportive of the anti-Nazi and antifascist forces in Central Europe, and provided considerable aid to non-Communist, German-speaking, trade unionists, socialists, and social democrats who attempted to leave Europe for the United States after the Nazi rise to power. Thus, though by no means an entity oriented towards academic research, the JLC was certainly attentive to the plight of left-wing exiles from Germany who had come to the United States in order to escape Nazi persecution (like those in the Institute).

This explains why Sherman was open to Gurland's pitch for JLC support of a research project on labor antisemitism to be conducted under the Institute's auspices – and why the Institute soon thereafter presented Sherman with a project proposal.[238] Adorno explained his views on antisemitism in an oral presentation to a meeting of the JLC in Los

Angeles in January 1944.[239] The JLC, therefore, was aware of a key element of the Institute's approach to this matter from a rather early point.

Not long thereafter, the Institute revised its proposal for the labor study, and began the edited version both by asserting that there had been "an ominous rise in antisemitism within labor organizations" in the United States and by suggesting that before that trend could be fought, it would be necessary to find out how far antisemitism had penetrated into the population.[240] The Institute indicated that it would investigate whether antisemitism in American labor was motivated by "bread-and-butter" issues or by other factors, the role of antisemitism in the psychology of American workers, the image of the Jew in the mind of workers, and the import of personal contacts on attitudes towards Jews, among other matters.[241] It also proposed that young non-Jewish workers be trained by the Institute to carry out "guided conversations" with fellow workers intended "to elucidate the nature, intensity and extent of antisemitic feeling among specific groups of workers."[242] It followed up by preparing a memorandum describing difficulties to be expected in conducting the proposed project, in which the Institute explained that it was its explicit intention "to present the problem under investigation as one of anti-democratic attitudes and subconscious leanings …"[243] The Institute's proposal ultimately led the JLC to award a substantial grant to be used by the Institute for its research project.[244]

The labor study was carried out in 1944–1945. Though Horkheimer feared that some American groups would criticize the project as entailing "a bunch of foreign-born intellectuals sticking their noses into the private affairs of American workers," he nevertheless helped the study to move forward.[245] A number of those affiliated with the Institute, including Gurland, Lowenthal, Pollock, and Massing, were responsible for analyzing data gathered by field workers, and were regularly given guidance by Adorno. In private correspondence, Adorno stated that he found the subject of antisemitism among workers to be a particularly interesting one.[246]

In a long memorandum on the labor study dated November 3, 1944, Adorno wrote that the Institute's interpretation of the data "should be based on the relationship of [the] class-consciousness of the underlying population to antisemitism" and put forth two major hypotheses.[247] The first of these was that "At the basis of Labor antisemitism – as far as class-consciousness is concerned – is the idea that the Jews, while actually belonging to the oppressed, identify themselves with the capitalists and thus appear as capitalists … the Jews, while being permanently threatened and without decisive social control, still seem to act according to middle-class patterns..."[248] Adorno's second hypothesis was that this "rational" component of the issue was overly one-sided. "[T]he Jewish urge for success and domination... is largely due to the worker's envy of those Jewish qualities which make for success and which the average worker himself lacks... [T]his trend is largely of a projective nature ... [T]he domineering features for which the Jews are blamed by the workers are actually inherent in the worker's mentality itself... In the last analysis it is the absence of power rather than its presence which evinces antisemitism."[249] Thus, from Adorno's perspective, antisemitism had an "essentially psychological, irrational nature... The object plays but a minor role as compared to the tendency of the subject..."[250] In the course of this memo, Adorno refers explicitly to "Elements of Anti-Semitism," particularly noting how a complex evident in workers interviewed for the Labor Project had been discussed in the fifth thesis of "Elements"[251] and that "[c]ertain proof of the interconnection between antisemitism and 'oppressed mimesis' may be gleaned from the interviews."[252]

The Institute's research team for the project on labor antisemitism ultimately wrote a 1449-page-long typescript. In describing the study's findings, Lowenthal stressed that though the study was primarily concerned with the nature and not with the extent of antisemitism, the study had found that antisemitism was widespread among those who had been surveyed. Massing, whose work for the project centered on the impact of fascism and of the Second World War on antisemitic attitudes, emphasized that the fact that the Nazis had succeeded in murdering millions of Jews had itself contributed to stereotypical antisemitic attitudes (by reinforcing pre-existing attitudes towards Jews) and also suggested that "the worker forms a good deal of his opinion and prejudice as a result of his consumer interests rather than his shop interests."[253] Gurland, who addressed the issues of the social and economic motivations of antisemitism, asserted that "the Jew, in the eyes of the worker, has become a substitute for social conditions that he does not like ... that cause him suffering and hardship" and indicated that this substitution could make the average American worker an easy target of fascist propaganda.[254]

The Institute initially intended to publish the study on antisemitism among American labor in book form, and reached a mutually agreeable arrangement with the JLC about that matter in 1946.[255] Paul Lazarsfeld (1901–1976), who was himself of Jewish origin, who had been born and raised in Vienna, who, like the members of the Horkheimer circle, was interested in both Marxism and psychoanalysis, and who had long had contact with Institute members,[256] worked on the typescript in the wake of the agreement. He met regularly with Lowenthal and Massing as he did so.[257] Both Lowenthal and Pollock, however, were dissatisfied with the results of Lazarsfeld's work. Indeed, in Lowenthal's opinion, "the Lazarsfeld version was a catastrophe."[258] Pollock, together with Adorno and Felix Weil, made an attempt to re-edit the manuscript,[259] even while Lazarsfeld continued his labors. These efforts, however, did not produce a satisfactory product. Pollock, for one, declared that the study was "beyond repair."[260]

Adorno, on the other hand, continued to believe that, given all the work that had been invested in the labor project by the Institute, it would be too demoralizing to allow attempts to whip it into publishable shape to come to naught.[261] But he too found that the edited version was very problematic. Though Horkheimer floated the idea of publishing the labor study as part of the "Studies in Prejudice" book series[262] alongside *The Authoritarian Personality* and the books by Massing, Lowenthal, and others that ultimately did appear in that series, the labor study was not integrated with these other works, and considered "neither the[ir] methods nor the[ir] results."[263] From Adorno's perspective, even the edited version of the labor study as it existed in 1949 did not sufficiently emphasize that "Antisemitism [among American workers] is due to the impact of the whole system of society upon the worker ... and to a peculiar break between the objective class situation and subjective class consciousness in American Labor..."[264] Adorno proposed at one point that he produce a concluding chapter for the labor study, which would have had a theoretical focus, and sketched out his ideas for this chapter in a letter to Lowenthal, indicating that the task of this chapter was to have been "to trace back the absence of proletarian class consciousness...." "The American working class," Adorno proclaimed, "is characterized by the contradiction between its objective position in the process of production – namely the proletarian position – and its subjective consciousness of itself... The objective function of the antisemitism of the worker is now to reconcile that contradiction. The Jews are particularly suitable for this ..."[265] But Pollock, it would appear, thought that "the book could not carry the weight of a theoretical chapter"[266] and, though Adorno disagreed,[267] he did not write up such a piece.[268]

*

When, in the summer of 1944, the Institute submitted its final report on the antisemitism project to the American Jewish Committee, the first phase of cooperation between the Institute of Social Research and the AJC formally came to an end. A conference on research in the field of antisemitism organized under the auspices of the AJC in New York in May 1944, however, had cemented the sense within the AJC that the initial grant provided by the AJC to the Institute had been fruitful, and that a mechanism should be sought by which to continue the ties that had been created through that grant. The AJC-sponsored conference was motivated not only by a "desire to evaluate the findings of" the studies that had been submitted by the Institute to the AJC but also by "the urgent need of validating the premises of a sound defense program."[269] Twenty-five prominent individuals participated in this conference, including psychologists, sociologists, a well-known rabbi, economists, psychiatrists and four representatives of the AJC. Horkheimer, Adorno, and Pollock were among those invited.

The extant record does not reveal precisely what Horkheimer said at this conference. However, Horkheimer is known to have "reported on the findings and suggestions which the Institute of Social Research had submitted" [to the AJC] and to have "outlined the necessary elaboration of various individual studies."[270] A summary of the discussion that took place at the AJC-sponsored conference on antisemitism notes that though "there was some difference of opinion with regard to the nature and causes of anti-Semitism, there was considerable agreement concerning the basic principles of a defense policy and the need of research for the implementation of a defense program."[271] The consensus view was that the defense program "should not be limited to a rational approach and that strong emphasis be placed upon latent anti-Semitism and upon the intrinsic relationship between anti-Semitism and anti-democratic attitudes."[272] It was also generally agreed by those participating that "economic and social dislocation after the war" was "likely to bring about a heightening of ... anti-Semitic agitation."[273] In all these ways, the conference of May 1944 corroborated contentions made by associates of the Institute in the initial studies conducted by it with the support of the AJC.[274]

This explains how and why it came about that the AJC publicly announced in September 1944 that it had appointed Max Horkheimer to the position of research consultant in its domestic defense program.[275] An early description of the work that Horkheimer's department, the Department of Scientific Research, intended to do mentioned three projects. The first was described as a "study of the nature and extent of antisemitism in America."[276] This project, it was explained, would be done in conjunction with a group (not explicitly identified in this description) operating out of the University of California at Berkeley and would make use of a scale of measurement created by the Berkeley group that allowed researchers both to differentiate between "high" and "low" cases of antisemitism, and to classify antisemites by type. By 1945, those responsible for this study – which provided the ground work for *The Authoritarian Personality* – had already concluded that "antisemitism is a symptom of destructive character structure which is generally anti-democratic."[277]

The second project that the Department for Scientific Research intended to support was an analysis of the speeches of antisemitic agitators. Preliminary work on these speeches – as described in Adorno's lecture in San Francisco at the psychiatric symposium on antisemitism held in June 1944 – had accented the psychological mechanisms used by such agitators. In its second project, the Department intended to expose these mechanisms, and thereby to undermine the activities of fascist agitators in the United States. "It is not enough to fight antisemitism by appealing to fair play. Prejudice is too deeply rooted in subconscious drives and feelings" a report of the Department stressed. "We must create a stereotype of the fascist agitator which can be recognized at once. Instead of just pitying the Jew, people should laugh at the agitator."[278]

The Department also planned – and this was the third of the projects it mentioned early on – "to develop new instruments for measuring subconscious feelings, and gauging antisemitism even among persons who are not aware that they have antisemitic leanings."[279]

Horkheimer rapidly established an advisory council for the Department, and attracted very prominent intellectuals to it. A meeting of the Advisory Council held on January 6, 1945, for example, was attended by Margaret Mead and Robert Merton, among others. Much of the meeting was taken up with reports by Horkheimer both on the work of the Institute on the projects he hoped to undertake in his new role at AJC, and by reactions by those attending to Horkheimer's plans. Horkheimer threw out a number of ideas, hypothesizing, for example "that antisemitic and similar feelings develop in human beings as forms of antagonistic reaction against the ideas in which they are supposed to believe. It is hostility against rational education and therefore rational education might not be the right form to fight this hostility."[280] He pitched the notion of a film to be used as a means of measuring antisemitism, a notion to which he had been attracted for quite some time,[281] and was careful to have invited as guests individuals who, while not regular members of the Advisory Council, were likely to support this project, such as Kracauer, who had arrived in the United States in 1941, and who had conducted research over a period of years on the history of German film, and the German-born film director and artist Hans Richter (1888–1976), who had come to the United States in the same year as had Kracauer.[282]

Within a matter of weeks, however, Horkheimer (without, by any means, abandoning the film idea or any of the other projects that had been proposed) became excited by a notion of an altogether different kind – a project that he eventually came to describe as a definitive treatise on antisemitism. At a meeting of the AJC's Committee on Scientific Research (to which Horkheimer reported regularly) Horkheimer introduced this idea as a project that "should become the point of crystallization for the ... work in the research department" and as a work that, he hoped, "might become as influential as Gunnar Myrdal's ... 'The American Dilemma'."[283] The Committee on Scientific Research responded cautiously, but agreed that Horkheimer should start the preparatory work for this project with two members of the Institute, and that a final decision as to whether or not to endorse the project should be postponed to a later date.

Drafts of the prospectus for the proposed treatise indicate that it would have had a comprehensive sweep, and would have included sections on the types of antisemitism, the theories put forth as explanations for the causes of antisemitism, the reasons why Jewish defense efforts in Europe had failed, the function of totalitarian antisemitism and the psychology of antisemitism, among other subjects. These drafts suggest that those proposing the treatise had anticipated that it would be co-edited, that Horkheimer would have been one of these editors, and that American scholars with the stature of MacIver or Gordon Allport (a psychologist and long-term member of the Harvard faculty) would be invited to work with Horkheimer on this project. The drafts also indicate that it was intended that the treatise be written in such a way as to appeal to a broad audience. One key thesis of the work would have been "that anti-Semitism is but one symptom of a certain character structure."[284]

By May 1945 planning had progressed far enough to create a tentative table of contents, including a preliminary indication of who the authors of the various components of the volume would be. MacIver, Massing, Lowenthal, Kirchheimer, Horkheimer, Pollock, and Allport are among those listed.[285] A progress report issued in June noted that a tentative agreement had been reached under which Horkheimer would be editor in chief and responsible for administration of the project, and under which

MacIver and Allport would advise on the overarching treatise and accept responsibility for coordinating particular sections of it.[286] Moreover, Lowenthal and Massing, it was reported, had actually begun their work on the portions of the proposed book assigned to them. A working meeting of those involved in the treatise took place in mid-June, at which time Horkheimer suggested that the thesis of the opening section of the work be that "anti-Semitism was a dangerous menace to western civilization."[287] During the summer and early fall of 1945, it would appear, work continued apace. Though the Department was involved in a number of projects, it was clear that Horkheimer intended the treatise to become one of its major foci in 1946–1947.[288]

In late October 1945, however, Horkheimer reported to the Committee on Scientific Research that his doctor had warned him to leave New York or risk very serious consequences to his health. Having decided that it was prudent to obey his physician's advice – and intensely interested, in any event, in getting back to his own theoretical work and away from the time-consuming activities involved in running an office at the AJC – Horkheimer made plans to return to California, where he had been living immediately before accepting the AJC staff position, and to turn over day-to-day operations of what had been his department at the AJC to Dr. Samuel H. Flowerman, who had previously served as an assistant to Horkheimer.[289]

Flowerman apparently continued work on the treatise in the months immediately following Horkheimer's return to California, and reported to Horkheimer in December 1945 that "[w]e are making good strides toward the launching of this project" and that there had been a meeting about the treatise attended by a number of people including Pollock, Massing, Lowenthal, Jahoda, and Flowerman himself.[290]

However, Horkheimer's absence from New York led directly to a diminution of his influence over the department that he had earlier headed. Flowerman allegedly insisted as early as December 1945 (when dealing with staff in New York) that he now had "the last word in all administrative and financial and technical matters."[291] And shortly after the beginning of the following year, Massing informed Horkheimer that, while Flowerman had expressed interest in the treatise, he had also accused the Institute of attempting to dominate the project. "I cannot help feeling," Massing wrote, "that it is essentially you against whom Flowerman is working."[292]

Whether or not Massing's opinion was correct, there is no question that the attitude of the AJC towards Horkheimer soured during this period.

At a meeting of the Committee on Scientific Research held on February 4, 1946, that was not attended by Horkheimer nor by any of the other members of the Institute of Social Research, the Committee's Chairman, Ira M. Younker, expressed the opinion "that the general relationship with ... Horkheimer had been difficult, and that a discontinuance of the relationship should be considered."[293] Others present at the meeting defended Horkheimer to some extent. John Slawson, for example, though he admitted that, in his opinion, Horkheimer had deficiencies as a methodologist, "regarded him as an extremely ingenious social philosopher, capable of producing ideas that rigid specialists cannot." The upshot of this discussion was that the Committee on Scientific Research agreed that Horkheimer should be retained by the AJC as a consultant, but also agreed that this relationship would be evaluated on the basis of whether it did or did not generate new ideas, and stipulated that it should be made clear to Horkheimer that he did not have the authority to initiate new projects without the approval of the New York staff and the Committee on Scientific Research. Horkheimer was informed of these decisions,[294] and, shortly thereafter, Flowerman told Horkheimer both that the funding that had earlier been allocated for a treatise on antisemitism had been halved, and that the project had been re-conceptualized as a series of monographs rather than a single, definitive treatise.[295]

In the following period, the relationship between Horkheimer and the members of his circle on the one hand and his one-time assistant Flowerman on the other became even more strained than it had been at an earlier point in time – leading Lowenthal to repeatedly denounce Flowerman in correspondence with Horkheimer. In May 1946, for example, Lowenthal declared that "Flowerman is a total zero: an insignificant scientist, an incompetent administrator and on top of it a paranoi[a]c psychopath. Consciously and unconsciously he sabotages a normal functioning of the Department."[296] Somewhat later, Lowenthal informed Horkheimer that he had had "the most violent scenes" with Flowerman "because of his lack of loyalty (to put it mildly) toward you and also toward our old group..."[297] Lowenthal also reported that Flowerman had a closer relationship with Slawson, a key figure in the AJC, than Lowenthal had earlier thought was the case, and that Flowerman was therefore able to influence policy decisions. Flowerman continued to correspond with Horkheimer on matters related to the progress of various projects.[298] But it should come as no surprise that Horkheimer's title at the AJC was downgraded from that of Chief Research Consultant to that of West Coast Consultant as of 1948.[299]

Despite the decidedly cool relationship between Horkheimer and Flowerman, some of the research initiated by Horkheimer and conducted by members of the Institute with the aid of the AJC ultimately bore fruit, notably as components of the book series, officially co-edited by Horkheimer and Flowerman, known as "Studies in Prejudice." Five books appeared in this series, all published by Harper and Brothers, and all bearing the imprimatur of the AJC, *The Authoritarian Personality*, in which Adorno played a crucial role, a book co-authored by Lowenthal on the rhetorical techniques used by American antisemitic agitators, a work by Massing (who, as we have noted above, though a long-term affiliate of the Institute, was not a member of Horkheimer's inner circle) on political antisemitism in imperial Germany, and two other works – *Dynamics of Prejudice* and *Anti-Semitism and Emotional Disorder* – written by individuals who were not closely associated with the Horkheimer circle or with the Institute or with Critical Theory.[300] Though the treatise on antisemitism never materialized, and much of the research on antisemitism conducted under the auspices of Horkheimer and Adorno in the 1940s remained unpublished, "Studies in Prejudice" stands as a considerable accomplishment.

The Authoritarian Personality, issued in 1950, is the most significant of the books published in this series, and has been characterized as "one of the key works of modern empirical social science."[301] Benjamin Beit-Hallahmi once noted that it "has achieved an extraordinary place in the history of the social sciences. Over more than fifty years, we find its influence in every discussion pertaining to psychological approaches to history, politics, and ideology."[302] *The Authoritarian Personality* is concerned primarily with ascertaining and describing the type of person whose character structure makes him (or her) a potential follower of fascist movements, and discusses the links between character structure and susceptibility to antisemitism.[303] It was, as Horkheimer saw it, focused on "the anthropological basis of totalitarianism," and found this basis in a psychological character syndrome, which, Horkheimer believed, was "more and more typical of the present phase of industrialism."[304] The study – which at one time had as its working title *The Fascist Personality*[305] – delineated a series of traits found in such a personality, including, as summarized by Adorno, "mechanical acceptance of conventional values, blind submission to authority combined with a violently aggressive attitude towards all those who … don't belong, anti-introspectiveness, rigid stereotypical thinking, a penchant for superstition, a … vilification of human nature, and … the habit to ascribe to the out-group the wishes and behavior patterns which one has to deny in oneself."[306] From the perspective of the Critical Theorists, the book suggested that a considerable portion of the American population was pre-conditioned to accept totalitarian ideas.

The Authoritarian Personality was written in a collaborative fashion by Adorno and individuals who were not members or associates of the Institute (including, notably, psychologists tied to the Public Opinion Study Group, based in Berkeley, California).[307] It cannot be read as an expression of Critical Theory pure and simple. Adorno's name is listed first on the title page not because those involved intended to suggest that he was the lead author (which was not in fact the case) but rather because the major authors chose to list their names alphabetically.[308] Nevertheless, Adorno's impact on the work is manifest, most noticeably in the section of the book devoted to qualitative analysis, of which Adorno was sole author.[309] In this section, we find that Adorno emphasized the functional aspect of antisemitism, asserting that antisemitism had "little to do with the qualities of those against whom it is directed" and that antisemitism "is not so much dependent upon the nature of the object as upon the subject's own psychological wants and needs" – points that had been made repeatedly in earlier writings on hatred of Jews written by the Critical Theorists, including "Elements of Anti-Semitism."[310]

Adorno cites *Dialectic of Enlightenment* (which had been published in German but not in English at that point in time) in *The Authoritarian Personality*.[311] *The Authoritarian Personality* also refers readers to the unpublished studies on antisemitism conducted by the Institute and submitted to the AJC, and makes repeated use of the labor study. But even when it does not explicitly refer to *Dialectic* or to the Institute's prior studies of antisemitism, Adorno's contribution to *The Authoritarian Personality* overlaps with the approach of these earlier works. *The Authoritarian Personality*, like the final (1947) version of "Elements of Anti-Semitism," for example, contains a discussion of the deleterious impact of ticket thinking.[312] More pointedly, the basic hypothesis of Adorno's contribution to *The Authoritarian Personality* was that antisemitism has a "largely projective character."[313] When, in 1944, Adorno was preparing a questionnaire ultimately used in conjunction with the studies discussed in *The Authoritarian Personality*, he told Horkheimer that he had distilled a number of the items in his questionnaire from "Elements" through a kind of translation process.[314] Indeed, as some critics of "Studies in Prejudice" sensed, Adorno used the project described in *The Authoritarian Personality* as a way to locate empirical verification for ideas he and Horkheimer had suggested in "Elements of Anti-Semitism."[315]

The links between *The Authoritarian Personality* and the earlier works on antisemitism written by Institute affiliates are most evident in an unpublished, contemporaneous, piece by Adorno, "Remarks on 'The Authoritarian Personality'," seemingly written in 1948, by which point the book was all but finished. "Remarks" reads as if it could have been published as an introductory section in *The Authoritarian Personality*.[316]

Adorno proclaims in his "Remarks" that the book as a whole "is in full harmony with psychoanalysis in its more orthodox, Freudian version."[317] He also notes, however, that while *The Authoritarian Personality* was devoted to the subjective aspects of bigotry, "We are convinced that the ultimate source of prejudice has to be sought in social factors which are incomparably stronger than the 'psyche' of any one individual involved."[318] At a later point in "Remarks" Adorno adds that the approach of the book is perfectly consistent with "the economic theory which sees in anti-semitism an essentially social rather than psychological phenomenon."[319] Prejudice is rooted in the totality of the socio-economic system.[320] Neither an economic nor a psychological explanation alone suffices to explain it.[321] Indeed, a key tenet of Critical Theory was that existing divisions between exclusively psychological and economic approaches ought to be overcome, ultimately, "by insight into the ... identity of the operative forces in both..."[322] At one and the same time, Adorno embraced core components of Freud's thought – Freud's understanding of the unconscious, of repression, and of the components of the psyche – and also stressed that there had been major changes since Freud's day, including a "decay of individuality brought about by the decline of free enterprise and market economy."[323] And he concludes: "If the individual, in the sense of an equilibrium between ego, superego, and Id, can no longer be regarded as the characteristic form of today's human beings, psychology may begin to become obsolescent inasmuch as individual actions can no longer be explained adequately in terms of the individual's own psychological household."[324] And yet, focusing on individuals makes sense, because "the mechanisms to which individuals are incessantly subject from without, are to be found in the depth of these same individuals."[325]

Changes in contemporary human beings mean that there are sharp differences between the forms of antisemitism that had existed in earlier times and contemporary antisemitism: "Modern anti-semitic ideology is the antidote against the sufferings entailed by rational civilization..."[326] It is not, Adorno insists, a result of spontaneous impulses, but rather a "concocted" doctrine "that utilizes powerful socio-psychological dispositions in the masses." In totalitarian societies "antisemitism is no longer a matter of primary hostilities on the part of the people... It is an administrative measure which uses existing prejudices..."[327] In brief, Adorno's "Remarks on 'The Authoritarian Personality'," close in spirit to "Elements of Anti-Semitism" but far more lucidly written, and created while *The Authoritarian Personality* was being prepared for publication, reflect Adorno's full and uncensored views on antisemitism in ways that *The Authoritarian Personality* itself does not.

*

The Authoritarian Personality was widely reviewed, and elicited a broad range of reactions.[328] A review that situated *The Authoritarian Personality* in the context of "Studies in Prejudice" as a whole and that was published in *The Annals of the American Academy of Political and Social Science* proclaimed that "the publication of this series represents what may perhaps be an epoch-making event in social science," and listed no fewer than five justifications for this assertion: (1) the series dealt with a significant problem, and one that urgently needed to be addressed; (2) the authors were genuinely interdisciplinary; (3) those involved had made use of a broad range of interdisciplinary tools; (4) Freudian ideas were appropriately used and acknowledged; and (5) the volumes arrived at new insights into prejudice.[329] Joseph H. Bunzel's review in *American Sociological Review* also had great praise for the series, describing the scales used by the authors as "ingenious," and the clinical material as "impressive." The authors of the books in the series are, moreover, commended by Bunzel for their clarity – and Adorno's section of *The Authoritarian Personality* is explicitly singled out as likely to be the most interesting portion of that volume for sociologists. Bunzel does suggest that he would have liked to read more about how the insights arrived at by Adorno and the other contributors could and should be acted upon – but his criticism is gently worded: "Perhaps we should not ask for more than was promised to us."[330] Alfred de Grazia, an Associate Professor at Brown University, finally, wrote a positive review for the *American Political Science Review*, the most important American journal in the field of political science, in which he asserted that *The Authoritarian Personality* would "serve political science well, both as to its findings and as to its techniques."[331]

Not all of the reviews, however, were equally laudatory. Allan W. Eister, in the course of a generally positive assessment, raised a fundamental issue by noting "the shortcomings that appear to be inevitable where psychoanalytic conjectures are permitted to intrude upon otherwise sound scientific research."[332] Harry C. Bredemeier, writing in *The Public Opinion Quarterly*, similarly, was generally impressed, but remarked on "the authors' compulsion to guess at unconscious mechanisms as explanatory variables."[333] A lengthy, serious, and insightful review that appeared in *Commentary* and that was written by Nathan Glazer was, to be sure, very positive. It concludes that the book leaves its readers "immeasurably richer."[334] But Glazer, while recognizing the work's strengths, does not shy away from raising a series of pertinent methodological questions, suggesting, among other matters, that the authors of *The Authoritarian Personality* had "certain rather simple and single-minded assumptions as to what is progressive or liberal" and, more generally, that the book rested on "unstated political and social assumptions."[335] He describes Adorno's contribution as "at once the most brilliant and the most debatable part of the volume, and yet finds Adorno's belief that he was living in "potentially fascist times" problematic.[336] Adorno's belief, Glazer notes, was an unproven hypothesis, and one for which empirical evidence had not been provided in *The Authoritarian Personality*.

Though Glazer's review was beyond doubt a scholarly one, it ought to be noted that *Commentary*, like "Studies in Prejudice," appeared with the support of the AJC, and that *Commentary* was not an academic publication. But other reviews published by eminent scholars or in scholarly periodicals also raised questions. A long review in *Ethics*, by Franz Alexander of the Institute for Psychoanalysis, who was an established and influential figure, found *The Authoritarian Personality* to be one-sided because of the authors' inclination to identify authoritarian tendencies all but exclusively with fascist tendencies and to disregard "the trend toward leftist authoritarianism." Alexander found the authors' depiction of the factors likely to make a person receptive to democratic ideas unconvincing – and traces what he believed to be the origins of this problem in the work under discussion to the authors' grouping of liberalism, socialism, and communism in one camp, and fascism in an opposing one. From Alexander's perspective, socialism and communism actually shared traits with fascism, and thus ought to have been contrasted to liberalism, not lumped together with it. Left-radicals and Right-radicals, Alexander asserts, manifest similar dynamic patterns. He concludes: "At this moment of human history, when all the major representatives of fascist ideology have been defeated in the last war, this book, with its sociological orientation which ignores the now existing threats to our still free society, appears strikingly out of date."[337] Herbert H. Hyman and Paul B. Sheatsley – among *The Authoritarian Personality*'s "most serious critics"[338] – objected to the book in part by arguing that the psychological interpretation offered in it ought to have been "controlled," by, for example, having the same data scored by various analysts.

Adorno responded to the points made by certain of his critics, privately, in 1953. He noted, for example, that the line of argument used by Hyman and Sheatsley had taken the concept of controlled experiments from the realm of the natural scientists and had attempted "somewhat naively" to apply it to an altogether different field. "I have stated the partly speculative nature of my interpretations quite frankly and my critics accept this statement – why then, do they blame me when they find that I actually *do* speculate? To argue pragmatically, I am pretty certain that, if Freud had been subjected to such a 'control', the whole bulk of psychodynamic theory would never have been evolved, which would mean, among other things, there would be no controversy about the Authoritarian Personality."[339]

Adorno answered those who agreed with critiques like that of Alexander by pointing out that

> The fact that less attention was given in the volume to the authoritarian communist party-line than to the potential fascist is solely due to the historical situation. At the time the questionnaire and interview schedule were set up and the material was gathered (1944–1945), the National Socialists were our enemies and Russians our allies. In the atmosphere then prevailing, the common denominator of anti-Nazism did not yet allow the difference between autonomous thinking and its perversion by the communist dictatorship to crystallize as clearly as later on.... [E]ven today a large percentage of non-authoritarian persons may be attracted by communism simply because they have not yet learned that communism has turned into a 'rightist party' ... and has become thoroughly identified with Russian imperialism.[340]

*

In the period following the drafting of the first theses of "Elements of Anti-Semitism" in 1943, Horkheimer attempted to explain antisemitism and Jewish history by pointing to both psychological and historical factors, stressing different factors when addressing different audiences. When speaking to the outside world, at the end of 1943, Horkheimer could write that "despite the tremendous importance of economic and social tendencies, antisemitism is fundamentally a psychological phenomenon."[341] When writing confidentially to Pollock during this period, on the other hand, Horkheimer stressed that "[o]ur real ideas on

Antisemitism attribute an infinitely greater part to economic and social factors than an isolated glimpse upon our work could suggest."[342]

Throughout the remainder of his American years, Horkheimer clearly believed that there was a constant interaction among social, economic, and religious factors contributing to antisemitism, to such an extent "that it is difficult to attribute this phenomenon to any isolated force. For instance, we must differentiate between the direct causes and the general conditions, between the frame of mind of the violent racists, on the one hand, and the educational and cultural background of their sympathizers on the other..."[343]

Adorno was doubtless in full agreement with these assertions. Both before and after the publication of *The Authoritarian Personality*, Adorno was worried that readers might come to believe, inaccurately, that the Institute's explanations of antisemitism were grounded primarily in psychology. To be sure, Adorno greatly contributed to this incomplete reading of the Critical Theorists' position by his choice of language. "Viewed from a purely psychological angle the idea of 'labor racketeering' seems to be of a nature similar to the stereotype of Jewish clannishness." Adorno writes in *The Authoritarian Personality*: "It dates back to the lack of an adequately internalized identification with paternal authority during the Oedipus situation. It is our general assumption that the typical high scorers [on a questionnaire administered in conjunction with the studies which formed the basis of *The Authoritarian Personality*], above all, fear the father and try to side with him in order to participate in his power."[344] Passages like these notwithstanding, Adorno regularly insisted that neither his approach to the study of antisemitism nor that of the Institute could be accurately characterized as solely psychological. In 1949, by which time Adorno was preparing to leave the United States and return to Frankfurt, he continued to attempt to transform the Institute's massive study of antisemitism among American workers into a publishable book. But, despite years of work, neither Adorno's "Remarks on 'The Authoritarian Personality' " nor the labor study ever did appear in print. And thus the misunderstanding that Adorno feared – that is, the sense that Horkheimer and Adorno came to embrace an understanding of antisemitism that was all but exclusively psychoanalytic and/or philosophical in its orientation – persisted for many years.

*

Prophets of Deceit, by Lowenthal and Norbert Guterman, is the second most important volume in "Studies in Prejudice" for our present purposes, for, like *The Authoritarian Personality*, it was co-authored by a core member of the Frankfurt School. *The Authoritarian Personality* was a far longer and more substantial book than was *Prophets of Deceit*. It has had a far greater and longer-lasting resonance than any other work issued as a part of "Studies in Prejudice." But Guterman was closer in spirit to the Frankfurt School, and more closely associated with the Institute, than were most of the co-authors of *The Authoritarian Personality*. *Prophets of Deceit* reveals more about the Frankfurt School's approach to the study of antisemitism than do those vast portions of *The Authoritarian Personality* not written by Adorno.

Guterman, who was Jewish, had been born in Warsaw in 1900, studied philosophy at the University of Warsaw, and continued his studies at the Sorbonne, where he focused on psychology and from which he earned degrees in 1922 and 1923.[345] He was, briefly, affiliated with the French Communist Party in the late 1920s (though allegedly not active in it) and collaborated over an extended period with the Marxist theorist Henri Lefebvre, with whom he worked on translations into French of works by Marx. Guterman emigrated from Europe to the United States in 1933, and eventually established himself as both a translator – he was proficient in Polish, Russian, French, German, and English – and an editor. His orientation was similar to that of the Frankfurt School in many respects, especially in terms of his sympathetic interest in Marx's early writings, his interest in psychology, and his tendency to be influenced by European philosophers more than by American social scientists. This helps to explain how and why Guterman became an associate member of the Institute in 1936. In that capacity, he participated in a number of Institute-related projects, and was eventually assigned to help prepare a study of the techniques of (antisemitic) American agitators. His initial work on what became known in Institute circles as the agitator study revolved around establishing a methodology for organizing relevant data.

Horkheimer's respect for Guterman is signaled by the fact that when, in 1946, Horkheimer was considering re-launching the *Zeitschrift*, he raised the notion of having Guterman (and Massing) serve on its staff, and commented to Lowenthal that "If you calculate that Guterman might devote at least part time to such an undertaking, we have, together with Massing an editorial staff which is indeed unique in the world today."[346] Horkheimer's respect for Guterman is also suggested by the fact that Guterman was given the task of helping to prepare Horkheimer's *Eclipse of Reason* for publication.[347]

Lowenthal kept closely in touch with Horkheimer while completing *Prophets*, which was based on the study of American agitators on which Guterman had worked, and solicited feedback from him. Horkheimer, in turn, read portions of the work when they were forwarded to him, and, at a relatively early phase in the book's creation, expressed great satisfaction with them. Referring to two parts of the study that had been sent to him in 1946, Horkheimer wrote to Lowenthal "They look like notes and drafts to a great book on our own line, and I am sure this is what it will finally be ... I am most happy with the two instal[l]ments. They show me more than anything else how closely your topic is related to my most urgent philosophical efforts."[348] Horkheimer's attitude towards the book remained positive as the book moved towards publication, though he did not shy away from disagreeing with the authors about specific points – sometimes fervently.[349] Significantly, Horkheimer encouraged Lowenthal to include a discussion of the economic context: "There is one thing which should not be omitted here: the agitators will probably be unleashed upon the people at a moment of economic depression. Therefore it seems necessary to me to bring in the economic motive much more clearly than the notes indicate so far... [W]e should not expose ourselves to the justified accusation that we ignore the role played by outright economic factors."[350] Specific points of contention notwithstanding, Lowenthal reported to Guterman in 1947, "Horkheimer has gone very carefully over your text and he wants you to know that in principle he agrees with almost everything and is in full harmony with your theoretical attitude."[351]

Adorno was also kept abreast of progress on the book. At one point, he suggested to Horkheimer that it be entitled *Pied Piper's Formula*.[352] The degree to which Adorno was aware of – and agreed wholeheartedly with – the major ideas of *Prophets* is manifested by the transcript of a talk that Adorno gave in Los Angeles in 1948. In the course of this talk, Adorno notes that the methods used by American fascist agitators can be understood by use of Freud's "Group Psychology and the Analysis of the Ego." "The agitator" Adorno proclaimed "can be defined as the man who consciously and manipulatively transforms individuals who attend his meeting into a passive, obedient, uncritical and highly irrational mass that is being held together by identification with ... the leader. We have reduced the technique of the agitators to ... standardized and ever-recurring tricks or devices... At present we are about to complete a short manual which describes these devices..."[353]

Horkheimer ultimately wrote an introduction for *Prophets* – edited by Adorno[354] – which argued that even in the realm of ideologies, attitudes are, in the modern era, often artificially created, and are created under pressure from those in power. In order to understand the attitudes of the people, therefore, it is necessary to study the stimuli to which they are subjected. Antisemitic agitation, Horkheimer emphasized, is an example of the far more widespread phenomenon of mass manipulation.

The authors of *Prophets* explicitly declared in their book that they drew on earlier work that had been conducted by the Institute of Social Research, including work that had been written by Adorno. Though not named, Lowenthal and Guterman likely had in mind the trial study written by Adorno and ultimately published as *The Psychological Technique of Martin Luther Thomas' Radio Addresses*, in which Adorno had analyzed the methods used by Thomas, an American fascist agitator, and included an analysis of Thomas's antisemitism.[355] Adorno's work, prepared in 1943, in which Adorno describes the ways in which Thomas appeals to the emotional needs of his audiences, Thomas's use of innuendo, and a variety of other techniques, seems to have provided a jumping off point for Lowenthal and Guterman, who ultimately examined the work of a larger number of agitators than had Adorno, but did so from a similar perspective.

The authors of *Prophets* also underscored that the notion, which lies at the core of their work, "of studying agitation as a surface manifestation of deeper social and psychological currents" was one that had been conceived by Horkheimer, and footnote an article by Horkheimer, "Egoism and the Freedom Movement," which had appeared in the Institute's *Zeitschrift* in 1936, and which, in the words of Lowenthal and Guterman, "set the historical frame of reference for our book."[356] They noted the prevalence of malaise in modern life, link this malaise with "growing doubt with relation to those universal beliefs that bound western society together" – and refer their readers to Horkheimer's *Eclipse of Reason* for additional discussion of that issue.[357]

Lowenthal and Guterman's study relied solely on analysis of agitators' texts. They did not actually attend meetings addressed by agitators in conjunction with their research for their book, nor did they make any attempt to directly ascertain the reactions of audiences to these agitators.[358]

Prophets of Deceit, which appeared in print in 1949, is devoted to qualitative analysis of the techniques and arguments that had been used in the years leading up to the book's publication by pro-fascist, antisemitic, American agitators, and argued – as had Adorno in his Los Angeles speech – that these agitators repeatedly relied on a set of motifs and devices as means by which to manipulate their audiences. Works by approximately a dozen agitators, including such figures as Father Coughlin, Joseph E. McWilliams, George Allison Phelps, and Gerald L. K. Smith, were examined in conjunction with this study.

The book begins with a composite speech, crafted by the American Jewish writer Irving Howe out of a number of statements that had been made by the agitators studied by Lowenthal and Guterman.[359] It then analyzes the themes used in this composite, and argues that the agitators make use of either subconscious or irrational phenomena, "a psychological Morse Code tapped out by the agitator and picked up by the followers."[360] It is the latent rather than the manifest meaning of the agitators' speeches that is of import – and the latent meaning is one that can be deciphered by use of psychoanalytic insights.

According to Lowenthal and Guterman, the agitators who they studied were neither classic reformers nor classic revolutionaries. These agitators, while advocating social change, did not have circumscribed grievances, as do reformers. On the other hand, the agitators did not declare that the problems they alluded to could be eliminated by a fundamental change in the social structure, as do revolutionaries. The American agitators suggested that the problems their audiences confronted were caused by specific people, or kinds of people, and that positive change would result from eliminating such people, not from eliminating institutions.

The agitators denounce many "enemies," including plutocrats, communists, and refugees, who are portrayed as ruthless. While claiming to repudiate antisemitism, the agitators devote particular attention to Jews, and to their connections, real and imagined, with all three of the categories of enemies just mentioned. The invective of the agitators is directed against any number of different sections of society – but it ultimately converges on the Jew: "The Jew becomes the symbol on which [the agitator] centers the projections of his own impotent rage against the restraints of civilization."

Jews are sometimes referred to directly. At other times, they are referred to by a variety of different code terms, including but not limited to "Pharisees, money changers, the goldmongers clan, the usurpers of Christian liberties."[361] Precisely by not explicitly mentioning Jews, attention is sometimes focused on Jews even more effectively. "Look into the rat holes, the agitator seems to say, I don't have to tell you whom you will find there."[362] Persecution of Jews is either characterized by the agitators as a natural phenomenon, which has recurred regularly throughout history and throughout the world, or the existence of genuine persecution is simply denied. Lowenthal and Guterman assert that in psychological terms persecution is reduced by the agitators to an ordinary part of life, and thus, it is suggested, is no cause for special concern. On the other hand, insofar as anti-Jewish animosity exists, agitators imply, it is justified, precisely because Jews are (allegedly) behind communism and capitalism, and, on another level, because of purportedly Jewish characteristics or behavior – such as clannishness or cunning. In effect, the agitators argued that Jews ought to be persecuted. Lowenthal and Guterman note: "In portraying the enemy as ruthless, the agitator prepares the ground for neutralizing whatever predispositions for sympathy for the underdog his audience may feel. If the enemy is ruthless, then there is no reason to feel sympathy for his simultaneous – if contradictory – helplessness. In this way the Jew as victim becomes legitimate prey."[363]

Tellingly, Lowenthal and Guterman, when describing the devices used by antisemitic agitators, footnote *Dialectic of Enlightenment*. Mimesis, the authors of *Prophets of Deceit* suggest, is among the most important stimuli of antisemitism. The American agitators mimic sounds purportedly made by Jews, and the imitations of alleged Jewish speech and behavior are enjoyed by the agitators' audiences. "The fact that the audience enjoys such caricatures and imitations of allegedly weird Jewish behavior," Lowenthal and Guterman write,

shows that this Jewish foreignness is not as external to them as it might seem. They feel it in their own flesh, it is latent in them; the Jew is not the abstract 'other,' he is the other who dwells in themselves. Into him they can conveniently project everything within themselves to which they deny recognition, everything they must repress. But this projection can be effected only on condition that they hate the Jews and are permitted to realize the repressed impulse in the form of a caricature of the enemy.[364]

Thus Lowenthal and Guterman suggest that the fifth thesis of "Elements of Antisemitism" – which was centered on the use of mimesis by antisemites – sheds light on analysis of the actual speeches and techniques used by American agitators in the 1940s.

Prophets also alludes to points that had been made in "Elements" in other passages. For example, the authors of *Prophets* note that American antisemitic agitators present Jews as if they did not engage in physical labor. But "[w]ork without hardship is identified with exploitation, and to the followers" of these agitators "the vision of a people who enjoy life without paying for it is intolerable... Domination by intellect is experienced as usurpation because it is not backed by actual physical power and ultimately depends on the consent of the dominated or on deception."[365]

The argument made at this point by Lowenthal and Guterman reads as a riff on the final paragraph of the second thesis of "Elements": "The idea of happiness without power is unendurable ... The fantasy of the conspiracy of lascivious Jewish bankers who finance Bolshevism is a sign of innate powerlessness, the good life an emblem of happiness. These are joined by the image of the intellectual, who appears to enjoy in thought what the others deny themselves and is spared the sweat of toil and bodily strength." Here as elsewhere, the theoretical work of the Critical Theorists on antisemitism and the empirical work of Institute members and associates on this same issue sparked and interacted with one another.

The major theorists of the Frankfurt School were clearly pleased by Lowenthal and Guterman's work. Adorno explicitly praised *Prophets* after it had appeared in print: "Many thanks for *Prophets*, which gives me great pleasure. I've read much of it and I think that you have succeeded in setting the proportions and achieving a tone which reveals the deadly without falling into the kind of gesticulations that are scarcely to be avoided with topics so inexpressibly emotion-laden as this one."[366]

The Frankfurt School worked hard at placing reviews in prestigious periodicals. As James Schmidt has pointed out, "[t]he notion that book reviews could be arranged by applying influence was consistent with the account of the culture industry in 'Dialectic of Enlightenment' ... As Horkheimer brought the fruits of his labor to market, he was not about to forget how the culture industry worked" and thus repeatedly pressed his associates to arrange for reviews to appear in major publications.[367] Lowenthal and Guterman's book received a glowing, short, review, by Carey McWilliams, in *The New York Times*.[368] McWilliams, who had himself written a book on antisemitism in America, and had referred to the work of the Institute in his own book, found the volume by Lowenthal and Guterman to be "beyond all doubt the most illuminating study of the techniques and the propaganda of the native American Fascist which has yet to appear," "uniquely well organized ... and extraordinarily well-written." In addition, McWilliams found the deciphering by Lowenthal and Guterman of the agitators' language to be "wholly convincing," even "brilliant." Though the Institute did in fact plant, or attempt to plant, other reviews, Horkheimer insisted that the Institute had "no advance knowledge of, or control over, Carey McWilliams' review..."[369]

There were also other positive (or mostly positive) reviews of *Prophets of Deceit*. Chester Jurczak, writing in *The American Catholic Sociological Review*, found *Prophets* to be "generally objective, well-annotated and documented."[370] Alfred McClung Lee of Brooklyn College proclaimed in

Public Opinion Quarterly that Lowenthal and Guterman "deserve praise for a wise and significant volume."[371] The review in *The New York Times* may help to explain why *Prophets* initially sold very well. One thousand nine hundred and thirty copies had been sold by April 1950.[372]

However, the scholarly reviews of *Prophets* that appeared in the wake of the piece in the *Times* were by no means uniformly positive. Indeed, the book was criticized by many, for any number of different reasons – including not only criticisms like those that were made of *The Authoritarian Personality*, but also criticisms that did not apply to that work.

Leibush Lehrer, who was associated with the YIVO Scientific Institute, damned *Prophets* with faint praise in *Jewish Social Studies*: "As far as they go, the authors performed a creditable job."[373] Lehrer was unconvinced by the ways in which Lowenthal and Guterman had distinguished between agitators and revolutionaries, and insisted that "no 'native-white-Protestant' agitator has ever in his abominable trade surpassed the level of agitation manifested by the communist trials....The authors would have been far better advised had they resolved to draw distinctions not between ideologies but between methods of persuasion."[374] Dennis Wrong of Princeton University published a review in *American Journal of Sociology* that echoed this criticism, arguing that Lowenthal and Guterman had neglected "to mention the techniques of the Communist agitator." The political insinuations of this comment were likely manifest to Wrong's readers. In addition, Wrong asserted that the authors' analysis, had, on occasion, outrun their data, and that they had been "too anxious to find exact parallels between the pronouncements of American agitators and the ideology of the Nazis and Fascists."[375] A review that appeared in *American Jewish Historical Quarterly* does not explicitly critique *Prophets* for failing to discuss Communist agitators, and comments favorably on the extent to which the book's analysis is "full and explicit," but also asserts "No future historian writing of our period in the United States can ignore the part played by pro-German, Fascist, Communistic and crackpot anti-Semitic propaganda..."[376] J. F. Brown found *Prophets of Deceit* to be "interesting and readable," but suggested that it would be "much less significant" viewed on its own than in the context of the series of which it was a part.[377] A reviewer for *Sociology and Social Research* was unhappy about several matters. "It does not appear to the reviewer ... that the authors have adequately shown what the *profits* of deceit may be... Furthermore, whether the agitator is himself aware of the subtle sign ificance and effects of his activities, the authors are not prepared to say."[378] The reviewer was not pleased by the psychoanalytic technique used by Lowenthal and Guterman, and, finally, suggests that the book's failure to analyze the kinds of people attracted by agitators is problematic. *American Sociological Review* printed a short, unsigned, review that griped "Sociologists may wonder why the authors felt the need for their new concept of *malaise* when Durkheim's widely accepted *anomie* was ready to hand ... Moreover, while the authors realize that their interpretations are tentative ... the hypotheses remain implicit ... More explicit and concise statement of their hypotheses would have added to the book's usefulness."[379] A major review of all of "Studies in Prejudice" by Harold D. Lasswell – a prominent American academic who had been associated with the University of Chicago in the early part of his career, and who, in 1946, became a professor at the Yale School of Law – also had critical comments about Lowenthal and Guterman's book:

If the material had been concurrently analyzed by quantitative methods, differentiations would have been possible that are beyond the range of the final typology. If there had been greater technical versatility in this project ... the qualitative and quantitative procedures would have been exhibited side by side, to the advantage of both.[380]

Prophets of Deceit, in sum, attracted attention, and was reviewed by prominent and respected authors. It also received a substantial amount of criticism, including criticism that suggested that Lowenthal and Guterman had political blinders, and criticism of these writers' methodology. Influenced by Critical Theory, and written by European-trained academics sympathetic to qualitative approaches and to left-wing ideas, *Prophets of Deceit*, was found wanting by American empirical social scientists writing in the context of the Cold War. These critiques shed light on the reasons why *Prophets* sold fewer than 500 copies between mid-1950 and the end of 1955, despite the fact that it had gotten off to a good start.[381]

*

As we have seen, Paul Massing first established ties to the Institute in 1927, before Horkheimer had become its director. Unlike Horkheimer or Lowenthal or Fromm, Massing was involved with the Communist Party of Germany in the Weimar years. In 1929, he became a research assistant of the International Agrarian Institute in Moscow. Although Massing returned to Germany in 1931, he focused his energies in the years immediately thereafter not so much on academic work, as did those around Horkheimer, as on anti-Nazi, pro-Communist, political struggle, and was based in Berlin rather than in Frankfurt. Massing initially remained in

Germany when the Nazis came to power. As a result of his political activities, he was incarcerated in a concentration camp for a portion of 1933. Despite the manifest risks involved, for much of the early- to mid-1930s, Massing remained in Europe, and continued to engage in activities on behalf of the Communist Party. By the late 1930s, however, Massing had become disillusioned with Communism, and had left the Party. He moved to the United States, and, in or around 1941, joined the Institute as a research associate. Massing's political position in the early 1940s – influenced by Marxism but not Communism – was roughly similar to that of most members of the Frankfurt School. But while Massing was a significant Institute associate in the years during which America participated in the Second World War, and was employed on the antisemitism project on a full-time basis, he did not have influence in the Institute comparable to those of Pollock or Adorno or Lowenthal or Marcuse, and was not a Critical Theorist. Thus, it is unsurprising that the book by Massing published as part and parcel of "Studies in Prejudice," *Rehearsal for Destruction. A Study of Political Anti-Semitism in Imperial Germany*, was rather different from the works in the series to which Adorno and Lowenthal contributed. But it too was a book embraced and endorsed by those surrounding Horkheimer.

Massing's study had a historical focus, and included sections on political antisemitism in Bismarck's Reich, the rise of racial antisemitism in late nineteenth-century Germany, antisemitism and imperialism, and the relationship of the German left to antisemitism in the period from 1863 to 1914. He began from the presumption that the history of German antisemitism could only be explained by situating it in the sociopolitical context in which it arose. Germany, he points out, did not make a radical break with its feudal past. As a result, it remained backward both economically and politically. Unlike in certain other Western countries, in which middle classes had come to power, feudal sectors retained considerable strength in Germany, and undermined liberalism. Antisemitism in imperial Germany was a part of the configuration of social and political forces. As Massing saw it, antisemitism had had a dual nature. On the one hand, it served as a political tool of ruling powers. On the other hand, it had also been an expression of social protest, albeit a confused expression. During some of the historic period that Massing studied, antisemitism was used by those in power to reinforce their position, and grew in significance. On the other hand, in the period from the beginning of the twentieth century until the beginning of the First World War, organized antisemitism was declining in Germany. This decline led some in

Germany – including German Social Democrats – to misunderstand the phenomenon. Massing provided a balanced and honest summary of problematic aspects of German socialist stances vis-à-vis antisemitism:

> Little attention has been paid in nonsocialist literature to the work of enlightenment and education which German socialism carried on among its followers. The Socialists, on the other hand, have done little in the way of critically reevaluating this work. On the whole they still refuse to acknowledge weaknesses which have by now become obvious, and cling steadfastly to a dogmatism that even the Nazi catastrophe has not shaken. Their chronic underestimation of anti-Semitism which they continue to view as a mere byproduct of the class struggle, is symptomatic of such dogmatic thinking.[382]

He concluded this portion of his book by labeling German Social Democratic understandings of antisemitism – altogether appropriately – as "incredibly naïve"[383]

Rehearsal for Destruction, like *Prophets of Deceit*, was reviewed in the *New York Times*. The review of Massing's book was signed by none other than Thomas Mann, who had lived near Adorno in Los Angeles. Mann, winner of the Nobel Prize for Literature in 1929, was one of the most distinguished German exiles in America. He and Adorno socialized together in California, and shared their opinions with one another. When Mann's *Doctor Faustus* was published in 1947, Mann had presented Adorno with a copy inscribed "For the Real Privy Councillor."[384] In a letter to Horkheimer in which he sketched his plans for placing a review in the *Times*, Adorno made it clear that Mann would be asked to sign off on a piece to be written by those in the Institute. Massing, Adorno indicated, would create a summary of his book for use in writing a draft of the review, this summary would be sent to Horkheimer for his input, and "Tommy" Mann would merely need to review an edited draft, make those changes that he believed to be desirable – and allow his name to be used to further the purposes of the Institute.[385] Though Adorno (who was in Frankfurt, on a trip intended to test the waters for a possible long-term return to Germany while this matter was being played out) did in fact write a draft,[386] and sent it to Horkheimer (who was in California) it actually arrived too late for Horkheimer to make use of it.[387] Nevertheless, it is clear that "Mann's" review was one that had been molded by the Critical Theorists, and, above all, by Horkheimer.

This explains how and why it happened that the review signed by Mann begins with the declaration that he had long been attracted to the Institute's work, and that Massing's book was "an excellent example" of that work.[388] The review in the *Times* summarizes the questions posed by Massing, and declares Massing's treatment of these questions to be "a model of objectivity." Massing's book is situated entirely in the context of the Institute and its work – so much so that Flowerman later protested to Horkheimer about the failure of the review to mention the AJC.[389] Whatever subtle differences there may have been between Massing's historical approach to the study of antisemitism [which was a left-wing approach but not psychoanalytically and philosophically informed, as were the approaches of the Critical Theorists during this period] on the one hand and those of the Horkheimer circle on the other, Horkheimer and Adorno had a vested interest in accenting Massing's ties to the Institute, and in allowing the Institute to get credit for yet another published book on an important topic.

Unfortunately, from the perspective of the Frankfurt School, the review of *Rehearsal for Destruction* in *American Sociological Review* never so much as mentions the Institute or Horkheimer. The reviewer found Massing's work "competent" and praised his "painstaking analysis" as "very successful," but may well have been wholly unfamiliar with Massing's background or affiliations.[390] Gordon Craig, who was appointed to a position at Princeton in the same year in which his review appeared, and who wrote on Massing's book for *The Public Opinion Quarterly*, similarly, does not mention the Institute – and found *Rehearsal for Destruction* to be "scholarly" and "persuasive." Massing, he concluded had "written a thoughtful and very thorough analysis of anti-Semitism in modern Germany."[391] *Sociology and Social Research* also published a very positive review of Massing's book, describing Massing's analysis of socialist positions on antisemitism as "extremely astute," and endorsing Massing's evaluation: "Massing shows brilliantly that the socialists 'missed the boat' in their interpretation of Germany's political and economic future..."[392]

The review published in *The American Historical Review* – a particularly prestigious and influential periodical among historians – offered a far more critical assessment. Roland Usher, the reviewer, *was* somewhat familiar with Massing's role in the Institute, and with Massing's background, and takes pains to note (correctly) that Massing was "not a professional historian." Usher points out that Massing had not made use of archival materials, and also notes that "experts will miss many titles they will deem important" in Massing's endnotes. From the perspective of the historian, "[m]uch of the information in the notes is ... familiar ... little in" the volume "...will be of use to specialists." But, he concludes, the general reader may well find "real value" in Massing's book.[393]

Raymond J. Sontag of the University of California, writing in *Political Science Quarterly*, was unhappy with Massing's approach, which he found to be "clamped in a deterministic frame." As Sontag saw it, Massing had attempted, inappropriately, to squeeze available evidence into this framework – and had thereby distorted reality. Since, Sontag wrote, the editors of "Studies in Prejudice" understood that education ought to be both psychological and personal, and since the stated purpose of "Studies in Prejudice" was education, Massing's book did not fit well in the series.[394]

A review by William O. Shanahan that appeared in *The Review of Politics* was even more negative. Shanahan describes Massing's book as "diffuse, poorly organized and in many places almost heedless of its central topic." He proclaims that "[i]t is part of the historian's craft to combine his material so that what is relevant will add luster or provide meaning to what he intends to emphasize" and bluntly asserts that "[l]ack of this skill obscures some of the author's most telling points." He, like Sontag, disapproved of Massing's approach to the topic, writing that "it is apparent that the author willingly subordinates the ideal to the material forces in history."[395]

Rehearsal for Destruction received a mixed reception from American academics. A fair proportion of the published reviews disapproved of its methodology or questioned its scholarship. Nevertheless, both Horkheimer and Adorno stood by *Rehearsal*.

Horkheimer did not write an introduction for the original, English-language, version of Massing's book, as he had for *Prophets of Deceit*. When, however, the Institute published a German translation of Massing's book, in 1959, it contained a foreword co-written by Horkheimer and Adorno, who were both living in Europe at that time. To be sure, the positions of Horkheimer and Adorno in 1959 were, on specific matters that are not relevant to our current concerns, no longer those of a decade earlier. It is, in addition, quite plausible that some of the formulations by Horkheimer and Adorno in the foreword concerning antisemitism differed from the ways in which they would have made parallel points when they had been living in exile. It is likely also significant that Massing's book had originally been written for an American audience. The foreword – like the translation itself – was aimed at a German audience. Nevertheless, Horkheimer and Adorno's foreword of 1959 is a revealing one, and suggests that the Critical Theorists had had a positive reaction to Massing's book when it first appeared, and that they continued to view it in a favorable light ten years after its initial publication.

The foreword emphasized that totalitarian antisemitism was in no way a specific German phenomenon, and that attempts to explain antisemitism by use of notions like national character downplay the importance of the phenomenon. Totalitarian antisemitism, Horkheimer and Adorno proclaim, triumphed in Germany not because of the characteristics of the German people or because of some kind of necessity written into history but rather because of an economic and social constellation. As Horkheimer and Adorno saw it in 1959, Massing's book had made a decided contribution. Moreover, they use the occasion to state flatly that "[a]ntisemitism has its basis in objective social conditions just as much as in the consciousness and unconsciousness of the masses... it actualizes itself as a means of politics..."[396]

*

Horkheimer allegedly hoped that all of the books in "Studies in Prejudice" – presumably including not only those to which the members and associates of the Institute had directly contributed, discussed above, but also those written by Nathan Ackerman and Marie Jahoda (*Anti-Semitism and Emotional Disorder*), and by Bruno Bettelheim and Morris Janowitz (*Dynamics of Prejudice*) that analyzed antisemitism from psychoanalytic or psychological perspectives but that were not influenced by the Frankfurt School's ideas – would eventually contribute to the creation of a series of booklets, written in a popular format, and meant for general distribution. Horkheimer's intent had been to contribute directly to the struggle against antisemitism in the United States: "Our aim is not merely to describe prejudice but to explain it in order to help in its eradication."[397] The booklet project would presumably have entailed making the ideas of the Critical Theorists somewhat more accessible than was otherwise the case. As Lowenthal described them, the booklets would have been distributed when necessary to extinguish antisemitic flare-ups, and would have been intended for use by teachers, politicians, students and others who had more direct contact with the masses than did the Frankfurt School per se.[398] The breakdown of Horkheimer's relationship with Flowerman ultimately undermined this plan. No such series of booklets was ever produced. The plan, however, is itself indicative of Horkheimer's motivations. The Institute's director believed that antisemitism needed to be fought, not merely studied, and hoped that the work done by the Frankfurt School would contribute to this fight.

*

The actualization of Adorno's foreboding prediction of 1938 led Adorno to underscore, as early as the autumn of 1944, that civilization had been profoundly altered: "The idea that after this war life will continue 'normally' or even that culture might be 'rebuilt' – as if the rebuilding of culture were not already its negation is idiotic. Millions of Jews have been murdered, and this is to be seen as an interlude and not the catastrophe itself. What more is this culture waiting for? And even if countless people still have time to wait, is it conceivable that what happened in Europe will have no consequences, that the quantity of victims will not be transformed into a new quality of society at large, barbarism?"[399] From Adorno's perspective, antisemitism had changed the whole world, let alone the world of the *Bildungsbürgertum* in which the term "culture" had been raised as the banner of righteousness.

Antisemitism also eventually changed Adorno's own relationship to his familial roots. Though not Jewishly identified in the pre-Holocaust years, Adorno increasingly empathized with Jewish Holocaust survivors as the enormity of events in Europe became apparent. *Minima Moralia*, written during and immediately after the Second World War, concludes with a passage that could easily have been written by Benjamin, and that echoes the influence that Jewish ideas had had on Adorno's friend:

The only philosophy which can be responsibly practiced in face of despair is the attempt to contemplate all things as they would present themselves from the standpoint of redemption. Knowledge has no light but that shed on the world by redemption: all else is reconstruction, mere technique. Perspectives must be fashioned that displace and estrange the world, reveal it to be, with its rifts and crevices, as indigent and distorted as it will appear one day in the messianic light.[400]

To be sure, Adorno's relationship to Jewishness remained complex, multifaceted, and conflicted. In 1946 he wrote to his parents that "...I am reluctant to correspond with you about the Jews, as that is not good for both our more or less broken hearts. After 6 million have been murdered, it goes against my instincts to dwell on the manners of those few who survived, whom I incidentally do not need to like. In addition to that, the 50% goy in me feels somehow responsible for the Jewish persecution, so I am therefore quite especially allergic to everything that is said against the chosen people, e.g. also by Max, whose anti-Semitism more or less matches that of WK [Oscar Wiesengrund], though he has the excuse of having spent a year working for the American Jewish Committee. Commentary the journal of 'our' (anti-Zionist) committee, is a revolting, lying gutter rag..."[401] And yet this "50% goy" also clearly thought of himself at that time as 50% Jewish – and this seems to have had an impact, in the wake of the Holocaust, on his self-perception, on his thought, and on his attitudes.

Shortly following Adorno's death, in 1969, Horkheimer received a letter from Otto Herz, a member of the B'nai B'rith Lodge in Vienna, which expressed regret that there had not been an "acknowledgment of his Jewishness" at Adorno's funeral.[402] Horkheimer replied that he had "a keen understanding" of this regret, and noted that "the external reasons" – the facts that Adorno's mother was Catholic, and that Adorno had been baptized a Catholic and confirmed a Protestant, among other matters – were "obvious." Horkheimer then adds:

I am telling you this in order to help you understand the complicated attitude of the deceased to religion and to a specific faith. On the other hand, I may say that Critical Theory, which we both developed, has its roots in Judaism. It derives from the idea that thou shalt make no image of God. That Adorno identified with the persecuted is proven by his declaration that no poem should be created after what happened in Auschwitz. Had he lived longer, and had we spoken about the funeral before he died, it is not impossible that the funeral would have been conducted in the manner suggested in your letter.[403]

Writing to a young Austrian scholar in 1988, Leo Lowenthal discussed matters relevant to Adorno's relationship to Jewishness and explicitly declared "[i]n conversations, although he was half Jewish, he always identified himself as a Jew, and ascribed an 'aristocratic' significance to this state of affairs."[404] Lowenthal does not differentiate here among the various periods of Adorno's life. But it appears to be the case that Adorno was more inclined to "identify" himself as a Jew in the second half of his life than he had been in the period before he arrived in the United States.

*

The single most important research project conducted by the Institute in the 1930s, results of which were published under the title *Studien über Autorität und Familie* in 1936,[405] has been analyzed by several leading scholars, including Richard Wolin. In an insightful piece on the Frankfurt School, Wolin argues that "the *mutual indifference* between theory and empirical research that colored *Studies on Authority and the Family* would also characterize much of the Institute's subsequent work" [emphasis in the original].[406] However, the works studied in this chapter suggest that the conclusion reached by Wolin (and others) as to the relationship between theory and empirical research in the work of the Institute is open to question. It could legitimately be argued that the empirical studies on antisemitism conducted by Institute affiliates in the 1940s were insufficiently meshed with the attempts by the Critical Theorists to offer a theoretical explanation of antisemitism and its significance.

It is not the case, however, that the Institute's empirical and theoretical works on antisemitism were mutually indifferent.

*

If one compares Horkheimer's essay on the Jews and Europe with relevant writings written over the course of the next few years, it becomes manifest that Horkheimer's thinking shifted considerably. In the period just before the War began, Horkheimer still placed particular stress on the primacy of economics, and on a Marxist framework, in explaining the phenomenon of antisemitism. In pieces by Horkheimer and by Adorno written during and immediately after the war, economics is one component of a multi-faceted explication of hatred of Jews. The shift in Horkheimer's perspective on antisemitism was part and parcel of a larger shift that deeply affected Critical Theory as a whole, and is best explained by the influence of Adorno, and by reflection on the part of Horkheimer on the destruction of the Jews, which was underway as he wrote the most important of the works he produced in exile.

But this shift did not signify a total rejection of previously held positions. Adorno had hoped, in the 1940s, to supplement his published writings on antisemitism with writings in which antisemitism would have been explained as intimately intertwined with economic and social conditions. The proposed "Treatise" initiated by Horkheimer, we can presume, would have taken this latter approach. The *published* pieces by Horkheimer and Adorno that grapple with antisemitism and that date from the post-1939 years are potentially misleading insofar as they may suggest that the Critical Theorists had given up altogether on their Marxist roots during the exile years. They had not. And yet, Horkheimer and Adorno never did actualize their intention to write a sequel to *Dialectic of Enlightenment*[407] (which, in any event, would have been unlikely to contain a sequel to "Elements of Anti-Semitism") and never did flesh out a fuller theory of antisemitism in later published works. "Elements of Anti-Semitism" remained a series of fragments. And yet "an aversion to closed philosophical systems," as Martin Jay first told us, "lies at the very heart of Critical Theory."[408] Thus the fact that the key writings of the Critical Theorists on antisemitism and the image of the Jew created in exile have remained "philosophical fragments" strikes me as ultimately not unfitting.

Chapter 3

Critical Theorists and the State of Israel

In 1950, Max Horkheimer moved back to Frankfurt. Two of his closest colleagues, Pollock and Adorno, also lived in Germany in the post-Holocaust era, and continued to work with Horkheimer for the rest of their lives. But a number of one-time members of the Horkheimer circle, including Fromm, Lowenthal, and Marcuse, did not relocate to Europe after the Second World War.[1] Over time, significant differences between those who had moved to Frankfurt after the war's end and those who had not became apparent.[2] Matters pertaining to Israel were by no means among the most important of these differences. However, the issue of Israel was an emotionally significant one for these theorists. The views towards Israel of key writers who had, at varying points in time, been associated with the Frankfurt School were heavily influenced by their relationships to Judaism. There was, among the writers under discussion, an inverse relation between knowledge of Jewish religious ideas and the depth of their criticisms of Israel. The deeper a given writer's familiarity with Judaism, the stronger that thinker's critique of the Jewish state.

Horkheimer, Lowenthal, Fromm, and Marcuse were all of Jewish origin, were all members of the same generational cohort, were all raised in Germany, and were all among those who succeeded in surviving the Nazi era by leaving the land of their birth. None of these men was sympathetic to Zionism in the period during which they were affiliated with the Institute. In the decades following the establishment of the State of Israel, however, subtle variations appeared in their attitudes towards that country. These variations – linked to their relationships with their Jewish backgrounds and with Judaism – reveal underlying distinctions among them. By analyzing the relationships of Critical Theorists to the State of Israel, therefore, we underscore the ways in which their Jewish family backgrounds continued to impact upon them in the last decades of their lives, and can also shed light on the reasons why these writers came to have distinctive stances on an issue that touched many of them rather personally.

*

By some accounts, the Jewish background of the Marcuse family was "largely a matter of indifference" to Herbert's parents during Herbert's childhood.[3] This wording, however, strikes me as too strong. Carl and Gertrud Marcuse, Herbert's father and mother, maintained affiliations, observed Jewish religious traditions, and evinced a set of prejudices, quite typical for German Jews of their time, place, and class. Carl, for one – like Moses Horkheimer – was a member of the Jewish service organization B'nai B'rith, and Herbert's family attended synagogue in Berlin, the city in which Herbert was born, albeit only on the Jewish High Holidays. Carl reportedly "even fasted" on Yom Kippur.[4] Indeed, Peter Marcuse, Herbert's son, has noted that, to the best of his knowledge, Carl and Gertrud were "relatively observant."[5] Herbert himself recalled that his grandparents hosted a seder on Passover – and it can be safely assumed that Herbert attended at least some of these seders.[6] Whatever their level of religious observance may have been, and there is no reason to think that it went beyond the level alluded to above, Carl and Gertrud made sure that their children received rudimentary Jewish religious instruction. This instruction, it should be noted, does not appear to have evoked any interest in Judaism in Herbert. Like his siblings, Herbert "attended synagogue indifferently, resistantly, and only under ... moral compulsion" exerted by his mother's parents.[7] He did not continue to receive instruction in matters related to Judaism after 1911, that is, the year in which he became a bar mitzvah. It is, moreover, quite clear that while Herbert's parents observed certain, specific, Jewish traditions, they ignored others. Herbert's nuclear family, for example, did not abide by traditional Jewish dietary restrictions. Additional indications of the attitudes of Carl and Gertrud may also be gleaned from the report that they expressed "a fashionable and probably self-conscious" distaste for East European Jews living in Berlin at the beginning of the last century and from the indication that they celebrated Christmas, or at least the more secular parts of it, alongside their celebrations of certain Jewish holidays.[8]

In all of these ways the relationship of the Marcuses, including Herbert, to Jewish matters was by no means exceptional. Many German Jews combined Hannukah and Christmas into one joyous event – *Weinukkah*.

Almost all German Jewish families in the neighborhood in Berlin in which Herbert was raised were likely to have been undergoing acculturation at the beginning of the twentieth century, signaled by an apparent fashion, even among some of those who remained observant of Jewish religious rituals, of giving their children decidedly non-Jewish names. "Marcuse used to joke that on Friday evenings one could hear mothers calling out 'Siegfried, Brunehilde, Shabbat!'"[9] Herbert's family, Herbert himself insisted, was integrated into German society, and, by his account, his upbringing was no different from that of other German upper-middle class youth.[10] It is manifestly the case that many German Jews (including not only Carl and Gertrud Marcuse, but also, as we suggested earlier, Oscar Wiesengrund and Victor Lowenthal, all of whom were of roughly the same generational cohort) did not like or identify with their East European co-religionists. In addition, according to Carl's grandson, Carl "refused to believe that, as a good German, he could possibly be the subject of discrimination or persecution, and refused to consider leaving Berlin until the very last moment before the war broke out."[11] Unlike, to take one prominent example, Gershom Scholem, Herbert did not feel "any contradiction between being German and being Jewish" in his formative years.[12]

Herbert Marcuse repeatedly told Helmut Dubiel that although he knew about the phenomenon of antisemitism in the Weimar period he was rarely directly victimized by it.[13] In an interview broadcast on German television in 1980, Marcuse also noted that the antisemitism that had existed in Germany before Hitler was different from the antisemitism that existed in America. He described German antisemitism of the pre-Hitler years as "more of an open and conservative" kind than its American counterpart, and as manifesting itself in relatively minor matters, such as Jews not going to specific vacation spots (where, presumably, they would not have been welcomed).[14] Marcuse's sense of German antisemitism in the years of his childhood and youth was strikingly parallel, therefore, to those of Horkheimer or Lowenthal or Adorno.

One significant chapter in Marcuse's life in the years preceding exile may have had an antisemitic element to it. Marcuse finished writing the work he had hoped would be his *Habilitationsschrift* – a study of Hegel's ontology – long before Hitler came to power. However, Marcuse did not complete the formal procedure by which he would have earned the *venia legendi* (and, thereby, official permission to lecture in Germany at the university level). The question as to just why he did not complete this procedure has not been definitively answered. Barry Kātz reports, seemingly on the basis of conversations that Kātz had with Marcuse, that Marcuse "never formally submitted" his work to his advisor at the University of Freiburg, Martin Heidegger, and that Heidegger "probably never read it."[15] In a postcard from Heidegger to Marcuse dated September 27, 1930, however, Heidegger explicitly states that he had read all of the work by Marcuse on Hegel, that he found it to be both very successful and valuable, and that he wanted to discuss the work with Marcuse.[16] But a letter from Edmund Husserl to Kurt Riezler of the University of Frankfurt notes that Heidegger (who publicly declared himself to be a Nazi in the spring of 1933, several months after Marcuse had left Germany) had "blocked" Marcuse's *Habilitation*.[17] Did Heidegger ultimately decide to prevent Marcuse from moving forward with his career – despite initially finding the latter's work on Hegel to be valuable – because Marcuse was Jewish? In 1953, Marcuse reported to Horkheimer that Heidegger had made a vulgar antisemitic remark about Marcuse – but he does not indicate when it was that Heidegger had made this remark.[18] In any event: Marcuse himself never publicly proclaimed that anti-Jewish prejudice on the part of Heidegger was a significant factor in their relationship in the years during which Marcuse was Heidegger's student.[19] He was more comfortable saying that "[t]he advent of the Nazi regime blocked the Habilitation" – a far more neutral statement – than with stating that Heidegger's attitude towards Marcuse's Jewish origins explains why the formal process of certifying Marcuse's *Habilitationsschrift* did not proceed.[20] In an interview published in 1977, Marcuse commented that "Now, from personal experience I can tell you that neither in [Heidegger's] lectures, nor in his seminars, nor personally, was there any hint of his sympathies toward Nazism" in the period prior to Hitler's ascent to power. "[H]is openly declared Nazism came as a complete surprise to us."[21] However, one could certainly harbor antisemitic sentiment without being publicly identified with the Nazis – antisemitism extended far beyond Nazi ranks among Germans of that era – and it seems quite likely that Heidegger harbored anti-Jewish prejudices before 1933.

Whether or not antisemitism on the part of Heidegger explains, in whole or in part, why Marcuse did not receive his *Habilitation* in Freiburg in the early 1930s, Marcuse, unlike Horkheimer or Adorno, did not develop a special interest in antisemitism per se – either before leaving Germany or thereafter – and rarely wrote about that theme.[22] It is telling, in this regard, that, unlike certain of his peers, Marcuse never attempted, in the decades following the end of the Second World War, to theorize about the larger significance of the extermination of European Jewry.[23]

This fact should not be taken as suggesting that Marcuse was altogether indifferent to antisemitism. In 1971, Marcuse reportedly signed a cable to Aleksei N. Kosygin, Premier of the Soviet Union, which deplored the treatment of Jews in that country. The cable noted that those signing were "deeply troubled by reports that the Soviet Union intends to proceed with its trial of Soviet Jews" and appealed to Kosygin to "recognize that ... present treatment of Jews is ... politically deleterious." The cable further requested that all Jews who wanted to leave the Soviet Union be permitted to do so.[24] During that same year, Marcuse sent a telegram to Gershom Scholem reading, in full: "I have protested [a]nd shall continue [to] protest against persecution of Jews in USSR. Herbert Marcuse."[25]

Particularly in the late 1960s, Marcuse was himself subjected to occasional antisemitic attacks. One Chetwood T. Schwarzkopf, an American veteran of both the First and the Second World Wars and a proud descendant of Andrew Jackson, wrote to Marcuse in the summer of 1968 in order to inform him that "[a]fter learning of your classroom antics, I have come to wonder – along with many another veteran of World War II – if Hitler wasn't right after all."[26] An unknown correspondent sent Marcuse a clipping of a review of Marcuse's *An Essay on Liberation* on which the correspondent had typed: "You damned phoney, talking about violence by armed forces. OUR armed forces. What about YOUR killers in Israeli uniforms? Are they – as usual – always exempt from your filthy attacks? Too bad Hitler let you go." On the same clipping, the correspondent also typed "Jew Boy" under the picture of Marcuse that had appeared with the review.[27]

In 1977, Marcuse was asked by an interviewer for a Jewish student newspaper whether he felt that antisemitism was "a real concern for Jews around the world, and especially for Jews in the U.S.". Marcuse's highly revealing answer was "Anti-semitism is rampant in all states, and still exists in all states. Anti-semitism may assume far more aggressive forms. This is a cause for concern, but not as long as things are running smoothly. If this situation changes drastically anti-semitism will be a greater cause for concern."[28]

Marcuse was strongly censured, in the late 1960s and in the 1970s, not only by antisemites, but also by (specific) self-identified Jews. An article published in *The American Zionist* in 1971 was very critical of Marcuse's analysis of contemporary society, but did not mention Marcuse's Jewish background, his comments on antisemitism, or his approach to the conflict between Israel and the Palestinians.[29] Later that year, the bulletin of a synagogue located in Brooklyn, Progressive Shaari Zedek, printed a condemnation of Marcuse written by the synagogue's rabbi, Theodore N. Lewis. Rabbi Lewis – who had read the article in *The American Zionist* – found it deeply disturbing that Marcuse, a refugee from Hitler, was a critic of contemporary American society and that he was, allegedly, "an ardent preacher of revolutionary Communism," and thus Rabbi Lewis rhetorically asked "if capitalism ... is so hateful, who prevents him from going to the... Soviet Union...?"[30]

Both in the 1960s and in the 1970s, Marcuse accepted invitations to speak before Jewish groups. In 1962, for example, he delivered a talk on humanism and humanity to a B'nai B'rith group on the occasion of the eightieth anniversary of the creation of the first European Lodge of B'nai B'rith.[31] At the end of the decade, he also agreed to speak on "The Role of Religion in Changing Society" at the request of Rabbi Robert E. Goldburg of Congregation Mishken Israel of Hamden, Connecticut.[32] A third such talk was given in Los Angeles at the Leo Baeck Temple in 1970.

In the last of these talks, Marcuse alluded to the fact that he was always uncomfortable with arguments as to Jewish exceptionalism. He noted that the Prophets of ancient days were "the first radicals." However, in his notes for this speech, he added immediately thereafter "but the critical spirit is not only part of the Jewish tradition: it is the weapon of all persecuted minorities ... Today, persecution of minorities is again rampant... this time not directed primarily against the Jews, but against the 'radicals' students, black and brown people."[33] While Marcuse never denied his Jewish origins, he was, as Michael Lerner has put it, "sharply anti-particularist... and ... particularly angered by anything even vaguely reminiscent of Jewish particularism."[34]

When asked how he defined himself as a Jew, Marcuse replied, in one notable interview:

That's one question I haven't been able to answer. I don't go around defining myself. I am Jewish by tradition and culture, but if culture includes dietary laws and the Bible as holy writ then I can't be classified in that way.

I've always defined myself as a Jew when Jews were unjustly attacked. In Germany, being Jewish in the face of overt anti-semitism was being on the left.[35]

On the same occasion, those interviewing Marcuse also asked him "How do you view the Jewish people?" Marcuse's answer, in full, reads:

My nationality is not Jewish but U.S. If I lived in Israel, I'd be Jewish or Israeli, or whatever you want to call it. You can't say Jews are a nation unless they all live in Israel. Jews are bound by the historical tradition (and the ghetto played an important part in this) which made for community and tradition.[36]

Marcuse was not what Isaac Deutscher called a "non-Jewish Jew" – though it may well be fair to describe him, using George Mosse's term, as a "German Jew beyond Judaism."[37] There was clearly a Jewish element to Marcuse's sense of himself – albeit of a very specific sort. He was strictly secular, and (unlike his parents) generally did not attend synagogue services in his adult years even on the High Holidays. When, in the summer of 1966, he travelled to Prague in order to take part in a conference on Hegel, he was invited by local Jews to come to services on the Sabbath. He is said to have replied that "he wouldn't go to prayer services at a synagogue."[38] He was, H. Stuart Hughes suggests, not as Jewish as was his friend Franz Neumann, and he spoke much less often about Jewry than did Neumann.[39] However, Marcuse's strict secularism should not be taken to mean that he was altogether devoid of Jewish consciousness. Peter Marcuse notes, "I remember at home hearing Jewish jokes, a smattering of Yiddish, Jewish friends, a Jewish intellectual circle."[40] Michael Lerner, who, in 1965, was chair of the Berkeley chapter of Students for a Democratic Society, visited with Marcuse at that time, stayed at his home, and eventually developed a friendship with him.[41] In the 1970s, by which point Lerner, who had, as a young man, served as president of the college students' organization of Conservative Judaism, and who had also attended, for three years, the Teachers' Institute of the Jewish Theological Seminary (a major educational institution and training facility for Conservative Jews in the United States), was leading Sabbath services for a group in Berkeley.[42] Marcuse was in Berkeley regularly, in that period, and, Lerner informs me, would sometimes come to those Sabbath services, "though often to argue rather than to daven [pray]."[43] On at least one occasion, like his grandparents before him, Herbert hosted a Passover seder. Shlomo Avineri, who attended a seder at Herbert's home in 1979, describes it as "a very normal one, with hagaddah etc."[44]

Marcuse's Jewish background, and his cognizance of antisemitism, unquestionably played a role in the development of his positions on Zionism and Israel. In the summer of 1967, shortly after the Six Day War (during which Israel, fearing that it was about to be attacked, occupied the Sinai desert, the Gaza Strip, East Jerusalem, the West Bank, and the Golan Heights) Marcuse travelled to Berlin at the invitation of the German SDS (Sozialistischer Deutscher Studentenbund) and participated in a series of discussions in that city with activists in the New Left–oriented German students' movement. In the course of these discussions, which were held at the Free University of Berlin, Marcuse noted:

> You will understand that I have personal, though not only personal, feelings of solidarity and identification with Israel. Though I have always stressed that emotions, moral concepts and sentiments belong to politics and even to science, and that you cannot motivate either politics or science without emotions, I must see more than a personal prejudice in this solidarity. I cannot forget that for centuries the Jews belonged to the persecuted and oppressed; that not too long ago six million of them were annihilated.... When finally a place is to be created for these people where they will not need to fear persecution and oppression that is a goal with which I must declare my sympathy... I agree with Jean-Paul Sartre, who has said that under all circumstances a new war of annihilation against Israel must be prevented.[45]

Marcuse went on, in his remarks, to criticize specific Israeli policies and then added "the fact is that Arabs in official positions... have loudly and explicitly declared that there must be a war of annihilation against Israel... it is under these circumstances that the preventive war [of 1967], which is what it was, against Egypt, Syria and Jordan must be understood and evaluated."[46] He concluded by advocating face to face talks between Israel and the Arab states, and by suggesting that the two sides might be able "to form a united front against the attacks of the imperialist powers."[47]

Marcuse repeated similar sentiments on other occasions. On the other hand, the emphasis of Marcuse's comments shifted from time to time. In an interview conducted with an American alternative newspaper, *Street Journal*, in 1970, Marcuse, responding to a question soliciting his opinion on the Arab-Israeli wars, proclaimed that

> Up to now I have always defended Israel, because I cannot forget the fact that 6 million Jews were exterminated and that under no circumstances should conditions arise in which the same may happen again. That is to say, as much as is humanly possible, the Jews must be protected against the recurrence of such a massacre. But it seems to me now, that the Israeli policy, far from preventing the recurrence of such conditions, may very well work toward their recurrence, unless the policies towards the Arabs radically change.[48]

Marcuse continued by noting that he had come to this belief in the wake of three incidents – the alleged bombing of a school in Egypt in which 32 children were reported to have been killed, the appearance of a report that accused Israel of torturing Arab prisoners, and the refusal by the Israeli government to endorse a visit to Egypt by Nahum Goldmann (who encouraged Israelis to make concessions to the Palestinians in the pursuit of peace, and who was, in 1970, the President of the World Jewish Congress). "[I]f these reports are correct" Marcuse noted "it seems to me that precisely as a Jew, and as a member of the New Left, I can no longer defend Israeli policies, and that I have to agree with those who are radically critical of Israel."

The interviewer (whose name is unknown) asked about the contention that had been made by some that the "Israelis have become a tool of ... US foreign policy and the oil interests." Marcuse responded by saying, in effect, that he did not support such a view, and added, at a later point in the interview, "I think US policy is changing in favor of the Arabs, certainly not in favor of Israel." The final question posed by *Street Journal* was "So you see another slaughter coming for the Jews?" Marcuse's answer reads:

I would say that unless Israel finally makes up its mind and goes out of its way to establish human relations with the Arabs and treat them as human beings, I am afraid that sooner or later such a condition may reoccur.

During this period, it ought to be underscored, Marcuse remained willing to criticize not only Israeli policies, but also Arab states. When asked to produce an introduction for the Hebrew language edition of his works *One-Dimensional Man* and *An Essay on Liberation*, Marcuse wrote, in part,

Military regimes and totalitarian parties do not assure freedom and independence, no matter whether or not they call themselves socialist, no matter whether they espouse white or black or brown, Arab or Jewish nationalism. Only a free Arab world can peacefully coexist with a free Israel.[49]

In December 1971, Marcuse traveled to Israel as a guest of the Van Leer Institute, a widely respected, mainstream, intellectual study center founded in the late 1950s and based in Jerusalem. He delivered a number of talks, while in that country, in Jerusalem, Beersheba, and Haifa and received a fair amount of attention.[50] A talk in the auditorium of the Van Leer Foundation in Jerusalem attracted a capacity crowd of 300. Approximately 300 other people, unable to fit into the auditorium, listened to Marcuse's talk over loudspeakers.[51] At Marcuse's request, the audience in Haifa was restricted to 200 – and the students of Haifa fought to enter the hall in which Marcuse was scheduled to speak. In the course of his remarks in Haifa, Marcuse noted that while he, personally, did not define the Jews as a nation, "[i]f you define the Jewish People as a nation, then Zionism is a national liberation movement."[52] When a student asked Marcuse about immigration by Jews to Israel, Marcuse responded: "I am trying to support every effort to prevent persecution, no matter whether it is for colour or religion, of oppressed minorities and individuals. One way to help (persecuted Jews) is to let them come to Israel; and I am in favour of this." When he was queried as to whether he would himself consider immigration to Israel, he replied, while smiling, "It depends on what goes on in this country." Marcuse also noted that he did not understand the New Left as contesting the right of the State of Israel to exist as a sovereign state, and stressed that "[a]s a Jew, I have the right to criticize the Government of the Jewish State."

Marcuse did not merely hold a number of lectures while in the State of Israel, but also met with prominent Israeli intellectual and political leaders during the course of his trip. Among those with whom he met were Israel's Minister of Defense, Moshe Dayan, the novelist Amoz Oz, Eliezer Beeri of Mapam (a significant left Zionist political party), and Moshe Sneh of the Israeli Communist Party.[53] Marcuse allegedly made a very positive impression on Oz. In a letter written years later to Marcuse, Arthur A. Cohen notes, in passing, that Cohen had spoken with Oz about Marcuse's visit to Kibbutz Hulda, on which Oz lived in the era during which Marcuse was in Israel, and that Oz had extolled Marcuse "with great warmth."[54]

While in Jerusalem, Marcuse (who was aware of stances taken by certain of those active on the Israeli left) issued a statement describing his position on matters pertaining to Israel.[55] As he had in 1967, Marcuse prefaced his remarks on the policies of the State of Israel and on his ideas as to the outlines of a settlement with a strong statement of support for the goal of the State as he perceived it:

I believe that the historical goal which motivated the foundation of the State of Israel was to prevent a recurrence of the concentration camps, the pogroms, and other forms of persecution and discrimination. I fully adhere to this goal which, for me, is part of the struggle for liberty and equality for all persecuted racial and national minorities the world over. Under present international conditions, pursuance of this goal presupposes the existence of a sovereign state which is able to accept and protect Jews who are persecuted or live under the threat of persecution.

Marcuse also stated that, in his opinion, the period of settlement by Jews in what became Israel proceeded "without due regard to the rights and interests of the native population," and that the foundation of the State involved the displacement of the Palestinians partly by force and partly voluntarily. In this and other ways, "the establishment of the Jewish State is not essentially different from the origins of practically all states in history."

Marcuse argued that annexation of territory by the State of Israel would harm its interests, and further argued that the first prerequisite for a solution to the problems confronting Israel was a peace treaty with the United Arab Republic "which would include the recognition of the State of Israel and free access to the Suez Canal and the Straits, and a settlement of the refugee problem." He suggested that Israel, which, in his opinion, was militarily stronger than Egypt, could afford to withdraw from Sinai and from the Gaza Strip for the sake of peace, recognized that "the status of Jerusalem may well turn out to be the hardest impediment to a peace treaty," and tentatively noted that keeping Jerusalem united while putting it under international administration might offer a solution.

In this statement, Marcuse describes Israel as an occupying power, and the Palestinian movement as one of national liberation. In a discussion of two possible, interim, solutions to questions revolving around Palestinian refugees, Marcuse noted that one route would entail resettlement in Israel of Palestinians either to the land that they had had before 1948, or to other land in the State. He responded to the possible objection that such a solution would transform the Jewish majority in the State into a Jewish minority by pointing out that policies aimed at maintaining a Jewish majority were "self-defeating" and proclaimed: "The Jewish population is bound to remain a minority within the vast realm of Arab nations from which it cannot indefinitely segregate itself without returning to ghetto conditions on a higher level ... lasting protection for the Jewish people cannot be found in the creation of a self-enclosed, isolated, fear-stricken minority, but only in the coexistence of Jews and Arabs as citizens with equal rights and liberties." Alternatively, Marcuse suggests, the aspirations of the Palestinians could be fulfilled on an interim basis by establishing a Palestinian state "alongside Israel." "Whether this state would be an independent entity, or federated with Israel or with Jordan would be" determined by a Palestinian referendum, under UN auspices. Marcuse made it clear that he thought of these alternative solutions as far from optimal. The best solution, he explicitly stated, would involve the coexistence of Israelis and Palestinians "in a socialist federation of Middle Eastern states." This optimal solution, he hastened to add, was still utopian. Thus, Marcuse urged that the interim solutions he had outlined not be rejected outright.[56]

On the same day on which Marcuse's statement was published in the prestigious Hebrew-language daily *Haaretz*, the newspaper also published an interview with Marcuse conducted by Uzi Benziman.[57] Benziman asked Marcuse "Are you a Zionist?" Marcuse responded:

"What is the definition of a Zionist? If Israel is an asylum for persecuted Jews, if its role is to protect Jews from a second Holocaust – the answer is positive. I am not a Zionist if it means that Israel is a home for all Jews." Benziman followed up by asking Marcuse about his "feeling as a Jew." Marcuse retorted: "I have a Jewish identity in the context of the expected dangers of the persecution of Jews. I have a difficult time identifying myself with them when they are the persecutors. I sense a connection to the cultural, socialist German heritage and in the same manner I feel a connection to the period in which the United States fought the Nazis. I have many loyalties." At a later point in the interview Marcuse explicitly stated "it is obvious I am against statements such as those which call for the destruction of Israel." He mentioned that he had met more groups in Israel than he had anticipated that opposed the policies of the Israeli government, and ended the interview by expressing admiration for those he had encountered "I was... impressed by the people I met, Jews as well as Arabs. As for the students, I found them vigorous, intelligent and even interested in politics, especially those in Haifa."

Marcuse discussed his position on Israel and the conflict in the Middle East on at least one other occasion. In the course of an interview conducted in April 1978 by Janguido Piani, an Italian journalist affiliated with the Rome-based *Lotta Continua*, Marcuse was asked whether he thought that Menachem Begin, Prime Minister of Israel, and Anwar Sadat, President of Egypt, who had entered into direct discussions with one another about the relations between their two countries, were sincere. Marcuse replied affirmatively, and added "but in my view, Begin's policy may be fatal... This doesn't mean that I would support the position of Arafat and the P.L.O. and in any case Israeli policy today seems disastrous."[58] Piani responded to this statement by declaring "Naturally you disagree both with Israeli retaliations in Lebanon and with the [P]alestinian attacks against Israeli people." Marcuse then commented "Well, this retaliation is an integral part of Begin's policy, always has been."

In sum, there was a Jewish component to Marcuse's sense of himself, but it was most definitely a secular rather than a religious component. Moreover, he was not necessarily inclined to characterize himself as Jewish first and foremost. He had German and American strands to his "identity" that existed alongside the Jewish strand, and one or another of these was, at many specific points in his life, probably more important to him than was his Jewish ancestry. Though he did not evince a strong interest in antisemitism, he was cognizant of it, and opposed it, just as he opposed mistreatment of racial or ethnic minorities in the United States and other places. Particularly in the wake of the Holocaust, Marcuse was well aware that antisemitism could well be extremely dangerous, and supported the existence of Israel, given the demonstrated need, in his opinion, for a place of asylum for Jews fleeing actual or potentially antisemitic milieus. Marcuse's stance vis-à-vis Zionism and Israel, finally, was linked by him to his Jewishness. He publicly proclaimed solidarity with Israel at the time of the 1967 war. In the wake of that war, however, he became quite critical of specific Israeli government policies vis-à-vis the Palestinians and neighboring Arab states, and, precisely because he thought of himself as a Jew, believed that he was entitled to state his criticism. However, even in the last decade of his life, Marcuse differentiated between the policies of Israeli governments and the rationale for the existence of Israel, opposing the former, in a number of instances, while steadfastly defending the need for a place of refuge from antisemitism. Herbert Marcuse's rather sympathetic stance towards Israel was manifestly influenced by his Jewish background. But it was precisely his *lack* of attachment to Jewish religious belief or tradition that led him to have a different and, in certain respects, somewhat softer stance towards the Jewish state than did his one-time colleagues in the Frankfurt School – whose views ranged, to some extent, along a continuum.

*

Marcuse's positions on Israel and Zionism in the post-Holocaust years can be fruitfully compared to those of other one-time members of the Horkheimer circle. Erich Fromm's position was perhaps furthest from that of his former colleague, and was characterized by ongoing rejection of the idea of a Jewish state, and by considerably harsher criticisms of the policies of that state.[59]

Fromm remained attentive to matters involving the Jews in Palestine long after the point – in the mid-1920s – at which he ceased to espouse Zionist ideas. Immediately after the Hebron pogrom of 1929, Fromm wrote to Ernst Simon (who was living in Palestine at that time), "Unfortunately these greetings are being written in a sad time for Palestine. I hope that when these lines reach you the acute danger will have been overcome. (I read your extra-ordinarily instructive and relevant essay in the *Jüdische Rundschau* [the major newspaper of the Zionist movement in Germany – JJ] with great interest)."[60]

Weeks before the declaration of independence of Israel in 1948, Fromm and Simon were involved in an initiative promoting the publication of a letter in the *New York Times* that condemned Arab and Jewish extremists and that urged peaceful coexistence in Palestine.[61] The initiative had been sparked by Judah Magnes and Martin Buber (among others), who had advocated the creation of a bi-national state in Palestine and who had helped to organize a group known as Ichud (which was established in Palestine in 1942).[62]

From at least 1950, if not earlier, Fromm was in touch with Isaac Nachman Steinberg (1888–1957), who was the head of the Freeland League, and who was a socialist. Steinberg had been a student at the University of Heidelberg from 1907 until 1910. While in Heidelberg, Steinberg studied Talmud with Salman Baruch Rabinkow (with whom, as we have seen, Fromm later studied).[63] Fromm became good friends with Steinberg in the final years of Steinberg's life, and repeatedly praised the orientation of the League.[64]

The Freeland League, a territorialist organization, was established in 1935, and advocated a non-Zionist solution to the problems confronting Jewish populations.[65] It was in favor of locating a large, unpopulated or undeveloped territory to which Jews in need of a place of refuge could move, and, at various points, considered potential locations around the world, but – both before and after the establishment of the State of Israel – did not believe that Palestine was the best place for a major concentration of Jews (because it recognized that there was already a large Arab population in Palestine and anticipated that the influx of Jews to that land would lead to conflict, and also because it believed that Israel could not absorb all Jews who were in need of a home or who would want to move to such a refuge).

Fromm published in the periodicals of the Freeland League, and served on the editorial board of the League's English-language organ, *Freeland*. An article by Fromm entitled "Jewish State and the Messianic Vision," written in 1950 – his first publication on Israel after it became an independent country – appeared in the Freeland League's Yiddish and English outlets, and set the tone for much of Fromm's later writings on Israel and Zionism.[66] Fromm begins this article by noting that the Zionist press had "greeted the establishment of the State of Israel as the fulfillment of the messianic hopes of the Jewish people."[67] He responds to this stance on the part of the Zionist press by flatly declaring that "[t]he claim that the state is a fulfillment of the Jewish messianic hopes is not only unjustifiable but contradicts the most fundamental principles and values of Jewish tradition."[68] Much of the piece is devoted to fleshing out Fromm's contentions that the Jewish religious tradition differentiated quite sharply between might and right, and that the prophetic notion of a messianic era "will be not only the cessation of oppression of the Jewish people, but equally the end of war between all nations."⁶⁹ He rhetorically asks "[c]an a Jewish State, as it establishes a precarious existence in a war-threatened world ... contain in its foundations the fulfillment of messianic hopes?"⁷⁰ His self-evident answer is quite firmly a negative one. Indeed from Fromm's perspective the "hysterical worship of the Jewish state as the fulfillment of messianic hopes" was "a betrayal of the very best in Jewish tradition."⁷¹ The article ends with a quote from Zachariah, thus underscoring that Fromm's critique of the State of Israel was grounded in his knowledge and understanding of Jewish text and thought, and in his firm belief that the leaders of Israel were acting in a manner contrary to the teachings of Judaism.⁷²

Several years later, unable to participate in person in a Freeland League-sponsored banquet held in New York, Fromm sent written greetings saluting the organization. He noted that the League was comprised of that sector of the Jewish population that believed that only moral principles would guarantee the future of the Jewish people, and explicitly declared that the League was, in his eyes, the expression of "the best Jewish traditions."⁷³

Fromm reiterated his view with regard to both the Freeland League and Israel at other points in the mid-1950s. He delivered a talk before a meeting of the League in 1953 on the "Jewish national character"⁷⁴ and allowed interviews conducted by Steinberg to be published in the Freeland League's organs. In the first of these interviews, Fromm discussed two Jewish groups, the Freeland League and the Ichud, as "voices raised in the cause of reason and true humanity."⁷⁵ He characterized the main task of the League as "the establishment of Jewish settlements without political aspirations, without displacement of other groups, based on the foundations of Jewish ethics and a just economy," noting that this task was "important enough," and praised the League as appealing "to the constructive forces in the Jew, in the Jewishness of generations."⁷⁶ Fromm described Ichud in much stronger terms as "a courageous avant-garde among the Israel population," representing "the oldest and trusted ideals of Jewishness in their universal scope," and as having "the spiritual strength to stand up to the forces of nationalism and militarism and [to] demand a sincere understanding with the Arabs."⁷⁷

Steinberg died in January 1957, and Fromm's ties to the Freeland League seem to have withered after his friend's death. In that same year, however, Fromm became a member of the Advisory Board of the American Friends of Ichud.⁷⁸ A flyer issued by the American Friends of Ichud after Fromm had joined the Board explained that its basic belief was that "the decisive factor for peaceful development of Israel is not material or military strength but a positive and fruitful relationship between Jews and Arabs."[79] In his letter accepting a position on the Board, Fromm wrote, "I have always been a warm admirer of Ichud, which, in fact, is to me the only bright and hopeful spot in the picture, politically as well as morally, of the State of Israel."[80]

Fromm worked actively in support of rapprochement between the Jews of Israel and the Arabs in the months following his adherence to the board of Ichud's American Friends. He attempted, for example, to arrange for a meeting between Martin Buber and Charles Malik (a prominent Lebanese diplomat and philosopher),[81] and met himself with Nahum Goldmann, Chairman of the Executive Committee of the Jewish Agency, and President of the World Zionist Organization.[82] Fromm's comments on his discussion with the latter in 1957 are highly revealing:

I was delighted to hear that Dr. Goldman[n] seemed to share the opinion that the Israeli government has the moral obligation to compensate the Arabs fully for their losses of property. I suggested to him how important it was that the Israeli government make such a declaration unequivocally and without being tied to peace negotiations. I added that I also thought it would be a good thing if the Israeli government would acknowledge the principle that all Arab refugees had a right to return, even though the Israeli government might add that for practical reasons the realization of this principle is not possible except, perhaps, for the return of let us say 100,000 refugees, and that therefore they offer the second-best, namely full financial restitution... I must confess that I recently had a rather violent attack of doubts as to whether I am really right in thinking that it is practically impossible for the Israeli government to take back all refugees.... I would assume that if all the Arabs went back it would really mean that Israel would be a truly bi-national state. This was Dr. Magnus' solution, and I still think the only reasonable one... I am not writing about all this as a practical solution, rather as a matter of conscience.[83]

Later that same year, Fromm described his position on Israel in a long letter to Norman Thomas, the most prominent leader of the Socialist Party of America. After describing his interactions with Goldmann and others, Fromm notes, "I think the whole position of a state, whose only moral justification is to find a home for homeless people, and who does so by depriving just as many other people of their homes is untenable, morally, and truly stupid politically... If all refugees came back, it would actually mean that the State of Israel would be a bi-national state, which is what it should have been in the first place. But it remains for me a revolting thing to accept the position that these Arab refugees should not be brought back to their homes. It is a sad thing to see how a nation which for 2,000 years was characterized by moral and pacifist ideals, changes its tune within a generation, if the opportunity arises."[84]

Unlike Marcuse, whose first inclination, at the time of the 1967 war, had been to voice solidarity with Israel, Fromm detailed his strong misgivings about Israeli government policies at that time. In a private letter written shortly after the end of the Six-Day War to Professor Karl D. Darmstadter of Howard University, who had, like Fromm (and Steinberg), studied Jewish texts with Rabinkow, Fromm expressed sadness "about the actions of the Israeli government, their flaunting of the U.N., their use of Napal[m] bombs, the plans to create an Arab satellite in West Jordan, which reminds me of the Apartheid program[me] of the South Africans. I am hesitant, because it is so different from what almost everybody thinks. But I have the confidence that you will think me neither cruel nor without compassion, when I say these things so sharply, and certainly it does not mean that I wish less than anybody else that the people of Israel may live."[85]

Fromm remained a strong critic of Israel in later years. Responding to a statement on the Arab-Israeli conflict endorsed by US Senator George McGovern and other Senators, Fromm noted in 1970: "As a Jew and one who is deeply rooted in the religious Jewish tradition and who all his life has followed closely the development of Zionism and since two decades of the State of Israel, I am certainly not without sympathy for the Jewish plight and not without knowledge about the history of Zionism which has led straight to the present situation." Fromm went on to mention "the problem of the aggressive spirit which has existed in Israel since the foundation of the State, and before that in the leading figures of Zionism." Fromm explained what he thought of as a "faith in force" in Israel by referring to the Holocaust, and to the psychological need on the part of Israeli Jews to demonstrate "that they know how to use force effectively." This, Fromm believed, had "led to an intransigence which runs through the whole history of ... Israel."[86]

Israeli policies gnawed at Fromm, and led him to return to some matters again and again. Thus, not long after writing to McGovern, Fromm informed Darmstadter that "[T]he Israelis ... have created a million homeless Arabs and they refuse to right the wrong. It is a peculiar thing, as if the Hitler trauma had completely reversed and perforated the minds of a people nursed on the prophetic tradition of peace and justice, and made them into the most fanatical believers in force as the only principle that can be applied in life."[87] One of his strongest remarks on Israel, dating from 1972, reads

Hitler destroyed half the Jewish people physically, but I am afraid the Zionist State is destroying the very essence of Judaism by its claims of representing the Messianic solution. Its whole militarism, its arrogance, lack of respect for the Arabs which arouse the admiration of the American military and reactionary circles is, indeed, the exact opposite of Prophetic teaching, and more than that; by this policy Israel is one of the greatest dangers to world peace... As long as the world is as it is each individual – whether Jewish or not – is, I believe, an exile, and from the traditional standpoint the Jewish people must be an exile too. To want to abolish "exile" in its spiritual meaning is to deny the discrepancy between what man is and what man could be... the voices that speak for the Messianic message among the Jewish people are rare, and met with more hostility by the other Jews than the dissenters are met with in other nations.[88]

Fromm was highly suspicious of Israeli intent in his later years, as evidenced by comments he made during the Yom Kippur War. "Since two days," he wrote on October 9, 1973, "we have the new war in the Near East, which it would seem the Egyptians have started, although I cannot help having a slight doubt even here, considering past Israeli behavior. At any rate I have the impression that [Moshe] Dayan," Israel's Minister of Defense, "who knew as he has said himself, of the coming attack for days, intentionally lured the Egyptians into the interior in order to destroy a large force of soldiers and weapons. With this he has a new basis for taking the position officially that he will not return any of the occupied land, and secures his own victory at the coming elections as the savior of the fatherland."[89] Fromm's tendency to strongly criticize Israeli actions was also quite manifest in a letter written fourteen months later: "I am terribly worried about the situation in Israel. It seems that their intransigence will lead to a new war... It is the same unwillingness to face the Palestinian government as shown through all these years, the same arrogance to build everything on force and retaliation... [W]hen the Nazis destroyed Lidice" in German-occupied Czechoslovakia "as a retaliation for the murder of one of their leaders" in 1942, "the world was indignant. What else are the bombing of the camps of Arab refugees but many small Lidices based on the same spirit of revenge and alleged intimidation, of which of course the opposite is true. I am particularly surprised that the constant statement that the government cannot deal with Arafat because he is a terrorist, is not answered by reminding the world that the methods used by the Stern group and the Irgun in 1947, of kidnapping British soldiers and connecting their bodies with booby traps, of blasting the King David Hotel, of sending explosive letters to many Englishmen, were in intensity and extent larger than the terror of the Arabs... I am opposed to the terrorist acts of the Palestinians. Those who know the situation however, say that the Arafat group itself has never approved of terror against innocent bystanders but has applied it only to military or similar kinds of installations."[90]

In 1976 Simon critiqued what he characterized as Fromm's "at times very aggressive anti-Zionism and anti-Israelism," and Fromm's "occasionally excessive" criticism of Israel, and suggested that Fromm had not only undergone a shift in terms of his attitudes towards Zionism but also an "externally perhaps even more blatant but internally much less radical" move away from Jewish tradition.[91] Fromm replied to Simon by acknowledging, "Indeed I am against the idea of a State as such, especially if it turns out as I see it to be an outpost of American imperialism in the Near East world and for a number of other reasons, as for instance that the State of Israel has occupied the Arab land, for which the flight of the Arabs, for me, is no excuse. So indeed I have turned away from Zionism... My whole attitude toward Israel and the Arabs cannot be separated from the analysis of the whole world situation of the strength of American and European imperialism ... I look at political events in the Near East from the standpoint of this total struggle and indeed I feel in no way identified with Israel."[92] As to Simon's comments concerning Fromm and the Jewish tradition, Fromm retorted, "If you say I have turned away from the Jewish tradition, this is true and not true, depending what is meant by the sentence. If you say I have turned away from the life of a practicing Jew ... you are of course perfectly right, but my interest in and love for the Jewish tradition has never died..."[93]

Fromm's last point deserves amplification. Throughout the latter decades of his life, Fromm retained admiration for (specific) Jewish teachings that he had first encountered in his youth. As he put it in a letter to Simon in 1964, "I am, deep in my heart, an old Orthodox Jew, but many reasons make it impossible for me to practice it except in the very general sense of what I believe to be the human core of Judaism. I am sure you understand the phenomenon I am describing ... I mean the particular fact of being consciously so very fond of the old Jewish tradition, and yet so completely separated from it in practice."[94] Several years later, Fromm made his position quite clear in a letter to Darmstadter: "[A]lthough I have removed myself from the practice of Judaism, I have not removed myself from its spirit, and have a deep respect and love for its practice."[95]

Fromm, who, as we have seen, had been a religiously observant Jew in his younger days, and who had studied Jewish texts for many years, retained strong emotional ties to the Jewish tradition long after he stopped practicing Judaism or believing in its tenets. In the late 1960s, he commented, in a private letter, that "Orthodox Jewish ritual has a great beauty. While I don't participate in it, I have a deep Heimweh [homesickness] for it and miss it."[96] He remained interested, in his later years, in matters pertaining to Jews, and, indeed, devoted some of his very last works to Jewish themes and to describing his own relationship to Judaism.[97]

Fromm had a severe heart attack in 1977.[98] While in hospital, he wrote to his old friend Simon about his thoughts as to German Jews, and noted that "German Jews have actually created fundaments for the development of the thought of the human race. I have in mind especially Marx, Einstein and Freud. It seems that this blending of German and Jewish thought is the most productive synthesis between two cultures... The question is what are the elements both in the German and in the Jewish culture which [are] the basis for such powerful fusion?"[99] These thoughts and questions led Fromm, early in 1978, to write an essay on Germans and Jews. While writing his work, Fromm mused that "political powerlessness is more prone to create cultural achievements, while political power tends to weaken the 'spirit' as it were. Related to this is a hypothesis about the root of anti-semitism. The Jews are a living example that one can survive without State and without political power and this is an intolerable idea for all those who believe in power, that is to say, almost everybody, because the Jews disprove by their very existence the necessity or even sanctity of power as a condition for survival."[100]

In the essay itself, Fromm argued that figures like Marx, Freud, and Einstein provide evidence of "a deep affinity between the Jewish and the German cultures," and that Jews and Germans, at one time, shared certain "essential qualities that make the fruitfulness of their relationship explainable."[101] One key similarity, in Fromm's opinion, was that both Germans and Jews were, for much of their histories, nations without power. For so long as neither Jews nor Germans had power, there was a positive interaction between them. According to Fromm, Nazi antisemitism could itself be explained by the "anti-power" example provided by Jews. From the Nazi perspective, the Jews were a danger precisely because "they proved that a people could survive ... without having any power."[102] In this piece, Fromm alludes to Israel only in passing.[103] But his piece was surely written with Israel in mind, and is implicitly critical of Zionism and of the Jewish state.[104]

The impact of Judaism on Fromm's ideas was repeatedly noted in the post–World War II era by those familiar with his writings on other topics (and unfamiliar with his early work touching on explicitly Jewish themes).

Reviewing Fromm's *The Art of Loving* in *Commentary* in 1956, Rabbi Jakob J. Petuchowski, for example, wrote that "There is a sense in which ... Fromm's new book ... might be said to represent a 20th century *midrash* – particularly on the early chapters of Genesis. This impression is created not only by several quotations from the Bible, but also by the many echoes from Biblical and rabbinic sources one seems to discern in the book."[105] In a later piece also published in *Commentary*, Edgar Z. Friedenberg found that the texture of Fromm's thought "is really more like that of Martin Buber than of Freud."[106]

To those who claimed that Fromm had left Judaism behind him, Steven S. Schwarzschild (1924–1989), a Frankfurt-born rabbi who was both a professor of philosophy at Washington University in St. Louis and editor of *Judaism*, and who corresponded with Fromm over a period of years, replied,

Fromm 'left Judaism'? Balderdash. Sure, Fromm had his profound misgivings about traditional theology and conventional religion. He wrote to me on Jan. 9, 1970: 'I am happy to do what God commands, without the support of the belief that God exists.' ... Fromm couldn't stomach the social politics of the Jewish 'establishment' ... But Fromm did not leave Judaism. Judaism left him, or rather Jewry left him. He identified (he, the 'Yekke') [German Jew] with the sparse remnants of Yiddishist, anti-Zionist territorialists and socialist folkists. He liked to listen to me talk about religion, intra-Jewish opposition to political Zionism, in which he, regretfully, could not partake because of his 'a-religionism.'[107]

In the mid-1960s, Fromm wrote a book about the Old Testament.[108] In describing this book to Adam Schaff, a Polish philosopher, Fromm stated – while he was still working on his project – that he was attempting to demonstrate that the Old Testament "has one core, which is a revolutionary one. That the liberation from social oppression is looked upon as a central event in Jewish history...." This led Fromm to comment, in the same letter, "Marxist socialism is ... the secular expression of a tradition which is to be found among the Jews, although there is, at the same time, a reactionary, nationalistic and clerical one."[109] In a later letter to Schaff, written after he had finished writing his book, Fromm once again summarized his thesis, and added "[i]t seems to me that Zionism has ended for most Jews the mostl[y] progressive elements of their past, and has led them back to the spirit of the conquerors of Canaan."[110] Similarly, in the wake of the Six-Day War, Fromm wrote a piece that began by noting that many Jews were proud of the victory by the Israeli army over the Arab armies, and impressed by the heroism displayed by members of the Israeli military, but that then went on to stress that the Jewish religious tradition most admired not heroism but martyrdom.[111] His piece concludes by proclaiming that if the inhabitants of Israel and many Jews outside of Israel now admired heroes, military victories, they had the right to do so. They ought to know, however, that when they slighted martyrs for the sake of heroes, they were slighting their own greatest traditions.[112] Here as elsewhere, Fromm's study of Jewish tradition and his interpretation of Jewish history seem to have reinforced his criticisms of Zionism and of Israel.

Thus, both Fromm's relationship to Jewish tradition and his position on Israel differed from that of Marcuse in the period beginning with the creation of the State of Israel in 1948 and ending with the deaths of Fromm and Marcuse more than thirty years later.[113] Fromm was far better informed about Judaism, and, simultaneously, more critical of the State of Israel, than was Marcuse. Even after 1948, Fromm was sympathetic to the notion of creating a bi-national state in Palestine. He never explicitly endorsed the idea of a two state solution. Marcuse, on the other hand, defended the need for Israel to exist and was more open than was Fromm to the possibility of creating Palestinian and Israeli states that would exist side-by-side, at least on an interim basis. It is, to be sure, certainly true – as noted above – that Fromm, like Marcuse, was an opponent of imperialism, and that Fromm insisted, on one occasion, that his position on Israel was merely part and parcel of his anti-imperialist perspective.[114] But Fromm's anti-imperialism does not actually get at the heart of the matter. His dyed-in-the-wool commitment to specific Jewish principles and traditions does. It is, I suspect, not mere coincidence that Fromm, unlike Marcuse, never visited the self-proclaimed Jewish state.

Erich Fromm, who had been a religiously observant Jew throughout his childhood and young adult years, and who had engaged in deep and sustained study of Jewish texts, retained strong emotional affinities for some portions of the Jewish religious tradition long after he stopped practicing Judaism. It was precisely these affinities, and his interpretations of Judaism, which explain the tenor of his condemnation of Israeli policies, and his continuing disavowal of the notion of a Jewish state in Palestine.

*

Other key members of the Frankfurt School did not agree with Fromm's position, but also staked out positions that differed from those of Marcuse. Both Horkheimer and Lowenthal expressed views on Israel that were, in important respects, between those of Marcuse on the one hand and those of Fromm on the other.

Horkheimer was more engaged with Jewish affairs in post-war Germany than he had been in Frankfurt in the pre-Nazi era.[115] He joined the Jüdische Gemeinde Frankfurt am Main [Jewish Community of Frankfurt] in February 1951, one year after his return.[116] According to Eva Reichmann (1897–1988), a German Jewish historian and sociologist who had been active in Jewish affairs in pre-war Germany, who immigrated to London in 1939 and who engaged in a friendly, multi-year, correspondence with Horkheimer, he "was one of the few re-migrants to Germany who immediately joined the Jewish congregation."[117] There had been some 30,000 Jews in Frankfurt in 1930.[118] In 1955, following the Nazi era and the emigration from Germany of many of the Jews who had been in displaced persons camps in Germany in the immediate post-war years, the Jewish Community had less than 1,400 formal members.[119] Since Horkheimer, who became Rector of the University of Frankfurt in November 1951, was a very visible public figure in Frankfurt after his return from the United States, the fact that he had chosen to join the modestly-sized Community was of considerable import to the latter. Indeed, Frankfurt's post-war Jewish Community clearly thought of Horkheimer as among its most distinguished members.

Horkheimer's obligations to the University and to the Institute made it difficult for him to play an active role in Community affairs. However, he did agree to speak under the auspices of the Community on several occasions. In 1955, for example, Horkheimer served as commentator for a talk on "Cultural Tasks of a Jewish Community in Our Time" in a series organized by the Jewish Community of Frankfurt.[120] Months later, Horkheimer also delivered a lecture on prejudice at a Jewish Community-sponsored event.[121]

In later years, Horkheimer received speaking invitations from Jewish communities and Jewish organizations in other places.[122] He accepted an invitation from the Jewish Community of Zurich in 1973, and tentatively proposed that he speak on "Jewry and the Crisis of Religion."[123] Is it wholly without symbolic import that the talk he ultimately delivered to the Community of Zurich was the very last talk that Horkheimer (who died in early July 1973) ever gave?[124]

Horkheimer's interest, in the post-war era, in his Jewish origins and in Judaism is clear from his correspondence, notes, and from other sources. He is said to have read often from Leopold Zunz's translation of the Bible – which had been widely known among German Jews of earlier times – and to have extensively annotated his copy.[125] He recited *kaddish*, the traditional prayer for the dead, at the graves of his parents, and of his wife.[126] In addition, Horkheimer reportedly attended synagogue on the Jewish High Holidays.[127] In 1971, he asked the Jewish Community of Stuttgart if it would be possible to ascertain (presumably on the basis of communal records) his Hebrew name. Horkheimer never explained why, at that late date, he wanted to know his Hebrew name.[128] However, it is standard practice in Jewish congregations to use a man's Hebrew name when calling him to the Torah during services.

Throughout the decades following the end of the Second World War, Horkheimer remained disturbed and worried about antisemitism.[129] Horkheimer discussed the possibilities of a renewed outbreak of antisemitic tendencies in 1952, in an interview published in the German Jewish press.[130] Antisemitism on the part of faculty members at the University of Frankfurt was a precipitating factor in his decision, in 1956, to request that he be allowed to retire early.[131] In the late 1950s, Horkheimer did in fact retire, to Switzerland.[132] Horkheimer participated in Passover *sdorim* in Lugano – and he is reported, on two such occasions, to have advised a young Jew who was apparently still living in Germany to leave that country, and to have explicitly told her that there was no future for Jews in that land.[133]

Horkheimer attributed the antisemitism evident among the adult population in post-war Germany to "unmastered, repressed, guilt feelings" and argued that it was essential to provide the younger generation of Germans with an education that would make them freedom-loving, and as free of *ressentiment*, as possible.[134] He returned to the role of education in combating contemporary German antisemitism several times, insisting that "[s]cholars, educators, politicians and statesmen must agree on a comprehensive plan of instruction within the various schools... This reorientation is necessary not only because we don't want antisemitism but because no people can live decently without a sound idea of their own role in history. Should we fail to enable the Germans to understand National Socialism as a complex phenomenon ... there is a danger that they will forget completely about historical justice and remember National Socialism without the horror and without the Jews."[135] When, in 1963, an article by the president of the Bundestag was published in a newspaper in Frankfurt under the title "There is No Longer Any Anti-Semitism," Horkheimer wrote a long letter arguing that "[t]o preserve their endangered culture the nations of this continent must ... consider that they are in jeopardy at every moment. They need the ability to renounce the illusion that the barbarism lurking within them is dead."[136] He is also reported to have spoken in January 1964 in a series devoted to

"Antisemitism and Political Education Today" sponsored by Frankfurt University's Deutsch-Israelischen Studiengruppe.[137]

Antisemitism, however, was not solely a German problem. In 1956, Horkheimer proclaimed that Jews "are endangered everywhere today. The justice which manifests itself in their nature and without their will is a protest against both the state capitalism in the East and the monopolistic society in the West. Jews are rooted in trade and liberalism, in the relations between individuals, in the bourgeoisie. To whatever extent the life of any one among them may fail to conform to this pattern, their existence points toward a society of free and equal men, not to a people's community."[138] Around 1968, Horkheimer stated that hatred of the Jews "is once against virulent, from the hypocritical Christians of South Africa to the atheists in the Kremlin..."[139] At the beginning of 1969, Horkheimer asserted that hatred of the Jews was spreading around the world, and was being stimulated by the existence of the State of Israel.[140] The continued existence, and continued danger, of antisemitism, in Germany and elsewhere, was an ongoing concern for Horkheimer throughout the latter decades of his life. However, Horkheimer also came to think that too much public talk about antisemitism could promote it rather than eliminate it. It was precisely because he believed that to be the case that he urged that emphasis be placed on educating youth in a manner that would leave them free of hate, and that would teach them to form opinions on the basis of their own knowledge (and not of inherited prejudices).[141]

Horkheimer explained his decision to return to Germany by stressing his desire to help those who had opposed the Nazis. In 1965, he wrote to the mayor of Frankfurt that "[m]y teaching and work has always and in every detail been determined by a solidarity with those who are persecuted, tortured, murdered. The decision to again accept an appointment to my former university in 1949 was made with those of my students in mind who risked or even lost their lives in order to fight against the executioners, just like quite a few others in Germany. By participating in the reconstruction I wanted, if only modestly, to help to educate such people once again. If I'm right, my true disciples are aware of this even today."[142] He expressed similar sentiments three and a half years later, in an interview with Martin Jay – but explicitly mentioned Jews in this latter comment. Jay reports that Horkheimer told him that the reestablishment of the Institute in Frankfurt "was not to be understood as acceptance of a *Wiedergutmachung* (compensation) by a repentant government, for nothing could make good what Germany had done. It was meant instead as a gesture to honor those Germans who had resisted Hitler by helping the Jews."[143] Was Horkheimer satisfied with the results of his work? His decision to retire early, and the reasons for his move to Switzerland, suggest that he found it too hard to continue to live "in the house of the hangman,"[144] as his friend Adorno once put it, that is, among the one-time torturers, executioners, ex-Nazis, and large number of other antisemites, who also lived there.[145] Indeed, in *Notizen*, which was not published until after Horkheimer's death, Horkheimer states in no uncertain terms that he ultimately came to believe that he had been a fool to return to the land of his birth, even if he had gone back in order to help ensure that what had occurred would not happen again, and that his considered opinion was that those who had remained in post-war Germany after realizing that Germany was making political and commercial deals on piles of cadavers deserved to be treated with contempt.[146]

Horkheimer did not support Zionism in the period before the creation of the State of Israel.[147] In September 1945 Horkheimer wrote to John Slawson of the AJC and described a conversation he had had with Dr. Maurice Karpf, a non-Zionist member of the Jewish Agency for Palestine. Horkheimer informed Slawson that Karpf was afraid that Zionist policies both inside and outside Palestine "might lead to an acute situation, possibly to rioting and bloodshed. Only a strong assertion of the non-Zionist Jewish friends of Palestine can, in his opinion, prevent Judaism, as a whole, being held morally responsible for the fallacies of Zionism. Any delicate diplomatic situation which might arise for our own government in this connection will not fail to have repercussions on American Jewry. Since apart from the shortsighted and completely insignificant utterances of the Council for Judaism no Jewish voice is heard in this country but the Zionist clarion, I find myself in agreement with Dr. Karpf on this point."[148] Horkheimer added that Karpf had suggested the organizing of a committee or agency "with a definite non-Zionist program," a suggestion Horkheimer found "perfectly reasonable." He pointed out that in the absence of such a body, the AJC itself might have to proclaim its non-Zionist position "in order to protect American Judaism against being identified with Zionism," but that having to do so would put the AJC "in an awkward position." Horkheimer clearly believed that the creation of a new (presumably Jewish) body that would take a non-Zionist stance could have a positive effect in several ways, and noted, for example, that "an independent non-Zionist body would ... be free to affirm, theoretically and practically, its active interest in the development of Palestine. It could, to some extent at least, collaborate with those Zionists who are interested in resolving the Jewish cause as a whole and helping in particular the harassed Jews in Europe, rather than furthering their own nationalistic philosophies." Thus, Horkheimer concludes, "this agency might prove to be a rung in our ladder to the ultimate goal of unity." This non-Zionist but empathetic approach remained typical of one strand of Horkheimer's attitude towards Israel in later years.

Horkheimer did not refer to Israel very often in the years following the establishment of the Jewish state. On one occasion in 1952, however, Horkheimer, who was then the Rector of the University of Frankfurt, wrote to his counterpart at Hebrew University, reported that the student parliament at Frankfurt had "resolved to do everything in its power to insure that the material and ideal prerequisites for peace with Israel are created here in Germany" and offered specific ideas as to how to foster positive ties between university students in Germany and Israel. Horkheimer justified his proposal by arguing "that every gesture of peace between young Germans and the Israeli generation that is not merely a gesture could have an immensely salutary effect and would, above all, strengthen the best elements in Germany."[149]

At a later point in the same decade, events in the Middle East led Horkheimer to take a stand that was sympathetic to Israeli needs. In 1956, Egypt blocked the Straits of Tiran, nationalized the Suez Canal, supported attacks by so-called *fedayeen* on Israel, and proclaimed that there was no place whatsoever for negotiations with the Jewish state. Israel, in turn, responded by attacking Egypt – with the encouragement of both England and France, both of which landed troops at Port Said after the Israelis had begun their attack. The United Nations condemned the actions of the English and the French. This condemnation led Julius Ebbinghaus, a philosopher and a professor at the University of Marburg, to publish a notice in *Der Spiegel* criticizing the United Nations' stance. Ebbinghaus's notice induced Horkheimer and Adorno to write to Ebbinghaus, and to inform him that they agreed with the position he had taken. Among other matters, they stated that no one talked about the "fact" that "Arabic robber-states" had lurked for years, waiting for an opportunity to pounce upon Israel and the Jews who had found refuge there. This, Horkheimer and Adorno added, was "a symptom of the public consciousness that's terribly hard to take."[150]

This sympathetic remark sets the stage for a slightly longer comment by Horkheimer found in an essay on German Jews, which Horkheimer first delivered as a lecture in Cologne in 1960. In the course of this essay, Horkheimer sketches out a variety of historic responses by Jews to

German civilization. He notes first those German Jews who had been inclined towards assimilation, accenting the links between assimilation and a critical spirit. He discusses, second, the emergence of liberal Judaism. Only after having done so does he discuss Zionism, which he sees as a reaction to history. He indicates that Theodor Herzl "had grown up in a Jewish circle that was no less assimilated than that of any highly educated Jew," mentions Herzl's exposure to antisemitism, and indicates that, as a result of this exposure, Herzl ultimately "lost faith in the prospects of pluralism amid a world that was rapidly becoming nationalistic and militaristic."[151] Horkheimer observes, "That about which he had forebodings appears today to be certain."[152] Horkheimer outlines how technological development and other factors had transformed civilization, and how antisemitism had become a means of manipulation. "The Zionist movement," Horkheimer concludes, "with its refusal to trust any longer in the prospects of pluralism or of the civilization of the autonomous individual in Europe, is the radical yet resigned reaction of Judaism to the possibilities thrown open in the last century." The passage ends: "it is a sad aspect of history, which has since played itself out, sad for Jewry as well as for Europe, that Zionism proved to be right in the end."[153]

Certain of Horkheimer's differences with contemporary Zionists are evident in a letter written in 1965. Horkheimer was sent a piece at that time by Heinrich Guttmann, president of the Frankfurt Lodge of B'nai B'rith – of which Horkheimer was a committed member.[154] The article sent by Guttmann, entitled "Our Tasks in Germany," had been written by Arno Lustiger, Chairman of the Zionist Organization in Germany, and had been published in a Frankfurt-based Jewish newspaper.[155] Lustiger proclaimed in his article that it was the life goal of a Zionist to immigrate to Israel. Horkheimer did not care for Lustiger's piece: "We certainly have every reason to affirm Israel, but the remark 'that the ultimate, personal, life-goal of the Zionist is aliyah to Eretz Israel' does not apply without very important addenda to Jews in general. However seriously they may take their Judaism, it is not exhausted by nationalism, not even Israeli nationalism. I believe it would be extremely important to put this topic up for debate some day in our circles."[156]

Unlike Marcuse, who, as we have seen, proclaimed at the time of the Six-Day War that he had "feelings of solidarity and identification with Israel," Horkheimer apparently declined to speak publicly about Israel while that conflict was underway.[157] Two sources make it quite clear that Horkheimer purposefully kept out of public discussions during the war.

A letter to him from Adorno notes, "I was supposed to speak at a pro-Israeli demonstration organized by [Berthold] Simonsohn, as one of the key speakers, together with Ernst Bloch and [Karl Heinrich] Rengstorf. I canceled, however, for a number of reasons. In this cancellation as well I show my unity with you."[158] A note by Horkheimer is somewhat more revealing: "The sympathy demonstrations for Israel are surface phenomena." As Horkheimer saw it, it was not these demonstrations but rather the foreign policy interests of the [German?] state or of its Establishment and the demand for a negative attitude towards Israel that was decisive: "The ideological preparation for this is the activation of antisemitism, which in any event, already lies quite closely under the surface among the masses."[159]

Horkheimer's misgivings about Zionism and Israel did not preclude his making charitable donations to various organizations with Zionist or pro-Zionist perspectives, or even joining pro-Zionist bodies.[160] He made a financial contribution, for example, to the WIZO [Women's International Zionist Organization] in 1969.[161] He also made a donation to Keren Hajessod Vereinigte Israel Aktion [Foundation Fund – United Israel Action].[162]

The precipitating causes for his financial contributions to the Keren Kajemeth Leisrael [Jewish National Fund] are quite striking. Keren Kajemeth, an initiative sparked by none other than Theodor Herzl, purchased large amounts of property in Palestine, and ultimately leased much of this land to Jews who wanted to settle on it. In some circles, it became common practice to donate funds to the Keren Kajemeth on special occasions, and for that organization to use these funds to plant trees on its property. Horkheimer made such donations at two fraught moments in his life. When, in 1971, Friedrich Pollock, Horkheimer's oldest friend, and a stalwart member of the Frankfurt School throughout his adult life, passed away, Horkheimer seems to have thought it a fitting tribute to donate funds to the Jewish National Fund in honor of Pollock, despite the fact that Pollock had never had a strong Jewish identity, and never manifested any particular sympathy for Zionism or Israel. The donation enabled the Keren Kajemeth to plant three trees.[163] In the following year, Horkheimer apparently made a contribution to the Jewish National Fund, sufficient for the planting of six trees, to mark the death of his wife, Maidon, who was not of Jewish origin, and who had never been to Israel.[164] We can only speculate as to why Horkheimer chose to mark the deaths of his spouse and his oldest friend in such a manner – but I would venture to guess that Horkheimer wanted to link profoundly felt losses with what he perceived as a positive and progressive phenomenon. Do these donations indicate a fundamental alteration in his attitude towards the State of Israel? Are they essentially in accord with his suggestion, in 1945, that it might be possible to cooperate with specific Zionists in order to foster "the development of Palestine"? However symbolically important gestures like his donations to the Jewish National Fund may be, Horkheimer's stance vis-à-vis Israel was a complicated one, and was impacted upon by his sense that the State was not fully in accord with the deepest teachings of the Jewish religious tradition.

Horkheimer's lack of ease with Zionism, I hasten to add, by no means suggests that Horkheimer was unwilling to take political steps to defend Israel. In 1963, at which point in time German scientists in Egypt were contributing to the development of that country's armaments program, Horkheimer, deeply concerned about this phenomenon, visited the German ambassador to the United States, and brought up the issue of the German scientists during this visit.[165]

It should, finally, be underscored that Horkheimer's continuing doubts about the Jewish state had nothing in common with "anti-Zionism." Horkheimer was well aware that purported anti-Zionism provided a (thin) screen both for neo-Nazis, such as those writing in the late 1960s for the *Deutsche National Zeitung*, and for Communists in Eastern Europe.[166] Horkheimer's critique of Zionism was in no way similar to the criticisms current at that time in the Soviet Union, or in the Arab world. His attitude was rooted not so much in specific policies of the state as in his understanding of the role that Jewry had historically played in the world, and of how the creation of Israel had altered that role.[167]

A note dating from the early 1960s, well worth quoting at length, reads:

Through millennia of persecution, the Jews held together for the sake of justice... Jewry was not a powerful state but the hope for justice at the end of the world. They were a people and its opposite, a rebuke to all peoples. Now, a state claims to be speaking for Jewry, to be Jewry. The Jewish people in whom the injustice of all peoples has become an accusation, the individuals in whose words and gestures the negative of what is reflected itself, have now become positive themselves. A nation among nations, soldiers, leaders, money-raisers for themselves.... Jewry is now to see the goal in the state of Israel. How profound a resignation in the very triumph of its temporal success. It purchases its survival by paying tribute to the law of the world as it is... It has adapted to the state of the world... it is a pity, for what was meant to be preserved through such renunciation disappears from the world as a result of it... The good is good, not because it is victorious but because it resists victory. It must be hoped that the national subjection to the law of this world not meet as drastic an end as that of the individuals did in the Europe of Hitler, Stalin and Franco, and as it may under their overdue successors.[168]

As Horkheimer put it in another place "Israel has ... become a nation structured fundamentally like every other nation. The originally messianic impulse has been weakened by the self-preservation inherent in national existence."[169] In yet another note, entitled "End of the Dream," Horkheimer compared Critical Theorists to messianists:

The dream of the Messiah, the dawning of justice on earth which holds together the Jews in the diaspora, is over and done with. It created no end of martyrs, caused untold suffering, and gave hope. Now the persecuted have gone to Zion, without a Messiah, have established their nation and their nationalism like other peoples, and Jewry has become a religion. Those remaining in the diaspora can decide either for Israel, for absorption in the nation into which fate has cast them ... or they must become provincial as Jews, romantic sectarians without historical substance. The diaspora is the backwoods. The Jews are remnants. Their situation is not dissimilar to that of communism and socialism... Those who adhere to critical theory can choose ... communist nationalism, or the social democratic variety. They may also become provincial, romantic sectarians. The realm of freedom is the backwoods. Those who remain loyal to theory are remnants, like those that cling to the Talmud and messianic hope.[170]

These notes notwithstanding, Horkheimer, at the end of his life, tended to explain his unwillingness to fully embrace Israel not by reference to the messianic tradition, but by alluding to the Third Commandment, and to his sense that Israel could not actualize millennia-long Jewish yearnings for Zion.[171] In a conversation with Georg Wolff and Helmut Gumnior that was published in *Der Spiegel* at the very beginning of 1970 – and that has often been cited in the years since its initial publication – Horkheimer suggested that Critical Theory had Jewish roots.[172] It is, however, somewhat less frequently noticed that, having made this point, Horkheimer goes on to accept that there are also parallels between his position on Israel and the general stance taken by Critical Theory vis-à-vis "graven images." Horkheimer began this portion of the interview by proclaiming: "Israel is an afflicted land, just as the Jews were always afflicted. One cannot oppose the establishment of the State, because otherwise all too many people would not know where they ought to flee. This is for me the decisive point. Israel, the asylum for many people. This notwithstanding: It appears to me not to be easy to reconcile it with the prophecies of the Old Testament." Horkheimer's interviewer summarized what he had just heard by stating that "[o]n the one hand, you think that the State of Israel is needed as a place of refuge for millions of Jews. On the other hand, however, this State ought to lead to the realization of a Jewish Utopia, Zion, the description or presentation of which is hardly less problematic than the image of the Supreme Being. Here as well parallels to your Critical Theory can quickly be made." Horkheimer's one word comment on this summary was "Certainly."[173]

In an excellent, unpublished, paper on Horkheimer and Israel, Jeremy Brown remarked, "It may have been empathy with the plight of other exiles and survivors which led Max Horkheimer to soften his tone, if not completely revoke his position on Israel" in this interview with *Der Spiegel*. But Horkheimer by no means revoked his earlier position in 1970. Indeed, his position on Israel at the end of his life – Horkheimer died in July 1973, that is, years earlier than Marcuse, Fromm, or, for that matter, Lowenthal – was fully consistent with the passing statements he had made on Israel in the decades following the creation of that state.[174] Horkheimer remained concerned about antisemitism not only during the Nazi era but in all the years thereafter. He explicitly described Israel as a place of refuge from antisemitism in 1957. He rarely criticized Israeli policies, and sometimes defended those policies. On the other hand, he was not a Zionist before the establishment Israel, and never became one. Horkheimer, a Critical Theorist, never did reconcile the modern State with longstanding Jewish traditions. Horkheimer's interpretation of the prohibition against graven images led him to be uneasy not only about positive depictions of a socialist society,[175] indeed about any formulations of the positive, but also about the creation of an independent Jewish state. His critique of Israel was rooted not in specific actions taken by that state but in his understanding of prophetic tradition and of the ways in which the creation of Israel conflicted with that tradition.

*

Lowenthal's attitude, finally, was similar to that of Horkheimer. On the other hand: Lowenthal – a close friend of Marcuse's in the 1960s and 1970s – certainly agreed with some components of Marcuse's views on matters related to Israel. In comments by Lowenthal on Israel, as in those by Marcuse, we find both willingness to defend the continued existence of the State and disapprobation for specific Israeli policies. Another indication of similarities between their stances is the fact that Marcuse and Lowenthal both happily accepted invitations to visit Israel. Horkheimer never did visit that country. However, Lowenthal was explicitly concerned with tension between the reality of the actually existing State of Israel and Jewish messianic tradition. Marcuse was not. Moreover, Lowenthal, but not Marcuse, tellingly, made reference to Horkheimer's views when explicating his position. On the issue of Israel – and on (some) other matters related to Critical Theory – Lowenthal's stance was closer to that of Horkheimer than was Marcuse's.

Lowenthal's correspondence from the 1960s and from later decades makes it crystal clear that Lowenthal, who knew people living in Israel, was concerned about them, and was sympathetic to the situation in which they found themselves. Immediately following the Six-Day War, Lowenthal wrote to his cousin Arye Ben-David, who lived in Jerusalem, that he had been "extremely worried about the fate of family and friends" during the war, and that he believed – or at least hoped – "that in the long run wisdom and moderation on both sides" would "win out over extremism."[176] Lowenthal continued: "it would be particularly tragic if the combination of the need for military defense paired with the problems of [a] highly depressed economy would lead to some form of authoritarian structure in Israel." He concluded his letter by noting "I hope that the generals will not carry the day, and I have enough confidence in the collective intelligenc[e] and morality of the country to hope faithfully that things will go all right." Writing, on the same day, to his old friend Ernst Simon, Lowenthal proclaimed "[n]ever was there so much of a chance to settle the basic problems between Jews and Arabs than there is now. But, who knows how the dialectical process will develop. I am no expert of the Arabic world, but I wouldn't be surprised if some of these States were conquered by a spirit of common sense led by the younger intellectuals. I am more worried about the potential dangers in the political structure and ethos of Israel – hoping, however, that the generals will not carry the day."[177] In yet another letter to Ben-David, Lowenthal clarified his stance in the following terms: "Needless to say that I pursue with profound empathy the news from Israel and the Near East and I am profoundly concerned, yet hoping that a livable solution may be found in the not too distant future. All the signs point toward tragedy, but I pray fervently as far as an agnostic can do, that Israel will not only survive but will grow and prosper in the years ahead."[178]

Like his friend Marcuse, Lowenthal was invited to Israel by the Van Leer Foundation. As early as 1976, the director of the Foundation wrote to Lowenthal, and inquired as to whether he would be willing to give a lecture at the Foundation on a topic of his choice.[179] Lowenthal, however – though unwilling to say as much to those who had invited him – worried that he could not afford such a trip, and replied that he was "not yet ready to suggest a date" because he was "not quite certain when and under what circumstances" he would be able to come to Israel.[180] But Lowenthal made it manifest, in a letter written on the same date to Simon, that he would very much like to travel to Israel, for several reasons, including that "encountering Israel" was "more than overdue at this point in my life."[181]

Roughly five years later, Lowenthal discussed his attitude towards matters in the Middle East during the course of a long interview with Paul Assall of Südwestfunk, a German radio network. When Assall asked whether Jewish settlement policies in Palestine (of which, as we have seen, Lowenthal had been critical in the mid-1920s) were the origins of the contemporary conflict in the Middle East, Lowenthal pointedly replied that that would be a crazy exaggeration. "I do not deny," Lowenthal continued, "that I believe that the original Zionist and then Israeli policies vis-à-vis the Arabs appear to be problematic to me to this very day." On the other hand: tracing these policies above all to actions that had taken place in the 1920s would be absurd. World history had come into the picture: "In any case I would like with absolute clarity to say that I do not have the least bit of sympathy for the radical chic that I find among many young people here, who are apparently ready to sacrifice the State of Israel out of love for the Palestine Liberation Movement. I consider this to be irresponsible and scandalous in light of that which has happened..."[182]

Lowenthal finally did visit Israel, for a total of nine days, in 1985.[183] In interviews conducted after his trip, Lowenthal stressed that he had been struck by the internal contradictions he found in Israel, including the simultaneous existence of a highly industrialized sector and what he described as a "primitive and not very developed Arabic style of living."[184] He had had conversations with Israeli intellectuals, writers, and artists (as had Marcuse before him), and discovered that virtually all of these individuals opposed the policies of the Israeli government, but he was also left with the feeling that though these people had "all the right slogans," they were completely powerless.[185] He observed, in the wake of his visit, that an overwhelming part of the Jewish population of Israel was secularized. Nevertheless, orthodox rabbis had great influence, forming what he described as a "pseudo-theocratic superstructure." Lowenthal was also apparently surprised to find that, by his reckoning, 60 to 65 percent of the Jewish population of Israel consisted of Jews from non-European countries. For this and other reasons, he explained "I had the feeling that I found myself in a land that was not so much a part of Europe as of Asia Minor..."[186]

Lowenthal took pains to stress the limits of his critique of Israel: "I certainly speak critically about Israel – just as I speak critically about everything in my life – but I do not for a moment question the right of Israel to exist."[187] Lowenthal added immediately thereafter that he was strongly influenced by events in Europe in the 1930s and 1940s, by which he clearly intended to make it known that his attitude to Israel was directly tied to the lessons he drew from the Nazi era. When Hajo Funke, who was German and who conducted the major interview in which Lowenthal described his attitude towards Israel, suggested that it was Jewish history that had led Jews in Israel to insist that they would never again be weak, and that this in turn had led to aggressiveness vis-à-vis Israel's neighbors, Lowenthal replied that it was perfectly understandable that Israelis could not tolerate a repetition of that which had occurred (to Jews in the Diaspora) in the past. He discussed the period of the Israeli war of independence, and informed Funke that at that time there had been discussions in Jewish circles as to whether or not weapons ought to be sent to those Jews who were fighting for independence. Lowenthal added that while these discussions were taking place, he was himself in New York, and was involved in talks with circles in the AJC that did not endorse either the sending of weapons or of funds to be used for the purchase of weapons. Lowenthal reported that he had a different opinion, and that he believed that his opinion had been one with which his colleagues in the Institute of Social Research agreed:

I was of the opinion that *one of the essential components of modern antisemitism was the Imago of the Jews as a colossus made of clay* [emphasis in the original – JJ], a colossus which could be smashed into pieces by the lightest kick, and that the picture of what a Jew is could radically change if it turned out: They can also use violence ... They can commit murder ... They are thus just like other peoples. This has something tragic to it. But in the situation in which one found oneself at that time and in which one finds oneself now, that was an extraordinarily important element of changing ... the image of Jews. You see it today again in the new anti-Semitic tendencies which are gaining ground in the Federal Republic of Germany.[188]

When pressed by Funke as to the differences between his position and that of Simon (who had, before 1948, reportedly urged that Zionists not move rapidly towards the declaration of an independent Jewish State, and who had worried at that time that the establishment of such a state would harm relations with Arabs) Lowenthal responded that if he had been in Palestine he would certainly have been on Simon's side in urging caution. Simon, Lowenthal continued, had, when still in Frankfurt in the 1920s, characterized the advocacy of a state as "intoxication with normality" – and Lowenthal made it clear that an intoxication of that kind stood in contradiction to the messianic conceptions of a Zionist ideal to which both Simon and Lowenthal had subscribed in their youth. Lowenthal explicitly stated that "as an American Jew of German origin with a strong Jewish past" he was ambivalent about "the whole enterprise."[189] Israel, he suggested was "very far from every dream of a socialist policy and society. It implies exploitation of a lower stratum by a dominant group in the population." If he lived in Israel, Lowenthal admitted, he would probably see these things in a somewhat different matter, but "I do not live there..."

Lowenthal was certainly ambivalent – but ambivalence is a very long way from antipathy or even hostility. "[T]here was no other possibility than to make a pact with the devil, with normality" Lowenthal informed Funke. "After the horrible things that happened ... I do not see any other possibility."[190] On the other hand, Lowenthal explained that, though, at that advanced point in his life – he was around eighty-five years old at that time – he could not simply sustain all of the messianic-utopian hopes of his youth, "the background music" of his life remained, to a certain extent, utopian.[191]

When he was nearly ninety, Lowenthal was asked by Herlinde Koelbl, a German photographer who compiled a series of portraits of Jewish figures, "What is the role that the specifically Jewish heritage plays for you?"[192] Lowenthal replied, "I can't say. It is an element. I am a Jew. I am a German. I am an American. I am a cosmopolitan and a Critical Theorist.... I really do still believe in ... the utopian element, in resistance. I do not know the extent to which the Jewish element plays an important role here." At a later point in the same reply, Lowenthal added, "[M]uch of that which the Jews in the so-called Diaspora and also in Israel do, I see as in contradiction to the prophetic-messianic heritage... It would perhaps be more appropriate if the intoxication with normality of the Israelis expressed itself somewhat less in the normal behavior of the Israelis... In this sense the messianic is still, justifiably, a raised finger ... which the Jews ought to hold before their eyes."

Significantly, Lowenthal had made much the same point some five years earlier, in 1985, but had added a formulation that he had first learned from Max Horkheimer – "The Jews ought to know better."[193] Lowenthal wholeheartedly agreed with Horkheimer's use of this phrase, and accepted it as his own. For Lowenthal, the phrase meant that much of what the Jews in the Diaspora and those in Israel did contravened the messianic tradition – and this tradition was a consequential one. In an essay on Benjamin initially drafted in 1982, Lowenthal, when sketching out elements of Benjamin's thought, writes:

Here we come ... to the third element ... which joins the messianic and the political: the Jewish. Some of us long denied its essential role in our development. In retrospect, this must be corrected.... The utopian-messianic motif, which is deeply rooted in Jewish metaphysics and mysticism, played a significant role for Benjamin, surely also for Ernst Bloch and Herbert Marcuse, and for myself. In his later years, when he ventured – a bit too far for my taste – into concrete religious symbolism, Horkheimer frequently said (and on this point I agree with him completely) that the Jewish doctrine that the name of God may not be spoken or even written should be adhered to. The name of God is not yet fulfilled, and perhaps it will never be fulfilled; nor is it for us to determine if, when, and how it will be fulfilled for those who come after us... The notion of something perhaps unattainable, perhaps unnameable, but which holds the messianic hope of fulfillment – I suppose this idea is very Jewish; it is certainly a motif in my thinking...[194]

Michael Löwy's masterful book, *Redemption and Utopia*, which was first published in 1988, but which was based in large part on research conducted at an earlier time (that is, before the publication of two of the interviews discussed above), contains a great deal of perceptive analysis of Lowenthal's pre-1926 perspective, stresses that Lowenthal's early work contains traces of Jewish mysticism, and also describes how Lowenthal's youthful writings were inspired, in part, by, messianic beliefs. Löwy – who conversed directly with Lowenthal in 1984 – concludes the section of his book devoted to Lowenthal, however, by proclaiming that "After 1926, Löwenthal became increasingly involved in scientific work at the Institute of Social Research ... and he abandoned his mystical and messianic concerns..."[195] But Lowenthal's late-in-life comments on Israel demonstrate that he had not in fact fully abandoned the messianism that characterized his early, pre-Institute, writings.

Lowenthal's position towards Israel was similar, in some respects, to that of Marcuse. He both defended the need for Israel in the post-Holocaust era and criticized the Israeli stance towards Arabs. But despite Lowenthal's insistence that the utopian-messianic motif played a significant role not only for himself but also for Marcuse, there were marked differences between their positions on Israel. Lowenthal's views on Israel were explicitly linked by him to his attitude towards Jewish messianism, and stemmed, in part from his (continued) strong sympathy for the prophetic tradition. Marcuse never indicated that his position on Israel was tied in any way to messianic or other Judaic doctrines – and Lowenthal to the contrary notwithstanding – it does not appear to be the case that messianism was of consequence to him. Moreover, unlike Marcuse, Lowenthal drew on Horkheimer's perspective as a touchstone for his ideas on Israel (and the Jews) long after his formal affiliation with the Institute of Social Research had come to an end.

*

Fromm, Horkheimer, Lowenthal, and Marcuse all had Jewish family backgrounds. Their backgrounds impacted upon their attitudes towards

Israel. None of these thinkers was a Zionist in the post-war era. But the positions of these thinkers towards the State of Israel differed from one another. Fromm, who was far more learned about Judaism than the other writers in question, was also the most critical of the continued existence of Israel. He clearly would have preferred to see the Jewish state replaced with a bi-national state. Horkheimer, who had considerably less substantive knowledge of Jewish texts than did Fromm, but who was nevertheless influenced by specific Jewish religious traditions, had misgivings about Israel linked to his understanding of the (Jewish) prohibition against graven images. He was, however, far more inclined than was Fromm to defend particular Israeli policies, and far less inclined to criticize policies with which he disagreed. Lowenthal's attitude was similar to that of Horkheimer. Just as Horkheimer focused on the message of the Third Commandment, Lowenthal could not fully reconcile the State of Israel with the utopian-messianic messages that he had embraced in his youth and to which he continued to be attracted for the rest of his life. Marcuse, finally, though he acknowledged his Jewish family background, was never as deeply influenced by Judaism per se as was Fromm, Lowenthal, or Horkheimer. Marcuse's approach to Israel was grounded in his understanding of imperialism and of great power conflicts, not on Jewish religious traditions or theological tenets. He openly criticized Israeli policies and attitudes. On the other hand, Marcuse did not call into question the legitimacy of the State.

In sum, there was, in the case of the members of what had earlier been the Horkheimer circle, something of an inverse relationship between knowledge of Judaism and positive attitudes towards Israel. Fromm, the Critical Theorist with the *strongest* grounding in Judaism, was also the Theorist most inclined to continue to doubt the desirability of the State in the post-Holocaust era. Marcuse, the *least* Jewishly knowledgeable, was least inclined to continue to raise fundamental questions about the state. Horkheimer and Lowenthal occupied a middle position. They were more familiar with Judaism than was Marcuse, but less familiar with Judaism than Fromm. Unlike Marcuse, both were concerned about the relationship between Israel and (specific) components of the Jewish religious tradition. But, unlike Fromm, they most definitely did not endorse the dismantling of the Jewish state at any point after its creation.[196]

Conclusion

The Institute of Social Research – the institutional context within which the Frankfurt School developed – was founded as a nonsectarian academic entity, devoted to research on "social life in its broadest sense."[1] The men who created the Institute, and those who worked for it in its earliest years, were initially linked to one another far more by their leftist political views than by other ties. The Institute devoted the bulk of its attention over the course of its history to matters having nothing to do with Jewish affairs. Nevertheless, it is the contention of this book that the history and development of the Frankfurt School can be clarified by exploring the relationships of the Critical Theorists to their own backgrounds, to antisemitism, and to Israel.

It is far from accidental that all of those most intimately involved in the Institute of Social Research in the period immediately preceding the Nazi seizure of power were of Jewish origin. Jews in Europe at the beginning of the twentieth century held a broad range of political views – but there was a noticeable tendency on the part of (some) Jews to gravitate towards the political left. Jews played highly visible roles in the leadership of a number of left-wing parties in pre-First World War Europe and in later decades, and also played such roles in journals and cultural groupings associated with leftist ideas in the inter-war years. The question of why this was the case has been hotly contested. One compelling analysis, famously advanced by Isaac Deutscher, revolves around the marginality of Jews in key European countries. Referring to individuals like Karl Marx, Rosa Luxemburg, and Leon Trotsky (as well as great figures of Jewish origin that were not identified with the Left, such as Freud), Deutscher once pointed out that "they dwelt on the borderlines of various civilizations, religions, and national cultures. They were born and brought up on the borderlines of various epochs.... . They lived on the margins or in the nooks and crannies of their respective nations. Each of them was in society and yet not in it, of it and yet not of it. It was this that enabled them to rise in thought above their societies, above their nations, above their times and generations, and to strike out mentally into wide new horizons and far into the future."[2] Deutscher noted that all of the people he discusses in his article moved beyond the limits of traditional Judaism. They were, in his phrase, "non-Jewish Jews." And yet Deutscher underscored that these men and women were nevertheless part of a well-known pattern in Jewish history: "[t]he Jewish heretic who transcends Jewry belongs to a Jewish tradition ... in some ways they were very Jewish indeed."[3]

Neither Horkheimer nor Fromm nor Lowenthal nor Marcuse fit neatly within Deutscher's category of "non-Jewish Jews" (because all of them had far more extensive familial ties to Jewishness than did figures like Marx or Trotsky). However, their affinity for the Institute can be partially explained using Deutscher's mode of analysis. The roads that brought these Critical Theorists to the Institute had Jewish markers. Like those in Deutscher's pantheon, key members of the Frankfurt School became Jewish "heretics" who remained "very Jewish indeed."

Moreover, the family backgrounds of the most prominent Critical Theorists of the exile period – Horkheimer and Adorno – ultimately impacted on their sense of the significance of antisemitism (and thus, in this one sense, though not necessarily in others, on the development of Critical Theory itself). Like Gershom Scholem, who proclaimed that "the writings of the most important ideologists of revolutionary messianism...", had been evidently influenced by "acknowledged or unacknowledged ties to their Jewish heritage,"[4] I have attempted to demonstrate that the insistence in the 1940s by the Frankfurt School's leading theorists on the importance of antisemitism was intimately connected to the Jewish backgrounds and experiences of these theorists.

Finally, it is my hope that by exploring the range of attitudes held by one-time members of the Horkheimer circle towards Israel in the decades following the Holocaust, I have shed light on the fissures that eventually emerged among members of the Frankfurt School, and on how knowledge of the Jewish backgrounds of these men help us to understand the differences among them. There were many sharp and cross-cutting distinctions among the members of the Frankfurt School in the post-Second World War era. Marcuse and Fromm, for example, had a famous and revealing debate, in the mid-1950s, revolving around their conflicting interpretations of Freud and the social implications of his ideas. In the late 1960s, Marcuse and Horkheimer had markedly different assessments of the student movement (with Horkheimer tending to see that movement as anti-American and pro-totalitarian, and Marcuse inclined to defend it). Israel was by no means the cause of the most significant fractures that were manifest in the years after the Second World War among the members of what had at one point been a circle of like-minded theorists. The Horkheimer circle manifestly did not break up because of differences of opinion on "the Jewish question." But the issue of Israel was an emotionally significant one for the Critical Theorists. The fact that key Critical Theorists had distinctive Jewish backgrounds clarifies why onetime members of the Frankfurt School ultimately took different positions on a matter of emotional import to them. Not only in the Weimar years, but also in the exile period and in the final decades of their lives, understanding the relationships of the Critical Theorists to Jewish matters helps us to understand the development of the Frankfurt School itself.

I take pains to note that my contentions that the life paths of key members of the Institute in Weimar were Jewish and that some of the Critical Theorists – including Horkheimer – were ultimately influenced, in specific instances, by Jewish ideas notwithstanding, I disagree rather strongly with those major discussions of Critical Theorists that accent the relationship of Critical Theory per se to Judaism. I find some of the relevant assertions of, for example, Lorenz Jäger, to be misguided. Jäger claims that "*Dialectic of Enlightenment* was a Jewish book not just in the sense of a critique and analysis of anti-Semitism: it was also a philosophical assertion of Jewishness at a time of its greatest danger."[5] I reject the notion that *Dialectic of Enlightenment* – or any of the other major works written by the first generation of Critical Theorists – is a Jewish book in any significant sense.

Critical Theory provides important insights into society. These insights are neither negated nor confirmed by research on the biographies of the Critical Theorists. Nevertheless, I conclude, the history of the Frankfurt School should be situated in multiple contexts, including that of Jewish history. One can't explain Critical Theory by reference solely to Judaism or Jewish history. But one can't explain the lives of the Frankfurt School's key writers without grappling with Jewish matters.

Notes

Acknowledgments

1 Leo, born Löwenthal, began to use Lowenthal (without an umlaut) as his family name after he moved to the United States. I use Lowenthal when referring to Leo throughout this book except in direct quotes which make use of Leo's original family name, when citing pieces which were signed by Leo with that name, or when citing letters written to or from Leo dating from the years before he went to America.

Introduction

1 Major works on Adorno's life include Lorenz Jäger, *Adorno. A Political Biography*, trans. Stewart Spencer (New Haven, CT, and London: Yale University Press, 2004); Stefan Müller-Doohm, *Adorno. A Biography*, trans. Rodney Livingstone (Malden, MA: Polity, 2005); and Detlev Claussen, *Theodor W. Adorno. One Last Genius*, trans. Rodney Livingstone (Cambridge, MA; London: The Belknap Press of Harvard University Press, 2008). Among the many books devoted, in whole or in part, to Adorno's ideas, special note ought to be made of Susan Buck-Morss, *The Origin of Negative Dialectics. Theodor W. Adorno, Walter Benjamin, and the Frankfurt Institute* (New York: The Free Press, 1977); Gillian Rose, *The Melancholy Science. An Introduction to the Thought of Theodor W. Adorno* (New York: Columbia University Press, 1978); Martin Jay, *Adorno* (Cambridge, MA: Harvard University Press, 1984); Peter Uwe Hohendahl, *Prismatic Thought. Theodor W. Adorno* (Lincoln, NE, and London: University of Nebraska Press, 1995); and Simon Jarvis, *Adorno. A Critical Introduction* (New York: Routledge, 1998). On Fromm see Rainer Funk, *Erich Fromm: The Courage to Be Human* (New York: Continuum, 1982), Rainer Funk, *Erich Fromm mit Selbstzeugnissen und Bilddokumenten* (Reinbek bei Hamburg: Rowohlt, 1983), and Daniel Burston, *The Legacy of Erich Fromm* (Cambridge, MA; London: Harvard University Press, 1991). See,

in addition, the collection of articles entitled *Erich Fromm und die Frankfurter Schule*, ed. Michael Kessler and Rainer Funk (Tübingen: Francke Verlag, 1992). The best book on the life and ideas of the early Horkheimer is John Abromeit's *Max Horkheimer and the Foundations of the Frankfurt School* (Cambridge: Cambridge University Press, 2011). Collections of articles on Horkheimer and his ideas include *Max Horkheimer heute: Werk und Wirkung*, ed. Alfred Schmidt and Norbert Altwicker (Frankfurt: Fischer Taschenbuch Verlag, 1986) and Seyla Benhabib, Wolfgang Bonss, and John McCole, eds., *On Max Horkheimer. New Perspectives* (Cambridge, MA; London: MIT Press, 1993). Among the first-rate books on Marcuse are those by Morton Schoolman, *The Imaginary Witness. The Critical Theory of Herbert Marcuse* (New York: New York University Press, 1984) and Douglas Kellner, *Herbert Marcuse and the Crisis of Marxism* (Berkeley and Los Angeles: University of California Press, 1984). Leo Lowenthal has received somewhat less attention than his colleagues. He has, however, certainly not been altogether ignored. See, in particular, Martin Jay, "Introduction to a *Festschrift* for Leo Lowenthal on his Eightieth Birthday," *Permanent Exiles. Essays on the Intellectual Migration from Germany to America* (New York: Columbia University Press, 1986), pp. 101–106; Jürgen Habermas, "Leo Lowenthal – A Felicitation," in *An Unmastered Past. The Autobiographical Reflections of Leo Lowenthal*, ed. Martin Jay (Berkeley, Los Angeles; London: University of California Press, 1987), pp. 9–14; and the pieces by Peter-Erwin Jansen, Helmut Dubiel, and Richard Wolin in *Das Utopische soll Funken schlagen ... Zum hundertsten Geburtstag von Leo Löwenthal*, ed. Peter-Erwin Jansen (Frankfurt am Main: Vittorio Klostermann, 2000). Important books containing chapters on the Frankfurt School or on several of the Critical Theorists include Richard Wolin, *The Terms of Cultural Criticism. The Frankfurt School, Existentialism, Poststructuralism* (New York: Columbia University Press, 1992); Stephen Bronner, *Of Critical Theory and Its Theorists* (London: Basil Blackwell, 1994); Gunzelin Schmid Noerr, *Gesten aus Begriffen. Konstellationen der Kritischen Theorie* (Frankfurt am Main: Fischer Taschenbuch Verlag, 1997); and Richard Wolin, *The Frankfurt School Revisited and Other Essays on Politics and Society* (New York, London: Routledge, 2006).

2 Martin Jay, *The Dialectical Imagination. A History of the Frankfurt School and the Institute of Social Research, 1923–1950* (Boston; Toronto: Little, Brown and Company, 1973); Helmut Dubiel, *Theory and Politics. Studies in the Development of Critical Theory*, trans. Benjamin Gregg (Cambridge, MA; London: MIT Press, 1985); Rolf Wiggershaus, *The Frankfurt School. Its History, Theories, and Political Significance*, trans. Michael Robertson (Cambridge, MA: MIT Press, 1994); Thomas Wheatland, *The Frankfurt School in Exile* (Minneapolis; London: University of Minnesota Press, 2009).

3 See, for example, Trent Schroyer, *The Critique of Domination. The Origins and Development of Critical Theory* (Boston: Beacon Press, 1975); David Held, *Introduction to Critical Theory. Horkheimer to Habermas* (Berkeley; Los Angeles: University of California Press, 1980); Seyla Benhabib, *Critique, Norm, and Utopia. A Study of the Foundations of Critical Theory* (New York: Columbia University Press, 1986); Douglas Kellner, *Critical Theory, Marxism, and*

Modernity (Baltimore: The Johns Hopkins University Press, 1989); David Ingram, *Critical Theory and Philosophy* (New York: Paragon House, 1990); Stephen Eric Bronner, *Of Critical Theory and its Theorists* (Oxford; Cambridge, MA: Blackwell, 1994); and Craig Calhoun, *Critical Social Theory. Culture, History and the Challenge of Difference* (Oxford; Cambridge, MA: Blackwell, 1995).

4 The creation and early history of the Institute of Social Research is discussed in Jay, *The Dialectical Imagination*; Ulrike Migdal, *Die Frühgeschichte des Frankfurter Instituts für Sozialforschung*. Campus Forschung, CCVII. (Frankfurt am Main; London: Campus Verlag, 1981); Wiggershaus, *The Frankfurt School*; and Michael Buckmiller, "Die 'Marxistische Arbeitswoche' 1923 und die Gründung des 'Instituts für Sozialforschung'," in *Grand Hotel Abgrund. Eine Photobiographie der Frankfurter Schule*, ed. Willem van Reijen and Gunzelin Schmid Noerr (Hamburg: Junius, 1990), pp. 145–183.

5 Max Horkheimer, "The State of Contemporary Social Philosophy and the Tasks of an Institute for Social Research," in *Critical Theory and Society. A Reader*, ed. Stephen Eric Bronner and Douglas MacKay Kellner (New York; London: Routledge, 1989), p. 32.

6 I have chosen to use the spelling "antisemitism" rather than "anti-Semitism" throughout this book (except where quoting or citing works that use another spelling), because Horkheimer was repelled by the latter and made a good point concerning why he was repelled: "I find the word Antisemitism spelt anti-Semitism in most of the publications on the subject. I know that we used to write it that way ourselves. On the other hand I found it so ugly that I asked Miss v. M. to write it in one word ... the Antisemites are not "Anti-Semites"; they are rather Anti-Jews" [Max Horkheimer to Friedrich Pollock, May 3, 1943, MHA, VI.33.542].

7 Hermann Weil was known to have made generous charitable contributions to both non-Jewish and Jewish institutions, and to have attempted to prevent certain explicitly antisemitic students from benefitting from his contributions [Migdal, *Die Frühgeschichte des Frankfurter Instituts für Sozialforschung*, p. 26]. Moreover, he was concerned about the growth of the antisemitic movement in Germany [Migdal, *Die Frühgeschichte des Frankfurter Instituts für Sozialforschung*, p. 46]. He may well have expressed this concern to his son, Feliks J. Weil, who sparked the efforts which ultimately resulted in the founding and funding of the Institute. Whether or not Hermann explicitly told Feliks of his concern, Feliks apparently feared that Hermann would be unwilling to endow an establishment devoted to Marxism, but would be sympathetic to the creation of an institution which would explore the sociological roots of antisemitism. Feliks, therefore, when approaching his father for financial support, described the proposed institute as a social scientific establishment which would be devoted "above all" else to the study of antisemitism [Migdal, *Die Frühgeschichte des Frankfurter Instituts für Sozialforschung*, p. 38].

8 See, for example, George Friedman, *The Political Philosophy of the Frankfurt School* (Ithaca, NY, and London: Cornell University Press, 1981), pp. 92–102; Joseph Maier, "Jüdisches Erbe aus deutschem Geist," in *Max Horkheimer heute: Werk und Wirkung*, ed. Alfred Schmidt and Norbert Altwicker (Frankfurt am Main: Fischer Taschenbuch Verlag, 1986), pp. 146–162; Judith Marcus and Zoltán Tar, "The Judaic Elements in the Teachings of the Frankfurt School,"

Notes to page xi

Leo Baeck Institute Year Book, XXXI (1986), pp. 339–353; Michael Löwy, Redemption and Utopia. Jewish Libertarian Thought in Central Europe. A Study in Elective Affinity, trans. Hope Heaney (Stanford, CA: Stanford University Press, 1992); F. Werner Veauthier, "'Jüdisches' im Denken der Frankfurter Schule," in Juden in Deutschland. Lebenswelten und Einzelschicksale. Ringvorlesung der Philosophischen Fakultät der Universität des Saarlandes im Wintersemester 1988/89, ed. Reinhard Schneider. Annales Universitatis Saraviensis Philosophische Fakultät, I (St. Ingbert: Röhrig Universitätsverlag, 1994), pp. 271–307; Amalia Barboza, "Die 'jüdische Identität' der Frankfurter Schule," in Die Frankfurter Schule und Frankfurt. Eine Rückkehr nach Deutschland, ed. Monika Boll and Raphael Gross ([Göttingen]: Wallstein, [2009]), pp. 162–169.

9 Adorno (whose father was born a Jew) had personal and other ties to the Institute before it went into exile, but did not become an official member of it until 1938. Walter Benjamin, Otto Kirchheimer, Herbert Marcuse, and Franz Neumann, all of whom were wholly of Jewish origin, and all of whom later wrote for the Institute's Zeitschrift für Sozialforschung and developed other links to the Institute, similarly, did not have formal memberships in the Institute while it was still based in Weimar Germany. Siegfried Kracauer – who, like Fromm and Lowenthal, had taught in the Freie Jüdische Lehrhaus in Frankfurt, and who was a long-term friend of Adorno's – attempted to write for the Zeitschrift, but never did publish in it. Though members of the Institute facilitated his emigration to the United States in 1941, the Institute per se stopped short of offering Kracauer a position as a member or even as a salaried associate [Martin Jay, "The Extraterritorial Life of Siegfried Kracauer," Permanent Exiles, p. 167; Martin Jay, "Politics of Translation: Siegfried Kracauer and Walter Benjamin on the Buber-Rosenzweig Bible," Permanent Exiles, pp. 206–207, 224].

10 Wittfogel (1896–1988), best known, in his later years, as an expert on China, moved from Frankfurt to Berlin in 1929 and was not actively involved in Institute affairs during the remainder of the Weimar era. He spoke before the Communist Youth Organization of Greater Berlin on the theme "How to Combat Anti-Semitism" in the spring of 1932 and was asked by the Organization to write a pamphlet on this subject. He completed the piece as requested, and submitted it to the Communist Party's General Secretary. However, the pamphlet apparently was not approved, and did not appear in print [G. L. Ulmen, The Science of Society. Toward an Understanding of the Life and Work of Karl August Wittfogel (The Hague; Paris; New York: Mouton Publishers, 1978), p. 147].

11 On Massing (1902–1979), see Max Horkheimer, Gesammelte Schriften, XVIII, ed. Gunzelin Schmid Noerr (Frankfurt am Main: Fischer Taschenbuch Verlag, 1985), p. 976.

12 Jay, The Dialectical Imagination, p. 170. Though Wittfogel was personally close to Massing in the 1920s and early 1930s, and was, like Massing, not part of the Institute's inner core once Horkheimer became Director, there is no evidence indicating that he too attributed his (outsider's) position in the Institute to his non-Jewish origins. It may be significant that the Institute was not the first organization with many Jewish members with which Wittfogel was affiliated. Near the end of the First World War, Wittfogel "became particularly

close to the Deutsche Wandervogel ... which had many Jewish members, and this at a time when some of its non-Jewish members were leaving because it was 'alien' to the true German spirit" [Ulmen, *The Science of Society*, p. 17]. Wittfogel once responded to an interviewer's characterization of him as a person who was not an Institute insider by stressing that he had been close to the original leadership of the Institute, and had been a favorite of Grünberg, but that a new inner circle formed around Horkheimer after the latter became Director [Rainer Erd, *Reform und Resignation. Gespräche über Franz L. Neumann* (Frankfurt am Main: Suhrkamp, 1985), pp. 104ff.].

13 Grossmann, who had studied under Grünberg, had been a core member of the Institute, and one of its most productive workers, while his one-time teacher was Director. Though he initially acted as a chief assistant to Horkheimer, and had a "harmonious" relationship with him in the Weimar era [Rick Kuhn, *Henryk Grossman and the Recovery of Marxism* (Urbana and Chicago: University of Illinois Press, 2007), p. 149], Grossmann was by no means politically or intellectually close to Horkheimer. Grossmann, an orthodox Marxist and a one-time member of the Polish Communist Party, never did display sustained sympathy for Critical Theory. While he retained an affiliation with the Institute for many years, his influence within it ebbed markedly once Horkheimer was installed [Jay, *The Dialectical Imagination*, p. 17; Migdal, *Die Frühgeschichte des Frankfurter Instituts für Sozialforschung*, pp. 96–97].

14 Wittfogel had moved to Berlin in August 1929, and devoted himself in the period thereafter to periodicals such as *Die Linkskurve*, to organizations like the Arbeitsgemeinschaft für Planwirtschaft, and to political activities [Ulmen, *The Science of Society. Toward an Understanding of the Life and Work of Karl August Wittfogel*, pp. 105–106]. He later rejoined the Institute in New York.

15 Works discussing the Critical Theorists' approach to antisemitism include Erich Cramer, *Hitlers Antisemitismus und die Frankfurter Schule. Kritische Faschismus-Theorie und geschichtliche Realität* (Düsseldorf: Droste, 1979); Martin Jay, "The Jews and the Frankfurt School: Critical Theory's Analysis of Anti-Semitism," *New German Critique*, 19 (Winter 1980), pp. 137–149; Ehrhard Bahr, "The Anti-Semitism Studies of the Frankfurt School: The Failure of Critical Theory," in *Foundations of the Frankfurt School of Social Research*, ed. Judith Marcus and Zoltán Tar (New Brunswick, NJ, and London: Transaction Books, 1984), pp. 311–321; Dan Diner, "Reason and the 'Other': Horkheimer's Reflections on Anti-Semitism and Mass Annihilation," in *On Max Horkheimer. New Perspectives*, ed. Seyla Benhabib, Wolfgang Bonss, and John McCole (Cambridge, MA; London: MIT Press, 1993), pp. 335–363; Lars Rensmann, *Kritische Theorie über den Antisemitismus. Studien zu Struktur, Erklärungspotential und Aktualität.* Edition Philosophie und Sozialwissenschaften 42 (Berlin and Hamburg: Argument Verlag, 1998); Anson Rabinbach, "'Why Were the Jews Sacrificed?' The Place of Antisemitism in Adorno and Horkheimer's *Dialectic of Enlightenment*," in *Adorno. A Critical Reader*, ed. Nigel Gibson and Andrew Rubin (Malden, MA: Blackwell Publishers Inc., 2002), pp. 132–149; Jonathan Judaken, "Between Philosemitism and Antisemitism: The Frankfurt School's Anti-Antisemitism," *Antisemitism and Philosemitism in the*

Twentieth and Twenty-first Centuries. Representing Jews, Jewishness, and Modern Culture, ed. Phylllis Lassner and Lara Trubowitz (Newark, DE: University of Delaware Press, 2008), pp. 23–46; Eva-Maria Ziege, *Antisemitismus und Gesellschaftstheorie. Die Frankfurter Schule im amerikanischen Exil* (Frankfurt am Main: Suhrkamp, 2009); Eva-Maria Ziege, "Arendt, Adorno und die Anfänge der Antisemitismusforschung," in *Affinität wider Willen? Hannah Arendt, Theodor W. Adorno und die Frankfurter Schule*, ed. Liliane Weissberg. Jahrbuch zur Geschichte und Wirkung des Holocaust (Frankfurt and New York: Campus Verlag, 2011), pp. 85–102; Jonathan Judaken, "Blindness and Insight: The Conceptual Jew in Adorno and Arendt's Post-Holocaust Reflections on the Antisemitic Question," *Arendt and Adorno. Political and Philosophical Investigations*, ed. Lars Rensmann and Samir Gandesha (Stanford, CA: Stanford University Press, 2012), pp. 173–196; Julia Schulze Wessel and Lars Rensmann, "The Paralysis of Judgment. Arendt and Adorno on Antisemitism and the Modern Condition," *Arendt and Adorno. Political and Philosophical Investigations*, pp. 197–225.
16 Schulze Wessel and Rensmann, "The Paralysis of Judgment. Arendt and Adorno on Antisemitism and the Modern Condition," p. 213.

Chapter 1

1 Leo Lowenthal, "Introduction," *Critical Theory and Frankfurt Theorists. Lectures – Correspondence – Conversations*. Communication in Society, IV (New Brunswick, NJ and Oxford: Transaction Publishers, 1989), p. 3.
2 Dubiel, *Theory and Politics*, pp. 173ff.
3 Max Horkheimer to Z. H. Wollach (of the Israelitische Religionsgemeinschaft Würtembergs), March 11, 1967, Max-Horkheimer-Archiv [Henceforth: MHA], Stadt- und Universitätsbibliothek, Frankfurt-am-Main, V.95.176; Max Horkheimer to Jüdische Gemeinde Stuttgart, June 7, 1971, MHA, V.95.170.
4 Max Horkheimer, "Das Schlimme erwarten und doch das Gute versuchen (Gespräch mit Gerhard Rein)," in Max Horkheimer, *Gesammelte Schriften*, VII, ed. Gunzelin Schmid Noerr (Frankfurt am Main: Fischer Taschenbuch Verlag, 1985), p. 443.
5 Helmut Gumnior and Rudolf Ringguth, *Max Horkheimer. Mit Selbstzeugnissen und Bilddokumenten* (Reinbek bei Hamburg: Rowohlt, 1973), p. 11.
6 M.C., "Frankfurt-Loge," *Allgemeine Jüdische Wochenzeitung*, XXIX, 6 (February 8, 1974), p. 11.
7 Max Horkheimer to Heinrich Guttmann, April 12, 1966, MHA, V.67.8.
8 Max Horkheimer to Jüdische Gemeinde Stuttgart, June 7, 1971, MHA, V.95.170.
9 Max Horkheimer, "Dokumente – Stationen [Gespräch mit Otmar Hersche]," in *Gesammelte Schriften*, VII, p. 319.
10 Max Horkheimer, "Nachwort," in *Porträts deutsch-jüdischer Geistesgeschichte*, ed. Thilo Koch (Cologne: Verlag M. DuMont Schauberg, 1961), p. 256.
11 Abromeit, *Max Horkheimer and the Foundations of the Frankfurt School*, p. 23. Abromeit asserts that Pollock's father "renounced" Judaism, but does not indicate whether this step was taken formally.

12 Gumnior and Ringguth, *Max Horkheimer*, p. 13.
13 Gumnior and Ringguth, *Max Horkheimer*, p. 18. Zvi Rosen, *Max Horkheimer* (Munich: C. H. Beck, 1995), p. 22.
14 Jay, *The Dialectical Imagination*, p. 35.
15 Rosen, *Max Horkheimer*, pp. 61ff.
16 Horkheimer, "Nachwort," in *Porträts deutsch-jüdischer Geistesgeschichte*, p. 256.
17 Abromeit, *Max Horkheimer and the Foundations of the Frankfurt School*, p. 21.
18 Abromeit, *Max Horkheimer and the Foundations of the Frankfurt School*, pp. 35–36.
19 Max Horkheimer, "Jochai," in *Gesammelte Schriften*, I, ed. Alfred Schmidt (Frankfurt am Main: Fischer Taschenbuch Verlag, 1988), pp. 266–267.
20 Max Horkheimer, "Gregor," in *Gesammelte Schriften*, I, pp. 295–296.
21 Julius Carlebach, *Karl Marx and the Radical Critique of Judaism*. The Littman Library of Jewish Civilization (London; Henley; and Boston: Routledge & Kegan Paul, 1978), p. 235. Carlebach apparently did not examine the manuscripts of the works of fiction by Horkheimer cited above, and probably did not know of their existence at the time he wrote his book.
22 Martin Jay, "The Jews and the Frankfurt School: Critical Theory's Analysis of Anti-Semitism," in *Permanent Exiles*, p. 90.
23 Max Horkheimer, *Dawn & Decline. Notes 1926–1931 and 1950–1969*, trans. Michael Shaw (New York: The Seabury Press, 1978), pp. 42–43.
24 Max Horkheimer, "Sociological Background of the Psychoanalytic Approach," *Anti-Semitism. A Social Disease*, ed. Ernst Simmel (New York: International Universities Press, 1946), p. 1.
25 Leo Lowenthal, "'We Never Expected Such Fame': A Conversation with Mathias Greffrath, 1979," *Critical Theory and Frankfurt Theorists*, p. 242.
26 Viktor Löwenthal, "Kindheit im orthodoxen Milieu," *Frankfurter jüdische Errinerungen. Ein Lesebuch zur Sozialgeschichte 1864–1951*, ed. Kommission zur Erforschung der Geschichte der Frankfurter Juden (Sigmaringen: Jan Thorbecke Verlag, 1997), p. 38.
27 Viktor Löwenthal, "Kindheit im orthodoxen Milieu," pp. 38–40, 45–47.
28 *Ibid.*, p. 47.
29 Wiggershaus, *The Frankfurt School*, p. 64.
30 Lowenthal, "I Never Wanted to Play Along," *An Unmastered Past. The Autobiographical Reflections of Leo Lowenthal*, ed. Martin Jay (Berkeley; Los Angeles; London: University of California Press, 1987), p. 27.
31 Gershom Scholem, "On the Social Psychology of the Jews in Germany: 1900–1933," *Jews and Germans from 1860 to 1933: The Problematic Symbiosis*, ed. David Bronsen. Reihe Siegen, IX (Heidelberg: Carl Winter; Universitätsverlag, 1979), pp. 18–20.
32 Hannah Arendt, "Walter Benjamin: 1892–1940," in Walter Benjamin, *Illuminations*, ed. Hannah Arendt; trans. Harry Zohn (New York: Schocken Books, 1969), p. 30.
33 Lowenthal, "I Never Wanted to Play Along," p. 34.

34 Michael Crasemann, Felicitas Gürsching, and Wolfgang Saalfeld, "Jüdische Schüler an der alten Wöhlerschule im Westend," *Wöhlerschule 88*. [Frankfurt am Main], [1988], p. 40.
35 Lowenthal, "I Never Wanted to Play Along," p. 18.
36 *Ibid.*, p. 45.
37 *Ibid.*, p. 45.
38 Cf. the comments by Simon in Hans Jürgen Schultz, ed., *Mein Judentum* (Stuttgart; Berlin: Kreuz Verlag, 1978), p. 94. Simon describes his experiences in the German army in Ernst Simon, "Wie ich Zionist wurde," *Entscheidung zum Judentum. Essays und Vorträge* (Frankfurt am Main: Suhrkamp 1979), pp. 30ff.
39 Simon was raised in Berlin, not in Frankfurt. Simon and Fromm first met around 1920 when they both were studying in the University of Heidelberg [Michael Bühler, *Erziehung zur Tradition – Erziehung zum Widerstand. Ernst Simon und die jüdische Erwachsenenbildung in Deutschland* (Berlin: Selbstverlag Institut Kirche und Judentum, 1986), p. 26]. One can obtain a sense of just how close Lowenthal and Simon were in the year in which they first became friends by reading Leo's letters to Ernst from that period. My thanks to Toni Simon, Ernst's widow, who generously gave me access to these and other letters, and who discussed them with me.
40 Lowenthal, "I Never Wanted to Play Along," p. 18. Lowenthal later wrote on Cohen for the Jewish press [Leo Löwenthal, "Die jüdische Religionsphilosophie Hermann Cohens," in *Frankfurter Israelitisches Gemeindeblatt*, VIII, 9, (Mai 1930), pp. 357–359].
41 Hans Liebeschütz, "Hermann Cohen and his Historical Background," *Leo Baeck Institute Year Book*, XIII, (1968), p. 27.
42 George L. Mosse, *Germans and Jews. The Right, the Left and the Search for a "Third Force" in Pre-Nazi Germany* (New York: Grosset & Dunlap, 1971), p. 205.
43 Lowenthal, "I Never Wanted to Play Along," pp. 38, 46, 111. Cf. Walter Kinkel, *Hermann Cohen. Eine Einführung in sein Werk* (Stuttgart: Strecker und Schröder, 1924).
44 Lowenthal, "I Never Wanted to Play Along," p. 47.
45 J. Toury, *Die politischen Orientierungen der Juden in Deutschland. Von Jena bis Weimar*. Schriftenreihe wissenschaftlicher Abhandlungen des Leo-Baeck-Instituts, XV (Tübingen: J. C. B. Mohr, 1966).
46 Peter Pulzer, "Jewish Participation in Wilhelmine Politics," *Jews and Germans from 1860 to 1933: The Problematic Symbiosis*, ed. David Bronsen, p. 89.
47 Richard Hunt, *German Social Democracy 1918–1933* (Chicago: Quadrangle Books, 1970), p. 196.
48 David W. Morgan, *The Socialist Left and the German Revolution. A History of the German Independent Social Democratic Party, 1917–1922* (Ithaca, NY, and London: Cornell University Press, 1975), p. 178.
49 Leo Löwenthal to Victor and Rosa Löwenthal, June 17, 1920, *Das Utopische soll Funken schlagen... Zum hundertsten Geburtstag von Leo Löwenthal*, ed. Peter-Erwin Jansen (Frankfurt-am-Main: Vittorio Klostermann, 2000), p. 37.

50 Walter Gross, "The Zionist Students' Movement," *Leo Baeck Institute Year Book*, IV (1959), p. 149.
51 Stephen N. Poppel, *Zionism in Germany, 1897–1933*, (Philadelphia: The Jewish Publication Society of America, 1977), tables 2 and 3.
52 Quoted in Poppel, *Zionism in Germany, 1897–1933*, pp. 105–106.
53 Scholem, "On the Social Psychology of the Jews in Germany: 1900–1933," p. 23.
54 Adolph Asch, *Geschichte des K.C.* (London: n.p., 1964).
55 Leo Löwenthal to Ernst Simon, September 4, 1920, Ernst Simon Papers, Jerusalem.
56 Leo Lowenthal, "In Memory of Walter Benjamin: The Integrity of the Intellectual," *An Unmastered Past*, p. 229.
57 Leo Löwenthal, "Ich will den Traum von der Utopie nicht aufgeben," *Die andere Erinnerung. Gespräche mit jüdischen Wissenschaftlern im Exil*, ed. Hajo Funke (Frankfurt am Main: Fischer Taschenbuch Verlag, 1989), p. 176.
58 Erich Fromm, Fritz Goithein, Leo Löwenthal, Ernst Simon, Erich Michaelis, "Ein prinzipielles Wort zur Erziehungsfrage," *Jüdische Rundschau*, XXVII, 103/104 (December 29, 1922), pp. 675–676. Also see: Leo Strauss, "Response to Frankfurt's 'Word of Principle,'" in Leo Strauss, *"The Early Writings" (1921–1932)*, trans. and ed. Michael Zank (Albany: State University of New York Press, 2002), pp. 64–75. The response by Strauss, who was active in Blau-Weiss, originally appeared in *Jüdische Rundschau* in January 1923. Robert Miner's understanding of Strauss's response is thrown askew by the fact that Miner confuses the grouping which wrote "Ein prinzipielles Wort zur Erziehungsfrage" with the neo-Orthodox separatists of Frankfurt [Robert Miner, "'Politics As Opposed to Tradition': The Presence of Nietzsche and Spinoza in the 'Zionist Essays' of Leo Strauss," *Interpretation. A Journal of Political Philosophy*, XXXVII, 2 (Winter 2010), p. 207], when those in the grouping were actually opposed to neo-Orthodox separatism.
59 Mosse, *Germans and Jews*, pp. 94–102; Poppel, *Zionism in Germany*, pp. 131–135.
60 Gross, "The Zionist Students' Movement," pp. 156–157.
61 Strauss, "Response to Frankfurt's 'Word of Principle,'" p. 64.
62 Fromm, Goithein, Löwenthal, Simon, Michaelis, "Ein prinzipielles Wort zur Erziehungsfrage," p. 676.
63 *Ibid.*, p. 676.
64 Arendt, "Walter Benjamin: 1892–1940," p. 34.
65 Lowenthal, "We Never Expected Such Fame," p. 240.
66 Hans Dieter Hellige, "Generationskonflikt, Selbsthaß und die Entstehung antikapitalistischer Positionen im Judentum. Der Einfluß des Antisemitismus auf das Sozialverhalten jüdischer Kaufmanns- und Unternehmersöhne im Deutschen Kaiserreich und in der K.u.K.-Monarchie," *Geschichte und Gesellschaft*, V (1979), pp. 476–518.
67 Despite the similarities in their backgrounds – that is the fact that both were the sons of successful German Jewish businessmen – Horkheimer's path and Pollock's path diverge here. Unlike Horkheimer's father, Pollock's parents ultimately came to sympathize with the political Left [Wheatland, *The*

Frankfurt School in Exile, p. 20]. Generational conflict was widespread in the world of German Jewry in the early decades of the twentieth century – but it was not universal.
68 Michael Brenner, "A Tale of Two Families: Franz Rosenzweig, Gershom Scholem and the Generational Conflict Around Judaism," *Judaism*, 42, (1993), p. 354.
69 Lowenthal, "I Never Wanted to Play Along," p. 18.
70 Lowenthal suggested around January 1921 that he had had visions of the messianic empire or the apocalypse, and that he saw these as realities, but the letter in which he did so has not survived. Cf. Siegfried Kracauer to Leo Löwenthal, January 14, 1921, *In steter Freundschaft: Leo Löwenthal – Siegfried Kracauer Briefwechsel 1921–1966*, ed. Peter Erwin Jansen and Christian Schmidt (Springe: zu Klampen Verlag, 2003), pp. 18–22.
71 Comments by Erich Fromm in Jacob J. Schacter, ed., "Reminiscences of Shlomo Barukh Rabinkow," a portion of the volume entitled *Sages and Saints*, ed. Leo Jung (Hoboken, NJ: Ktav Publishing House, Inc., 1987), p. 104. Lowenthal was reportedly introduced to the circle around Rabbi Nobel by Fromm [Rainer Funk, *Erich Fromm mit Selbstzeugnissen und Bilddokumenten* (Reinbek bei Hamburg: Rowohlt, 1983), p. 30].
72 Nobel's life and work are discussed in Oskar Wolfsberg, *Nehamia Anton Nobel, 1871–1922, Versuch einer Würdigung*, (Frankfurt am Main: J. Kaufmann Verlag, 1929); Eugen E. Mayer, "Nehemiah Anton Nobel," *Guardians of Our Heritage (1724–1953)*, ed. Leo Jung (New York: Bloch Publishing Company, 1958), pp. 565–580; Ernst Simon, "N. A. Nobel (1871–1922) als Prediger," *Brücken. Gesammelte Aufsätze* (Heidelberg: Verlag Lambert Schneider, 1965), pp. 375–380; Bühler, *Erziehung zur Tradition*, pp. 27–28; Rachel Heuberger, "Orthodoxy versus Reform. The Case of Rabbi Nehemiah Anton Nobel of Frankfurt a. Main," *Leo Baeck Institute Year Book*, XXXVII, (1992), pp. 45–58 and in Rachel Heuberger, *Rabbi Nehemiah Anton Nobel. The Jewish Renaissance in Frankfurt am Main*. Schriftenreihe des Jüdischen Museums Frankfurt am Main, X (Frankfurt am Main: Societäts-Verlag, 2007).
73 Lowenthal describes Nobel as not "technically orthodox, but conservative and well-educated in philosophy" [Lowenthal, "I Never Wanted to Play Along," p. 19], a description which could be misleading for contemporary American Jews. Nobel was also described as a conservative rabbi by Glatzer [Nahum N. Glatzer, "The Frankfort Lehrhaus," in *Leo Baeck Institute Year Book*, I, (1956), p. 109]. German "conservative rabbis" of the inter-war era were not at all like contemporary American Conservative rabbis, the similarities in these labels notwithstanding. Jews in Germany in the post–World War I period used the term "conservative rabbi" as a way to differentiate such men from "liberal rabbis." Heuberger reports that Nobel "was very strict in ritual observance and fulfilled all the commandments with great precision," while also noting that Nobel, a complex man, "embodied many contradictions" [Heuberger, *Rabbi Nehemiah Anton Nobel. The Jewish Renaissance in Frankfurt am Main*, p. 12]. She describes Nobel's feelings about the label "Orthodox" on p. 32 of her book.

74 Max Horkheimer was not involved in the circle around Rabbi Nobel. "I did not know the Rabbi" Horkheimer later told an interviewer. "I had never seen him [...] I didn't belong already for the reason that this Rabbi was the complete opposite of liberal Judaism, he represented a most conservative Judaism" [Abromeit, *Max Horkheimer and the Foundations of the Frankfurt School*, p. 64]. However, Horkheimer's wording strongly suggests that he was aware of the Nobel circle (or, at the very least, became cognizant of it shortly after Nobel's death at the beginning of 1922) and that, in his opinion, Nobel was "a very great man" [*ibid.*].
75 Gershom Scholem, *From Berlin to Jerusalem. Memories of My Youth*, trans. Harry Zohn (New York: Schocken Books, 1980), p. 153. Also see Gershom Scholem, "Ernst Simon," typescript, Gershom Scholem Archive, 1599/277/II 37, Jerusalem, in which Scholem notes the continuing impact of Nobel, Franz Rosenzweig, and Martin Buber on Simon, and Ernst Simon, "Selbstdarstellung," *Pädagogik in Selbstdarstellungen*, I, ed. Ludwig J. Pongratz (Hamburg: Felix Meiner Verlag, 1975), pp. 300ff.
76 It ought to be noted that Jews were a small minority in both cities. Jews made up 4.3 percent of the total population in Berlin in 1925, and 6.29 percent of the population of Frankfurt a. M. Moreover, the proportion of the population in Frankfurt which was Jewish decreased over time [Ld, "Die Frankfurter Juden in Zahlen und Bildern," in *Frankfurter Israelitisches Gemeindeblatt*, IX, 10 (June 1931), pp. 317–319].
77 Glatzer, "The Frankfort Lehrhaus," p. 109.
78 Lowenthal, "I Never Wanted to Play Along," p. 21.
79 Lowenthal was in curative institutions, in St. Blasien and elsewhere, until March 1922 [Ingrid Belke and Irina Renz, "Siegfried Kracauer 1889–1966," *Marbacher Magazin*, 17 (1988), p. 37; Rachel Heuberger, "Die entdeckung der jüdischen Wurzeln. Leo Löwenthal und der Frankfurter Rabbiner Nehemias Anton Nobel," *Das Utopische soll Funken schlagen ... Zum hundertsten Geburtstag von Leo Löwenthal*, p. 65; *In steter Freundschaft*, p. 29].
80 Nehemiah Anton Nobel to Leo Löwenthal, September 30, 1921, Leo-Löwenthal-Archiv [Henceforth: LLA], unsorted material, Stadt- und Universitätsbibliothek, Frankfurt-am-Main. Nobel had reason to be concerned about Lowenthal's spirits. Lowenthal was in fact quite lonely during the holiday [Leo Löwenthal to Ernst Simon, October 4, 1921, Ernst Simon Papers, Jerusalem].
81 Nehemiah Anton Nobel to Leo Löwenthal, October 10, 1921, *Das Utopische soll Funken schlagen*, pp. 68–69.
82 Nehemiah Anton Nobel to Leo Löwenthal, October 17, 1921, *Das Utopische soll Funken schlagen*, pp. 70–71. In another postcard [Nehemiah Anton Nobel to Leo Löwenthal, October 21, 1921, LLA, unsorted material], Nobel suggests that "we can also ask a specialist here" in Frankfurt for medical advice, clearly offering to play a role that would typically be played by a close relative or friend.
83 Leo Löwenthal, *Untergang der Dämonologien. Studien über Judentum, Antisemitismus und faschistischen Geist* (Leipzig: Reclam Verlag, 1990), pp. 10–25.

84 Michael Löwy, *Redemption and Utopia*, p. 70.
85 Lowenthal, "We Never Expected Such Fame," p. 240. Lowenthal's contribution was received with reservations both by Franz Rosenzweig and by Lowenthal's friend and mentor, Siegfried Kracauer [Franz Rosenzweig to Leo Löwenthal, October 11, 1921, and Siegfried Kracauer to Leo Löwenthal, December 4, 1921, Leo Löwenthal, *Mitmachen wollte ich nie. Ein autobiographisches Gespräch mit Helmut Dubiel* (Frankfurt am Main: Suhrkamp, 1980), pp. 242–247]. Lowenthal initially rejected Rosenzweig's critique of his contribution [Leo Löwenthal to Ernst Simon, October 8, 1921, Ernst Simon Papers, Jerusalem].
86 One component of the blow (albeit by no means the most important one) may well have been that Lowenthal was unable to afford to continue to remain in curative institutions for extended periods. [*In steter Freundschaft*, p. 29].
87 As translated in Heuberger, *Rabbi Nehemiah Anton Nobel. The Jewish Renaissance in Frankfurt am Main*, p. 93. Nobel had requested that there be no speakers at his funeral. Lowenthal published a short piece about Rabbi Nobel three years after his teacher's death, discussing the meaning of that request [Leo Löwenthal, "Rabbiner N. A. Nobel. Ein Prinzipielles Vorwort zu einem Nekrolog," in *Jüdisches Wochenblatt*, II, 3 (January 16, 1925), p. 25].
88 Leo Löwenthal, "Rabbiner Dr. N. A. Nobel, verschieden am 24. Januar 1922" *Der jüdische Student. Zeitschrift des kartells jüdischer Verbindungen*, XIX, 2 (March 1922), pp. 87–88.
89 Lowenthal, "I Never Wanted to Play Along," p. 19. Compare also a letter from Betty Scholem to her son Gershom in which Betty informs Gershom that Leo and Golde had sent Rosh Hashanah greetings [Betty Scholem to Gershom Scholem, September 21, 1923, in Betty Scholem and Gershom Scholem, *Mutter und Sohn im Briefwechsel*, ed. Itta Sheletzky with Thomas Sparr, (Munich: Verlag C. H. Beck, 1989), p. 81].
90 Funk, *Erich Fromm mit Selbstzeugnissen und Bilddokumenten*, p. 49. Fromm had first become acquainted with Ginsburg in 1920–1921.
91 Lowenthal, "Recollections of Theodor W. Adorno," *An Unmastered Past*, p. 207. Just as both Betty Scholem, mother of Gershom, and Adele Rosenzweig, mother of Franz, "displayed much more understanding for their sons' feeling about Judaism" [Brenner, "A Tale of Two Families," p. 357] than did the young men's fathers, so too did Rosie Löwenthal display more sympathy for her son Leo's choice than did Rosie's husband Victor. Rosie apparently did attend the wedding of Leo and Golde. Leo's path, once again, was not unique, but rather similar to that of (certain) other German Jewish men.
92 Lowenthal, "We Never Expected Such Fame," p. 240; Lowenthal, "I Never Wanted to Play Along," p. 20.
93 Lowenthal, "The Utopian Motif in Suspension: A Conversation with Leo Lowenthal. Interview with W. Martin Lüdke," *An Unmastered Past*, p. 244.
94 Lowenthal, "I Never Wanted to Play Along," p. 20.
95 Löwy, *Redemption and Utopia*, p. 68.
96 Lowenthal, "Recollections of Theodor W. Adorno," p. 203. A report on the activities of the Advisory Board in the period immediately preceding Lowenthal's affiliation with that organization was published in a periodical

aimed at Jewish youth in Frankfurt in 1922 ["Tätigkeitsbericht der Beratung [s]stelle für ostjüdische Flüchtlinge für die Zeit vom 1. August 1921 bis. 1. März 1922," *Frankfurter Jüdische Jugendblätter*, II, 24 (April 21, 1922, pp. 2–3]. During that period, the Advisory Board was apparently focused on "productivization," that is, on finding productive work for the refugees.

97 The work of the Arbeiterfürsorgeamt is discussed in Salomon Adler-Rudel, *Ostjuden in Deutschland 1880–1940. Zugleich eine Geschichte der Organisationen, die sie betreuten.* Schriftenreihe wissenschaftlicher Abhandlungen des Leo-Baeck-Instituts, 1. (Tübingen: J. C. B. Mohr, 1959), pp. 71ff. and in Trude Maurer, *Ostjuden in Deutschland 1918–1933*. Hamburger Beiträge zur Geschichte der deutschen Juden, XII (Hamburg: Hans Christians Verlag, 1986), pp. 508–522.

98 Walter Mannheim to Alfred Berger, November 22, 1923, LLA, A.25.5–10; Arbeiter-Fürsorgeamt der jüdischen Organisationen Deutschlands, Berlin, "Zeugenis," July 24, 1924, LLA, A.25.3. Cf. Leo Löwenthal to Ernst Simon, March 10, 1923, Ernst Simon Papers, Jerusalem, in which Lowenthal discusses matters related to his work for the Advisory Board, such as his interest in obtaining data about the situations of East European Jews near the Belgian and French borders, including information as to any legal limitations and/or work possibilities, the cultural situation of and numbers of East European Jews already there, etc.

99 Studies of the attitudes of German Jews towards Jews from Eastern Europe, and of the ways in which these attitudes changed over time, include Steven E. Aschheim, *Brothers and Strangers. The East European Jew in German and German Jewish Consciousness, 1800–1923* (Madison: The University of Wisconsin Press, 1982); Jack Wertheimer, *Unwelcome Strangers. East European Jews in Imperial Germany* (New York and Oxford: Oxford Univesity Press, 1987), and Shulamit Volkov, "The Dynamics of Dissimilation. *Ostjuden* and German Jews," *The Jewish Response to German Culture. From the Enlightenment to the Second World War*, ed. Jehuda Reinharz and Walter Schatzberg (Hanover, NH, and London: University Press of New England, 1985), pp. 195–211.

100 Peter Gay, *Freud, Jews and Other Germans. Masters and Victims in Modernist Culture* (Oxford: Oxford University Press, 1978), p. 187.

101 Lowenthal, "Recollections of Theodor W. Adorno," p. 203.

102 Lowenthal, "I Never Wanted to Play Along," p. 25.

103 A letter from Alfred Berger of the Arbeiterfürsorgeamt suggests that Lowenthal had expressed a desire to leave the position by April 1, 1923 (and attempts to dissuade him from doing so) [Alfred Berger to Leo Löwenthal, February 26, 1923, LLA, A.25.1–2].

104 Arbeiter-Fürsorgeamt der jüdischen Organisationen Deutschlands, Berlin, "Zeugenis," July 24, 1924, LLA, A.25.3.

105 Works on the Lehrhaus include: Richard Koch, "Das Freie Jüdische Lehrhaus in Frankfurt am Main," *Der Jude*, 7 (1923), pp. 116–120; Nahum N. Glatzer, "The Frankfort Lehrhaus," *Leo Baeck Institute Year Book*, I, (1956), pp. 105–122; Ernst Simon, "Franz Rosenzweig und das jüdische Bildungsproblem," *Brücken*, pp. 393–406; Jehuda Reinharz, "The Lehrhaus

in Frankfurt am Main: A Renaissance in Jewish Adult Education," *The Yavneh Review. A Student Journal of Jewish Studies*, 7 (1969), pp. 7–29; Erich Ahrens, "Reminiscences of the Men of the Frankfurt Lehrhaus," *Leo Baeck Institute Year Book*, XIX (1974), pp. 245–253; Wolfgang Schivelbusch, *Intellektuellendämmerung. Zur Lage der Frankfurter Intelligenz in den zwanziger Jahre* (Frankfurt am Main: Insel Verlag, 1982), pp. 27–41; Bühler, *Erziehung zur Tradition*, pp. 38ff.; Brigitte Kern-Ulmer, "Franz Rosenzweig's Jüdisches Lehrhaus in Frankfurt: A Model of Jewish Adult Education," *Judaism*, 39 (1990), pp. 202–214; Michael Brenner, *The Renaissance of Jewish Culture in Weimar Germany* (New Haven and London: Yale University Press, 1996), pp. 69–90; Martin Jay, "1920. The Free Jewish School is founded in Frankfurt am Main under the leadership of Franz Rosenzweig," *Yale Companion to Jewish Writing and Thought in German Culture 1096–1996*, ed. Sander L. Gilman and Jack Zipes (New Haven and London: Yale University Press, 1997), pp. 395–400.
106 Brenner, *The Renaissance of Jewish Culture in Weimar Germany*, p. 90.
107 Lowenthal, "In Memory of Walter Benjamin: The Integrity of the Intellectual," p. 232.
108 Jay, "1920. The Free Jewish School is founded in Frankfurt am Main under the leadership of Franz Rosenzweig," p. 399.
109 Glatzer, "The Frankfort Lehrhaus," p. 114.
110 Franz Rosenzweig to Joseph Prager, May 30, 1923 [Franz Rosenzweig, *Briefe*, ed. Edith Rosenzweig, with the assistance of Ernst Simon (Berlin: Schocken Verlag, 1935), p. 481]; Bühler, *Erziehung zur Tradition*, p. 60.
111 Bühler, *Erziehung zur Tradition*, p. 68.
112 [Liebmann?], Jüdisches Lehrhaus (Verein für jüdische Geschichte und Literatur), Wiesbaden to Leo Löwenthal, September 12, 1927, LLA; Verein für jüdische Geschichte und Literatur in Wiesbaden, Jüdisches Lehrhaus, "Winterprogramm 1927/28," LLA. Lowenthal was also helpful during that period to an altogether different Jewish institution: the Yeshiva [Rabbinische Lehranstalt] of Frankfurt. For a number of years, Lowenthal helped to prepare pupils of the Frankfurt Yeshiva for their matriculation examinations [Rabbi (Jakob) Hoffmann, Rabbinische Lehranstalt Frankfurt am Main to Leo Löwenthal, May 8, 1928, LLA]. The Rabbinische Lehranstalt was an Orthodox, non-separatist, institution.
113 Leo Lowenthal to Paul Mendes-Flohr, May 23, 1988, LLA, A.579.5. Rosenzweig and Lowenthal corresponded intermittently during the first half of the 1920s [Franz Rosenzweig to Leo Löwenthal, October 11, 1921, LLA, A.742.4-6; Franz Rosenzweig to Leo Löwenthal, August 23, 1922, LLA, A.742.11-12; Franz Rosenzweig to Leo Löwenthal, May 6, 1925, LLA, A.742.13; Franz Rosenzweig to Leo Löwenthal, May 18, 1925, LLA, unsorted material]. In 1925, Lowenthal drafted a project on "Judaism and Jewishness in Recent German Philosophy," and solicited support from Rosenzweig and Buber, who responded positively and who attempted to obtain funds for Lowenthal from the Moses Mendelssohn Foundation. Despite the efforts of Rosenzweig and Buber, Lowenthal did not receive a grant [Lowenthal, "I Never Wanted to Play Along," pp. 112].

114 Kracauer was raised, in part, in the home of his uncle Isidor Kracauer, who was a prominent historian of the Jewish community of Frankfurt [Jay, "The Extraterritorial Life of Siegfried Kracauer," pp. 152–154]. S. Kracauer contributed an article on friendship to the Festschrift in honor of Nobel. He co-taught a course sponsored by the Lehrhaus on contemporary religious and political movements [Glatzer, "The Frankfort Lehrhaus," p. 111].

115 Martin Jay, "Politics of Translation: Siegfried Kracauer and Walter Benjamin on the Buber-Rosenzweig Bible," pp. 198–216. An article by Martina Lesch and Walter Lesch ["Verbindungen zu einer anderen Frankfurter Schule. Zu Kracauers Auseinandersetzung mit Bubers und Rosenzweigs Bibelübersetzung," *Siegfried Kracauer. Neuen Interpretationen. Akten des internationalen, interdisziplinären Kracauer-Symposions Weingarten, 2.-4. März 1989. Akademie der Diözese Rottenburg-Stuttgart*, ed. Michael Kessler and Thomas Y. Levin (Tübingen: Stauffenburg Verlag, 1990), pp. 171–193] is also useful.

Lowenthal had had direct contact with Buber prior to the appearance of the Buber/Rosenzweig translation [Martin Buber to Leo Löwenthal, January 13, 1923, LLA, A.122.1-2; Martin Buber to Leo Löwenthal, March 23, 1925, LLA, unsorted materials; Martin Buber to Leo Löwenthal, May 3, 1925, LLA, A.122.3-4; Martin Buber to Leo Löwenthal, May 24, 1925, LLA, unsorted materials]. In 1923, Buber wrote a short statement recommending Lowenthal as "a young person with considerable intellectual talents," from whom Jewish philosophy and science could expect important accomplishments if he were given the possibility to devote himself to these fields with the required level of concentration and time [Martin Buber, Transcript of a recommendation of Leo Löwenthal, August 7, 1923, LLA, unsorted materials]. In 1990, however, Lowenthal publicly proclaimed that he had already had a "a very ambivalent relationship" with Buber before the publication of *Das Buch im Anfang* [Leo Lowenthal, "As I Remember Friedel," *New German Critique*, 54 (Fall 1991), p. 11].

116 Georg Salzberger, *Leben un Lehre*, ed. Albert H. Friedlander (Frankfurt am Main: Waldemar Kramer, 1982), pp. 105–106.

117 Brenner, *The Renaissance of Jewish Culture in Weimar Germany*, pp. 103–111.

118 Thomas Y. Levin, *Siegfried Kracauer. Eine Bibliographie seiner Schriften* (Marbach am Neckar: Deutsche Schillergesellschaft, 1989).

119 Siegfried Kracauer, "The Bible in German," *The Mass Ornament. Weimar Essays*, trans. Thomas Y. Levin (Cambridge, MA, and London: Harvard University Press, 1995), p. 192.

120 *Ibid.*, p. 198.

121 Jay, "Politics of Translation: Siegfried Kracauer and Walter Benjamin on the Buber-Rosenzweig Bible," p. 208.

122 Kracauer, "The Bible in German," p. 195.

123 *Ibid.*, p. 199.

124 *Ibid.*, p. 201.

125 Martin Buber and Franz Rosenzweig, "The Bible in German: In Reply," *Scripture and Translation*, trans. Lawrence Rosenwald with Everett Fox.

Indiana Studies in Biblical Literature (Bloomington and Indianapolis: Indiana University Press, 1994), pp. 159, 155.
126 When, in 1922, Kracauer got into a dispute with Ernst Bloch (to whom Kracauer had first been introduced by Lowenthal) over a review by Kracauer of a book by Bloch, Lowenthal responded by breaking off his friendship with Bloch [Lowenthal, "As I Remember Friedel," pp. 6, 10].
127 Leo Lowenthal to Paul Mendes-Flohr, May 23, 1988, LLA, A.579.5.
128 Paul Mendes-Flohr to Leo Lowenthal, April 22, 1988, LLA, A.579.21. The letter which Lowenthal wrote to Rosenzweig at that time is no longer extant. Lowenthal later claimed that the return of the letter had been "a very traumatic shock", and that he "probably tore it up" [Leo Lowenthal to Paul Mendes-Flohr, May 23, 1988, LLA, A.579.5].
129 At a later point, however, Rosenzweig, who was dying of amyotrophic lateral sclerosis, let it be known to Lowenthal via an intermediary that he would like to see Lowenthal one more time. Lowenthal acceded to this request, and went to visit Rosenzweig, who, by that point in his illness, could no longer speak [Leo Lowenthal to Paul Mendes-Flohr, May 23, 1988, LLA, A.579.5]. Rosenzweig died in December 1929. Lowenthal's final judgment of Rosenzweig was that he had had an "autocratic personality" but had been a "great man" and "generous enough" to have invited Lowenthal into his home despite the fact that Lowenthal had hurt him.
130 Leo Lowenthal to Paul Mendes-Flohr, May 23, 1988, LLA, A.579.5.
131 Ernst Simon sided with Rosenzweig and Buber in this dispute [Ernst Simon to Siegfried Kracauer, May 7, 1926, Siegfried Kracauer Nachlass, 72.2971/1, Deutsches Literaturarchiv, Schiller-Nationalmuseum, Marbach am Neckar; Ernst Simon to Siegfried Kracauer, May 17, 1926, Siegfried Kracauer Nachlass, 72.2971/2; Siegfried Kracauer to Ernst Simon, May 12, 1926, and May 21, 1926, Ernst Simon Papers, Jerusalem; Cf. Jay, "Politics of Translation: Siegfried Kracauer and Walter Benjamin on the Buber-Rosenzweig Bible," pp. 209–211. Jay did not have access to the letters from Kracauer to Simon cited above]. Did Simon's position strain his friendship with Lowenthal? There are no extant letters between Lowenthal and Simon dating from this period.
132 Gershom Scholem, *Briefe*, I, 1914–1947, ed. Itta Shedletzky (Munich: Verlag C. H. Beck, 1994), p. 400.
133 Wiggershaus mistakenly claims that Fromm co-edited the *Wochenblatt* with Simon [Wiggershaus, *The Frankfurt School*, p. 666]. Scholem, who had already immigrated to Palestine by the time Simon and Lowenthal took over the paper, sharply criticized the periodical as having three flaws – "it is dumb, not clear, and intellectual." Scholem was particularly unhappy about what he perceived as the periodical's support for Mizrachi, and advised Simon to drop his position and come to Palestine [Gershom Scholem to Ernst Simon, January 24, 1925, in Scholem, *Briefe*, I, pp. 223–225].
134 Lowenthal, "I Never Wanted to Play Along," p. 24.
135 Ernst Simon to Felix Rosenblüth, December 11, 1925, transcript in the Ernst Simon Papers, Leo Baeck Institute, Jerusalem, quoted, in part, in Ernst A. Simon, *Sechzig Jahre gegen den Strom. Briefe von 1917–1984*. Schriftenreihe

wissenschaftlicher Abhandlungen des Leo-Baeck-Instituts, 59 (Tübingen: J. C. B. Mohr [Paul Siebeck], 1998), p. 25. Simon also noted in this letter that the official position of the periodical on Zionism notwithstanding, he attempted to accentuate the matter of Palestine as strongly as possible in its pages, and that he had had to struggle in order to do so.

136 Golde Löwenthal, "Der Traum des jüdischen Schusterjungen," *Jüdisches Wochenblatt*, II, 3 (January 16, 1925), p. 26; Golde Löwenthal, "Die Reise nach England," *Jüdisches Wochenblatt*, II, 5 (January 30, 1925), p. 53; Golde Löwenthal, "Der Sabbath der Natur," *Jüdisches Wochenblatt*, II, 8 (February 20, 1925), p. 89; Golde Löwenthal, "Der gestohlene Afikaumen," *Jüdisches Wochenblatt*, II, 15 (April 8, 1925), p. 176; Golde Löwenthal, "Der Mond," *Jüdisches Wochenblatt*, II, 37 (September 18, 1925), p. 401. She also contributed a non-fictional piece for children on the significance of Chanukah [G(olde) L(öwenthal), "Die Bedeutung des Chanukkahfestes," *Jüdisches Wochenblatt*, II, 48 (December 11, 1925), p. 520].

137 L[eo] L[öwenthal], "Philosophisches," *Jüdisches Wochenblatt*, II, 9, (February 27, 1925), p. 100; L[eo] L[öwenthal], "Ein Heinrich Heine-Film," *Jüdisches Wochenblatt*, II, 24 (June 19, 1925), p. 267; L[eo] L[öwenthal], "Potasch und Perlmutter," *Jüdisches Wochenblatt*, II, 25 (June 26, 1925), p. 277; L[eo] L[öwenthal], "Jüdische Erzähler," *Jüdisches Wochenblatt*, II, 27 (July 10, 1925), p. 300; L[eo] L[öwenthal], "Einer von unsere Leut'," *Jüdisches Wochenblatt*, II, 28 (July 17, 1925), pp. 307–308; L[eo] L[öwenthal], "Doktor Stieglitz," *Jüdisches Wochenblatt*, II, 28 (July 17, 1925), p. 308; L[eo] L[öwenthal], "Eine Dostojewsky-Biographie," *Jüdisches Wochenblatt*, II, 33 (August 21, 1925), p. 359; L[eo] L[öwenthal], "Die große Passion," *Jüdisches Wochenblatt*, II, 35 (September 4, 1925), p. 380; L[eo] L[öwenthal], "Die Jagd Gottes," *Jüdisches Wochenblatt*, III, 4 (January 22, 1926), pp. 30–31.

138 L[eo] L[öwenthal], "Das Konzessionsgesetz in Polen," *Jüdisches Wochenblatt*, II, 23 (June 12, 1925), p. 257; L[eo] L[öwenthal], "Die Lage der Juden in Polen," *Jüdisches Wochenblatt*, II, 26 (July 3, 1925), pp. 287–288.

139 Haereticus [Leo Löwenthal], "Die Lehren von China," *Jüdisches Wochenblatt*, II, 25 (June 26, 1925), p. 279.

140 As quoted in Lowenthal, "I Never Wanted to Play Along," p. 113.

141 Ernst Simon to Martin Buber [June 7, 1925], Martin Buber Archive, 730:45, Jerusalem. Simon also inquired as to whether Buber would be willing to recommend Lowenthal to those seeking lecturers and essayists, so that Lowenthal would still have an income after he ceased working for the *Wochenblatt*.

142 The summary of "Die Lehren von China" provided by Lowenthal to Dubiel ["I referred to contemporary events in China and wrote that dealings of these organizations with the rich Arab landowners would result in the creation of a great mass of discontented, landless Palestinian peasants and rural poor, a development that sooner or later would have negative consequences for the entire Zionist movement" (Lowenthal, "I Never Wanted to Play Along," p. 25)], was obviously an extemporaneous one, rather than one based on a recent re-reading by Lowenthal of his text.

143 The following section on Reichmann and the sanatorium she created draws heavily on Ursula Engel, "Das Heidelberger 'Thorapeutikum'," *PsA-Info*, 30 (1988), pp. 4–16, on Reinhard Blomert, "Das vergessene Sanatorium," *Jüdisches Leben in Heidelberg. Studien zu einer unterbrochenen Geschichte*, ed. Norbert Giovannini, Jo-Hannes Bauer, and Hans-Martin Mumm, Heidelberg: Wunderhorn, 1992, pp. 249–262; and on Ursula Engel, "Vom 'Thorapeutikum' nach Chestnut Lodge. Frieda Fromm-Reichmann (1889–1957)," *Psychoanalyse in Frankfurt am Main: zerstörte Anfänge, Wiederannäherung, Entwicklungen*, ed. Tomas Plänkers, Michael Laier, Hans-Heinrich Otto, Hans-Joachim Rothe, and Helmut Siefert (Tübingen: Edition Diskord, 1996, pp. 141–152).

144 Frieda Fromm-Reichmann, autobiographical interview, circa 1954, transcript in Erich-Fromm-Archiv, Tübingen, p. 12.

145 Frieda Fromm-Reichmann, "Reminiscences of Europe," *Psychoanalysis and Psychosis*, ed. Ann-Louise S. Silver (Madison, CT: International Universities Press, 1989), p. 479.

146 Leo Löwenthal, *Mitmachen wollte ich nie*, p. 27. The relevant sentence has been inexplicably left out of the published English translation of this passage. Fromm was already living in Heidelberg when Reichmann moved to that city [Blomert, "Das vergessene Sanatorium," p. 251].

147 Reichmann-Fromm broke off her analysis of Fromm when they fell in love with one another [Fromm-Reichmann, "Reminiscences of Europe," p. 480].

148 Ernst Simon, "Selbstdarstellung," pp. 307–308). Also see Walter Benjamin to Gerhard Scholem, July 7, 1924, in Walter Benjamin, *The Correspondence of Walter Benjamin 1910–1940*, ed. Gershom Scholem and Theodor W. Adorno (Chicago: University of Chicago Press, 1994), p. 245, suggesting that Simon was in Heidelberg between April and July 1924 (if not longer). Simon ended his analysis in the Autumn of 1924, under pressure from his fiancé, Toni Rapaport [Simon, *Sechzig Jahre gegen den Strom*, p. 171]. In the course of conversations that I had with Toni Simon in 1997, in her home in Jerusalem, she informed me that she had told Ernst that she would not marry him if he remained in analysis. Toni and Ernst Simon married in 1925.

149 Ernst Simon, "Erinnerungen an Erich Fromm," Stadtarchiv, Frankfurt am Main, S/8101.

150 Ernst Simon, "Erinnerungen an Erich Fromm." I follow here the translation provided by Wiggershaus, *The Frankfurt School*, p. 54. Kracauer was in Heidelberg for business in July 1924, spoke with Golde Löwenthal, Fromm, and Simon while he was there, and probably visited the sanatorium at that time [Siegfried Kracauer to Leo Löwenthal, July 28, 1924, *In steter Freundschaft*, pp. 59–60]. Kracauer planned to spend a four-week period at the sanatorium. However, in the sole meeting Kracauer had with Reichmann, she informed Kracauer that he knew too much about Freud, and was too skeptical about Freud, for her to conduct a psychoanalysis of him [Siegfried Kracauer to Marianne Kamnitzer, October 26, 1960, quoted in Belke and Renz, "Siegfried Kracauer 1889–1966," p. 41].

151 Lowenthal, "I Never Wanted to Play Along," p. 26. Writing to Paul Mendes-Flohr of Hebrew University about Reichmann's clinic at a later point in time,

Lowenthal added that "There was, of course, nothing specific[ally] Jewish in her psychoanalytical technique. I couldn't even fathom what this could mean.... I do not any longer know the address of the house (it was indeed a whole house), and I cannot exactly tell you how many people lived there at the same time. I stayed there for a while with my wife who also helped Frieda in the management of the house..." [Leo Lowenthal to Paul Mendes-Flohr, March 2, 1988, LLA, A.579.4].

152 Scholem, *From Berlin to Jerusalem*, p. 156. In a letter to Mendes-Flohr, Lowenthal commented that a pun like Torah-peuticum was "not very enlightening" and that the passage in which Scholem described the clinic was "typical Scholem. It is witty but supercilious" [Leo Lowenthal to Paul Mendes-Flohr, May 23, 1988, LLA, A.579.5].

153 Scholem, *From Berlin to Jerusalem*, p. 156.

154 Frieda Fromm-Reichmann, autobiographical interview, p. 15; Reichmann herself left Germany in 1933. After a brief period in Palestine, where she lived in the household of the prominent Hebrew-language writer Shmuel Agnon (to whose spouse Fromm-Reichmann was related), she went on to the United States [Eran J. Rolnik, *Freud in Zion. Psychoanalysis and the Making of Modern Jewish Identity*. The History of Psychoanalysis Series (London: Karnac, 2012), p. 23].

155 Leo Lowenthal to Paul Mendes-Flohr, May 23, 1988, LLA, A.579.5.

156 Lowenthal, "As I Remember Friedel," p. 9.

157 Leo Löwenthal, "Moses Mendelssohn und der deutsche Geist," *Frankfurter Israelitisches Gemeindeblatt*, VIII, 1 (September 1929), pp. 7–9; Löwenthal, "Die jüdische Religionsphilosophie Hermann Cohens," *Frankfurter Israelitisches Gemeindeblatt*, VIII, 9 (May 1930), pp. 357–359; Leo Löwenthal, "Judentum und deutscher Geist, I. Salomon Maimon," *Bayerische Israelitische Gemeindezeitung*, VI, 14 (July 15, 1930), pp. 217–219; Leo Löwenthal, "Judentum und deutscher Geist, II. Sigmund Freud," *Bayerische Israelitische Gemeindezeitung*, VI, 19 (October 1, 1930), pp. 299–300; Leo Löwenthal, "Judentum und deutscher Geist, III. Ferdinand Lassalle," *Bayerische Israelitische Gemeindezeitung*, VII, 16 (August 15, 1931), pp. 245–247. Also see Ludwig Feuchtwanger [Bayerische Israelitische Gemeindezeitung] to Leo Löwenthal, January 7, 1930, LLA, in which Feuchtwanger discussed the series of articles to be written by Lowenthal, and in which he proposed that Lowenthal submit articles not only on Maimon, Freud, and Lassalle but also on Heine, Börne, Moses Hess, Karl Marx, and Hermann Cohen. Lowenthal also wrote on a non-Jewish writer for the Jewish press: Leo Löwenthal, "Tolstoi und die Judenfrage," *Frankfurter Israelitisches Gemeindeblatt*, VII, 11 (July 1929), pp. 381–383.

158 Lowenthal, "Ferdinand Lassalle and Karl Marx," *Critical Theory and Frankfurt Theorists*, p. 32.

159 Lowenthal, "Sigmund Freud," *Critical Theory and Frankfurt Theorists*, p. 45.

160 Lowenthal, "I Never Wanted to Play Along," pp. 28, 29.

161 Feliks Weil to Martin Jay, June 1, 1969, as quoted in Jay, *Dialectical Imagination*, p. 32.

162 Gershom Scholem, "Jews and Germans," *On Jews and Judaism in Crisis. Selected Essays*, ed. Werner J. Dannhauser (New York: Schocken Books, 1976), p. 89.
163 For one example among many of a memoir corroborating Lowenthal's perspective, see the work of Selmar Spier, a Jew who lived in Frankfurt until early in 1936, who has described Frankfurt as a tolerant city in the pre-Nazi era, and as one in which those who lived there were willing to make compromises in order to get along with others [Selmar Spier, *Vor 1914. Erinnerungen an Frankfurt geschrieben in Israel* (Frankfurt am Main: Verlag Waldemar Kramer, 1961), p. 36].
164 See Ludwig Feuchtwanger to Leo Löwenthal, June 9, 1931, LLA, and the article by Löwenthal on Marx, which was published in the issue of the *Bayerische Israelitische Gemeindezeitung* dated April 1, 1932.
165 Jay, *Dialectical Imagination*, p. 25. The core members of the Institute, like Lowenthal, accepted Horkheimer's dominant position as positive and necessary. Similarly, Rosenzweig was once described as a "dictator" by someone particularly close to him. Cf. Brenner, *The Renaissance of Jewish Culture*, p. 82.
166 Lowenthal, "I Never Wanted to Play Along," p. 112.
167 On Fromm's Jewish antecedents and involvements, and on his relationship to Judaism, see Rainer Funk, "Von der jüdischen zur psychologischen Seelenlehre. Erich Fromms Weg von der einen über die andere Frankfurter Schule," *Das Freie Jüdische Lehrhaus – ein andere Frankfurter Schule*, ed. Raimund Sesterhenn. Schriftenreihe der Katholische Akademie der Erzdioezese Freiburg (Munich, Zurich: Verlag Schnell und Steiner, 1987), pp. 91–108; Rainer Funk, "The Jewish Roots of Erich Fromm's Humanistic Thinking," *Symposium. Erich Fromm. Life and Work. Locarno May 12–14, 1988. Centro didattico cantonale* (International Erich Fromm Society: Tübingen, [1988]); Jochack Shapira, "Fromm and Judaism," *Incontro con Erich Fromm. Atti del Simposio Internazionale su Erich Fromm: "Dalla necrofilia alla biofilia: linee per una psicoanalisi umanistica". Firenze, novembre 1986 – Palazzo Vecchio* (Firenze: Edizioni medicea, 1988, pp. 223–235); Zoltan Tarr and Judith Marcus, "Erich Fromm und das Judentum," *Erich Fromm und die Frankfurter Schule. Akten des internationalen, interdisziplinären Symposions Stuttgart-Hohenheim, 31.5. – 2.6.1991*, ed. Michael Kessler and Rainer Funk (Tübingen: Francke Verlag), 1992, pp. 211–220; Löwy, *Redemption and Utopia*, pp. 150–158; and Svante Lundgren, *Fight Against Idols. Erich Fromm on Religion, Judaism and the Bible* (Frankfurt am Main: Peter Lang, 1998).
168 See Funk, *Erich Fromm mit Selbstzeugnissen und Bilddokumenten*, for additional details on Fromm's family background.
169 Funk, "Von der jüdischen zur psychologischen Seelenlehre. Erich Fromms Weg von der einen über die andere Frankfurter Schule," pp. 96–97. An article signed "Achad ha'talmidim" [One of the students] and entitled "Rabbiner Nobel als Führer der Jugend," was published in *Neue Jüdische Presse* on February 2, 1922, p. 3. The article reads, in part, "[T]hat which compelled us was not the fact that he knew, but rather this: that he practiced

what he preached and only preached what he practiced ... He was a poet – and thus was able to make us understand that the paths of Torah are paths of beauty. He taught love as the force uniting the people – and we understood – because he loved us. Humbly he cried for prophets – and in mourning we cry for the leader" [Heuberger, *Rabbi Nehemiah Anton Nobel. The Jewish Renaissance in Frankfurt am Main*, p. 85]. A copy of this article owned by the Leo Baeck Institute in New York contains a handwritten notation reading "Erich Fromm." Though the source of this notation is unknown, the attribution of "Rabbiner Nobel als Führer der Jugend" to Fromm has been widely accepted.

170 Salzberger, *Leben un Lehre*, p. 98.
171 Ibid., p. 103; Erich Fromm to Martin Jay, May 14, 1971, "Ein Memorandum in eigener Sache," *Erich Fromm und die Frankfurter Schule*, p. 250. Fromm not only taught in the Lehrhaus, but studied in it as well: he participated in a course on the Zohar given by Gershom Scholem [Glatzer, "The Frankfort Lehrhaus," p. 114; Scholem, *From Berlin to Jerusalem*, p. 156].
172 Brenner, *The Renaissance of Jewish Culture*, p. 88.
173 I. Nathan Bamberger, "A Note on Erich Fromm's Rabbinic Roots," *Tradition*, XXIX, 3 (1995), p. 52.
174 Eric Fromm to Karl D. Darmstadter, March 3, 1966, Erich Fromm Papers, New York Public Library, Box 25.
175 Funk, "The Jewish Roots of Erich Fromm's Humanistic Thinking," p. 2.
176 Erich Fromm, "Zur Tagung der Agudas-Jisroel-Jugendorganisation," *Der Jüdische Student. Zeitschrift des Kartells Jüdischer Verbindungen*, XV, 5/6 (November 1918), pp. 80–81.
177 Erich Fromm, "V. J. St. Achduth, Frankfurt a. M.," *Der Jüdische Student*, XVI, 3 (May 1919), p. 107; "Der Kartelltag," *Der Jüdische Student*, XVI, 8 (December 1919), p. 325. Scholem reports that a humorous pun, "Gebet der kleinen K.J.V.er" [Prayer of the little KJVer] circulated among Zionist students in the early 1920s: "Mach mich wie den Erich Fromm/Dass ich in den Himmel komm" [Gershom Scholem, *Walter Benjamin. The Story of a Friendship*, trans. Harry Zohn (New York: Schocken Books, 1981), p. 117]. Fromm's involvement in the KJV is also noted in a memoir by Bruno Ostrovsky [Monika Richarz, ed., *Jüdisches Leben in Deutschland*, III. Selbstzeugnisse zur Sozialgeschichte, 1918–1945 (Stuttgart: DVA, 1982), p. 195].
178 "V. J. St. 'Ivria', Heidelberg," *Der Jüdische Student*, XVII, 4 (August–September, 1920), p. 197.
179 *Mitteilungen der jüdisch-nationalen Jugendorganisationen in Frankfurt am Main*, I, 1 (June 3, 1921); II, 16 (December 30, 1921). More than half a century later, Fromm asserted that he had denounced Jewish nationalism at a meeting of the Blau-Weiss when he was eighteen or nineteen years old, had asserted at that time that "This Jewish nationalism is not a bit better than the National-Socialism" and had left thereafter. However, the historical record does not confirm Fromm's account [Lundgren, *Fight Against Idols. Erich Fromm on Religion, Judaism and the Bible*, p. 106].
180 Erich Fromm, *Das jüdische Gesetz. Zur Soziologie des Diaspora-Judentums. Dissertation von 1922*, ed. Rainer Funk and Bernd Sahler. Schriften aus dem

Nachlaß, II (Weinheim and Basel: Beltz, 1989). Also see David Groiser, "Jewish Law and Tradition in the Early Work of Erich Fromm," *The Early Frankfurt School and Religion*, ed. Margarete Kohlenbach and Raymond Geuss (Houndmills, Basingstoke, Hampshire: Palgrave Macmillan, 2005), pp. 128–144.
181 Fromm, *Das jüdische Gesetz*, pp. 70–83.
182 *Ibid.*, p. 134.
183 *Ibid.*, p. 113.
184 Franz Rosenzweig to Joseph Prager, October 6, 1922 [Rosenzweig, *Briefe*, p. 446].
185 Abraham L. Udovitch, "Foreword," in S. D. Goitein, *A Mediterranean Society. The Jewish Communities of the Arab World as Portrayed in the Documents of the Cairo Geniza*, V: The Individual: Portrait of a Mediterranean Personality of the High Middle Ages as Reflected in the Cairo Geniza (Berkeley; Los, Angeles; London: University of California Press, 1988), p. xiv. My thanks to Prof. Harvey Goldberg of Hebrew University for making me aware of this source.
    Fromm later claimed that when he was in his early twenties, he had known Buber "quite well" [Erich Fromm to Karl D. Darmstadter, February 6, 1968, Erich Fromm Papers, Box 25, New York Public Library]. But however well he knew Buber, Fromm did not have particularly warm relations with Buber or, for that matter, with Scholem [Rainer Funk, "Von der jüdischen zur psychologischen Seelenlehre. Erich Fromms Weg von der einen über die andere Frankfurter Schule," p. 98]. Scholem's assertion that Fromm later became "an enthusiastic Trotskyite" [Scholem, *From Berlin to Jerusalem*, p. 156] is inaccurate.
186 Erich Fromm to Ernst Simon, November 29, 1925, Ernst Simon Papers, Jerusalem.
187 Frieda Fromm-Reichmann, autobiographical interview, pp. 12, 14.
188 *Ibid.*, p. 16. Reichmann delivered the talk which formed the basis for her article in December 1926 in Berlin at the German Psychoanalytic Society. It appeared in *Imago* under the title "Das jüdische Speiseritual" in 1927.
189 As quoted in Wiggershaus, *The Frankfurt School*, p. 54. Fromm broke, at some point, not only from observant Judaism but also from Zionism. It has been claimed that Fromm "repudiated" his earlier Zionist beliefs in 1927 [Burston, *The Legacy of Erich Fromm*, p. 12].
190 Lowenthal, "I Never Wanted to Play Along," p. 51.
191 Funk, *Erich Fromm mit Selbstzeugnissen und Bilddokumenten*, p. 14.
192 Erich Fromm, "Some Biographical Notes," *In the Name of Life. Essays in Honor of Erich Fromm*, Bernard Landis and Edward S. Tauber, eds. (New York: Rinehart and Winston, 1971), p. xi.
193 Erich Fromm, *You Shall be as Gods. A Radical Interpretation of the Old Testament and Its Tradition* (New York: Holt, Rinehart and Winston), pp. 12–13.
194 Bühler, *Erziehung zur Tradition*, p. 29.
195 Fromm provided different dates at different times: Erich Fromm, "Memories of Rav Zalman Boruch Rabinkow," Erich-Fromm-Archiv; Erich Fromm to Leo Jung, June 10, 1970, Erich-Fromm-Archiv.

196 Erich Fromm to C. A. Goldschmidt, November 18, 1966, Erich Fromm Papers, Box 25, New York Public Library. Fromm was in Munich during parts of 1925, and noted at the end of that year that he had not seen Rabinkow for many months [Erich Fromm to Ernst Simon, November 29, 1925, Ernst Simon Papers, Jerusalem].
197 Fromm reports that Rabinkow also spoke of Eugen Leviné, a leader of the German Spartacists and head of the Munich Soviet in 1919, "with deep sympathy", and that Rabinkow apparently knew someone who knew Leviné well [Erich Fromm to Ernst Simon, July 21, 1973, Ernst Simon Papers, Leo Baeck Institute, Jerusalem].
198 Erich Fromm to Karl D. Darmstadter, November 18, 1966, Erich Fromm Papers, Box 25, New York Public Library.
199 Erich Fromm to Karl D. Darmstadter, September 15, 1972. Erich Fromm Papers, Box 25, New York Public Library.
200 On Rabinkow, cf. Schacter, "Reminiscences of Shlomo Barukh Rabinkow," pp. 93ff.; Peter Honigmann, "Der Heidelberger Talmudistenkreis um Salman Baruch Rabinkow. Aus Anlass von Rabinkows 50. Todestag am 28. Mai 1991," *Frankfurter Jüdische Nachrichten* (March/April 1991), pp. 38–39; Peter Honigmann, "Jüdische Studenten zwischen Orthodoxie und moderner Wissenschaft. Der Heidelberger Talmudistenkreis um Salman Baruch Rabinkow," *Menora. Jahrbuch für deutsch-jüdische Geschichte* (1992), pp. 85–96.
201 Honigmann, "Jüdische Studenten zwischen Orthodoxie und moderner Wissenschaft," p. 89.
202 Comments by Fritz Gumpertz in Schacter, "Reminiscences of Shlomo Barukh Rabinkow," p. 114.
203 *Ibid.*, p. 101.
204 *Ibid.*, p. 102.
205 *Ibid.*, p. 103. Also see Erich Fromm to T. E. Rabinkow-Rothbard, July 9, 1964, Erich-Fromm-Archiv.
206 Fromm, *You Shall be as Gods*, p. 14.
207 Marcus and Tar, "The Judaic Elements in the Teachings of the Frankfurt School," p. 344.
208 The following information on Grossmann draws heavily on an unpublished paper by Rick Kuhn, "Henryk Grossman in Galicia." My thanks to Professor Kuhn for providing me with a copy of his work. An earlier (but not necessarily more accurate) source indicates that Grossmann was born in 1882 [Zalmen Reyzen, *Leksikon fun der yidisher literatur, prese un filologie*, I (Vilna: Farlag fun b. kletskin, 1926), p. 616].
209 Kuhn, *Henryk Grossman and the Recovery of Marxism*, pp. 17–18.
210 For additional information on the ŻPSD see Y[ankef] Bros, "Tsu der geshikhte fun der i.s.d.p. in galitsie," in *Royter pinkes. tsu der geshikhte fun der yidisher arbeter-bavegung un sotsialistisher shtremungen bay yidn*, II (Warsaw: Farlag kultur lige, 1924), pp. 22–48; V[iktor] Shulman, "25 yor. tsum yobiley fun der yidisher s. d. partay in galitsie ('galitsianer bund') 1-ter may 1905–30," *Naye folkstsaytung* (April 30 1930), p. 5, Yoysef Kisman, "Di yidishe sotsial-demokratishe bavegung in galitsie un bukovine," in

Di geshikhte fun bund, III, ed. G. Aronson, S. Dubnow-Erlich [Dubnov-erlikh], J. S. Hertz [I. Sh. Herts], E. Nowogrudski [Novogrudski], Kh. Sh. Kazdan, and E. Scherer [Sherer] (New York: Farlag unzer tsayt, 1966), pp. 369–482; Feliks Gutman, "An araynfir-vort in shaykhes mit der antshteyung un antviklung fun z.p.s.d. bizn yor 1911," typescript, Bund Archives of the Jewish Labor Movement [henceforth: Bund Archives], YIVO Institute for Jewish Research [New York], and Rick Kuhn, "Organizing Yiddish-Speaking Workers in Pre-World War I Galicia: The Jewish Social Democratic Party," *Yiddish Language and Culture. Then and Now*, ed. Leonard Jay Greenspoon. Studies in Jewish Civilization, IX (Omaha, NE: Creighton University Press, 1998), pp. 37–63.

211 For information on the reply by the executive of the *Gesamtpartei* to this invitation see Jack Jacobs, *On Socialists and "the Jewish Question" after Marx* (New York and London: New York University Press, 1992), p. 92.

212 Henryk Grossmann to Victor Adler, October 23, 1905, Adler-Archiv, Mappe 176, Verein für Geschichte der Arbeiterbewegung [Vienna].

213 H[enryk] Grossman[n], "Vegen unzere agitatsie un propaganda," in *Der sotsial-demokrat. Organ fun di yudishe sotsial-demokratishe partay in galitsien*, II, 33 (August 24, 1906), pp. 2–3; 36 (September 14, 1906), pp. 2–3. H[enryk] Grossman[n], "Der bundizm in galitsien," in *Der sotsial-demokrat*, III, 37 (September 13, 1907), pp. 2–3; 38 (September 20, 1907), pp. 1–2; 39 (September 27, 1907), pp. 2–3; 40 (October 4, 1907), pp. 2–3; 44 (November 8, 1907), pp. 1–2; 46 (November 22, 1907), pp. 1–2; 47 (November 29, 1907), pp. 1–2. The articles on Bundism in Galicia were published in pamphlet form both in Yiddish and in Polish.

214 Kuhn, "Henryk Grossman in Galicia," p. 18.

215 Bund Archives, MG 2 #130. I have discussed the work of the Lassalle Verein in "Written Out of History. Bundists in Vienna and the Varieties of Jewish Experience in the Austrian First Republic," in *In Search of Jewish Community. Jewish Identities in Germany and Austria, 1918–1933*, ed. Michael Brenner and Derek J. Penslar (Bloomington and Indianapolis: Indiana University Press, 1998), pp. 115–133.

216 Kuhn, *Henryk Grossman and the Recovery of Marxism*, pp. 73, 244.

217 *Ibid.*, pp. 83, 248.

218 In the altogether different climate of eastern Germany in the late 1940s, at which time Grossmann became a professor of political economy at the University of Leipzig, he chose to list himself as "without religion" rather than as Jewish on a questionnaire. He also chose, when preparing c.v.s for the university, not to list his leadership positions in the ŻPSD (while listing other political memberships, such as his one-time affiliation with the Polish Communist Party) [Kuhn, *Henryk Grossman and the Recovery of Marxism*, pp. 215, 216]. Grossmann evinced no interest in Jewish matters in the last decades of his life.

219 Reijen and Schmid Noerr, *Grand Hotel Abgrund*, p. 48.

220 By the end of the Weimar years, I hasten to add, there were virtually no individuals of Jewish origin still prominent in the KPD's top ranks. None of

the Reichstag deputies elected on the Communist Party ticket in 1932 were Jewish [Henry M. Pachter, Letter to the editor, *Commentary*, LI, 3, March 1971, p. 34].
221 Istvan Deak, *Weimar Germany's Left-Wing Intellectuals. A Political History of the Weltbühne and Its Circle* (Berkeley and Los Angeles: University of California Press, 1968), p. 24.
222 Isaac Deutscher, *The Non-Jewish Jew and other Essays*, ed. Tamara Deutscher (New York: Hill and Wang, 1968), pp. 25–41.
223 Mosse, *Germans and Jews*, p. 207.
224 Deak, *Weimar Germany's Left-Wing Intellectuals*, p. 24.
225 George L. Mosse, *German Jews beyond Judaism* (Bloomington: Indiana University Press; Cincinnati: Hebrew Union College Press, 1985), pp. 61–62. Also see Steven E. Aschheim, *Culture and Catastrophe. German and Jewish Confrontations with National Socialism and Other Crises* (Houndmills, Basingstoke, Hampshire: Macmillan, 1996), pp. 31–44, which accepts certain of Mosse's insights, and which also insightfully critiques other portions of Mosse's work, and Steven E. Aschheim, *In Times of Crisis. Essays on European Culture, Germans, and Jews* (Madison: The University of Wisconsin Press, 2001), pp. 168–169. Despite Aschheim's criticisms of Mosse, he generally believes, as he made clear in the course of a conversation with me in 1997, that the lives and thought of core members of the Frankfurt School tend to confirm rather than to undermine Mosse's thesis.
226 Lowenthal did so in the course of a visit that he made to Israel in 1985. During that visit, Steven E. Aschheim, who had never previously met Lowenthal, went to hear a lecture given by Lowenthal in Jerusalem and sponsored by the Van Leer Foundation. In a discussion following Lowenthal'a talk, a question concerning the Frankfurt School's Jewishness was raised, and Aschheim (following Mosse) noted the link between *Bildung* and the Jewishness of German Jews. Lowenthal, who had apparently never thought about the matter in quite that way before, replied that Aschheim had just given him an *Erlebnis*, and that Lowenthal felt that, as a result of Aschheim's remark, he now understood something he could previously not have articulated [E-mail messages of Steven E. Aschheim to Jack Jacobs, August 19, 2010, and January 29, 2011].
227 My use of constellation imagery, and my identification of Jewish identity as one star in the constellation under consideration, is derived from Jay, *Adorno*, pp. 14ff.
228 Jay, *Dialectical Imagination*, p. 32.
229 Quoted and translated in Claussen, *Theodor W. Adorno. One Last Genius*, p. 3.
230 Deutscher, *The Non-Jewish Jew and other Essays*, p. 26.
231 Scholem, *From Berlin to Jerusalem*, p. 131.
232 Like Wittfogel, Feliks Weil (1898–1975) left Frankfurt for Berlin in 1929. Weil worked in Berlin with several publishing ventures, and with a radical theater, and moved back to Argentina (where his family's business was based) in 1930. Though he contributed financially to the Institute both before

and after he left Germany, he was not closely involved with the Institute's academic work during the period under discussion [Jay, *Dialectical Imagination*, p. 24].

Chapter 2

1 Werner E. Mosse, "German Jews: Citizens of the Republic," *Die Juden im nationalsozialistischen Deutschland. The Jews in Nazi Germany. 1933–1943*, ed. Arnold Paucker with Sylvia Gilchrist and Barbara Suchy. Schriftenreihe wissenschaftlicher Abhandlungen des Leo-Baeck-Instituts, 45 (Tübingen: J. C. B. Mohr [Paul Siebeck], 1986, p. 52).
2 Lowenthal, "I Never Wanted to Play Along," pp. 53–55; Jay, *The Dialectical Imagination*, pp. 29, 37; Wiggershaus, *The Frankfurt School*, pp. 110; 127–128.
3 Barry Kātz, *Herbert Marcuse and the Art of Liberation. An Intellectual Biography* (London: Verso, 1982), pp. 86, 87. Marcuse joined the Institute as of January 30, 1933 [Wiltrud Mannfeld, "Fragen an Herbert Marcuse. Ein Interview zu seiner Biographie," *Befreiung denken – Ein politischer Imperativ*, ed. Peter-Erwin Jansen, 2nd edition (Offenbach: Verlag 2000 GmbH, 1990), p. 34], the date on which Hitler was appointed Chancellor of Germany (and the date on which the house in the suburbs of Frankfurt in which Horkheimer and Pollock had resided was occupied by the Nazis and converted by them into barracks) [Wiggershaus, *The Frankfurt School*, p. 127].
4 Wiggershaus, *The Frankfurt School*, p. 143; Wheatland, *The Frankfurt School in Exile*, pp. 31–32. Müller-Doohm reports that the decision to leave Europe was made "above all because [Horkheimer] feared the outbreak of a European war" [Müller-Doohm, *Adorno*, p. 196]. Lowenthal, on the other hand, flatly proclaims "at that time we still did not anticipate a war" [Lowenthal, "I Never Wanted to Play Along," p. 56].
5 Lowenthal, "I Never Wanted to Play Along," p. 56.
6 Helmut Dubiel in Lowenthal, "I Never Wanted to Play Along," p. 27.
7 Wiggershaus, *The Frankfurt School*, pp. 146–148. Erich Fromm was in Switzerland for a significant portion of the years 1932–1934, but he was only rarely able to work at the Institute in Geneva during that period. He fell ill with tuberculosis in the summer of 1931, and lived primarily in Davos during the era in question [Rainer Funk, *Erich Fromm. His Life and Ideas. An Illustrated Biography*, trans. Ian Portman and Manuela Kunkel (New York, London: Continuum, 2000), pp. 74–77]. Grossmann spent several years in London and Paris after the Nazis came to power. He too, however, eventually went to the United States, arriving in 1937 [Jay, *The Dialectical Imagination*, p. 151].
8 Douglas Kellner, "The Frankfurt School Revisited: A Critique of Martin Jay's *The Dialectical Imagination*," *The Frankfurt School. Critical Assessments*, ed. Jay Bernstein, vol. I (London and New York: Routledge, 1994), pp. 44, 50.
9 Helmut Dubiel, *Theory and Politics. Studies in the Development of Critical Theory*, trans. Benjamin Gregg (Cambridge, MA; London: MIT Press, 1985), p. 105.
10 Martin Jay, "The Jews and the Frankfurt School: Critical Theory's Analysis of Antisemitism," *Permanent Exiles*, pp. 90–100.

11 Wiggershaus reports that the text of this article was finished at the end of 1938 [Wiggershaus, *The Frankfurt School*, p. 257]. Horkheimer edited and amended his work during the course of the following year [Max Horkheimer to Katharina von Hirsch, July 14, 1939, Max Horkheimer, *Gesammelte Schriften*, XVI, ed. Gunzelin Schmid Noerr (Frankfurt am Main: Fischer Taschenbuch Verlag, 1995), p. 614; Max Horkheimer to Leo Lowenthal, July 20, 1939, Horkheimer, *Gesammelte Schriften*, XVI, pp. 618–619.].
12 According to Gershom Scholem, basing himself on information he obtained directly from Adorno, the title was suggested by Adorno and not by Horkheimer [Scholem, *Walter Benjamin*. p. 224].
13 Max Horkheimer, "The Jews and Europe," *Critical Theory and Society. A Reader*, ed. Stephen Eric Bronner and Douglas MacKay Kellner (New York, London: Routledge, 1989), p. 77.
14 K[arl] A. Wittfogel, "The History of Prehistoric China," *Zeitschrift für Sozialforschung*, VIII, (1939–1940), pp. 138–186.
15 Mannfeld, "Fragen an Herbert Marcuse. Ein Interview zu seiner Biographie," p. 35.
16 Dan Diner, "Von Universellem und Partikularem: Max Horkheimer," *Kritische Theorie und Kultur*, ed. Rainer Erd, Dietrich Hoss, Otto Jacobi, and Peter Noller (Frankfurt am Main: Suhrkamp, 1989), p. 174.
17 Horkheimer, *Dawn & Decline*, pp. 42–43.
18 Horkheimer, "The Jews and Europe," p. 77.
19 *Ibid.*, p. 93.
20 Donald L. Niewyk, *The Jews in Weimar Germany* (Baton Rouge and London: Louisiana State University Press, 1980), pp. 175–176.
21 Yehuda Eloni, "German Zionism and the Rise to Power of National Socialism," *Studies in Zionism*, VI, 2 (1985), pp. 248ff.
22 *Ibid.* p. 89.
23 Enzo Traverso, *The Marxists and the Jewish Question. The History of a Debate (1843–1943)*, trans. Bernard Gibbons (Atlantic Highlands, NJ: Humanities Press, 1990), p. 183.
24 Horkheimer, "The Jews and Europe," p. 92.
25 Diner, "Reason and the 'Other': Horkheimer's Reflections on Anti-Semitism and Mass Annihilation," p. 337. Horkheimer, I would add, continued to write in such terms, from time to time, even after he had become aware of the extermination of much of European Jewry (though, to be sure, he did so in a more empathetic manner). See, for example, Max Horkheimer to Theodor W. Adorno, November 13, 1944, Max Horkheimer, *A Life in Letters. Selected Correspondence*, ed. Manfred R. Jacobson and Evelyn M. Jacobson (Lincoln, NE, and London: University of Nebraska Press, 2007), p. 224: "The best that could be said of the Jews is that they belong to the most liberal clique of entrepreneurs that is breaking up, or rather that they are precisely the ones on whom revenge is being exclusively taken for the sins of the clique."
26 Jay, *The Dialectical Imagination*, p. 133.
27 Horkheimer, "The Jews and Europe," p. 94.
28 *Ibid.*, p. 92.

29 Otto Heller, *Der Untergang des Judentums. Die Judenfrage. Ihre Kritik. Ihre Lösung durch den Sozialismus* (Vienna; Berlin: Verlag für Literatur und Politik, 1931), pp. 126–150.
30 Dubiel, *Theory and Politics*, p. 42; Horkheimer, *Gesammelte Schriften*, XVI, p. 619.
31 Horkheimer, "The Jews and Europe," pp. 78, 88. I derive my analysis of this issue from Wiggershaus, *The Frankfurt School*, pp. 257–258.
32 I disagree with Cramer's description of "The Jews and Europe" as the high point of Horkheimer's identification with Marxism [Cramer, *Hitlers Antisemitismus und die Frankfurter Schule*, p. 76]. By the time that he published "The Jews and Europe," Horkheimer was edging down from that high point.
33 Max Horkheimer to Hans Mayer, December 17, 1937, Horkheimer, *A Life in Letters*, p. 122.
34 Bahr, "The Anti-Semitism Studies of the Frankfurt School", p. 312.
35 Buckmiller, "Die 'Marxistische Arbeitswoche' 1923 und die Gründung des 'Instituts für Sozialforschung'," p. 155; Katharina von Hirsch to Max Horkheimer, July 24, 1939, Horkheimer, *Gesammelte Schriften*, XVI, p. 622; Horkheimer, *Gesammelte Schriften*, XVIII, p. 949.
36 Katharina von Hirsch to Max Horkheimer, July 24, 1939, Horkheimer, *Gesammelte Schriften*, XVI, pp. 622–623.
37 Horkheimer, *Gesammelte Schriften*, XVIII, p. 977.
38 Hans Mayer to Max Horkheimer, September 29, 1939, Horkheimer, *Gesammelte Schriften*, XVI, p. 637.
39 Reijen and Schmid Noerr, *Grand Hotel Abgrund*, p. 124.
40 Andries Sternheim to Max Horkheimer, March 24, 1940, *Gesammelte Schriften*, XVI, p. 707.
41 Siegfried Kracauer to Max Horkheimer, June 11, 1941, Siegfried Kracauer Nachlass, 72.1439/17, Deutsches Literaturarchiv, Schiller- Nationalmuseum, Marbach am Neckar.
42 Olga Lang to Max Horkheimer, April 15, 1940, Horkheimer, *Gesammelte Schriften*, XVI, p. 711.
43 Momme Brodersen, *Walter Benjamin. A Biography*, trans. Malcolm R. Green and Ingrida Ligers; ed. Martina Derviş (London and New York: Verso, 1996), pp. 212–215.
44 Brodersen, *Walter Benjamin. A Biography*, p. 224. Benjamin may have exacerbated his financial predicament, at some points, by gambling, and may also have exaggerated his financial precariousness [Howard Eiland and Michael W. Jennings, *Walter Benjamin. A Critical Life* (Cambridge, MA and London: The Belknap Press of Harvard University Press, 2014), p. 484] – but his situation was a very problematic one nevertheless.
45 Max Horkheimer to Walter Benjamin, February 23, 1939, Horkheimer, *Gesammelte Schriften*, XVI, p. 567.
46 Eiland and Jennings, *Walter Benjamin. A Critical Life*, p. 631; Walter Benjamin to Gerhard Scholem, March 14, 1939, *The Correspondence of Walter Benjamin and Gershom Scholem 1932–1940*, ed. Gershom Scholem; trans. Gary Smith and Andre Lefevere; intro. Anson Rabinbach (Cambridge, MA: Harvard University Press, 1992), p. 248.

47 Theodor W. Adorno to Walter Benjamin, July 15, 1939, Theodor W. Adorno and Walter Benjamin, *The Complete Correspondence 1928–1940*, ed. Henri Lonitz; trans. Nicholas Walker (Cambridge, MA: Harvard University Press, 1999), p. 313.
48 Walter Benjamin to Max Horkheimer, November 30, 1939, *The Correspondence of Walter Benjamin 1910–1940*, ed. Gershom Scholem and Theodor W. Adorno; trans. Manfred R. Jacobson and Evelyn M. Jacobson (Chicago and London: The University of Chicago Press, 1994), p. 619.
49 Anson Rabinbach, "Between Apocalypse and Enlightenment. Benjamin, Bloch, and Modern German-Jewish Messianism," *In the Shadow of Catastrophe. German Intellectuals between Apocalypse and Enlightenment* (Berkeley; Los Angeles; London: University of California Press, 1997), pp. 35–43; Susan A. Handelman, *Fragments of Redemption. Jewish Thought and Literary Theory in Benjamin, Scholem, and Levinas* (Bloomington and Indianapolis: Indiana University Press, 1991), pp. 3–173.
50 Walter Benjamin to Max Horkheimer, December 15, 1939, *The Correspondence of Walter Benjamin 1910–1940*, p. 622.
51 Walter Benjamin to Gretel Adorno, January 17, 1940, *The Correspondence of Walter Benjamin 1910–1940*, p. 627.
52 Walter Benjamin to Gerhard Scholem, January 11, 1940, in Walter Benjamin, *The Correspondence of Walter Benjamin 1910–1940*, p. 624.
53 Gerhard Scholem to Walter Benjamin, November 6–8, 1938, *The Correspondence of Walter Benjamin and Gershom Scholem 1932–1940*, pp. 235.
54 *Ibid.*, 235–236.
55 *Ibid.*, p. 236.
56 Scholem, *Walter Benjamin*, p. 222.
57 *Ibid.*, p. 223. Scholem's letter of February 1940 was apparently the last he wrote to Benjamin. He did not receive a reply to it (but suggests that Benjamin may well have written a response and that this response may have been lost in the mail). Benjamin committed suicide, in Spain, on September 25, 1940.
58 Brodersen, *Walter Benjamin. A Biography*, p. 247.
59 Theodor W. Adorno to Walter Benjamin, November 10, 1938, Adorno and Benjamin, *The Complete Correspondence 1928–1940*, p. 284.
60 The differences of opinion between Adorno and Benjamin are perceptively and thoroughly analyzed in Buck-Morss, *The Origin of Negative Dialectics*, pp. 136ff.
61 Walter Benjamin to Theodor W. Adorno, December 9, 1938, Adorno and Benjamin, *The Complete Correspondence 1928–1940*, p. 289.
62 Arendt, "Walter Benjamin: 1892–1940," p. 16.
63 Lowenthal, "I Never Wanted to Play Along," pp. 67–69; Lowenthal, "In Memory of Walter Benjamin: The Integrity of the Intellectual," p. 217: "I have spoken out with indignation against insinuations from some quarters concerning allegedly humiliating dependence and intellectual suppression in Benjamin's dealings with the Institute…", and Leo Lowenthal to Gershom Scholem, September 19, 1980, private collection, examined in the home of Mrs. Toni Simon, Jerusalem: "Not with one word … not even with the slightest intimation, was it suggested that Benjamin could lose his stipend.

None of us thought of such a thing. The money that was regularly sent by us was supposed to make his life in exile possible and not exclusively defined and intended as an honorarium for journal contributions." ["Mit keinem Wort ... wurde auch nur die leiseste Andeutung gemacht, daß Benjamin sein Stipendium verlieren könnte. An so etwas dachte niemand von uns. Das von uns regelmäßig geschickte Geld sollte sein Leben im Exil möglich machen und war nicht ausschließlich definiert und intendiert als ein Honorar für Zeitschriftenbeiträge."]

64 Gershom Scholem to George Lichtheim, October 21, 1968, Gershom Scholem, *Briefe*, II, 1948–1970, ed. Thoma Sparr (Munich: Verlag C. H. Beck, 1995), p. 214.

65 Scholem, *Walter Benjamin*, p. 216.

66 Buck-Morss, *The Origin of Negative Dialectics*, p. 153.

67 Scholem, *Walter Benjamin*, p. 217.

68 *Ibid.*, p. 222. Wolin finds the accusation, made by the editors of the periodical *Alternative* in the late 1960s, "that Benjamin's *financial* dependence on the Institute in the late 1930s also entailed an *intellectual* dependence" to be "scurrilous" [Richard Wolin, *Walter Benjamin. An Aesthetic of Redemption* (Berkeley; Los Angeles; London: University of California Press, 1994), p. 276]. The Institute did not demand that Benjamin follow a party line, and did not press him to become intellectually subservient. But Benjamin had good reason to curry favor with Horkheimer, and may well have done so in specific instances.

69 Gerhard Scholem to Theodor W. Adorno, April 15, 1940, Scholem, *Briefe*, I, p. 280.

70 G[erhard] Scholem to Theodor W. Adorno, October 28, 1943, Scholem, *Briefe*, I, p. 291.

71 Theodor W. Adorno, "Fragmente über Wagner," *Zeitschrift für Sozialforschung*, VIII (1939–1940), pp. 16–17.

72 Cf. Theodor W. Adorno to Max Horkheimer, August 10, 1939, Theodor W. Adorno and Max Horkheimer, *Briefwechsel*, II, ed. Christoph Gödde and Henri Lonitz, (Suhrkamp: Frankfurt am Main, 2004), p. 58, in which Adorno comments on a draft of Horkheimer's article. The language of several key passages in Horkheimer's article had been softened. "Daß mich jede Milderung brennt," Adorno writes, "versteht sich von selbst. Aber der Substanz des Aufsatzes ist kein leid geschehen." During this period, Adorno, like Horkheimer, remained committed to Marxism (of a particular kind): "Alle sagen, der Marxismus sei erledigt. Dem gegenüber sagen wir, nein, er ist nich erledigt, sondern es kommt darauf an, ihm die Treue zu halten. Aber wenn man ihm wirklich die Treue haelt, dann bedeutet das die Weiterbewegung des dialektischen Prozesses" ["Verhältnis zum Marxismus. Entwurf des 'Manifests' (II)," November 20, 1939, Horkheimer, *Gesammelte Schriften*, XII, (1985), p. 524].

73 Theodor W. Adorno to Max Horkheimer, February 15, 1938, Horkheimer, *Gesammelte Schriften*, XVI, p. 392; Gunzelin Schmid Noerr, *Gesten aus Begriffen. Konstellationen der Kritischen Theorie* (Frankfurt am Main: Fischer Taschenbuch Verlag, 1997), p. 133.

74 Marion A. Kaplan, *Between Dignity and Despair. Jewish Life in Nazi Germany* (New York; Oxford: Oxford University Press, 1998), p. 5.
75 Theodor W. Adorno, "Fragmente über Wagner," *Zeitschrift für Sozialforschung*, VIII, (1939–1940), p. 12, as translated in Theodor Adorno, *In Search of Wagner*, trans. Rodney Livingstone (London; New York: Verso, 2005), p. 14.
76 Adorno, "Fragmente über Wagner," pp. 12–13, as translated in Adorno, *In Search of Wagner*, p. 15.
77 *Ibid.*, p. 17.
78 Buck-Morss, *The Origin of Negative Dialectics*, p. 59.
79 Wiggershaus, *The Frankfurt School*, pp. 66–67; Stefan Müller-Doohm, *Adorno. A Biography*, p. 494, footnote 16.
80 Wolfram Schütte, ed., *Adorno in Frankfurt. Ein Kaleidoskop mit Texten und Bildern* (Frankfurt am Main: Suhrkamp Verlag, 2003), p. 11.
81 Schütte, ed., *Adorno in Frankfurt*, p. 12. Adorno was baptized in the Roman Catholic cathedral in Frankfurt on October 4, 1903 [Evelyn Wilcock, "Negative Identity: Mixed German Jewish Descent as a Factor in the Reception of Theodor Adorno," *New German Critique*, 81 (Fall, 2000), p. 170].
82 Max Horkheimer to Otto O. Herz, September 1, 1969, Hokheimer, *Gesammelte Schriften*, XVIII, p. 743. Müller-Doohm notes that "In the baptism book of the Catholic parish of St. Bartholomäus, there is nothing to show that Adorno ever left the church." [Müller-Doohm, *Adorno. A Biography*, p. 495, footnote 20]. In light of the letter from Horkheimer cited above, we may conclude that Adorno converted to Protestantism without bothering to tell the Catholic Church that he had done so.
83 Theodor W. Adorno to Ernst Krenek, October 7, 1934, Theodor W. Adorno and Ernst Krenek, *Briefwechsel* (Suhrkamp: Frankfurt am Main., 1974), p. 46.
84 Theodor W. Adorno, "The Curious Realist: On Siegfried Kracauer," *New German Critique*, 54 (Fall 1991), pp. 159–160.
85 Leo Lowenthal, "As I Remember Friedel," *New German Critique*, 54 (Fall, 1991), p. 6.
86 Nahum N. Glatzer, "The Frankfort Lehrhaus." *Leo Baeck Institute Year Book*, I, (1956), p. 111.
87 Siegfried Kracauer to Leo Löwenthal, December 4, 1921, *In steter Freundschaft*, p. 31.
88 Müller-Doohm, *Adorno. A Biography*, p. 494. Decades later, Adorno described what he had come to recognize as a deeply problematic result of the prejudice against East European Jews: "In Germany ... the 'autochthonous' Jews used to discriminate heavily against refugees and immigrants from the East and often enough comforted themselves with the idea that the Nazi policies were directed merely against the '*Ostjuden*.' Distinctions of this sort seem to promote gradual persecution of Jews, group by group, with the aid of the smooth rationalization that only those are to be excluded who do not belong anyway.... . The division between 'whites' [the 'white Jews'] and 'kikes,' arbitrary and unjust in itself, invariably turns against the so-called 'whites' who become the 'kikes' of tomorrow." [T(heodor) W. Adorno et al.,

The Authoritarian Personality, Studies in Prejudice, ed. Max Horkheimer and Samuel H. Flowerman (New York: Harper & Brothers, 1950), p. 624].
89 Lowenthal, "Recollections of Theodor W. Adorno," p. 205; Theodor W. Adorno to Leo Löwenthal, August 22, 1923, *In steter Freundschaft*, p. 45.
90 Peter von Haselberg, "Wiesengrund-Adorno," *Theodor W. Adorno*, ed. Heinz Ludwig Arnold. 2nd edition (Munich: Edition Text + Kritik, 1983), p. 12.
91 Jäger, *Adorno*, p. 30, 97.
92 Claussen, *Theodor W. Adorno. One Last Genius*, p. 58. Cf. Jäger, *Adorno*, p. 9.
93 Adorno, "The Curious Realist: On Siegfried Kracauer," p. 161.
94 Theodor W. Adorno to Alban Berg, September 8, 1933, Theodor W. Adorno and Alban Berg, *Correspondence 1925–1935*, ed. Henri Lonitz; trans. Wieland Hoban (Cambridge: Polity, 2005), p. 193; Theodor W. Adorno to Alban Berg, November 13, 1933, Adorno and Berg, *Correspondence 1925–1935*, p. 196.
95 Wiggershaus, *The Frankfurt School*, p. 157.
96 Alban Berg to Theodor W. Adorno, November 18, 1933, Adorno and Berg, *Correspondence 1925–1935*, p. 200.
97 Theodor W. Adorno to Alban Berg, November 28, 1933, Adorno and Berg, *Correspondence 1925–1935*, p. 201.
98 Erich Pfeiffer-Belli, "Frankfurt um 1900 und danach," in *Adorno in Frankfurt*, p. 29.
99 Steven S. Schwarzschild, "Adorno and Schoenberg as Jews. Between Kant and Hegel," *Leo Baeck Institute Year Book*, XXXV (1990), p. 455; Wilcock, "Negative Identity: Mixed German Jewish Descent as a Factor in the Reception of Theodor Adorno," pp. 178–182.
100 Theodor W. Adorno to Ernst Krenek, October 7, 1934, Adorno and Krenek, *Briefwechsel*, p. 43.
101 Theodor W. Adorno to Oscar and Maria Wiesengrund, February 12, 1940, *Letters to his Parents 1939–1951*, ed. Christoph Gödde and Henri Lonitz; trans. Wieland Hoban. Malden, MA: Polity, 2006, p. 41.
102 Theodor W. Adorno to Ernst Krenek, October 7, 1934, Adorno and Krenek, *Briefwechsel*, pp. 43–44.
103 Walter Benjamin to Theodor W. Adorno, May 7, 1940, Adorno and Benjamin, *The Complete Correspondence 1928–1940*, p. 330.
104 Theodor W. Adorno, "Scientific Experiences of a European Scholar in America," *The Intellectual Migration. Europe and America, 1930–1960*, ed. Donald Fleming and Bernard Bailyn (Cambridge, MA: The Belknap Press of Harvard University Press, 1969), p. 341. While based at Oxford from 1934 to 1938, Adorno repeatedly returned to Germany during the first three of those years [Jäger, *Adorno. A Political Biography*, pp. 87–90].
105 Theodor W. Adorno to Max Horkheimer, January 14, 1940, Horkheimer, *Gesammelte Schriften*, XVI, p. 696.
106 Max Horkheimer to Katharina von Hirsch, July 14, 1939, Horkheimer, *Gesammelte Schriften*, XVI, p. 615.

107 Adorno wrote to his parents in the summer of 1939 that "In the next two weeks you will be receiving ... the extensive project of a scientific study of anti-Semitism; Max had the idea to begin with, and then the two of us wrote it together with Gretel and my old American secretary... We are absolutely convinced ... that the only meaningful way to counteract the persecution of Jews is to get to the heart of the matter, rather than simply reeling off the customary phrases. Admittedly such attempts will not always meet with approval – least of all from those in whose interests it is being undertaken." [Theodor W. Adorno to Oscar and Maria Wiesengrund, July 25, 1939, Adorno, *Letters to his Parents 1939–1951*, pp. 10–11].

108 Max Horkheimer to Juliette Favez, April 25, 1939, Horkheimer, *Gesammelte Schriften*, XVI, p. 472. The initial project proposal seems to have been completed in April 1939, at which time it was sent by Horkheimer to Ernst Simmel [Max Horkheimer to Ernst Simmel, April 21, 1939, Horkheimer, *Gesammelte Schriften*, XVI, pp. 585–586].

109 Theodor W. Adorno to Max Horkheimer, July 29, 1940, Horkheimer, *Gesammelte Schriften*, XVI, p. 734. Cf. Franz Neumann to Max Horkheimer, August 5, 1940, MHA, VI.30.105.

110 Theodor W. Adorno to Charles E. Merriam, July 30, 1940, Horkheimer, *Gesammelte Schriften*, XVI, p. 743.

111 Horkheimer, *Gesammelte Schriften*, XVI, p. 746.

112 Theodor W. Adorno to Oscar and Maria Wiesengrund, February 12, 1940, Adorno, *Letters to his Parents 1939–1951*, pp. 40–41.

113 Max Horkheimer to Franz Neumann, July 10, 1940, MHA, VI.30.117.

114 Franz Neumann to Theodor W. Adorno, August 14, 1940, MHA, VI.1a.22.

115 Neumann was by no means opposed to having the Institute conduct a study of antisemitism, and indicated, in a letter to Horkheimer dated July 20, 1940, that he believed that a project which would study the anti-Jewish policy of the Nazis and the effects of that policy would be extraordinarily important. Leo Lowenthal responded to Neumann's critique of Adorno's proposal by noting that Neumann's comments on the antisemitism project had, in general, disappointed him [Leo Lowenthal to Friedrich Pollack, August 20, 1940, Leo Lowenthal Papers, Harvard, bMS Ger 185 (82) folder 3]. A project proposal all but certainly based on the proposal prepared by Adorno was published as "Research Project on Anti-Semitism" in *Studies in Philosophy and Social Science*, IX, 1941, pp. 124–143.

116 Theodor W. Adorno to Max Horkheimer, August 5, 1940, as translated in Wiggershaus, *The Frankfurt School*, p. 275. Horkheimer was receptive to Adorno's suggestion "I'm sticking to our mutual conviction that we want to tackle anti-Semitism with or without a grant" [Max Horkheimer to Theodor W. Adorno, September 16, 1940, Horkheimer, *A Life in Letters*, p. 165]. Cf. Max Horkheimer to Paul and Gabrielle Oppenheim, January 5, 1942, Horkheimer, *Gesammelte Schriften*, XVII, p. 240, in which Horkheimer proclaims that he is "determined not to abandon" the topic of antisemitism "whether the Institute is able to pursue it on a grand scale or not."

117 Rolf Tiedemann, "Introduction: 'Not the First Philosophy, but a Last One': Notes on Adorno's Thought," in Theodor W. Adorno, *Can One Live after Auschwitz? A Philosophical Reader*, ed. Rolf Tiedemann; trans. Rodney Livingstone and others (Stanford, CA: Stanford University Press 2003), p. xix.
118 *Ibid.*
119 "Research Project on Anti-Semitism," *Studies in Philosophy and Social Science*, IX, (1941), p. 124.
120 *Ibid.*, pp. 124, 129.
121 *Ibid.*, p. 124.
122 *Ibid.*, p. 126.
123 *Ibid.*, pp. 142–143.
124 See Wheatland, *The Frankfurt School in Exile*, pp. 219–242 for a very useful discussion of the history of the antisemitism project.
125 Anson Rabinbach, "The Cunning of Unreason: Mimesis and the Construction of Antisemitism in Horkheimer and Adorno's *Dialectic of Enlightenment*," In the Shadow of Catastrophe. German Intellectuals between Apocalypse and Enlightenment (Berkeley; Los Angeles; London: University of California Press, 1997), p. 174.
126 Gershom Scholem, "Walter Benjamin," *On Jews and Judaism in Crisis*, pp. 190–197.
127 Rabinbach, "'Why Were the Jews Sacrificed?' The Place of Antisemitism in Adorno and Horkheimer's *Dialectic of Enlightenment*," p. 137. More recently, Rabinbach has caught – and corrected – this slip, but accidently misdated the letter in question [Anson Rabinbach, "The Frankfurt School and the 'Jewish Question,' 1940–1970," *Against the Grain. Jewish Intellectuals in Hard Times*, ed. Ezra Mendelsohn, Stefani Hoffman, and Richard I. Cohen (New York, Oxford: Berghahn, 2014), p. 273].
128 Theodor W. Adorno to Max Horkheimer, October 2, 1941, as translated in Wiggershaus, *The Frankfurt School*, p. 309. Cf. MHA, VI.32.29.
129 *Ibid.*, p. 309.
130 Max Horkheimer to Friedrich Pollock, November 23, 1941, MHA, VI.32.29.
131 MHA, IX.43A. There is no extant information as to the occasion on which Horkheimer delivered this speech, the place at which he delivered it, or the audience for which it was prepared [Horkheimer, *Gesammelte Schriften*, XII, p. 165]. Horkheimer, however, reiterated his point, word for word, in another speech, delivered on April 30, 1943, at Temple Israel [MHA, IX 44A, p. 9]. Cf. Horkheimer, *Gesammelte Schriften*, XII, p. 180.
132 Leonard Dinnerstein, *Uneasy at Home. Antisemitism and the American Jewish Experience* (New York: Columbia University Press, 1987), p. 35.
133 *Ibid.*, p. 183.
134 Marcia Graham Synnott, "Anti-Semitism and American Universities: Did Quotas Follow the Jews?" *Anti-Semitism in American History*, ed. David A. Gerber (Urbana and Chicago: University of Illinois Press, 1986), p. 234.
135 Leonard Dinnerstein, *Antisemitism in America* (New York, Oxford: Oxford University Press, 1994), p. 91.

136 Naomi W. Cohen, *Not Free to Desist. A History of the American Jewish Committee 1906–1966* (Philadelphia: The Jewish Publication Society of America, 1972), p. 205.
137 Dinnerstein, *Antisemitism in America*, pp. 118, 121.
138 Dinnerstein, *Uneasy at Home*, pp. 178–179.
139 Lowenthal, "I Never Wanted to Play Along," pp. 30–31.
140 Max Horkheimer to Friedrich Pollock, March 20, 1943, MHA, VI.33: "You know very well that it [was] our finances which gave birth to these efforts ... Naturally, I shall see to it that it is also worth while in connection with our own theoretical interests".
141 Adorno reports that Horkheimer "got investigations under way on the problem of anti-Semitism" "under the impress of the gruesome things happening in Europe" [Adorno, "Scientific Experiences of a European Scholar in America," p. 355].
142 Wiggershaus, *The Frankfurt School*, p. 690. Wiggerhaus indicates that Horkheimer made this statement in a letter dated March 10, 1941. However, there is no such statement in the letter from Horkheimer to Laski written on that date and published in Horkheimer, *Gesammelte Schriften*, XVII, pp. 17–18. I have not been able to ascertain whether there is an additional letter from Horkheimer to Laski written on the same date, or whether Horkheimer wrote a letter to someone else on that date with the words quoted by Wiggershaus.
143 Leo Lowenthal to Max Horkheimer, October 27, 1942, MHA, VI.15.315.
144 Leo Lowenthal to Max Horkheimer, October 29, 1942, MHA, VI.15.306.
145 Max Horkheimer to Leo Lowenthal, October 31, 1942, Horkheimer, *Gesammelte Schriften*, XVII, p. 366. Cf., on Horkheimer's motivation, Max Horkheimer to Herbert Marcuse, April 3, 1943, MHA, VI.27A.21.
146 Max Horkheimer to Leo Lowenthal, November 27, 1942, Horkheimer, *Gesammelte Schriften*, XVII, p. 384.
147 Max Horkheimer to Herbert Marcuse, April 3, 1943, MHA, VI.27A.21.
148 Leo Lowenthal to Max Horkheimer, August 20, 1943, Leo Lowenthal Papers, Harvard, bMS Ger 185, [78], folder 23.
149 Jay, *The Dialectical Imagination*, pp. 150, 170; Reijen and Schmid Noerr, *Grand Hotel Abgrund*, p. 56.
150 Paul Massing and Arkady Gurland to Max Horkheimer, September 29, 1944, MHA, IX.147.3.
151 M[assing] and G[urland], "Some Remarks on L.L.'s Memorandum," pp. 1–2, MHA, IX.147.4.
152 Theodor W. Adorno to Leo Lowenthal, October 3, 1944, Leo Lowenthal Papers, Harvard, bMS Ger 185 (8) folder 4; Max Horkheimer to Paul Massing and Arkady Gurland, October 5, 1944, MHA, VI.17.197–199; Friedrich Pollock to Leo Lowenthal, September 25, 1944, MHA, VI.17.220–222.
153 Leo Lowenthal to Theodor W. Adorno, October 13, 1944, *Critical Theory and Frankfurt Theorists*, pp. 132–133.
154 See the memo sent with Theodor W. Adorno to Max Horkheimer, September 18, 1940, Horkheimer, *Gesammelte Schriften*, XVI, pp. 760–761.

155 Wiggershaus, *The Frankfurt School*, pp. 276–277. Horkheimer replies: "I am ... convinced that the Jewish question is the question of contemporary society – we're in agreement with Marx and Hitler on this but, in other respects, we are in no more agreement with them than with Freud" [Max Horkheimer to Theodor W. Adorno, September 24, 1940, Horkheimer, *A Life in Letters*, p. 166].
156 Anna Friedman to Franz Neumann, April 17, 1940, MHA, I.26.32; Max Horkheimer to Edward S. Greenbaum, June 18, 1940, Horkheimer, *Gesammelte Schriften*, XVI, p. 719.
157 Cohen, *Not Free to Desist*, p. 143.
158 Wheatland has perceptively analyzed the Institute's initial proposal for a project on antisemitism and has pointed to the weaknesses of that proposal. He notes that the character types listed in the initial proposal "lacked the scientific rigor" that had been evident in other, earlier, work conducted under the auspices of the Institute, and suggests that the project initially failed to attract widespread support from Americans because it did not address "the needs of American social scientists" [Wheatland, *The Frankfurt School in Exile*, pp. 228–229].
159 Leo Lowenthal to Max Horkheimer, September 10, 1947, Leo Lowenthal Papers, Harvard, bMS Ger 185 (78), folder 38. John Slawson and "Sandy" Flowerman, Lowenthal wrote in this letter, "are united in the spirit of politicians and, as I suppose, also by the common mentality of Eastern Judaism and its resentment against our kind".
160 Cohen, *Not Free to Desist*, pp. 195ff.
161 Wheatland, *The Frankfurt School in Exile*, p. 230. "I have been extremely busy with the Anti-Semitism Project," Franz Neumann wrote to Horkheimer late in 1941 [Franz Neumann to Max Horkheimer, December 20, 1941, MHA, VI.30.1–4]. Adorno also continued to keep a hand in this project [Theodor W. Adorno to Max Horkheimer, October 18, 1941, Horkheimer and Adorno, *Briefwechsel*, III (2005), p. 271].
162 Institute of Social Research, "Anti-Semitism, a Research Project," p. 2, November 10, 1941, MHA, IX.92.7a (II). Neumann continued to advocate the notion of antisemitism as a spearhead when, at a later point in time, he went to work for the Office of Strategic Services [OSS], a component of the United States government which provided intelligence services. In a report published in 1943, for example, Neumann argued that "Anti-Semitism is ... the spearhead of terror" and that, for the Nazis, "the extermination of the Jews is only the means to the attainment of the ultimate objective, namely, the destruction of free institutions, beliefs, and groups" [Franz Neumann, "Anti-Semitism: Spearhead of Universal Terror," in Franz Neumann, Herbert Marcuse and Otto Kirchheimer, *Secret Reports on Nazi Germany. The Frankfurt School Contribution to the War Effort*, ed. Raffaele Laudani (Princeton, NJ and Oxford: Princeton University Press, 2013), p. 28.] Lowenthal was not persuaded by the spearhead approach – but Neumann's argument influenced the approach taken by the OSS [Raffaele Laudani, "Introduction," *Secret Reports on Nazi Germany*, pp. 19–20].

163 Institute of Social Research, "Anti-Semitism, a Research Project," p. 6, November 10, 1941, MHA, IX.92.7a (II).
164 Cohen, *Not Free to Desist*, p. 199.
165 Quoted in Cohen, *Not Free to Desist*, p. 260.
166 Draft of "Annual Report on the Activities of the Social Studies Association, Inc.", to be presented on March 2, 1942, MHA, VI.32.330; Wheatland, *The Frankfurt School in Exile*, p. 382.
167 Franz Neumann to Max Horkheimer, August 21, 1942, Leo Lowenthal Papers, Harvard, bMS Ger 185 (78), folder 20. See as well a later letter in which Neumann described a follow-up conversation he had with Rosenblum [Franz Neumann to Max Horkheimer, October 17, 1942, MHA, VI.30.322–323]. Neumann remained interested in the antisemitism project for some time, and suggested, in November, 1942, that he should be the person to write the work resulting from this undertaking [Friedrich Pollock, "Memo re F. Neumann," November 2, 1942, MHA, VI.33.114]. Pollock, however, while happy to accept Neumann's help in obtaining funding, did not trust Neumann [Friedrich Pollock, Memo, November 5, 1942, MHA, VI.33.104], and resisted Neumann's bid to become the antisemitism project's central figure.
168 "Memo on Luncheon Discussion Lynd-Pollock Re: Anti-Semitism Project," October 30, 1942, MHA, VI.15.305.
169 Abraham G. Duker, a Jewish historian who taught at the Jewish Theological Seminary in the 1940s, wrote a critique of one version of the Institute's proposed project and accented major shortcomings in the proposal, including that it concentrated too much on Central and Western Europe, that the authors knew nothing of Jewish history, and that it had an "almost exclusively" economic orientation. I first learned of this critique through my reading of Christian Fleck, *Transatlantische Bereicherungen. Zur Erfindung der empirischen Sozialforshung* (Frankfurt am Main: Suhrkamp, 2007), pp. 361–363. My thanks to Prof. Fleck for having sent me the typescript of his work prior to its publication.
170 Max Horkheimer, "Notes on Horkheimer's Remarks," Horkheimer, *Gesammelte Schriften*, XVII, p. 526.
171 Speech by Max Horkheimer delivered at Temple Israel, April 30, 1943, MHA, IX.44A. Cf. Horkheimer, *Gesammelte Schriften*, XII, p. 172.
172 Max Horkheimer, "Notes on Horkheimer's Remarks," pp. 521–522.
173 Herbert Marcuse to Max Horkheimer, July 28, 1943, Horkheimer, *Gesammelte Schriften*, XVII, p. 467.
174 Max Horkheimer to Herbert Marcuse, September 11, 1943, Horkheimer, *Gesammelte Schriften*, XVII, p. 470. For Lowenthal's response to Marcuse's critique of the spearhead theory see Leo Lowenthal to Herbert Marcuse, June 29, 1943 [Peter-Erwin Jansen, ed., *Das Utopische soll Funken schlagen ... Zum hundertsten Geburtstag von Leo Löwenthal*, pp. 100–114).
175 Adorno et al., *The Authoritarian Personality*, p. 653.
176 "Final arrangements between P. and Mr. David Rosenblum re Antisemitism Project," March 2, 1943, MHA, II.2.370.
177 David Rosenblum to Friedrich Pollock, March 3, 1943, MHA, II.2.377. Adorno was in fact very engaged with work on the antisemitism project in

the following weeks and months: "I absolutely cannot leave here on account of the anti-Semitism project, which involves not only the actual scientific work, but in addition all sorts of contacts ... The anti-Semitism project is a true blessing. Incidentally, I agree entirely with WK [Oscar Wiesengrund] that abolishing the racial distinction would be the only right thing to do, and God knows our study espouses no less. But the *others* do not want to. And at a time when millions of Jews are being murdered, it would not be so appropriate to reproach those people for isolating themselves. The problem lies with the Christians. I hope with all my heart that we really can do something – however modest – to help." [Theodor W. Adorno to Oscar and Maria Wiesengrund, March 29, 1943, Adorno, *Letters to his Parents 1939–1951*, pp. 130–131]. Later that spring, Adorno informed his parents that he found his work on the antisemitism project to be "*exceptionally interesting*" [Theodor W. Adorno to Oscar and Maria Wiesengrund, May 31, 1943, Adorno, *Letters to his Parents 1939–1951*, p. 136] and repeatedly expressed the hope that it would do some good in the struggle against fascism.

178 Institute of Social Research, "Notes on Some Methodological Principles and Some Tentative Assumptions for the Work on the Anti-Semitism Project," March 15, 1943, MHA, IX.102, p. 1.

179 Max Horkheimer to Friedrich Pollock, April 11, 1943, MHA, VI.33.218. Cf. Max Horkheimer to Leo Lowenthal, March 26, 1943, Horkheimer, *Gesammelte Schriften*, XVII, pp. 439–440.

180 "Joint Meeting of the A.J.C. and the Institute on May 7, 1943," MHA, IX.100, p. 3.

181 *Ibid.* Cf. Arkady Gurland, "Problems involved in the Study of the Decrease in Efficiency of the Fight against Antisemitism in Germany," paper presented at joint meeting of the AJC and the Institute, May 7, 1943, MHA, IX.100.

182 "Joint Meeting of the A.J.C. and the Institute on May 7, 1943", MHA, IX.100, p. 3.

183 *Ibid.*, p. 4. Cf. Paul Massing, "Problems involved in the Study of the Dynamics of Antisemitism in Germany," paper presented at joint meeting of the AJC and the Institute, May 7, 1943, MHA, IX.100.

184 Friedrich Pollock, "Structural Analysis of a Hypothetical Situation in USA where Antisemitism in its 'political' variety would be used as a main weapon for destroying the democratic system," paper presented at joint meeting of the AJC and the Institute, July 8, 1943, MHA, IX.100, p. 3.

185 *Ibid.*

186 *Ibid.* Cf. "Why Research on Antisemitism?" November 12, 1943, MHA, IX.113. A. Pollock described this to Horkheimer as "a joint work, based on a draft of mine" [Friedrich Pollock, "Memorandum No. 18," November 12, 1943, MHA, VI.34.122], and intended it to be used when approaching potential funders and other interested individuals. "Why Research on Antisemitism?" notes that "Our own studies, though incomplete and in need of careful verification, have led us to the tentative conclusion that the average susceptibility to Antisemitism is probably greater in this country than it was in pre-Hitler Germany."

187 Reijen and Schmid Noerr, *Grand Hotel Abgrund*, p. 74.
188 "Memorandum on work's progress of AS project," September 15, 1943, MHA, Frankfurt, IX.110.2. Kirchheimer's research results were not well received by at least one prominent leader of the AJC, Judge Joseph M. Proskauer, who was eager not to be associated with any criticism of the Catholic church [Notes, apparently taken by Joseph Freeman, of a joint meeting of the AJC and the Institute, December 9, 1943, Joseph Freeman Papers, Box 57, Folder 7, Hoover Institution].
189 Wiggershaus, *The Frankfurt School*, p. 358.
190 Theodor W. Adorno, "Anti-Semitism and Fascist Propaganda," *Anti-Semitism. A Social Disease*, ed. Ernst Simmel (New York: International Universities Press, 1946), pp. 125–126.
191 Adorno, "Anti-Semitism and Fascist Propaganda," p. 130.
192 *Ibid.* p. 131.
193 *Ibid.*, p. 133.
194 *Ibid.*, p. 133. "My lecture" in San Francisco on antisemitism and fascist propaganda, Adorno told his parents, "was the greatest success that I have ever had as a speaker in emigration... I received by far the most applause of all the speakers" [Theodor W. Adorno to Oscar and Maria Wiesengrund, June 22, 1944, Adorno, *Letters to his Parents 1939–1951*, p. 189].
195 Max Horkheimer, "Antisemitism as a Social Phenomenon," June 17, 1944, MHA, IX.46.1A, pp. 2–3. A revised version of this talk was published as Max Horkheimer, "Sociological Background of the Psychoanalytic Approach," *Anti-Semitism. A Social Disease*, pp. 1–10.
196 Horkheimer, "Antisemitism as a Social Phenomenon," p. 3.
197 *Ibid.*, p. 6.
198 "Re: Editing of Report to the A.J.C. (Dr. Klein) August 1944. Notes – Dr. Adorno," MHA, VI.1b.217–225.
199 *Ibid.*, p. 8.
200 Institute for Social Research, "Studies in Anti-Semitism: A Report on the cooperative project for the study of antisemitism for the year ending March 15, 1944, jointly sponsored by the American Jewish Committee and the Institute of Social Research," August 1944, MHA, IX.121, p. 24.
201 *Ibid.*, pp. 25–26.
202 *Ibid.*, p. 30.
203 *Ibid.*, p. 31.
204 Max Horkheimer and Theodor W. Adorno, *Dialectic of Enlightenment. Philosophical Fragments*, ed. Gunzelin Schmid Noerr; trans. Edmund Jephcott (Stanford, CA: Stanford University Press, 2002), p. xix.
205 For an excellent, exceptionally lucid, reconstruction of the history of *Dialectic of Enlightenment* see James Schmidt, "Language, Mythology, and Enlightenment: Historical Notes on Horkheimer and Adorno's Dialectic of Enlightenment," *Social Research*, LXV, 4 (Winter 1998), pp. 807ff.
206 Horkheimer and Adorno, *Dialectic of Enlightenment*, pp. xiv, 253. "Elemente des Antisemitismus" initially appeared as a constituent component of the mimeographed work issued under the title "Philosophische

Fragmente" and presented to Pollock in May 1944 on the occasion of his fiftieth birthday [Wiggershaus, *The Frankfurt School*, p. 325]. *Dialektik der Aufklärung*, of which "Elemente" is the final chapter, was first published in book form in 1947. Specific terms in the 1944 edition of "Philosophical Fragments" which suggested that the authors were linked to Marxism were removed and replaced (by Adorno) as he prepared *Dialectic of Enlightenment* for publication [Willem van Reijen and Jan Brensen, "The Disappearance of Class History in 'Dialectic of Enlightenment'. A Commentary on the Textual Variants (1947 and 1944)," in Horkheimer and Adorno, *Dialectic of Enlightenment*, pp. 248–252]. My quotations of passages from *Dialectic of Enlightenment* in this section of my book follow Jephcott's translations, but make use of the terminology used by Horkheimer and Adorno in 1944 [and published by the editors of the Jephcott translation, pp. 272–276] rather than the terms Horkheimer and Adorno used in 1947. There is a typescript of the 1944 version of "Elemente des Antisemitismus" in the Max-Horkheimer-Archiv [MHA, XI.6.1].

207 Max Horkheimer to Theodor W. Adorno, December 27, 1944, Horkheimer, *Gesammelte Schriften*, XVII, p. 614.

208 For another early sign of the direction which would be taken in "Elements" see Max Horkheimer to Egon Wissing, August 1941, Horkheimer, *A Life in Letters*, p. 184: "An examination of anti-Semitism leads back to mythology, and, in the end, to physiology... . This is not meant as a point against economic theory. Rather, economic theory must maintain its preeminence..."

209 "The joint work with Max has now settled into a very comfortable routine... There is always a unification of our opinions before anything is written down. There is not a single line in the Dialektik der Aufklärung, the Culture Industry and 'Elements of Anti-Semitism' that we did not formulate together, often many times over." [Theodor W. Adorno to Oscar and Maria Wiesengrund, November 22, 1944, Adorno, *Letters to his Parents 1939–1951*, p. 205]. Cf., similarly, Adorno, "Scientific Experiences of a European Scholar in America," p. 356, in which Adorno asserts that "Horkheimer and I ... literally dictated together..." "Elements of Anti-Semitism". According to Gunzelin Schmidd Noerr, "Elements" was, by and large, "originally written by Horkheimer and intensively revised by Adorno" [Gunzelin Schmid Noerr, "The Position of *Dialectic of Enlightenment* in the Development of Critical Theory," in Horkheimer and Adorno, *Dialectic of Enlightenment*, p. 224]. Rabinbach, who reports that "Elements" "can be attributed to Adorno..." appears to be mistaken on this point (though he is extremely compelling in much of his analysis) [Rabinbach, "The Cunning of Unreason: Mimesis and the Construction of Antisemitism in Horkheimer and Adorno's *Dialectic of Enlightenment*," p. 167].

210 Wiggershaus, *The Frankfurt School*, pp. 323–324.

211 Lowenthal spent several months in Los Angeles with Horkheimer and Adorno in 1943 and helped to develop certain portions of "Elements" during his stay in California. Horkheimer and Adorno, in acknowledgements

penned in May 1944, stated that "We wrote the first three theses jointly with Leo Löwenthal [Horkheimer and Adorno, *Dialectic of Enlightenment*, p. xix]. While Lowenthal was still in California, Horkheimer, describing progress on the work, seems to have given Lowenthal somewhat less credit: "Lowenthal ... has had an opportunity to watch what is going on and to take a certain part in it" [Max Horkheimer to Herbert Marcuse, July 17, 1943, MHA, VI.27A.12]. In the fall of 1943, Lowenthal left Los Angeles and returned to New York. He attempted, however, to continue to have an impact on the development of "Elements" by sending memos on relevant themes to Horkheimer.

212 Horkheimer and Adorno, *Dialectic of Enlightenment*, p. 137.
213 *Ibid.*, p. 138.
214 Max Horkheimer to Isaac Rosengarten, September 12, 1944, Horkheimer, *Gesammelte Schriften*, XVII, p. 599.
215 Horkheimer and Adorno, *Dialectic of Enlightenment*, p. 138.
216 *Ibid.*, p. 139.
217 Max Horkheimer, *Eclipse of Reason* (New York: Continuum, 1992), pp. 3, 5.
218 *Ibid.*, p. 21.
219 Horkheimer and Adorno, *Dialectic of Enlightenment*, p. 140.
220 *Ibid.*, p. 142.
221 *Ibid.*, p. 143.
222 *Ibid.*
223 Dan Diner stresses differences between the ways in which the relationship of Jews to the sphere of circulation is discussed in "The Jews and Europe" and in "Elements of Anti-Semitism" [Diner, "Reason and the 'Other'," pp. 355–356].
224 Horkheimer and Adorno, *Dialectic of Enlightenment*, p. 147.
225 *Ibid.*, p. 144.
226 Wessel and Rensmann, "The Paralysis of Judgment. Arendt and Adorno on Antisemitism and the Modern Condition," pp. 201–202.
227 Simon Jarvis, *Adorno. A Critical Introduction* (New York: Routledge, 1998), p. 31. Cf. Rabinbach, "The Cunning of Unreason: Mimesis and the Construction of Antisemitism in Horkheimer and Adorno's *Dialectic of Enlightenment*," p. 177: "the concept of mimesis is not understood as mere imitation, but as a form of mimicry or semblance that appropriates rather than replicates its object in a nonidentical similitude."
228 Horkheimer and Adorno, *Dialectic of Enlightenment*, p. 148.
229 *Ibid.*, p. 153.
230 Rabinbach, "The Cunning of Unreason: Mimesis and the Construction of Antisemitism in Horkheimer and Adorno's *Dialectic of Enlightenment*," pp. 184. Cf. James Schmidt, "Genocide and the Limits of Enlightenment: Horkheimer and Adorno Revisited" in *Enlightenment and Genocide, Contradictions of Modernity*, ed. James Kaye and Bo Stråth. Series: Philosophy and Politics, 5. Brussels: P.I.E.–Peter Lang, 2000, p. 94: "Fascism ... has discovered the secret of miming mimesis in the interest of domination."

Notes to page 72

231 Horkheimer and Adorno, *Dialectic of Enlightenment*, p. 153.
232 *Ibid.*, p. 151.
233 Two important additional theses were added to "Elements" at later dates. Because I am interested in analyzing the *development* of Horkheimer and Adorno's approaches towards the study of antisemitism (and not merely the positions at which they ultimately arrived), I think it best to discuss the final theses separately from the earlier components of "Elements."

In November, 1943, Lowenthal wrote to Horkheimer "I have just written a page on projection and the Jews which attempts to add a few points of view to what we started to say about the concept of idiosyncrasy." [Leo Lowenthal to Max Horkheimer, November 16, 1943, MHA, VI.16.222]. He enclosed a draft thesis dealing with this theme. Lowenthal followed up by sending other comments on reification and on fascism in which antisemitism is used as a major example. Lowenthal describes antisemitism in these comments as a "blindness by which human beings look at their likes and by their very looking transform them into their unlikes, into frozen nature" [MHA, VI.16.211–212; Lowenthal's comments accompanied Leo Lowenthal to Max Horkheimer, November 20, 1943, MHA, VI.16.182–195]. Horkheimer replied that he liked Lowenthal's comments on fascism and reification, and "would not contradict any particular statement you made" [Max Horkheimer to Leo Lowenthal, December 2, 1943, Horkheimer, *Gesammelte Schriften*, XVII, p. 517]. During the following spring, Horkheimer informed Lowenthal that he thought "we should add a paragraph on projection to the 'Thesen.' After all, the projection of aggression or destruction is the most obvious psychological fact of Antisemitism." [Max Horkheimer to Leo Lowenthal, March 17, 1944, Horkheimer, *Gesammelte Schriften*, XVII, p. 549].

The subject of projection was incorporated into the sixth thesis, among the most important and lengthiest parts of "Elements", which was ultimately completed in April 1944. Indeed, thesis six is devoted to the notion that antisemitism is based on false or morbid projection, "the reverse of genuine mimesis... If mimesis makes itself resemble its surroundings, false projection makes its surrounding resemble itself." [Horkheimer and Adorno, *Dialectic of Enlightenment*, p. 154]. The antisemite, Horkheimer and Adrono argues, attributes his own desires to the Jew. Echoing themes sketched out by Adorno in his memo to Horkheimer of September 1940 [described above] the sixth thesis notes that "No matter what the makeup of the Jews may be in reality, their image, that of the defeated, has characteristics which must make totalitarian rule their mortal enemy: happiness without power, reward without work, a homeland without frontiers, religion without myth. These features are outlawed by the ruling powers because they are secretly coveted by the ruled. The former can survive only as long as the latter turn what they yearn for into an object of hate. They do so through pathic projection..." [*Ibid.*, pp. 164–165]. Schmidt critiques this thesis by arguing that it operates "on too deep a level to account for the historical particularity of Nazi genocide. If pathological projection is the spectre that haunts every act of cognition ... what accounts for the historical emergence of Nazi genocide in one country at one particular moment?" [Schmidt, "Genocide and the Limits of Enlightenment," p. 95]

A final, seventh thesis, written after the end of World War II, appeared in the first published edition of *Dialectic of Enlightenment*, but not in "Philosophical Fragments." It begins with a rhetorical flourish "But there are no longer any anti-Semites" [*Dialectic of Enlightenment*, p. 165]. Antisemitism, the authors proclaim, "has practically ceased to be an independent impulse and has become a plank in the [fascist] platform" [*Ibid.*, p. 166]. The appearance of this "ticket" thinking, however, provides a glimmer of light at the end of the tunnel: "The tendency according to which anti-Semitism now exists only as one item on an interchangeable ticket gives irrefutable reason to hope for its end. The Jews are being murdered at a time when the leaders could replace the anti-Semitic plank in their platform just as easily at their followers can be transplanted from one location of wholly rationalized production to another" [*Ibid.*, pp. 171–172]. Cf. MHA, XI.6.43 for a typescript of this thesis, including handwritten corrections and alterations.

234 Jonathan Judaken, "Between Philosemitism and Antisemitism: The Frankfurt School's Anti-Antisemitism," pp. 36, 39. Cf. Jonathan Judaken, "Blindness and Insight: The Conceptual Jew in Adorno and Arendt's Post-Holocaust Reflections on the Antisemitic Question," pp. 185–196.

235 Jürgen Habermas, "Remarks on the Development of Horkheimer's Work," *On Max Horkheimer. New Perspectives*, p. 57.

236 Ziege, *Antisemitismus und Gesellschaftstheorie. Die Frankfurter Schule im amerikanischen Exil*, pp. 12–13. Ziege's fine discussion of the labor study appeared after I had already completed my research on that project.

237 "Memorandum re: Jewish Labor Committee," MHA, IX.146.13. The Institute had initially proposed to the AJC that a study of labor and the Jews in the USA be conducted as a portion of the AJC-sponsored antisemitism project ["Memorandum on a Research Project on Anti-Semitism prepared for the American Jewish Committee by the Institute of Social Research," October 30, 1942, MHA, IX, 95B, pp. 9–10]. Whereas Pollock thought that the notion of conducting a research project devoted to labor antisemitism was a good idea – arguing on its behalf that it could be done comparatively rapidly and easily, that it would be possible to make use of Massing and Kirchheimer on such a project, that Neumann was not needed for it, and that "We can make here concessions to American positivism ... without doing any harm to the other sections" [Friedrich Pollock, Memo, November 5, 1942, MHA, VI.33.108], Horkheimer had been highly skeptical, at that time, of the idea of a study on labor antisemitism, had been "inclined to drop it entirely" [Leo Lowenthal to Friedrich Pollock, October 8, 1942, Leo Lowenthal Papers, Harvard, bMS Ger 185 (82) folder 6] and had at one point described Neumann's advocacy of such a project as "idiotic" [Max Horkheimer to Friedrich Pollock, December 11, 1942, MHA, VI.15.225]. The JLC had been encouraged to embark on a study of labor antisemitism by Horace Kallen, and had budgeted for such an undertaking in 1942 [Horace Kallen to Adolph Held, September 17, 1942, Horace Kallen Papers, RG 317,

File 252, Item 13453, YIVO Institute for Jewish Research, New York [henceforth: YIVO]; Horace Kallen to Jacob Pat, October 8, 1942, Horace Kallen Papers, RG 317, File 252, Item 13467, YIVO]. Once funds for the JLC-supported project were awarded to the Institute, Horkeimer cooperated with those members of the Institute who were directly involved with the study, his earlier misgivings notwithstanding. The day-to-day work on the Labor Study, however, was led by Pollock, not Horkheimer, and the qualitative work on this project was done primarily by Adorno [Ziege, *Antisemitismus und Gesellschaftstheorie*, p. 190].

238 The first known draft of the proposal is dated December 1943 [Institute of Social Research, "Project on Antisemitism and American Labor," December 1943, Joseph Freeman Collection, Box 57, Folder 9, Hoover Institution], and was apparently sent by Pollock to Sherman at that time [Friedrich Pollock to Charles B. Sherman, December 31, 1943, MHA, IX.146.23]. Sherman was enthusiastic about the Institute's memorandum, and informed Adorno that he was eager to have the project carried out [Theodor W. Adorno, "Memorandum on telephone conversation with Mr. Sherman, January 28, 1944, MHA, VI.1b.259].

239 "A[d]dress to a meeting of the Jewish Labor Committee," p. 2, January 20, 1944, MHA, IX.146.11.

240 Institute of Social Research, "Project on Antisemitism and American Labor," February 29, 1944, Jewish Labor Committee Collection, Wagner Archives, Tamiment Institute, New York [henceforth: JLC Collection)].

241 Institute of Social Research, "Project on Antisemitism and American Labor," p. 3.

242 *Ibid.*, p. 5.

243 Institute of Social Research, "Re: Project on Labor and Antisemitism. Difficulties to be expected," March 21, 1944, Horace Kallen Papers, RG 317, File 252, Item 13490, YIVO.

244 The initial grant was in the amount of $9100 [Frederick Wild to Jewish Labor Committee, June 15, 1944, JLC Collection]. When, at a later point in time, the Institute informed the JLC that its expenses had far exceeded the amount of the original grant, the JLC provided an additional grant of $4000 [Friedrich Pollock to Adolph Held, January 8, 1946, JLC Collection; Jacob Pat to Friedrich Pollock, May 7, 1946, JLC Collection].

245 Max Horkheimer to Leo Lowenthal, July 26, 1944, Horkheimer, *Gesammelte Schriften*, XVII, p. 576.

246 Theodor W. Adorno to Oscar and Maria Wiesengrund, August 28, 1944, Adorno, *Letters to his Parents 1939–1951*, p. 196.

247 "Memorandum from T. W. Adorno re Evaluation of Participant Interviews (Labor Project)," p. 6, November 3, 1944, P. F. Lazarsfeld Collection, Box 20, Columbia University.

248 *Ibid.*

249 *Ibid.*, p. 7.

250 *Ibid.*, p. 16.

251 *Ibid.*, p. 24.

252 *Ibid.*, p. 41. Approximately a month later, Adorno wrote a second long memorandum in order to help the team working on the Labor Project with its final report [Theodor W. Adorno, "(R)e: Write-up of final report," December 1, 1944, P. F. Lazarsfeld Collection, Box 20, Columbia University].

253 Adolph Held to H[orace] M. Kallen, September 19, 1945, Horace Kallen Papers, RG 317, File 942, Item 46282, YIVO.

254 "Stenographic Report to the National Executive Committee of the Jewish Labor Committee on the Susceptibility of American Labor to Antisemitic Propaganda presented by the Institute of Social Research on March 10, 1945 at Hotel Pennsylvania, New York City," pp. 66, 68, JLC Collection. The full, four volume, typescript of the Institute's labor study, "Antisemitism Among American Labor. Report on a Research Project conducted by the Institute of Social Research (Columbia University) in 1944–1945," is in the JLC Collection.

255 Friedrich Pollock to Jacob Pat, April 24, 1946, JLC Collection.

256 Wheatland, *The Frankfurt School in Exile*, p. 48.

257 Leo Lowenthal to Friedrich Pollock, September 27, 1946, Leo Lowenthal Papers, Harvard, bMS Ger 185 (82) folder 10.

258 Leo Lowenthal to Friedrich Pollock, May 12, 1948, Leo Lowenthal Papers, Harvard, bMS Ger 185 (82), folder 13.

259 Friedrich Pollock to Leo Lowenthal, April 23, 1948, May 6, 1948, Leo Lowenthal Papers, Harvard, bMS Ger 185 (122) folder 14.

260 Friedrich Pollock to Leo Lowenthal, July 26, 1948, Leo Lowenthal Papers, Harvard, bMS Ger 185 (122) folder 15.

261 Theodor W. Adorno to Leo Lowenthal, June 6, 1949, Leo Lowenthal Papers, Harvard, bMS Ger 185 (8) folder 7.

262 Max Horkheimer to Samuel H. Flowerman, July 5, 1948, MHA, II.7.184.

263 Memorandum, Theodor W. Adorno to Max Horkheimer, Frederick Pollock, Leo Lowenthal, re: Antisemitism among American Labor, as edited by the Bureau of Applied Social Research, July 15, 1949, p. 4, P. F. Lazarsfeld Collection, Box 20, Columbia University.

264 Memorandum, Theodor W. Adorno to Max Horkeheimer, Frederick Pollock, Leo Lowenthal, re: Antisemitism among American Labor, as edited by the Bureau of Applied Social Research, July 15, 1949, p. 3.

265 Theodor W. Adorno to Leo Lowenthal, May 4, 1949, Leo Lowenthal Papers, Harvard, bMS Ger 185 (8) folder 7.

266 "Supplement to the Memorandum by T.W.A. of July 15, 1949, re Antisemitism among American Labor, as edited by the Bureau of Applied Social Research," July 30, 1949, P. F. Lazarsfeld Collection, Box 20, Columbia University.

267 Theodor W. Adorno to Leo Lowenthal, "Supplement to the Memorandum of 7/28/49 by F.P. re Labor Study," August 18, 1949, P. F. Lazarsfeld Collection, Box 20, Columbia University.

268 The members of the Institute reached an agreement with the Free Press in the early 1950s to publish the labor study. In 1954, the Press was about to list the volume in its catalogue of forthcoming titles – when the Institute

reluctantly but definitively pulled the plug. Reasons offered by the Institute as to why the labor study could not be published included the sense that it was "too late in the day, critics might ask why now, not earlier", fear that publication "may stir up a hornet's nest in [the] present situation", and the fact that "opinion of [the] Institute's members was divided pro [and] con" with the "cons" ultimately carrying the day [Notes by Friedrich Pollock to Leo Lowenthal, added to copy of letter by Jeremiah Kaplan to Leo Lowenthal, March 15, 1954, Leo Lowenthal Papers, Harvard, bMS Ger 185, [122], folder 25].

269 *Conference on Research in the Field of Anti-Semitism. Summary of Proceedings and Suggestions for a Program* (New York: American Jewish Committee, 1945), p. 3.

270 "Report on the Scientific Department of the American Jewish Committee – Dr. Max Horkheimer, Chairman," p. 4, January 5, 1945, Joseph Freeman Papers, Box 57, Folder 9, Hoover Institution.

271 *Conference on Research in the Field of Anti-Semitism*, p. 3.

272 *Ibid.*, pp. 3–4.

273 *Ibid.*, p. 8.

274 Horkheimer attempted to obtain additional funding for the Institute from the AJC by writing a lengthy memo to John Slawson in which he summarized the Institute's ideas as to the nature and causes of antisemitism and in which he described the work the Institute had not yet done but proposed to do ["Memorandum to Dr. John Slawson by Dr. Max Horkheimer on Research Project on Antisemitism," n.d., MHA.II.2.322–334].

Adorno's evolving ideas as to antisemitism during this period may also be gleaned from memoranda he wrote to Horkheimer. In one such memo, he emphasized that totalitarian antisemitism was linked to the tendency towards monopolization, and that it was thus closely related to the "racket-ification" of society. "Every group," Adorno proposed, "develops under the pressure of monopoly the tendency to numerus clausus … This economic tendency to numerus clausus … is one of the reasons for the ostracizing of the Jews…The Jews are … victims of the abrogation of competition." [Theodor W. Adorno to Max Horkheimer, November 3, 1944, Horkheimer, *Gesammelte Schriften*, XVII, p. 601].

275 "American Jewish Committee Launches New Program of Scientific Research in Anti-Semitism Under Direction of Noted Social Scientist," September 11, 1944, AJC Archives, Jacob and Hilda Blaustein Human Relations Research Library, NY, (henceforth: Blaustein), File: Horkheimer, Max.

276 "Report on the Department for Scientific Research – Dr. Max Horkheimer – AJC," p. 6. n.d. AJC Archives, Blaustein, Box 24, File: Departments and Divisions/Scientific Research/Reports/AD 45-58.

277 *Ibid.*

278 *Ibid.*, p. 7.

279 *Ibid.*

280 American Jewish Committee, "Meeting of the Advisory Council to Dr. Horkheimer," p. 9. AJC Archives, Blaustein, Box 23, File: Departments and Divisions/Scientific Research/Advisory Council/AD 45.

281 The notion of making an experimental film which would be used as a way of studying American antisemitism had been presented by the Institute in "Research Project on Anti-Semitism," *Studies in Philosophy and Social Science*, IX, 1941, pp. 142–143. Horkheimer batted around the idea that the Institute should try to make use of a film or films as a way of uncovering antisemitic attitudes at a number of different points in time. See, for example, "Notes for An Experimental Film to Be Made by the Institute of Social Research," May 28, 1943, MHA, II.10.386.

282 Belke and Renz, "Siegfried Kracauer. 1889–1966," pp. 101–106; Horkheimer, *Gesammelte Schriften*, XVIII, pp. 989–990. For additional information on a screenplay prepared by Kracauer in 1945 for what he hoped would be a test film to be used in assessing antisemitism see Graeme Gilloch and Jaeho Kang, "Below the Surface: Siegfried Kracauer's 'Test-film' Project." *New Formations*, 61 (Summer 2007), pp. 149–160.

283 "Meeting of the Committee on Scientific Research," February 22, 1945, AJC Archives, Blaustein, Box 23, File: Departments and Divisions/Scientific Research/Committee/AD 45–63.

284 "Notes for the Outline of the Book on Prejudice," p. 2, March 15, 1945, Records of the American Jewish Committee, YIVO, Folder: Treatise on Anti-Semitism, 1945.

285 "Tentative Outline of Contents of Book on Antisemitism As Revised up to May 28, 1945," Records of the American Jewish Committee, YIVO, Folder: Treatise on Anti-Semitism, 1945.

286 "Progress on the Project of a Treatise on Antisemitism – As of June 1, 1945," Records of the American Jewish Committee, YIVO, Folder: Treatise on Anti-Semitism, 1945.

287 "Treatise on Anti-Semitism. Notes on Meeting of June 13, 1945," p. 2, Records of the American Jewish Committee, YIVO, Folder: Treatise on Anti-Semitism, 1945.

288 "Progress Report of the Scientific Department," p. 13, June 22, 1945, AJC Archives, Blaustein, Box 24, File: Departments and Divisions/Scientific Research/Reports/AD 45–58.

289 "Committee on Scientific Research," Minutes for meeting of October 24, 1945, AJC Archives, Blaustein, Box 23, File: Departments and Divisions/Scientific Research/Committee/AD 45–63.

290 Samuel H. Flowerman to Max Horkheimer, December 14, 1945, MHA, II.7.134.

291 Leo Lowenthal to Max Horkheimer, December 3, 1945, Horkheimer, *Gesammelte Schriften*, XVII, p. 683.

292 Paul Massing to Max Horkheimer, January 3, 1946, MHA, VI.28.132–137.

293 "Meeting of the Committee on Scientific Research," first draft of minutes of a meeting held on February 6, 1946, AJC Archives, Blaustein, Box 23, File: Departments and Divisions/Scientific Research/Committee/AD 45–63.

294 John Slawson to Max Horkheimer, February 8, 1946, Leo Lowenthal Papers, Harvard, bMS Ger 185 (137). Fleck provides a very negative assessment of Horkheimer, claiming that Horkheimer devoted a great deal of time to perfecting "office intrigues," that Horkheimer was not capable

of judging his own abilities correctly, and that his letters reveal a suspicious nature, bordering on paranoia [Fleck, *Transatlantische Bereicherungen*, pp. 395–396]. Fleck also argues that a mythological version of the Frankfurt School's exile years, rooted in the works of Horkheimer, came into being in the 1970s [*Ibid.*, pp. 426–427]. Fleck's conclusions concerning Horkheimer (though not his conclusions concerning the mythology of the Frankfurt School) strike me as overly harsh. Fleck, for one thing, seems not to take Flowerman's attitudes and actions into account in assessing Horkheimer's relationship with the AJC. It should also be noted that at a crucial point in his contacts with the AJC and Flowerman, Horkheimer explicitly declined to take part in office "intrigues" and "struggles for the budget" [Max Horkheimer to Leo Lowenthal, February 6, 1946, Horkheimer, *Gesammelte Schriften*, XVII, p. 695]. It is, however, true, that certain of the proclamations later made by members of the Frankfurt School as to their motivations and ideas must be taken with a grain of salt.

295 Samuel H. Flowerman to Max Horkheimer, March 29, 1946, AJC Archives, Blaustein, File: Departments and Divisions/Scientific Research/Horkheimer, Max/AD 45–48.

296 Leo Lowenthal to Max Horkheimer, May 15, 1946, Leo Lowenthal Papers, Harvard, bMS Ger 185 (78), folder 31.

297 Leo Lowenthal to Max Horkheimer, July 23, 1947, Leo Lowenthal Papers, Harvard, bMS Ger 185 (78), folder 37. Lowenthal eventually concluded that it had been Flowerman's intent from the moment he had obtained his position to sever connections with the initiatives initially undertaken by Horkheimer [Leo Lowenthal to Theodor W. Adorno, September 26, 1947, Leo Lowenthal Papers, Harvard, bMS Ger 185 (73), folder 4].

298 Samuel H. Flowerman to Max Horkheimer, April 30, 1947, MHA, II.7.38; Samuel H. Flowerman to Max Horkheimer, October 16, 1947, MHA, II.7.9–10.

299 "Relationship between Dr. Horkheimer and Dept. of Scientific Research," January 20, 1948, AJC Archives, Blaustein, File: Departments and Divisions/Scientific Research/Horkheimer, Max/AD 45–48. Horkheimer ceased acting as a consultant for the AJC once he moved back to Frankfurt. However, he did not burn his bridges, and, almost a decade later, he spoke at a meeting of the AJC Foreign Affairs Committee on matters related to contemporary thinking in Germany and elsewhere [Ralph Friedman to Max Horkheimer, January 12, 1959, Records of the American Jewish Committee, 44–62, YIVO]. In 1960 John Slawson proposed that the AJC re-engage Horkheimer as a consultant [John Slawson to Zachariah Shuster, March 23, 1960, Records of the American Jewish Committee, YIVO]. It was anticipated that Horkheimer would concern himself with a number of matters including "[a]ction research on the degree of authoritarianism in Germany and perhaps other countries; relation between Nazism, fascism, and anti-Semitism" and the "depth of authoritarian trends in Germany" ["Memorandum on Max Horkheimer as Consultant on Germany," March 22, 1960, Records of the American

Jewish Committee, YIVO]. Horkheimer, who accepted this position, was given responsibility for selecting German educators interested in visiting the United States under a program sponsored by the Institute of International Education, and also coordinated certain activities for these educators when they returned to Germany [Cohen, *Not Free to Desist*, p. 495].

300 For additional information on "Studies in Prejudice" and the individual works appearing in that series cf. Jay, *The Dialectical Imagination*, pp. 234–252; Wiggershaus, *The Frankfurt School*, pp. 408–430; Stuart Svonkin, *Jews Against Prejudice. American Jews and the Fight for Civil Liberties* (New York: Columbia University Press, 1997), pp. 34–40.

301 Zoltán Tar, *The Frankfurt School. The Critical Theories of Max Horkheimer and Theodor W. Adorno* (New York: Schocken Books, 1985), p. 102.

302 Benjamin Beit-Hallahmi, "Authoritarianism and Personality – Some Historical Reflections," *Tel Aviver Jahrbuch für deutsche Geschichte*, XXXII, (2004), pp. 173–174.

303 The study was based primarily on questionnaires completed in 1945–1946 and on interviews which were also conducted during those years. The individuals who responded to the questionnaires were not told of the actual interests of the study's organizers, and were not asked directly about their views of Jews (because the researchers feared that doing so might lead interviewees to mask their true feelings), but were instead asked "indirect" questions intended both to probe susceptibility to bigoted thinking and to provide indicators of antisemitic and other attitudes. The results, in Adorno's eyes, established that there was a significant correlation between specific personality traits and a tendency towards bigotry. There was no attempt made to obtain what would currently be called a representative sample. Answers received from members of minority groups (such as Jews and Blacks) were excluded, and the sample was heavily weighted towards younger people. Many of those who participated in the study were on the West Coast of the United States, though some questionnaires were completed by individuals in Washington DC. Individuals from different, sectors of the population were surveyed. However, most were from "the middle socioeconomic class" [Adorno et al., *The Authoritarian Personality*, p. 22]. There were, all told, more than 2,000 questionnaires completed.

304 Max Horkheimer to Paul Lazarsfeld, August 21, 1947, Horkheimer, *Gesammelte Schriften*, XVII, p. 878.

305 Max Horkheimer to Samuel H. Flowerman, May 15, 1946, MHA, II.7.100.

306 Theodor W. Adorno, [Talk to the "Young Men's Christian Association – Veterans" of UCLA], June 1, 1948, Adorno and Horkheimer, *Briefwechsel*, III, p. 533.

307 The members of the Public Opinion Study Group were R. Nevitt Sanford, Daniel J. Levinson, and Else Frenkel-Brunswick, all of whom were

associated, in various capacities, with the Psychology Department of the University of California at Berkeley, and all of whom were interested in and sympathetic to Freudian psychoanalysis. The bulk of *The Authoritarian Personality* was written not by Adorno but by the members of the Berkeley group. Horkheimer had become interested in Sanford's work in 1943, and established contact with him via Frenkel-Brunswick, who was herself a German-speaking refugee and with whom Horkheimer had had prior connections [Jay, *The Dialectical Imagination*, p. 239; Wiggershaus, *The Frankfurt School*, p. 359].
308 Fleck, *Transatlantische Bereicherungen*, pp. 421–423.
309 A generation after the publication of *The Authoritarian Personality*, R. Nevitt Sanford, among the book's co-authors, quipped that one of Adorno's main functions had been to teach American academics some Marxist theory and some Critical Theory [Samelson, "Authoritarianism from Berlin to Berkeley: On Social Psychology and History," p. 199].
310 Adorno et al., *The Authoritarian Personality*, pp. 607, 609.
311 *Ibid.*, p. 729. Compare Adorno, "Scientific Experiences of a European Scholar in America," p. 356: "[T]he chapter 'Elemente des Antisemitismus' in *Dialektik der Aufklärung* ... anticipated my later investigations ... published in The Authoritarian Personality."
312 Adorno et al., *The Authoritarian Personality* pp. 663–671.
313 *Ibid.*, p. 638. The Critical Theorists recognized the need to examine not only antisemites, but also the objects of antisemitism. Horkheimer, for example, wrote to Pollock in May 1943 that "it is not only imperative to enter into a thorough study of the antisemitic reactions, but of Jewish psychology as well" [Max Horkheimer to Friedrich Pollock, May 19, 1943, MHA, VI.33.506]. In October 1944, as he was reviewing the interviews conducted as part of the study of labor antisemitism, Adorno sent a memorandum to Horkheimer in which he proposed that a manual for distribution among Jews be prepared. The idea for such a manual was purportedly motivated by Adorno's sense that "not all the ever recurring objections against the Jews are of an entirely spurious, projective, paranoid character. There are a number among them which, though distorted within the framework of general aggressiveness, have their basis in certain Jewish traits which are either really objectionable or at least likely to evince actual hostile reactions" [Theodor W. Adorno to Max Horkheimer, Memorandum, October 30, 1944, re: "Manual for distribution among Jews," Adorno and Horkheimer, *Briefwechsel*, II, p. 336]. Adorno's plan was to create a manual which would list the traits he had in mind and which would contain suggestions as to how they could be overcome. Rabinbach indicates that the memo in which Adorno proposes this manual is meant to be humorous, and suggests that "this ironic text... should be taken just so seriously" [Rabinbach, "The Cunning of Unreason: Mimesis and the Construction of Antisemitism in Horkheimer and Adorno's *Dialectic of Enlightenment*," p. 195]. It is my sense, however, that Adorno really

did believe that some of the objections made by antisemites "may have some basis in reality" [Adorno et al., *The Authoritarian Personality*, p. 639].

Horkheimer prepared a few thoughts on the psychology of Jews for the speech on "Anti-Semitism as a Social Phenomenon," which he gave in 1944 in San Francisco at the conference organized by Simmel, noting that "the psychology of the Jews ... often mirrors the psychology of the anti-Semite" and that "It would be ideal and a great contribution to the solution of our problem, if all Jews would undergo psychoanalysis" but seems to have left these thoughts out of the speech he ultimately delivered. [Max Horkheimer, "Antisemitism as a Social Phenomenon," June 17, 1944, MHA, IX.46.1A, p. 10]. There is a handwritten notation on this typescript, "close here," immediately preceding Horkheimer's comments on the psychology of the Jews.

314 Theodor W. Adorno to Max Horkheimer, November 9, 1944, Adorno and Horkheimer, *Briefwechsel*, II, p. 347.

315 Wheatland, *The Frankfurt School in Exile*, p. 256.

316 By 1948, Adorno was suspicious of Flowerman, and worried that Flowerman had "some kind of monkey business in mind" [Theodor W. Adorno to Leo Lowenthal, May 24, 1948, Leo Lowenthal Papers, Harvard, bMS Ger 185, (8), folder 5]. Did Flowerman intercede to prevent Adorno's "Remarks" from being included in *The Authoritarian Personality*? Wiggershaus reports merely that Adorno's "Remarks" had "originally been conceived as part of the book" and that "Adorno did not manage to push their publication through" [Wiggershaus, *The Frankfurt School*, p. 417].

317 Theodor W. Adorno, "Remarks on 'The Authoritarian Personality' by Adorno, Frenkel-Brunswik, Levinson, Sanford," p. 7 [1948], MHA, VI.1d.77. This statement should not be taken to mean that Adorno endorsed Freud's explanations as to the origins of antisemitism, which Adorno feared "tend to reduce anti-semitism genetically to the psychological events" [*Ibid.*, p. 27, MHA, VI.1d.97].

318 *Ibid.*, p. 3, MHA, VI.1d.72.

319 *Ibid.*, p. 12, MHA, VI.1d.82.

320 *Ibid.*, p. 18, MHA, VI.1d.88.

321 Similarly, Adorno found neither the explanations of antisemitism propounded by mainstream sociologists nor traditional religious explanations of antisemitism compelling in and of themselves. He did, on the other hand, find much to praise in Sartre's work on antisemitism [*Ibid.*, pp. 21–24, MHA, VI, 1d. 91–94].

322 *Ibid.*

323 *Ibid.*, p. 28, MHA, VI.1d.98.

324 *Ibid.*

325 *Ibid.*, p. 29, MHA, VI.1d.99.

326 *Ibid.*, p. 4, MHA, VI.1d.74.

327 *Ibid.*, p. 9, MHA, VI.1d.79.

328 Wheatland, *The Frankfurt School in Exile*, pp. 254–257.

329 J. F. Brown, Review of *The Authoritarian Personality, Dynamics of Prejudice, Anti-Semitism and Emotional Disorder, Rehearsal for Destruction*, and *Prophets of Deceit*, Annals of the American Academy of Political and Social Science, CCLXX (July 1950), p. 176.
330 Joseph H. Bunzel, Review of *The Authoritarian Personality, Dynamics of Prejudice*, and *Anti-Semitism and Emotional Disorder*, American Sociological Review, XV, 4 (August 1950), pp. 572–753.
331 Alfred de Grazia, Review of *The Authoritarian Personality*, The American Political Science Review, XLIV, 4 (December 1950), p. 1006.
332 Allan W. Eister, Review of *The Authoritarian Personality, Dynamics of Prejudice, Anti-Semitism and Emotional Disorder, Rehearsal for Destruction*, and *Prophets of Deceit*, Southwest Review, XXXV (Autumn 1950), p. 294.
333 Harry C. Bredemeier, Review of *The Authoritarian Personality*, The Public Opinion Quarterly, XIV, 3 (Autumn 1950), p. 573.
334 Nathan Glazer, "The Authoritarian Personality in Profile. Report on A Major Study of Race Hatred," Commentary, IX, 6 (June 1950), p. 583.
335 Nathan Glazer, "The Authoritarian Personality in Profile," p. 577.
336 Ibid., pp. 579, 580.
337 Franz Alexander, Review of *Authoritarianism and the Individual* and *The Authoritarian Personality*, Ethics, LXI, 1 (October 1950), pp. 76–80.
338 Jay, *The Dialectical Imagination*, p. 227.
339 Theodor W. Adorno to Marie Jahoda, June 22, 1953, Adorno/Horkheimer, *Briefwechsel*, IV, p. 872.
340 Ibid., pp. 872–873.
341 Max Horkheimer, "Notes on Horkheimer's Remarks," Horkheimer, *Gesammelte Schriften*, XVII, p. 521. The piece in which Horkheimer made this comment was produced for a leading figure in the AJC, Morris Waldman, and was clearly written in such a way as to present the Institute's ideas in a manner which Horkheimer believed was in accord with what the AJC wanted to hear. Similarly, in a draft of a memorandum to John Slawson of the AJC, Horkheimer stated that "antisemitism is largely based upon subconscious reactions ... it is hardly necessary to further point out the close affinity of our approach to psychoanalysis. We have in the back of our minds something like a 'mass-psychoanalysis'." [Max Horkheimer, Memorandum to John Slawson on the research project on antisemitism, MHA, II.2.327].
342 Max Horkheimer to Friedrich Pollock, July 3, 1943, MHA, VI.33.419.
343 "Broadcast: College of Jewish Studies, KFMV, Sunday December 12, 1948, 1:30 p.m. – 1:45 p.m.," MHA, X.6.6a, p. 2.
344 Adorno et al., *The Authoritarian Personality*, p. 709.
345 See Guterman's unpublished autobiographical sketch, an obituary written by Francis Steegmuller in 1984, and other materials in the Norbert Guterman Papers, Columbia University, Box 10. Cf. Adorno and Horkheimer, *Briefwechsel*, III, p. 46.
346 Max Horkheimer to Leo Lowenthal, July 5, 1946, Horkheimer, *Gesammelte Schriften*, XVII, p. 743.

347 Max Horkheimer to Norbert Guterman, September 6, 1946, Horkheimer, *Gesammelte Schriften*, XVII, p. 757.
348 Max Horkheimer to Leo Lowenthal, July 5, 1946, Horkheimer, *Gesammelte Schriften*, XVII, pp. 744–745.
349 Max Horkheimer to Samuel H. Flowerman, February 15, 1947, Horkheimer, *Gesammelte Schriften*, XVII, p. 789.
350 Max Horkheimer to Leo Lowenthal, July 29, 1946, Lowenthal, *Critical Theory and Frankfurt Theorists*, p. 209.
351 Leo Lowenthal to Norbert Guterman, February 25, 1947, Norbert Guterman Papers, Columbia University, Box 3.
352 Theodor W. Adorno to Max Horkheimer, July 1, 1948, Adorno and Horkheimer, *Briefwechsel*, III, p. 236.
353 Theodor W. Adorno, "Ansprache Adornos vor den 'Young Men's Christian Association – Veterans' der UCLA am 1. Juni 1948," Adorno and Horkheimer, *Briefwechsel*, III, p. 534.
354 Theodor W. Adorno to Max Horkheimer, June 16, 1949, Adorno and Horkheimer, *Briefwechsel*, III, p. 276.
355 Theodor W. Adorno, *The Psychological Technique of Martin Luther Thomas' Radio Addresses* (Stanford, CA: Stanford University Press, 2000), pp. 120–126.
356 Leo Lowenthal and Norbert Guterman, *Prophets of Deceit. A Study of the Techniques of the American Agitator*. Studies in Prejudice, ed. Max Horkheimer and Samuel H. Flowerman (New York: Harper & Brothers, 1949), p. xvi.
357 Lowenthal and Guterman, *Prophets of Deceit*, p. 18.
358 Wiggershaus, *The Frankfurt School*, p. 410.
359 Lowenthal, "I Never Wanted to Play Along," p. 134.
360 Lowenthal and Guterman, *Prophets of Deceit*, p. 140.
361 *Ibid.* p. 77.
362 *Ibid.*, p. 77.
363 *Ibid.*, p. 72.
364 *Ibid.*, p. 80.
365 *Ibid.*, p. 85.
366 Theodor W. Adorno to Leo Lowenthal, January 3, 1949, Lowenthal, *Critical Theory and Frankfurt Theorists*, p. 142.
367 James Schmidt, "The 'Eclipse of Reason' and the End of the Frankfurt School in America," *New German Critique*, XXXIV, 1 (Winter 2007), p. 67.
368 Carey McWilliams, "The Native Fascist," *The New York Times*, Book Review, December 4, 1949.
369 Max Horkheimer to Samuel H. Flowerman, January 9, 1950, Horkheimer, *Gesammelte Schriften*, XVIIII, p. 86.
370 Chester A. Jurczak, Review of *Prophets of Deceit* and *Rehearsal for Destruction*, *The American Catholic Sociological Review*, XI, 1 (March 1950), p. 51. His comment applied not only to *Prophets* but also to Massing's *Rehearsal for Destruction*.
371 Alfred McClung Lee, Review of *Prophets of Deceit*, *Public Opinion Quarterly*, XIV, 2 (Summer 1950), p. 348.

372 Samuel H. Flowerman to Norbert Guterman, April 21, 1950, Norbert Guterman Papers, Columbia University, Box 2.
373 Leibush Lehrer, Review of *Prophets of Deceit*, *Jewish Social Studies*, XII, 3 (July 1950), p. 259.
374 Lehrer, Review of *Prophets of Deceit*, *Jewish Social Studies*, p. 260.
375 Dennis H. Wrong, Review of *Prophets of Deceit*, *American Journal of Sociology*, LVI, 3 (November 1950), p. 279.
376 Lee M. Friedman, Review of *Prophets of Deceit* and *Rehearsal for Destruction*, *American Jewish Historical Quarterly*, XL (1950), p. 199.
377 J. F. Brown, Review of *The Authoritarian Personality*, *Dynamics of Prejudice*, *Anti-Semitism and Emotional Disorder*, *Rehearsal for Destruction*, and *Prophets of Deceit*, *Annals of the American Academy of Political and Social Science*, pp. 176–177.
378 Melvin Nadell, Review of *Prophets of Deceit*. *Sociology and Social Research*, XXXV (1950), p. 60.
379 Review of *Prophets of Deceit*. *American Sociological Review*, XV, 1 (February 1950), p. 161.
380 Harold D. Lasswell, "Personality, Prejudice, and Politics," *World Politics*, III, 3 (April 1951), pp. 406–407.
381 The total number of copies sold as of June 1956 was 2427 [Marshall Sklare to Leo Lowenthal, June 18, 1956, Norbert Guterman Papers, Columbia University, Box 3]. *Prophets* was later translated into several languages, and was reissued in English in the late 1960s.
382 Paul Massing, *Rehearsal for Destruction. A Study of Political Anti-Semitism in Imperial Germany*. Studies in Prejudice, ed. Max Horkheimer and Samuel H. Flowerman (New York: Harper & Brothers, 1949), p. 151.
383 *Ibid.*, p. 205.
384 Claussen, *Theodor W. Adorno. One Last Genius*, p. 115.
385 Theodor W. Adorno to Max Horkheimer, November 9, 1949, Adorno and Horkheimer, *Briefwechsel*, III, pp. 315–316. It was Flowerman who first raised the idea of asking Mann to write a review of Massing's book [Theodor W. Adorno to Max Horkheimer, October 20, 1949, Adorno and Horkheimer, *Briefwechsel*, III, pp. 298–299].
386 Adorno's draft is reproduced in full in Adorno and Horkheimer, *Briefwechsel*, III, pp. 552–559.
387 Max Horkheimer to Theodor W. Adorno, December 6, 1949, *Briefwechsel*, III, p. 369.
388 Thomas Mann, "The Pre-Nazi Architects of Hitler's Atrocities," *The New York Times*, Book Review, December 11, 1949.
389 Samuel H. Flowerman to Max Horkheimer, December 14, 1949, Horkheimer, *Gesammelte Schriften*, XVIII, p. 75.
390 Bart Landheer, Review of *Rehearsal for Destruction*, *American Sociological Review*, XV, 2 (April 1950), p. 319.
391 Gordon A. Craig, Review of *Rehearsal for Destruction*, *The Public Opinion Quarterly*, XIV, 2 (Summer 1950), pp. 349–350.
392 Melvin Nadell, Review of *Rehearsal for Destruction*, *Sociology and Social Research*, XXXV (1950), p. 66.

393 Roland G. Usher, Review of *Rehearsal for Destruction*, *The American Historical Review*, LVI, 1 (October 1950), pp. 105–106.
394 Raymond J. Sontag, Review of *Rehearsal for Destruction*, *Political Science Quarterly*, LXV, 4 (December 1950), pp. 600–602.
395 William O. Shanahan, "The Germans and Modern History," *The Review of Politics*, XIII, 2 (April 1951), pp. 250–251.
396 Max Horkheimer and Theodor W. Adorno, "Vorwort," in Paul W. Massing, *Vorgeschichte des politischen Antisemitismus*, trans. Felix J. Weil. Frankfurter Beiträge zur Soziologie, VIII, ed. Theodor W. Adorno and Walter Dirks (Frankfurt am Main: Europäische Verlagsanstalt, 1959), p. viii.
397 Max Horkheimer and Samuel H. Flowerman, "Foreword to Studies in Prejudice," in T. W. Adorno et al., *The Authoritarian Personality*, p. vii.
398 Lowenthal, "I Never Wanted to Play Along," p. 136.
399 Theodor Adorno, *Minima Moralia. Reflections from a Damaged Life*, trans. E. F. N. Jephcott (London: Verso, 1974), p. 55. Cf. Max Horkheimer to Paul Massing and Arkady Gurland, October 5, 1944, MHA, VI.17.199: "After the murder of millions of Jews, Antisemitism has become one of the essentials of the social and political struggle and is no longer a mere epiphenomenon."
400 Adorno, *Minima Moralia*, p. 247. Rabinbach points to "innumerable indications of Adorno's interest in Jewish theological motifs in his writings during the 1930s" [Rabinbach, " 'Why Were the Jews Sacrificed?'," p. 137].
401 Theodor W. Adorno to Oscar and Maria Wiesengrund, March 11, 1946 [Adorno, *Letters to his Parents 1939–1951*, p. 248].
402 Max Horkheimer to Otto O. Herz, September 1, 1969, Horkheimer, *A Life in Letters*, p. 361. Herz had written to Horkheimer on August 15, 1969, and had stated that he had been "very disappointed" by Adorno's funeral because it had not been conducted in accord with Jewish ritual. Cf. Horkheimer, *Gesammelte Schriften*, XVIII, pp. 743, 948.
403 Horkheimer to Otto O. Herz, September 1, 1969, Horkheimer, *A Life in Letters*, p. 361.
404 "In Gesprächen hat er sich immer, obwohl er Halbjude war, als Jude identifiziert und diesem Umstand eine 'aristokratische' Bedeutung beigelegt." [Leo Lowenthal to Evelyn Adunka, April 11, 1988, Leo-Löwenthal-Archiv, Stadt- und Universitätsbibliothek, Frankfurt-am-Main, A. 8.1].
405 Max Horkheimer, Erich Fromm, Herbert Marcuse et al., *Studien über Autorität und Familie. Forschungsberichte aus dem Institut für Sozialforschung*. Schriften des Instituts für Sozialforschung, V (Lüneburg: Dietrich zu Klampen Verlag, 1987).
406 Richard Wolin, *The Terms of Cultural Criticism. The Frankfurt School, Existentialism, Poststructuralism* (New York: Columbia University Press, 1992), pp. 57–58.
407 Schmidt, "The 'Eclipse of Reason' and the End of the Frankfurt School in America," pp. 58–59.
408 Jay, *The Dialectical Imagination*, p. 41.

Chapter 3

1 Among the discussions of the return to Frankfurt by members of the Frankfurt School are those by Jay, *The Dialectical Imagination*, pp. 281–299; Wiggershaus, *The Frankfurt School*, pp. 397ff.; Wheatland, *The Frankfurt School in Exile*, pp. 258–261; and Ludwig von Friedeberg, "Die Rückkehr des Instituts für Sozialforschung," in *Die Frankfurter Schule und Frankfurt. Eine Rückkehr nach Deutschland*, pp. 40–46.
2 There was never any question as to whether or not Fromm (who had been severed from the Institute long before the end of the war, and who was no longer on good terms with Horkheimer in the post-war era) would return to Germany with Horkheimer. But relations between Horkheimer on the one hand and both Marcuse and Lowenthal on the other were rather more complex. As late as 1953, Horkheimer asked Marcuse whether he was ready to move at that time to Frankfurt [Wiggershaus, *The Frankfurt School*, p. 464]. Nothing came of this query, however, and the political differences between Marcuse and his one-time colleagues in Germany became quite stark as the years past – for one thing because Marcuse remained politically engaged with left-wing politics, while Horkheimer and Adorno did not. Lowenthal hoped, at one point, that he too would be invited to return to Germany. He was, however, not asked back by Horkheimer – and a bitter dispute in the 1950s that revolved around Lowenthal's pension claims further hurt their relations [Wiggershaus, *The Frankfurt School*, p. 654]. In 1963 Lowenthal wrote to Kracauer "The most traumatic event of my whole life which I probably will never overcome ... is the estrangement from the old group.... It is not a nice story and it is quite possible to say that I have committed more mistakes and acted more wrongly than M[ax] H[orkheimer]. The provocations, however, defy description. I have little respect for Teddie's so-called solidarity which led him to break off any connections with me and has led to such absurdities as the complete silence for my name and work in the circles of the Institute. I must frankly say that I find it rather degrading for them and for me to use the occasion of private fights for intellectual defamation." [Leo Lowenthal to Siegfried Kracauer, December 13, 1963, Siegfried Kracauer Nachlass, 72.2642/15, Deutsches Literaturarchiv, Marbach am Neckar].
3 Andrew Feenberg and William Leiss, eds. "Introduction. The Critical Theory of Herbert Marcuse," *The Essential Marcuse. Selected Writings of Philosopher and Social Critic Herbert Marcuse* (Boston: Beacon Press, 2007), p. vii.
4 "An Interview with Herbert Marcuse: thoughts on Judaism, Israel, etc...," *L'Chayim*, IV, 2 (Winter 1977), p. 1. *L'Chayim* was published by Jewish students at the University of California San Diego. The interview, originally conducted on March 10, 1977 by Marty Gaynor, Ralph Grunewald, and Harlan Simon, has been republished in Herbert Marcuse, *The New Left and the 1960s*. Collected Papers of Herbert Marcuse, III, ed. Douglas Kellner (London and New York: Routledge, 2005), pp. 179–182.
5 Peter Marcuse, "Herbert Marcuse's 'Identity'," *Herbert Marcuse. A Critical Reader*, ed. John Abromeit and W. Mark Cobb (New York and London: Routledge, 2004), p. 249.

6 "An Interview with Herbert Marcuse: thoughts on Judaism, Israel, etc...," *L'Chayim*, IV, 2 (Winter 1977), p. 1.
7 Barry Kātz, *Herbert Marcuse and the Art of Liberation*, p. 20.
8 Kātz, p. 17.
9 Feenberg and Leiss, "Introduction. The Critical Theory of Herbert Marcuse," p. vii.
10 Douglas Kellner, *Herbert Marcuse and the Crisis of Marxism*, p. 13.
11 Peter Marcuse, "Herbert Marcuse's 'Identity'," p. 249.
12 *Ibid.*
13 Lowenthal, "I Never Wanted to Play Along," p. 27.
14 Wiltrud Mannfeld, "Fragen an Herbert Marcuse zu seiner Biographie," *Befreiung Denken – Ein Politischer Imperativ. Ein Materialenband zu einer politischen Arbeitstagung über Herbert Marcuse am 13 u. 14 Oktober 1989 in Frankfurt*, ed. Peter-Erwin Jansen. 2nd edition (Offenbach/Main: Verlag 2000 GmbH, 1990), p. 36.
15 Kātz, *Herbert Marcuse and the Art of Liberation*, p. 84. Seyla Benhabib finds this explanation plausible [Seyla Benhabib, "Translator's Introduction," in Herbert Marcuse, *Hegel's Ontology and the Theory of Historicity*, trans. Seyla Benhabib (Cambridge, MA, and London: MIT Press, 1987, p. x]. Wolin comments "Marcuse, appraised of the fact that Heidegger would not accept it, refrained from submitting it in order to avoid the ignominy of having it formally rejected." [Richard Wolin, "Introduction. What is Heideggerian Marxism?" in Herbert Marcuse, *Heideggerian Marxism*, ed. Richard Wolin and John Abromeit. (Lincoln, NE, and London: University of Nebraska Press, 2005), p. xxii].
16 Peter-Erwin Jansen, "Marcuses Habilitationsverfahren – eine Odyssee," *Befreiung Denken*, p. 145.
17 Wiggershaus, *The Frankfurt School*, p. 104. Jürgen Habermas reportedly was told by Marcuse that Heidegger rejected his *Habiltationsschrift* [Kellner, *Herbert Marcuse and the Crisis of Marxism*, p. 406, footnote 1].
18 Herbert Marcuse to Max Horkheimer, April 15, 1953, Max Horkheimer Archiv, Frankfurt am Main. Marcuse reported to Horkheimer that Karl Löwith – who had defended his *Habilitationsschrift* under Heidegger's direction in 1928 – knew about Heidegger's comment. Marcuse adds "Nur aus psychopathischen Gruenden wuerde mich interessieren, was H[eidegger] gesagt hat."
19 Peter-Erwin Jansen, "Establishing Lives in Exile – Herbert Marcuse and Leo Löwenthal in America," address delivered at the conference entitled "Marcuse and the Frankfurt School for a New Generation," York University, Toronto, Canada, October 29, 2009, http://www.marcusesociety.org/. Wolin, exploring the fact that Heidegger had a number of students of Jewish origin in the years before the Third Reich (including not only Marcuse, but also Karl Löwith, Hannah Arendt, and Hans Jonas), and knowing full well that his generalizations did not apply in this instance to Jonas, claims that "The explanation lies in the fact that, for the most part, these students did not regard themselves as Jewish, nor did Heidegger so regard them. Instead, they viewed themselves as fully assimilated Germans. Heidegger never shared the Nazis' version of biological antisemitism. Rather, his distaste for Jews was of

the traditional cultural order – a mentality that, as a rule, was accepting of acculturated or baptized Jews" [Richard Wolin, *Heidegger's Children. Hannah Arendt, Karl Löwith, Hans Jonas, and Herbert Marcuse* (Princeton, NJ, and Oxford: Princeton University Press, 2001), p. 83].

20 Sidney Lipshires, *Herbert Marcuse: From Marx to Freud and Beyond* (Cambridge, MA: Schenkman Publishing Company, Inc., 1974), p. 3. Lipshires adds "Marcuse's statement" [that it was the advent of the Nazi regime that prevented him from becoming *habilitiert*] "does not explain ... why he dropped his efforts ... at Freiburg and went to Frankfurt instead. Perhaps he is somewhat sensitive in regard to his relationship to Heidegger". Several years after the publication of Lipshires book, Marcuse discussed the matter of why he left Freiburg and affiliated with the Institute in response to a question ["What did you know of the Institute in 1932?"] posed to him by Habermas. Marcuse's reply reads: "1932 war vom Instiut nur erschienen der erste Band der *Zeitschrift für Sozialforschung*. Das war das einzige, was ich wußte. Ich wollte dringend ans Institut gehen wegen der politischen Situation. Es war ganz klar, Ende 1932, daß ich mich niemals unter dem Nazi-Regime würde habilitieren können. Und das Institut hatte damals schon Vorbereitungen getroffen zu emigrieren, mit der Bibliothek usw." [(Herbert Marcuse), *Gespräche mit Herbert Marcuse*. Gesprächsteilnehmer: Herbert Marcuse, Jürgen Habermas, Tilman Spengler, Silvia Bovenschen, Marianne Schuller, Berthold Rothschild, Theo Pinkus, Erica Sherover, Heinz Lubasz, Alfred Schmidt, Ralf Dahrendorf, Karl Popper, Rudi Dutschke, Hans Christoph Buch (Frankfurt am Main: Suhrkamp Verlag, 1978), p. 12].

Even if Heidegger blocked Marcuse, it is altogether possible that he did so because of misgivings as to Marcuse's work rather than because of Marcuse's Jewish background. Marcuse is known to have expressed questions about both the style and the substance of Heidegger's work as early as 1929–1930 [John Abromeit, "Herbert Marcuse's Critical Encounter with Martin Heidegger 1927–33," *Herbert Marcuse. A Critical Reader*, pp. 140–141, 149, footnote 46] – but it ought to be noted that Heidegger never expressed any such misgivings to Marcuse. Cf. Wolin, *Heidegger's Children*, p. 162.

21 "Heidegger's Politics: An Interview," in Marcuse, *Heideggerian Marxism*, p. 169. Cf. Kātz, *Herbert Marcuse and the Art of Liberation*, pp. 84–85; Wolin, "Introduction. What Is Heideggerian Marxism?" in Marcuse, *Heideggerian Marxism*, pp. xxi–xxii. Henry Pachter, who, like Marcuse, had been a student in Freiburg before the Nazi era, thought that it would be strange if Marcuse had been surprised by Heidegger's involvement with the Nazis, for any number of reasons, including the fact that Heidegger attracted many Nazi students, and that Heidegger's wife was widely known to have been a member of the Nazi party before the Nazis came to power [Kellner, *Herbert Marcuse and the Crisis of Marxism*, pp. 406–407].

22 In 1943, at which point Horkheimer was deeply involved in discussions as to the nature of antisemitism, Marcuse once commented on the approach to that subject being taken by his colleagues: "Perhaps I wrote you already that the 'spearhead' theory in the form in which we formulated it originally seems to me inadequate, and this inadequacy seems to increase with the development of

fascist anti-Semitism. The function of this anti-Semitism is apparently more and more the perpetuation of an already established pattern of domination in the character of men. Note that in the German propaganda, the Jew has now become an 'internal' being, which lives in Gentiles as well as Jews, and which is not conquered even with the annihilation of the 'real' Jews. If we look at the character traits and qualities which the Nazis designate as the Jewish elements in the Gentiles, we do not find the so-called typical Jewish traits (or at least not primarily), but traits which are regarded as definitely Christian and 'human'." [Herbert Marcuse to Max Horkheimer, July 28, 1943, Horkheimer, *Gesammelte Schriften*, XVII, p. 467].

Marcuse apparently wrote a report on "Anti-Semitism in the American Zone" as part and parcel of his job with the State Department's Office of Intelligence Research. The report, however, may well have been an assignment rather than a task undertaken by Marcuse because of any particular interest on his part in the subject with which it was concerned. The report is preserved in Marcuse's archive [HMA 137.00].

23 Zvi Tauber, "Herbert Marcuse: Auschwitz und My Lai?" *Zivilisationsbruch. Denken nach Auschwitz*, ed. Dan Diner (Frankfurt am Main: Fischer, 1988), p. 90.

24 "Group Here Sends Plea for Aid of Soviet Jews," *Evening Tribune* (January 26, 1971), A-3. Though eager to avoid aiding in any way those who wanted to use the issue of Soviet Jewry to support a pro-Cold War perspective, Marcuse reportedly recognized that "there was a real problem of discrimination against Soviet Jewry" [Michael Lerner to Jack Jacobs, May 26, 2010].

25 Telegram, Herbert Marcuse to Gershom Scholem, 1971, Gershom Scholem Archives, Jerusalem.

26 Chetwood T. Schwarzkopf to Herbert Marcuse, July 27, 1968, HMA.

27 The unlabeled and undated clipping containing these remarks is among the unsorted material in the HMA. A letter from a Rena Rogers of Downey, California asserts "Any man who has lived as long as you and still retained any truths within Karl Marx's philosophy is either a Zionist or a fool..." [Rena Rogers to Herbert Marcuse, April 7 1969], HMA.

28 "An Interview with Herbert Marcuse: thoughts on Judaism, Israel, etc...," *L'Chayim*, IV, 2 (Winter 1977), p. 12.

29 Rachel Wirnik, "The New Left In Its Own Image," *The American Zionist*, October 1971, pp. 20–23. Wirnik's article was based on a piece by Arthur Lermer which had appeared in a Yiddish-language, decidedly non-Zionist, organ of the Jewish Labor Bund, *Unzer tsayt*.

30 "From the Rabbi," *Temple Topics*, November 15, 1971, p. 2. Marcuse was provided with a copy of this article by Rabbi Robert E. Goldburg, who had a friendly relationship with Marcuse [see Robert E. Goldberg to Herbert Marcuse, January 10, 1969, HMA 371.03]. Cf. the response to Rabbi Lewis written by Rabbi Goldburg [Robert E. Goldburg to Theodore N. Lewis, December 2, 1971, HMA 371.12]. For another example of unhappiness on the part of self-identified Jews with Marcuse see the letter signed "An American Jew", written to Marcuse and dated March 12, 1968, HMA, unsorted material.

31 Herbert Marcuse, "Humanismus und Humanität," June/July 1962, HMA.
32 Herbert Marcuse to Robert E. Goldburg, January 24, 1969, HMA 371.04.
33 Talk by Marcuse delivered at the Leo Baeck Temple, Los Angeles, California, May 6, 1970 [HMA 0407.01].
34 Michael Lerner to Jack Jacobs, May 25, 2010.
35 "An Interview with Herbert Marcuse: thoughts on Judaism, Israel, etc...," p. 1.
36 *Ibid.*, p. 12.
37 Isaac Deutscher, *The Non-Jewish Jew and other Essays*, ed. Tamara Deutscher (New York: Hill and Wang, 1968); George L. Mosse, *German Jews beyond Judaism* (Bloomington: Indiana University Press; Cincinnati: Hebrew Union College Press, 1985).
38 Shlomo Avineri, "Prague Summer: The Altneuschul, Pan Am, and Herbert Marcuse," *Jewish Review of Books* (Fall 2010), p. 50.
39 Rainer Erd, ed., *Reform und Resignation. Gespräche über Franz. L. Neumann* (Frankfurt am Main: Suhrkamp, 1985), p. 29. Henry Ehrmann recalled that in 1940 or 1941 he visited Neumann at home, and that Neumann had sat with his son, with his head covered, and sung songs by candle light – "a real Jewish father". Ehrmann also noted that Neumann had raised his children "with certain Jewish traditions" [Erd, *Reform und Resignation*, p. 30].
40 Peter Marcuse, "Herbert Marcuse's 'Identity'," p. 249.
41 Michael Lerner to Jack Jacobs, May 25, 2010.
42 Michael P. Lerner, "Jewish New Leftism at Berkeley," *Judaism*, XVIII, 4 (Fall, 1969), p. 473; Michael Lerner to Jack Jacobs, May 25, 2010.
43 In 1969, a statement on the Middle East written by Michael Lerner and Mario Savio on behalf of the Berkeley Chapter of the Committee for a Progressive Middle East was published in *Judaism* (Fall, 1969), pp. 483–487. Lerner reports that Marcuse "was very much supportive" of this statement, and that in Lerner's opinion "the statement summed up his position on Israel at the time... and this is part of what drew him to attend my religious services" [Michael Lerner to Jack Jacobs, May 25, 2010].
44 Shlomo Avineri to Jack Jacobs, March 9, 2010. Was the seder initiated primarily by Erica Sherover, to whom Marcuse was married beginning with 1976, rather than by Marcuse? Sherover developed a strong interest in Jewish matters, and became active in New Jewish Agenda following Marcuse's death. According to Michael Lerner, Sherover "was central to Marcuse's transformation on the Judaism issue" [Michael Lerner to Jack Jacobs, May 26, 2010]. In a telephone conversation with me on June 18, 2010, Sherover's sister, Yeshi Neumann, noted that, though their mother was "very" secular, and their father had left the family home, Sherover decided to get confirmed, and, when in her twenties, travelled to Israel. Neumann also stated that she too believed that Sherover had an impact on Marcuse's attitudes about Jewish matters.
45 Herbert Marcuse, "The Problem and the Hope," *New Outlook*, XI (July/August, 1968), p. 56. Cf. Herbert Marcuse, *Das Ende der Utopie. Vorträge und Diskussionen in Berlin 1967* (Frankfurt: Verlag Neue Kritik, 1980), pp. 141–142.

46 Marcuse, "The Problem and the Hope," p. 57. Marcuse continued to see the 1967 war as a "defensive war" in later years ["Protocol of the Conversation between the Philosopher Herbert Marcuse and Israel's Minister of Defense, Moshe Dayan, December 29, 1971," *Telos*, 158 (Spring 2012), p. 186].
47 Marcuse, "The Problem and the Hope," p. 58.
48 "Marcuse on The University Music New Culture Ecology Personal & Social Liberation Workers The Mideast," *Street Journal* (April 1970), p. 12. All other quotes in this paragraph are derived from the same source.
49 Herbert Marcuse, "Only a Free Arab World Can Co-exist with a Free Israel", [HMA 402.00]. Marcuse penned his introduction in October 1969.
50 Herbert Marcuse, *Nachgelassene Schriften*, IV. Die Studentenbewegung und ihre Folgen, ed. Peter-Erwin Jansen (Springe: zu Klampen, 2004), p. 146. Marcuse actually delivered two talks in Jerusalem, on December 21 and December 23, 1971. In a question and answer period following one of these two talks, Marcuse was asked whether "dual loyalty ... to the struggle for socialism and ... to Jewish history" could "in any way be reconciled with the notion of the new sensibility" [HMA 445.04]. Marcuse began his answer by asserting "I cannot see any insurmountable contradiction between being a Jew and a socialist" and ended by stating that the new sensibility was not limited to any particular ethnic group. Marcuse also addressed one hundred and fifty students at the university in Beersheva on January 2. He answered questions for roughly an hour, in the course of which he reportedly noted, among other matters, "that the kibbutz movement was very impressive, but [that] he did not know if it would be able to survive" [H. Ben-Adi, "Marcuse: Up women's lib, the kibbutz," *Jerusalem Post* (January 3, 1972), p. 7].
51 "Prof. Marcuse talks in J'lem," *Jerusalem Post* (December 22, 1971), p. 10.
52 "Haifa students fight to hear Marcuse," *Jerusalem Post* (December 27, 1971), p. 9.
53 Herbert Marcuse, *Nachgelassene Schriften*, IV, p. 146; "Protocol of the Conversation between the Philosopher Herbert Marcuse and Israel's Minister of Defense, Moshe Dayan, December 29, 1971," pp. 185–191.
54 Arthur A. Cohen to Herbert Marcuse, January 17, 1979, HMA 1095.1.
55 The typescript of Marcuse's statement, dated December 30, 1971, is in the Marcuse Archive [HMA 443.00]. The statement was published in English in the *Jerusalem Post* on January 2, 1972, and on the same date, in the Hebrew-language newspaper *Haaretz*. An Arabic translation was published shortly thereafter. Cf. the editorial note published in conjunction with Herbert Marcuse, "Israel ist stark genug für Zugeständnisse" in Marcuse, *Nachgelassene Schriften*, IV, p. 146, and Herbert Marcuse, *The New Left and the 1960s*. Collected Papers of Herbert Marcuse, III, ed. Douglas Kellner (London and New York: Routledge, 2005), pp. 54–56.

A statement written by the Israeli New Left (SIAH) entitled "What Shall the Next War Defend?" and dated November 1971, is preserved in Marcuse's Archive [HMA 2084.03], and suggests that Marcuse was aware of the positions being taken on the left in Israel at the time that he issued his own statement on the situation.

56 Daniel Amit, who was active on the Israeli left, kept in touch with Marcuse after Marcuse's visit to Israel, as evidenced by the typescript of a book review written by Amit, entitled "The Left and the Middle East", dated December 1974, and containing a hand-written inscription – "with warm regards, Daniel" – preserved in Marcuse's archive [HMA 2084.05].

Marcuse never made a return trip to Israel – but he was encouraged to consider such a trip by Shlomo Avineri of Hebrew University, who, while visiting the University of California San Diego (the institution at which Marcuse had taught in the last part of his academic career) in 1979, wrote to Marcuse in order to find out whether Marcuse would be open to the idea of coming to Jerusalem as a Fellow of Hebrew University's Institute for Advanced Studies in 1980–1981. Avineri noted "Needless to say how much Dvora [Avineri's spouse] and I – and many others in Israel and the university – would like you to come..." [Shlomo Avineri to Herbert Marcuse, May 17, 1979, HMA 1021.1]. I have not located a reply by Marcuse to Avineri's letter.

57 Uzi Benziman, "It is up to Israel to initiate moves which will promote a settlement," *Haaretz* (January 2, 1972) [in Hebrew]. My thanks to Asaf Shamis for his help in translating this piece. Cf. Tauber, "Herbert Marcuse: Auschwitz und My Lai?" p. 97.

58 Janguido Piani, "An Interview with Herbert Marcuse," p. 5, HMA 2121.05.

59 Fromm had been formally separated from the Institute, against his will, in 1939. The matters that led to this separation revolved, in part, around Adorno's long-term criticism of Fromm's critique of Freud – a criticism which Horkheimer seems to have come to share – and had nothing to do with differences on Jewish affairs [Wiggershaus, *The Frankfurt School*, pp. 265–273]. In the wake of the parting of ways between Horkheimer and Fromm, differences between them which had not been evident in earlier years became apparent, or came into being. "It was no accident" Martin Jay points out "that increased pessimism about the possibility of revolution" on the part of the Horkheimer circle "went hand in hand with an intensified appreciation of Freud's relevance" [Jay, *The Dialectical Imagination*, p. 105]. Fromm, who jettisoned key components of Freud's theory, was involved in left-wing political affairs in the United States in the post–World War II years. Horkheimer (and Adorno) on the other hand, kept the German left at arm's length when they returned to the country in which they were born. This general political difference between Fromm and Horkheimer may help to explain certain latent differences in attitude between the two on Israel.

60 Erich Fromm to Ernst Simon, September 2, 1929. My thanks to Dr. Dafna Mach for allowing me to have access to this and other transcripts of letters to and from Simon.

61 Erich Fromm, *Ethik und Politik. Antworten auf aktuelle politische Fragen*, ed. Rainer Funk (Weinheim, Basel: Beltz, 1990), pp. 227–235.

62 Fromm's old friend Simon was also one of the founding members of Ichud. The history and orientation of Ichud are described in Ernst Simon, "Ihud," *Struggle for Tomorrow. Modern Political Ideologies of the Jewish People*, ed. Basil Vlavianos and Feliks Gross (New York: Arts, Incorporated, 1954), pp. 100–108.

63 *I. n. shteynberg. Der mentsh. Zayn vort. Zayn oyftu. 1888–1957* (New York: Dr. i. n. shteynberg bukh-komitet, 1961), pp. 12, 57–67. Fromm first began studying Talmud in Heidelberg with Rabinkow after the end of the First World War – by which point Steinberg was in Russia. As a result, Fromm did not actually meet Steinberg until they were both in New York [Erich Fromm, "Memories of Rav Zalman Boruch Rabinkow," pp. 1–2, Erich-Fromm-Archiv, Tübingen].

64 The depth of their friendship is evident in letters by Fromm to Steinberg [Isaac Nachman Steinberg Collection, RG 366, folder 239, YIVO]. Also see the short statement by Fromm about Steinberg written after the death of the latter [Eric Fromm, "Dr. I. N. Steinberg," *Freeland* (January–March, 1957), p. 4; *I. n. shteynberg*, p. 607].

65 Isaak N. Steinberg, "Territorialism," *Struggle for Tomorrow*, 112–129; Michael Astour [Mikhel Astur], *Geshikhte fun der frayland-lige un funem teritorialistishn gedank*, 2 vols. (Buenos Aires: Frayland lige, 1967).

66 Fromm's article appeared first in the Yiddish-language organ of the Freeland League [Erich Fromm, "Yidishe melukhe un moshiakh-vizie," *Oyfn shvel* (June 1950), pp. 6–8.], and was only published in English at a later date [Erich Fromm "Jewish State and the Messianic Vision," *Freeland* (September – October, 1951), pp. 11–12.], but was doubtless not written in Yiddish, a language which Fromm could read, but only with difficulty. The Yiddish-language version of Fromm's article elicited a number of positive responses from readers of *Oyfn shvel* [Erich Fromm to Isaac Nachman Steinberg, 1 December 1950, Isaac Nachman Steinberg Collection, RG 366, folder 239, YIVO].

67 Fromm, "Jewish State and the Messianic Vision," p. 11.

68 *Ibid.*, p. 11.

69 *Ibid.*, pp. 11–12.

70 *Ibid.*, p. 12.

71 *Ibid.*, p. 12.

72 Fromm continued to hold these views for decades thereafter. See, for example, Erich Fromm, "Religious Humanism and Politics," *Judaism*, XII, 2 (Spring, 1963), p. 223, in which he proclaimed that "the Zionists and the leaders of Israel... in spite of quoting the prophets frequently" were "not in the spirit of Jewish religious tradition".

73 Erich Fromm, "Vegn moralishe printsipn," *Oyfn shvel* (March 1952), p. 12.

74 Mita Charney, "Erich Fromm on the 'Jewish National Character'," *Freeland* (March–April, 1953), p. 11. In the course of this talk, Fromm reportedly described Zionist policy as "unrealistic," and bemoaned both that the state and power were "being worshipped in their own right" in Israel, and that the return of Jews to Israel had polished off long-standing Jewish attitudes towards power.

75 Fromm, "On the Mental Health of the Jewish People. A talk between Dr. Erich Fromm and Dr. I. N. Steinberg," *Freeland* (June–August, 1952)," p. 4. This piece also appeared as Erich Fromm, "Vegn dem gaystikn gezunt fun yidishn folk," *Oyfn shvel* (May–July, 1952), pp. 3–4.

76 Fromm, "On the Mental Health of the Jewish People. A talk between Dr. Erich Fromm and Dr. I. N. Steinberg," p. 4. Fromm also spoke of the

Freeland League in positive terms in another such interview with Steinberg [Erich Fromm, " 'The Sane Society'. Conversation on the new book by Erich Fromm, between Dr. I. Steinberg and Dr. Erich Fromm," *Freeland* (November-December, 1955), p. 9; Erich Fromm, "Di gezunte gezelshaft," *Oyfn shvel* (November–December, 1955), p. 6].

77 Fromm, "On the Mental Health of the Jewish People. A talk between Dr. Erich Fromm and Dr. I. N. Steinberg," p. 4.
78 Steinberg had had longstanding ties with Ichud [*I. n. shteynberg*, pp. 303–306].
79 http://www.spiritualprogressives.org/fmd/files/ICHUD_brochure_sm.pdf
80 Erich Fromm to Joseph Ben David, January 7, 1957, Erich-Fromm-Archiv, Tübingen.
81 Erich Fromm to Ernst Simon, February 14, 1957; March 7, 1957; March 20, 1957, Erich-Fromm-Archiv, Tübingen.
82 Erich Fromm to Ernst Simon, June 24, 1957, Erich-Fromm-Archiv, Tübingen. Fromm had had contact with Goldmann decades earlier, but had not seen him in 40 years.
83 Erich Fromm to James Pike, June 13, 1957, Erich-Fromm-Archiv, Tübingen. See as well the follow-up letters from Fromm also discussing relevant questions: Erich Fromm to James Pike, October 23 and November 22, 1957, Erich-Fromm-Archiv, Tübingen.
84 Erich Fromm to Norman Thomas, July 18, 1957, Erich-Fromm-Archiv, Tübingen. In the same letter, Fromm informs Thomas that while Pike had responded positively to his ideas, Martin Buber's reaction "was rather negative".
85 Erich Fromm to Karl D. Darmstadter, July 26, 1967, Erich Fromm Papers, Box 25, New York Public Library. Fromm corresponded with Darmstadter over a period of years, and commented on Israel very regularly in his letters to Darmstadter. Not long after the letter cited above, for example, Fromm wrote "I ... do not believe that Israel was in as much danger as the people of Israel and many others believe it to have been... The plans to annex Western Jordan and to make the Arabs into a colony are based on strategic reasons. I believe that the hate engendered by the procedure will, in the long run, be much more dangerous to the existence of Israel than the advantage of another piece of land... I am speaking as a Jew who loves the Jewish tradition. Would the prophets, speaking today, approve ... of making hundreds of thousands of refugees, when we have had a history of our own in which we were refugees, and still are? To me, this State, with its admiration of the principles of power, and its lack of concern for the Arabs is a negation of the spirit of the Jewish tradition." [Erich Fromm to Karl D. Darmstadter, September 20, 1967, Erich Fromm Papers, Box 25, New York Public Library].
86 Erich Fromm to George McGovern, July 18, 1970, Erich-Fromm-Archiv, Tübingen.
87 Erich Fromm to Karl D. Darmstadter, October 14, 1970, Erich Fromm Papers, Box 25, New York Public Library.
88 Erich Fromm to Karl D. Darmstadter, March 11, 1972, Erich Fromm Papers, Box 25, New York Public Library. Cf. Erich Fromm to Karl D. Darmstadter,

January 27, 1975, Erich Fromm Papers, Box 25, New York Public Library: "I am more and more convinced that political Zionism is one of the false Messiahs."
89 Erich Fromm to Karl Darmstadter, October 9, 1973, Erich-Fromm-Archiv, Tübingen.
90 Erich Fromm to Karl Darmstadter, December 16, 1974, Erich Fromm Papers, Box 25, New York Public Library. Daniel Burston, who communicated with a woman who had been supervised by Fromm at the William Alanson White Institute [Anna Antonovsky], reports that she recalled "Fromm's passionate denunciations of the injustices perpetrated by Israeli settlers on Palestinian Arabs" [Burston, *The Legacy of Erich Fromm*, p. 13].
91 Ernst Simon to Erich Fromm, December 26, 1976, Simon, *Sechzig Jahre gegen den Strom*, p. 258. The differences between Simon and Fromm on matters relating to Israel were apparent to them long before 1976. See, for example, Ernst Simon to Erich Fromm, October 25, 1967, Leo Baeck Institute, Jerusalem, and Erich Fromm to Ernst Simon, October 31, 1967, Erich Fromm Papers, Box 25, New York Public Library.
92 Erich Fromm to Ernst Simon, January 7, 1977, Erich-Fromm-Archiv, Tübingen.
93 *Ibid*. Simon was not convinced by Fromm's rejoinder [Ernst Simon to Erich Fromm, January 30, 1977, Leo Baeck Institute, Jerusalem]. Their political differences notwithstanding, Fromm and Simon continued to correspond with one another for some time following this exchange.
94 Erich Fromm to Ernst Simon, April 25, 1964, Ernst Simon Collection, Jerusalem.
95 Erich Fromm to Karl D. Darmstadter, October 21, 1966, Erich Fromm Papers, Box 25, New York Public Library. Commenting on a draft of what eventually became chapter 3 of Martin Jay's *Dialectical Imagination*, Fromm noted that Jay had written "although Fromm lost the outward trappings of his orthodoxy the remnants of his faith remained with him in all his later work". Fromm was unhappy with this formulation, and wrote to Jay: "This could easily sound as if I continued my religious faith in God and only gave up my outward religious practice. This, however, would be incorrect. I gave up all theistic belief, but retained an attitude which I would describe as religious, if one does not imply by this belief in God." [Erich Fromm to Martin Jay, May 14, 1971, "Ein Memorandum in eigener Sache," *Erich Fromm und die Frankfurter Schule. Akten des internationalen, interdisziplinären Symposions Stuttgart-Hohenheim, 31.5. – 2.6.1991*, ed. Michael Kessler and Rainer Funk (Tübingen: Francke Verlag, 1992), p. 250]. In an undated letter written in the 1950s in which Fromm discussed a personal matter with his friend Steinberg, he notes that even if he was not a religious Jew in the narrow sense of the term, he could, in situations such as the one Steinberg was apparently confronting, only return to the elementary principles of a religious position, and especially a Jewish position, in deciding how to proceed [Erich Fromm to Isaac Nachman Steinberg, labeled as having been received November 13, but without a year noted on the letter, Isaac Nachman Steinberg Collection, RG 366, folder 239, YIVO].

96 Eric Fromm to Karl D. Darmstadter, February 28, 1969, Erich Fromm Papers. Box 25, New York Public Library.
97 Fromm dipped into the Talmud upon occasion long after he ceased to be an observant Jew, and wrote to Simon about passages in the Talmud [Erich Fromm to Ernst Simon, August 20, 1964]. My thanks to Dr. D. Mach of Jerusalem for providing me with a transcript of this letter, and of a number of other such letters. For an indication of the ways in which Fromm made use of the Talmud in the 1960s, see Adam Schaff, "Erich Fromm zum Gedächtnis," Leo Baeck Institute, Jerusalem. Steven S. Schwarzschild (who both met Fromm and corresponded with him) asserts that Fromm and Simon "got together every morning, into their old age, to study Talmud" [Steven S. Schwarzschild, "Remembering Erich Fromm," *The Jewish Spectator* (Fall, 1980), p. 31]. However, Fromm and Simon met very rarely in the post–World War II decades. Much of Schwarzschild's analysis of Fromm is correct, but he seems to have gotten this point wrong.

Fromm also corresponded with Darmstadter about matters related to Jewish traditions, texts, and doctrines, in the 1960s and 1970s. See, for example, Eric Fromm to Karl D. Darmstadter, November 18, 1966, September 1, 1967, September 20, 1967, January 27, 1975, Erich Fromm Papers. Box 25, New York Public Library.

Works grappling with the relationship between Fromm and Judaism in the last decades of his life include Jochack Shapira, "Fromm and Judaism," *Incontro con Erich Fromm. Atti del Simposio Internazionale su Erich Fromm: "Dalla necrofilia alla biofilia: linee per una psicoanalisi umanistica." Firenze, novembre 1986 – Palazzo Vecchio* (Firenze: Edizioni medicea, 1988), pp. 223–235.
98 Editorial note in Erich Fromm, *On Being Human* (New York: Continuum, 1994), p. 105.
99 Erich Fromm to Ernst Simon, October 24, 1977, Leo Baeck Institute, Jerusalem. Also see Simon's reply: Ernst Simon to Erich Fromm, November 1, 1977, Ernst A. Simon, *Sechzig Jahre gegen den Strom*, pp. 261–262.
100 Erich Fromm to Adam Schaff, January 18, 1978, Erich-Fromm-Archiv, Tübingen.
101 Erich Fromm, "Remarks on the Relations between Germans and Jews," *On Being Human* (New York: Continuum, 1994), p. 107. I have examined the English-language typescript of Fromm's "Remarks" in the Erich-Fromm-Archiv in Tübingen, but follow here the published version of the text.
102 Fromm, "Remarks on the Relations between Germans and Jews," p. 108.
103 "When I speak of the Jews I speak of those generations before the present. The power of Hitler and the trauma of the Holocaust have so deeply affected later Jews that most of them surrendered spiritually and believed they had found an answer to their existence in founding a state— which however lacks none of the evils inherent more or less in all states, precisely because they are based on powers" [Erich Fromm, "Remarks on the Relations between Germans and Jews," p. 108].
104 A short document by Fromm entitled "Mein Judentum," dating from the late 1970s and stored in the Erich Fromm Archiv, was probably produced

in conjunction with the series aired on South German Radio also entitled "Mein Judentum" and discussed in Hildegunde Wöller [of the Kreuz Verlag] to Erich Fromm, February 23, 1978, Erich Fromm Archiv, Tübingen. Fromm writes "I cannot even speak of mein Judentum because I do not belong to any Jewish religious organization and when asked, give the answer 'no religion.' If anyone suspected me of wanting to hide that I am a Jew, he must consider that such an attempt would be rather ridiculous ... if he knows me and my work, he will have ... no reason to believe that I want to hide my Jewish origins."

105 Jakob J. Petuchowski, "Erich Fromm's Midrash on Love. The Sacred and the Secular Forms," *Commentary*, XXII (1956), p. 543.

106 Edgar Z. Friedenberg, "Neo-Freudianism and Erich Fromm," *Commentary*, XXXIV (1962), p. 305.

107 Schwarzschild, "Remembering Erich Fromm," p. 31. For a contrary perspective – that is, the view that Fromm "abandoned Judaism", see I. Nathan Bamberger, "A Note on Erich Fromm's Rabbinic Roots," *Tradition*, XXIX, 3 (1995), p. 52. Bamberger, who was an orthodox Rabbi, was distantly related to Fromm, and like Schwarzschild, had corresponded with Fromm.

108 Erich Fromm, *You Shall Be as Gods: A Radical Interpretation of the Old Testament and Its Tradition* (Greenwich, CT: Fawcett Premier Books, 1966).

109 Eric Fromm to Adam Schaff, January 13, 1965, Erich-Fromm-Archiv, Tübingen. Years later, Fromm made a similar remark about Marx: "I have always looked on Marx as a representative of the Jewish tradition ... [W]hen the Jews made contact with the outside world, the boldest and most radical forms of the messianic tradition were pursued in a form of Marxist socialism..." [Erich Fromm to Steven S. Schwarzschild, October 11, 1974, Erich-Fromm-Archiv, Tübingen].

110 Erich Fromm to Adam Schaff, March 21, 1966, Erich-Fromm-Archiv, Tübingen.

111 Erich Fromm, "Märtyrer und Helden," *Ethik und Politik. Anworten auf aktuelle politische Fragen*, ed. Rainer Funk. Schriften aus dem Nachlaß, IV (Weinheim and Basel: Beltz, 1990), pp. 216, 222.

112 Fromm, "Märtyrer und Helden," p. 226. Fromm discussed these matters in letters to Darmstadter [Eric Fromm to Karl D. Darmstadter, July 26, 1967, September 1, 1967, September 20, 1967, Erich Fromm Papers. Box 25, New York Public Library]. In the first of these letters he wrote: "I find repugnant the frequently shown contempt for the Jewish past in the Diaspora ... One central issue seems to me to be this: the highest traditional ideal for human conduct was the *Martyr* [emphasis in the original]. He risks and sacrifices his life for the affirmation of his faith. This is the greatest or most admirable act a human being can perform. In contrast to the martyr is the *Hero* [emphasis in the original]. He risks or sacrifices his life ... for the assertion of his life, of survival.... The Israelis look down on the Jews [who] have died without fighting, because they do not understand the martyr..." In the second of the letters, Fromm discusses the notion of dying "al kdushas hashem", that is for sanctification of the divine name, and asked Darmstadter "Am I right in assuming that to die al kdushas hashem was considered the greatest virtue

anyone is capable of, although by no means was martyrdom something one was seeking...?" Cf. Karl D. Darmstadter to Erich Fromm, October 9, 1967, Erich Fromm Papers, Box 25, NYPL, in which Dramstadter replies to Fromm's comments.
113 Fromm died on March 18, 1980 [Reijan and Schmid Noerr, *Grand Hotel Abgrund*, p. 44].
114 Erich Fromm to Ernst Simon, January 7, 1977, Erich-Fromm-Archiv, Tübingen.
115 I have learned a great deal from the work of Dan Diner, but do not fully agree with a central premise of his work on Max Horkheimer: "Es ist schlechte, der schwankenden Laune des Zeitgeistes geschuldete Praxis, einen Denker wie Max Horkheimer, gar sein Oeuvre, in den Kontext herkunftsbezogener Kontinuitäten zu stellen. Solcher Umgang wird weder den wirklichen Brüchen der Biographie noch den historischen Verwerfungen seiner Zeit gerecht werden können" [Dan Diner, "Von Universellem und Partikularem: Max Horkheimer," *Kritische Theorie und Kultur*, ed. Rainer Erd, Dietrich Hoss, Otto Jacobi and Peter Noller (Frankfurt am Main: Suhrkamp, 1989), p. 270].
116 Tobias Freimüller, "Max Horkheimer und die jüdische Gemeinde Frankfurt am Main," *Die Frankfurter Schule und Frankfurt*, pp. 150–157. I do not know whether there is any significance to the fact that Horkheimer waited a year before joining the Jewish Community. On the one hand: Horkheimer was extremely busy in the months after his arrival with other matters. On the other hand, it is possible that, in 1950, Horkheimer did not yet know how long he would be remaining in Frankfurt, and that he therefore was hesitant to put down roots at that time.
117 Eva G. Reichmann, "Max Horkheimer the Jew. Critical Theory and Beyond," *Leo Baeck Institute Year Book*, XIX (1974), p. 194. On Reichmann see Horkheimer, *Gesammelte Schriften*, XVIII, p. 989.
118 Ld.,"Die Frankfurter Juden in Zahlen und Bildern," *Frankfurter Israelitisches Gemeindeblatt*, IX, 10 (June 1931), p. 317.
119 Freimüller, "Max Horkheimer und die jüdische Gemeinde Frankfurt am Main," p. 154.
120 MHA, V.67.181.
121 MHA, V.67.177.
122 Horkheimer agreed to deliver a talk sponsored by the Swiss Section of the World Union for Progressive Judaism [Max Horkheimer to Eugen J. Messinger, March 6, 1958, MHA, V.95.105]. In 1962, he received a request by the Jewish Community of Munich that he deliver a lecture, and made a proposal in response [M. Weinbrenner to H.E. Blumenthal, July 3, 1962, MHA, III.21.92], but ultimately did not deliver this talk [Ruth Miriam Ralle to Max Horkheimer, July 5, 1962, MHA, III.21.91]. Horkheimer responded warmly to an invitation from the Jewish students' organization of Frankfurt in 1965, and was "sincerely pleased" to learn that such an organization had been established, but, for a variety of (technical rather than ideological) reasons, found it difficult to simply accept [Max Horkheimer to Georg Heuberger, September 17, 1965, MHA, V.91.94].

123 Max Horkheimer to S. Bendkower, February 5, 1973, MHA, V.90.247.
124 Ernst Ludwig Ehrlich, "Max Horkheimer – ein Leben 'um der Wahrheit willen'," *Israelitisches Wochenblatt*, LXXIII, 13 (July 13, 1973), p. 29.
125 M[artin] C[ohn], "Frankfurt-Loge," *Allgemeine Jüdische Wochenzeitung*, XXIX, 6 (February 8, 1974), p. 11.
126 Reichmann, "Max Horkheimer the Jew. Critical Theory and Beyond," p. 194; C[ohn], "Frankfurt-Loge," p. 11. Maidon Horkheimer did not formally convert to Judaism [Max Horkheimer to Eugen Weill-Strauss, October 2, 1955, Horkheimer, *Gesammelte Schriften*, XVIII, pp. 309–310]. Jewish cemeteries run under orthodox auspices traditionally bury only Jews within their boundaries. However, the Jewish Community of Bern was willing, under exceptional circumstances, to allow the non-Jewish spouses of its members to be buried in the Jewish cemetery of Bern [Eugen Weill-Strauss to Max Horkheimer, October 7, 1955, MHA, V.95.151]. It was because he was informed of this custom that Horkheimer – who was very eager to make sure that he and his wife would ultimately be buried in the Jewish cemetery in Bern, as were his parents – requested that he be allowed to become a member of the Jewish Community of Bern [Max Horkheimer to the Vorstand der Israelitischen Kultusgemeinde Bern, November 15, 1955, MHA, V.95.152–153]. Horkheimer's application was ultimately accepted [Israelitische Kultusgemeinde Bern to Max Horkheimer, February 27, 1956, MHA, V.95.134]. Cf. Max Horkheimer to René Weil, November 18, 1962, MHA, V.95.76, in which Horkheimer describes the reasons for his desire that he and his wife be buried in Bern. Cf. as well Max Horkheimer to the Vorstand of the Jewish Community of Frankfurt, February 27, 1970, MHA, XIX.11.29.
127 Zvi Rosen, "Ueber die gesellschaftliche Rolle des Judaismus bei Max Horkheimer," *Kritische Theorie und Religion*, ed. Matthias Lutz-Bachmann. Religion in der Moderne (Würzburg: Echter, 1997), p. 33.
128 Max Horkheimer to Jüdische Gemeinde Stuttgart, June 7, 1971, MHA, V.95.170. Cf. Z.H. Wollach [Israelitische Religionsgemeinschaft Würtembergs] to Max Horkheimer, June 11, 1971, MHA, V.95.169: "Your Jewish name is Mayer ben Moische."
129 Notes written by Horkheimer, or transcribed by Pollock on the basis of conversations which Pollock had with Horkheimer, such as "Unschuldiger Antisemitismus" (1959–1960) [Horkheimer, *Gesammelte Schriften*, XIV, pp. 103–104]; "Zur Funktion des Antisemitismus heute" (1969) [Horkheimer, *Gesammelte Schriften*, XIV, p. 139]; "Dialektik des Judentums," (1957–1967) [Horkheimer, *Gesammelte Schriften*, XIV, pp. 314–315]; "Die tiefste Wurzel des Antisemitismus in Deutschland" (1957–1967) [Horkheimer, *Gesammelte Schriften*, XIV, p. 362]; "Warum der Haß auf die Juden?" (1957–1967) [Horkheimer, *Gesammelte Schriften*, XIV, p. 389]; "Anti-Amerikanismus, Antisemitismus und Demagogie und die Lage der Jugend heute (1967) [Horkheimer, *Gesammelte Schriften*, XIV, pp. 408–409]; and "Judenfeindschaft" (1968) [Horkheimer, *Gesammelte Schriften*, XIV, pp. 481–482] provide evidence of Horkheimer's ongoing interest in antisemitism in the era following his return from the United States to Europe.

Adorno was also concerned with antisemitism in the decades following the Holocaust. For an example of Adorno's thoughts on antisemitism during that period see Theodor W. Adorno, "Zur Bekämpfung des Antisemitismus heute," *Gesammelte Schriften*, ed. Rolf Tiedemann. XX, part 1 (Frankfurt am Main: Suhrkamp, 1986), pp. 360–383. Adorno delivered this speech in 1962.

Pollock thought it worthy of note, in 1969, that, though there had been attacks made by the Association of German Socialist Students [SDS] on Adorno – because of disappointment on the part of the students' movement with Adorno's stance on the appropriate relationship between theory and practice – SDS had never made insinuations concerning Adorno's Jewish background in the course of these attacks [Frederick Pollock to Leo Lowenthal, June 16, 1969, Leo Lowenthal Papers, 185 (122), folder 27, Harvard]. The Israeli Ambassador to Germany, Asher Ben-Natan, had been repeatedly shouted down at a series of discussions which Ben-Natan had attempted to have in June 1969 with students at German universities [Hans Kundnani, *Utopia or Auschwitz. Germany's 1968 Generation and the Holocaust* (New York: Columbia University Press, 2009), p. 89]. It was precisely the fact that Ben-Natan had been shouted down that led Pollock to make his comment to Lowenthal. As Pollock saw it, one could rationalize the treatment received by Ben-Natan as stemming from an anti-Israeli position or some other factor, but "no one can be in doubt as to its objective significance."

There can, similarly, be no question whatsoever that radical German students were familiar with the fact that Adorno had some Jewish roots. In 1968, Adorno reported to Horkheimer that there had been a rumor among the students that he (Adorno) wanted to attend a meeting called by a group which was critical of the Critical Theorists while wearing a Jewish star. Adorno commented "If that is not projection..." Theodor W. Adorno to Max Horkheimer, December 5, 1968, Adorno and Horkheimer, *Briefwechsel*, IV (2006), p. 835.

130 Wolfgang Kraushaar, ed. *Frankfurter Schule und Studentenbewegung. Von der Flaschenpost zum Molotowcocktail 1946 bis 1995*, I (Hamburg: Rogner & Bernhard bei Zweitausendeins, 1998), p. 86.

131 The incident which sparked Horkheimer's decision revolved around a faculty meeting in which the promotion of Adorno to the rank of professor was discussed: "The historian and orientalist Helmut Ritter was ... scathing in discussion of the appointment ... He said that this was an instance of favouritism. To make a career in Frankfurt, you had only to be a Jew and a protégé of Horkheimer. Horkheimer was present at the meeting. He accused Ritter of anti-Semitism and left the room, slamming the door. He then applied to the ministry in Wiesbaden for early retirement" [Müller-Doohm, *Adorno. A Biography*, pp. 368–369]. Cf. Notker Hammerstein, *Die Johann Wolfgang Goethe-Universität Frankfurt am Main. Von der Stiftungsuniversität zur staatlichen Hochschule*, I (Neuwied, Frankfurt: Alfred Metzner Verlag, 1989), p. 801.

132 Available sources provide marginally different information as to precisely when Horkheimer retired. Jay [*The Dialectical Imagination*, p. 287] and

Müller-Doohm [*Adorno. A Biography*, p. 368] assert that Horkheimer retired in 1958, and that Adorno took over the directorship of the Institute at that time. Reijen and Schmid Noerr suggest that Horkheimer actually retired in 1959 [Reijen and Schmid Noerr, *Grand Hotel Abgrund*, p. 62]. Cf. Wiggershaus, *The Frankfurt School*, p. 468 for additional details. It is clearly the case, in any event, that Horkheimer continued to be engaged with Institute affairs for years following his official retirement.

133 Sonja Latasch-Herskovits to Liliane Weissberg, October 16, 2009. My thanks to Liliane Weissberg for forwarding this e-mail message to me.

134 Max Horkheimer to Franz Spelman, May 20, 1956 [Horkheimer, *Gesammelte Schriften*, XVIII, p. 351].

135 Max Horkheimer to John J. McCloy, February 1, 1960 [Horkheimer, *A Life in Letters*, p. 314]. Cf. Max Horkheimer, "Sozialpsychologische Forschungen zum Problem des Autoritarismus, Nationalismus und Antisemitismus," in *Autoritarismus und Nationalismus – ein deutsches Problem? Bericht über eine Tagung veranstalt vom Institut für staatsbürgerliche Bildung Rheinland-Pfalz im Fridtjof-Nansen-Haus in Ingelheim geleitet von Prof. Dr. Karl Holzamer. Politische Psychologie. Eine Schriftenreihe*, ed. Wanda von Baeyer-Katte, Gerhard Baumert, Walter Jacobsen, Theodor Scharmann, Heinz Wiesbrock, II (Frankfurt am Main: Europäische Verlagsanstalt, 1963), pp. 61–66, which is concerned with the question of how nationalistic and antisemitic attitudes among Germans could be overcome by education.

136 Max Horkheimer to Eugen Gerstenmaier, June 10, 1963 [Horkheimer, *A Life in Letters*, pp. 318–322].

137 Kraushaar, ed. *Frankfurter Schule und Studentenbewegung*, I, p. 208.

138 Horkheimer, *Dawn & Decline*, p. 165.

139 Max Horkheimer, "Judenfeindschaft," Horkheimer, *Gesammelte Schriften*, XIV, p. 481.

140 Max Horkheimer, "Zur Funktion des Antisemitismus heute," Horkheimer, *Gesammelte Schriften*, XIV, p. 139.

141 See the transcript of an interview with *Der Spiegel*, May 1971, MHA, V.147.119.

142 Max Horkheimer to Willi Brundert, October 30, 1965, Horkheimer, *A Life in Letters*, p. 334.

143 Jay, *The Dialectical Imagination*, p. 282, citing an interview by Jay with Horkheimer conducted on March 12, 1969.

144 Theodor W. Adorno, "Reply to Peter R. Hofstätter's Critique of Group Experiment," in Theodor W. Adorno, *Guilt and Defense. On the Legacies of National Socialism in Postwar Germany*, ed. Jeffrey K. Olick and Andrew J. Perrin (Cambridge, MA: Harvard University Press, 2010), p. 208. Adorno's words – "in the house of the hangman, one should not mention the noose; otherwise one might be suspected of harboring resentment" – were first published in 1957.

145 Adorno was seen as a Jewish figure by many post-war Germans (some of whom had antisemitic inclinations and others of whom did not). See, for example, a letter written during the early 1950's to Friedrich Wilhelm by

Gottfried Benn: "I got to know Herr *Adorno*, who gave another lecture, a *highly* intelligent, not very prepossessing Jew but with the intelligence that is really only found in Jews, good Jews." [As quoted in Jäger, *Adorno*, p. 163].

146 Monika Boll, "Konzeptionen des Judentums zwischen Säkularisierung und Marxismus: Hannah Arendt und Max Horkheimer," in *Affinität wider Willen? Hannah Arendt, Theodor W. Adorno und die Frankfurter Schule*, ed. Liliane Weissberg. Jahrbuch zur Geschichte und Wirkung des Holocaust (Frankfurt and New York: Campus Verlag, 2011), p. 116, citing Horkheimer, *Gesammelte Schriften*, VI, p. 361.

147 The following discussion of Horkheimer's views on Zionism has benefitted from my reading of an unpublished paper by Jeremy Brown, "Max Horkheimer's Israel," distributed by the author at the conference held at Bard College in August 2002, "Contested Legacies: The German-Speaking Intellectual and Cultural Emigration to the United States and the United Kingdom, 1933-45", of Stephan Grigat, "Befreite Gesellschaft und Israel. Zum Verhältnis von Kritischer Theorie und Zionismus," *Feindaufklärung und Reeducation. Kritische Theorie gegen Postnazismus und Islamismus*, ed. Stephan Grigat. Freiburg: ça ira-Verlag, 2006, pp. 115-129, and of Rabinbach, "Israel, die Diaspora und das Bilderverbot in der Kritischen Theorie," *Die Frankfurter Schule und Frankfurt. Eine Rückkehr nach Deutschland*, pp. 252-263.

148 See the excerpts from Horkheimer's letter to Slawson included in Max Horkeheimer to S. Flowerman, November 17, 1945, American Jewish Committee Archives, New York. File: Departments and Divisions/Scientific Research/Horkhemer, Max AD 45-48. Brown mentions a series of studies proposed to the AJC and touching on matters having to do with either Palestine or Zionism which were drafted during the period in which Horkheimer was associated with the AJC. Horkheimer's letter to Flowerman, and the relevant studies proposed to the AJC, are also mentioned by Rabinbach, "Israel, die Diaspora und das Bilderverbot in der Kritischen Theorie," pp. 252-253. Cf. the minutes of the meetings of the Committee on Scientific Research, February 21, 1946, and October 24, 1946, American Jewish Committee Archives, NY, Box 23, File: Departments and Divisions/Scientific Research Committee, AD 45-63, at which certain of the proposed studies were discussed. Horkheimer was not present during either of these meetings.

149 Max Horkheimer to Moshe Schwabe, March 24, 1952, Max Horkheimer, *A Life in Letters*, pp. 290-292. Schwabe replied to Horkheimer that, in light of the traumatic experiences of those Jews who had immigrated to Israel from Europe and of other factors, the time for initiatives such as those suggested by Horkheimer had not yet arrived [Horkheimer, *Gesammelte Schriften*, XVIII, p. 232].

150 Max Horkheimer and Theodor W. Adorno to Julius Ebbinghaus, January 7, 1957, Horkheimer, *A Life in Letters*, p. 305. It is also revealing that, in 1958, Horkheimer requested that an author not publish excerpts from Horkheimer's 1939 article "Die Juden und Europa", and that he cited, as one of his reasons for this request, that the article could be read as a renunciation of Israel [Max Horkheimer to Achim von Borries, June 7, 1958, Horkheimer, *Gesammelte Schriften*, XVIII, p. 423].

151 Max Horkheimer, "The German Jews," *Critique of Instrumental Reason* (New York: Continuum, 1994), p. 109.
152 Max Horkheimer, *Über die deutschen Juden*. Germania Judaica. Kölner Bibliothek zur Geschichte des deutschen Judentums, III (Cologne: DuMont, 1961), pp. 10–11.
153 Horkheimer, *Über die deutschen Juden*, pp. 11–12. At another point in this essay, Horkheimer compares the German experience to that of the Jews, noting that "The Germans became free citizens at a later date than other Western peoples; only at a late date did they create a centralized political state and a position of equality ... Once admitted on terms of equality to competition with other countries, the Germans won a high place through mercantile proficiency and scientific brilliance, such as were attributed to no other people except the Jews" [Horkheimer, "The German Jews," p. 111]. He also accents analogies between "the Jewish and German mentalities" [Horkheimer, "The German Jews," p. 111]. Horkheimer's thinking on these issues is obviously similar to the thoughts on Germans and Jews later expressed by Fromm and discussed above. For additional thoughts by Horkheimer on the issue of the relationship between Germans and Jews see Horkheimer, "Nachwort," in *Porträts deutsch-jüdischer Geistesgeschichte*, ed. Thilo Koch, pp. 255–272. The typescript of this piece is in MHA, X.85.1a. Cf. Max Horkheimer to Gershom Scholem, January 12, 1967, Gershom Scholem Archive, Jerusalem.
154 Horkheimer's understanding of the tasks of B'nai B'rith is manifest in a letter to Heinrich Guttmann: "Beim ersten Jubiläum der wiedergegrundeten Loge vermag ich die Erinnerung an meinen Vater als hingebungsvolles Mitglied der alten Loge in Stuttgart nicht abzuweisen. Was und wie er über den Sinn von B'nai B'rith in Deutschland erzählte, die Bedeutung, die seine Zugehörigkeit für ihn besass, unsere Teilnahme an den öffentlichen Feiern und Zusammenkünften haben meine Jugend mitbestimmt. Zu den Ideen, die für mich mit der Loge verbunden waren, gehörten ein freies und gerechtes Deutschland, in dem die Juden ohne furcht zu ihrem glauben sich bekennen und ihn pflegen durften... Ohne solchen einfluss von B'nai B'rith auf meine Jugend wäre ich anders geworden. [I]ch sehe die wesentliche Aufgabe der Frankfurt-Loge darin, die alten Ideen in der neuen Realität zu bewahren, für die Rechts jedes Menschen, für Demokratie, Humanität, für eine offene Gesellschaft in brüderlicher Verbundenheit zu zeugen und einzustehen." [Max Horkheimer to Heinrich Guttmann, April 12, 1966, MHA, V.67.8]. Horkheimer was elected to one of the commissions of the Frankfurt Lodge in 1963 [Martin Cohn to Max Horkheimer, June 26, 1964, MHA, V.67.27]. At a later point, Horkheimer wrote "Ich fühle unserer Gemeinschaft mich mehr verbunden, als ich in wenigen Worten sagen kann. Natürlich leide ich darunter, dass ich so selten an den Veranstaltungen teilnehmen kann, in Gedanken bin ich oft dabei" [Max Horkheimer to Max Schüftan, March 4, 1966, MHA, V.67.11].
155 Lustiger's article, issued under the title "Unsere Aufgaben in Deutschland", was published in a Rosh Hashanah edition of *Frankfurter Jüdische Nachrichten*.

156 Max Horkheimer to Heinrich Guttmann, November 15, 1965, MHA, V.67.18.
157 There is nothing surprising about the fact that Horkheimer and Marcuse took different approaches in 1967 towards matters related to Israel. They also differed rather significantly from one another during that period on other contemporary political matters, including the Vietnam War, and, as became apparent over time, the tactics of the student movement.
158 Theodor W. Adorno to Max Horkheimer, June 20, 1967, Horkheimer, *Gesammelte Schriften*, XVIII, p. 660. Unlike Horkheimer, Adorno made his feelings about Israel known both in public and in private during that period. On June 5, 1967, for example, Adorno wrote to his friend Lotte Tobisch, "Wir machen uns schreckliche Sorgen wegen Israel. Armer [Gershom] Scholem. In einem Eck meines Bewusstseins habe ich mir immer vorgestellt, dass das auf die Dauer nicht gut gehen wird, aber dass sich das so rasch akutualisiert, hat mich doch völlig überrascht. Man kann nur hoffen, dass die Israelis einstweilen immer noch militärisch den Arabern soweit überlegen sind, dass sie die Situation halten können" [Theodor W. Adorno and Lotte Tobisch, *Der private Briefwechsel*, ed. Bernhard Kraller and Heinz Steinert. ([Graz]: Literaturverlag Droschl, [2003]), p. 197]. A day later, Adorno began a lecture by referring to "the terrible threat to Israel, the home of countless Jews who fled from horror" [Adorno and Horkheimer, *Briefwechsel*, IV, p. 809].

Adorno had had very little to say about Zionism in the years prior to the establishment of Israel. During the Second World War, he expressed sympathy for a (non-Zionist) solution to the "Jewish question", that is, a proposal to create a refuge for Jews in Alaska, and described this notion as "very interesting and sensible" [Theodor W. Adorno to Oscar and Maria Wiesengrund, July 15, 1939, Theodor W. Adorno, *Letters to his Parents 1939–1951*, p. 8; cf. Theodor W. Adorno to Oscar and Maria Wiesengrund, July 25, 1939, and June 30, 1940, Adorno, *Letters to his Parents 1939–1951*, pp. 10, 58].

In 1944, the Yiddish Scientific Institute – YIVO solicited from Horkheimer and others answers to a questionnaire concerning the classification of Jewish immigrants to the United States [Max Weinreich and Jacob Lestchinsky to Max Horkheimer, July 28, 1944, MHA, II.16.62–63; *The Classification of Jewish Immigrants and its Implications: A Survey of Opinion* (New York: YIVO, 1945)]. The questions revolved around whether or not those whose opinions were requested believed that it was important to have exact data on the immigration of Jews into the United States, and whether or not those receiving the questionnaire agreed with current practices of the Immigration and Naturalization Service [MHA, II.16.64-66]. Adorno drafted a reply on Horkheimer's behalf, and advised the latter (incorrectly) that the YIVO "should be treated somewhat cautiously. They are apparently fanatical Zionists and their questions are a kind of a nationalist Jewish trap. I have tried a little 'Eiertanz' in order to avoid the fallacies of both naïve assimilation and Jewish Nationalis[m].... I have the distinct feeling that this whole business is very hot" [Theodor W. Adorno to Max Horkheimer, August 21, 1944, Adorno and Horkheimer, *Briefwechsel*, II, pp. 318].

Several weeks before the establishment of the State of Israel, Adorno solicited information from Lowenthal on what Lowenthal had found in his agitator studies concerning Palestine, Zionism and related matters because the AJC had requested advice concerning the psychological effects of "the entire Palestine complex" [Theodor W. Adorno to Leo Lowenthal, April 8, 1948, Leo Lowenthal Papers, 185 (8), folder 5, Harvard]. In a follow up, Adorno writes "Ich bin somewhat at a loss: auf der einen Seite müssen wir all das urgieren, was jüdische Kraft beweist, auf der andern Seite bin ich gar nicht so sicher, ob nicht auch das Wasser auf die antisemitischen Mühlen ist, weil es sich ja bis zu einem gewissen Grad mit dem deckt, was die Antisemiten projizieren. Wieder einmal die Quadratur des Zirkels – mit anderen Worten, was auch die Juden tun, und was man darüber sagt, wird irgendwie gegen sie gehalten. Trotzdem ist mein eigenes Gefühl, daß z. B. öffentliche Sympathiekundgebungen für die jüdische Sache in Palästina g u t sind, vorausgesetzt, daß sie selber stark genug besucht und propagiert warden. Aber davon werden gerade die wieder Angst haben, mit denen wir hauptsächlich zu rechnen haben." [Theodor W. Adorno to Leo Lowenthal, April 13, 1948, Leo Lowenthal Papers, 185 (8), folder 5, Harvard].

Near the end of his life, Adorno corresponded with Gershom Scholem about the possibility of coming to Israel (for the first time) and giving lectures at Hebrew University. Though Adorno was open to the idea, and proposed potential dates, the dates that Adorno suggested did not work well for those in Jerusalem. Scholem therefore informed Adorno that he saw no possibility of having Adorno make a visit during the academic year 1969–1970 of the kind Scholem had hoped to facilitate [Gershom Scholem to Theodor W. Adorno, April 20, 1969, Gershom Scholem, *Briefe*, II, ed. Thomas Sparr (Munich: Verlag C. H. Beck, 1995), p. 222]. Adorno, who died on August 6, 1969, thus never did travel to Israel.

159 Max Horkheimer, "Israel Blitzkrieg und der Antisemitismus," Horkheimer, *Gesammelte Schriften*, XIV, p. 413.

160 Horkheimer was a member of the board of the Union of Friends of Hebrew University, and a member of the Honorary Committee of United Israel Action Keren Hayessod [Freimüller, "Max Horkheimer und die jüdische Gemeinde Frankfurt am Main," pp. 156–157]. He was also a founding member of the Kuratorium humanitärer Hilfsmaßnahmen zugunsten israelischer Bürger, founded in June 1967, immediately following the Six-Day War [Kraushaar, ed. *Frankfurter Schule und Studentenbewegung*, I, p. 261].

161 WIZO Gruppe Bern to Max Horkheimer, September 5, 1969, MHA, V.95.25.

162 R. Lang, R. Braunschweig, and E. Weil, Keren Hajessod to Max Horkheimer, March 29, 1971, MHA, V.91.96.

163 J. Holzman to Dr. Dembitzer, February 3, 1971, MHA, V.91.99.

164 A certificate noting this donation, issued by the President of the Marcus Melchior Lodge of B'nai B'rith and dated March 28, 1972, is in the Horkheimer archive [MHA,V.95.3.].

165 Max Horkheimer, "Aide Memoire," May 22, 1963, MHA, V.16.36. Horkheimer worked on this issue in conjunction with the AJC. The latter organization's Foreign Affairs Committee drafted a statement on German scientists in Egypt at the AJC's 56th Annual Meeting, held from May 16–19, 1963. Horkheimer participated in the Annual Meeting immediately before his meeting with the German ambassador.

166 Max Horkheimer to Zachariah Shuster, May 5, 1969, Horkheimer, *Gesammelte Schriften*, XVIII, p. 722.

167 Horkheimer did criticize specific decisions made by the Israeli government from time to time, such as the decision to put Eichmann on trial [Max Horkheimer, "The Arrest of Eichmann," *Critique of Instrumental Reason*, pp. 118–123].

168 Horkheimer, *Dawn & Decline*, pp. 206–207. See, similarly, "In Israel there is being repeated in miniature what Christendom did on a mass scale. From a people without power and without territory, the Jews became a nation-state analogous to the way in which Christendom fell apart into nations which war with one another" [Max Horkheimer, "Israel oder der Verrat," Horkheimer, *Gesammelte Schriften*, XIV, p. 370] and, perhaps most revealingly: "Judaism, in all its problematic, creates another meaning of nation; for centuries its existence was not one with its power. The symbol of the crisis in which Judaism finds itself today is Israel, whose establishment is contingent on the persecution of the Jews and the salvation of the Jews, which, not improbably, allows one to predict the end of Judaism in the spiritual sense. A bad dialectic, but one characteristic of the present" [Max Horkheimer to Hans Jürgen Schultz, March 15, 1967, Horkheimer, *A Life in Letters*, p. 336].

169 Brown, "Max Horkheimer's Israel," p. 6, quoting Max Horkheimer and Friedrich Pollock, "Von der Familie, dem Stamm, dem Volk, der Religionsgemeinschaft, der richtigen Gesellschaft, der Nation und dem Fanatismus," in Horkheimer, *Gesammelte Schriften*, VII.

170 Horkheimer, *Dawn & Decline*, pp. 221–222.

171 Whether or not Horkheimer continued to be influenced by (secular) messianic traditions, Adorno's ideas certainly appear to have been linked to messianism. The relationship of Adorno's thought to messianism is discussed in Micha Brumlik, "Theologie und Messianismus im Denken Adornos," *Ende der Geschichte. Abschied von der Geschichtskonzeption der Moderne?*, ed. Hartmut Schröter and Sabine Gürtler (Münster: Edition liberación, 1986), pp. 36–52; Evelyn Adunka, "Das messianische Denken Adornos. Eine Studie zur jüdischen Philosophie und Identität in diesem Jahrhundert," Diplomarbeit. Universität Wien, 1988; and F. Werner Veauthier, "'Jüdisches' im Denken der Frankfurter Schule," *Juden in Deutschland. Lebenswelten und Einzelschicksale. Ringvorlesung der Philosophischen Fakultät der Universität des Saarlandes im Wintersemester 1988/89*, ed. Reinhard Schneider. Annales Universitatis Saraviensis Philosophische Fakultät, I (St. Ingbert: Röhrig Universitätsverlag, 1994), pp. 302–306.

172 When his interviewer noted that "caution in dealing with the name of God is ... Jewish heritage", Horkheimer replied "Yes. And in the same way that

this caution entered into our theory of society, that we called Critical Theory. The Bible says 'Thou shalt not make a graven image of God'. You cannot depict the absolute good... What moves me is applying the theological idea to a reasonable theory of society" ["Was wir 'Sinn' nennen, wird verschwinden," *Der Spiegel*, XXIV, 1–2 (January 5, 1970), p. 81; Horkheimer, *Gesammelte Schriften*, VII, p. 352]. Horkheimer repeated his understanding as to the relationship between Critical Theory and Judaism in other interviews ["Die Sehnsucht nach dem ganz Anderen," Horkheimer, *Gesammelte Schriften*, VII, p. 387]. However, Horkheimer's assertions have been questioned by some. One article in a popular (as distinguished from scholarly) periodical, which refers to Horkheimer and Adorno's alleged "internalized antisemitism" in its opening paragraph, begins its final section as follows: "The tendency has been to take Horkheimer's utterances about Judaism and his reasons for returning to Germany at face value, rather than to examine them skeptically in psychodynamic terms. Horkheimer's rather tenuous claims concerning the Jewish elements of critical theory are analyzable as rationalizations of his guilt and a 'return of the repressed' identification with the father" [Adam Weisberger and Gerda Lederer. "Horkheimer and Adorno," *Midstream* (August/September, 1994), pp. 19, 22].

173 "Was wir 'Sinn' nennen, wird verschwinden," p. 82. Gershom Scholem was apparently moved by the statements made by Horkheimer about Jewry in this interview [Gershom Scholem to Max Horkheimer, February 5, 1970, Gershom Scholem Archives, Jerusalem].

Joachim von Zedtwitz wrote to Horkheimer in January 1971, and suggested, in his letter, that Israel was "like an idol made out of stone", and that this made the fact that there were very observant Jews who objected to Israel explicable, but that this stance was not a smart one since there needed to be a place to which one could go if one could not go anywhere else. Thus, the writer, concluded, the State of Israel was a "practical solution" [Horkheimer, *Gesammelte Schriften*, XVIII, p. 774]. Horkheimer replied; "your ideas are so close to me that I have a great need to speak with you... it does me a world of good that you articulate the difficult problem of reconciling the state of Israel with the Jewish expectation of a Messiah. It is not only the pious but also others, not least myself, who find it difficult to overcome their reservations. I too know only the one answer that you give, namely, that what is needed is a 'practical solution'." [Max Horkheimer to Joachim von Zedtwitz, January 31, 1971, Horkheimer, *A Life in Letters*, p. 367].

174 Marcuse died on July 29, 1979 [Reijen and Schmid Noerr, *Grand Hotel Abgrund*, p. 44]. Lowenthal died on January 21, 1993 [Helmut Dubiel, "Mehr als ein Zeitzeuge...," in *Das Utopische soll Funken schlagen ... Zum hundertsten Geburtstag von Leo Löwenthal*, ed. Peter-Erwin Jansen (Frankfurt am Main: Vittorio Klostermann, 2000), p. 9].

175 Horkheimer's critique of Israel paralleled his critique of Marx: "Marx betrayed the Jews. The betrayal does not consist of his antisemitism. Rather, that one can bring God into this world..." [Max Horkheimer, "Marx, die Juden und der Marxismus als Religion," Horkheimer, *Gesammelte Schriften*, XIV, p. 351].

The significance of the prohibition against graven images for Critical Theory is discussed by, among others, Veauthier, " 'Jüdisches' im Denken der Frankfurter Schule," pp. 296–302; Rosen, "Ueber die gesellschaftliche Rolle des Judaismus bei Max Horkheimer," pp. 37–42; and Rabinbach, "Israel, die Diaspora und das Bilderverbot in der Kritischen Theorie," pp. 260–263.

176 Leo Lowenthal to Arye Ben-David, June 21, 1967, LLA A.63.14.
177 Leo Lowenthal to Ernst Simon, June 21, 1967, LLA A.808.15.
178 Leo Lowenthal to Arye Ben-David, December 10, 1974, LLA A.63.31. Lowenthal also discussed his feelings about events in Israel in letters to Paul Mendes-Flohr, a professor at Hebrew University who wrote on Martin Buber and with whom Lowenthal was on good terms. In one such letter, Lowenthal wrote "We are of course here all very disturbed about the situation in Israel which in a way I had predicted sixty years ago... I am afraid that the next elections will be a catastrophe" [Leo Lowenthal to Paul Mendes-Flohr, March 2, 1988, LLA A.579.4]. Lowenthal made his comments in response to remarks made by Mendes-Flohr on the situation in Israel [Paul Mendes-Flohr to Leo Lowenthal, February 18, 1988, LLA A.579.18]. In a second letter to Mendes-Flohr, Lowenthal stated that "[t]he situation in Israel seems to deteriorate with every day, and I share your feelings with empathy and compassion" [Leo Lowenthal to Paul Mendes-Flohr, May 23, 1988, LLA A.579.6].
179 Yehuda Elkana to Leo Lowenthal, March 14, 1976, private collection, examined in the home of Mrs. Toni Simon, Jerusalem.
180 Leo Lowenthal to Yehuda Elkana, April 6, 1976, private collection, examined in the home of Mrs. Toni Simon, Jerusalem.
181 Leo Lowenthal to Ernst Simon, April 6, 1976, private collection, examined in the home of Mrs. Toni Simon, Jerusalem.
182 Paul Assall, ed. "Zeitgenossen. Leo Löwenthal im Gespräch mit Paul Assall," transcript of a broadcast on Sudwestfunk Baden-Baden. Sendung vom 1.2.1981. 2. Programm. 17:00–18:00 Uhr, p.11, LLA.
183 Lowenthal's trip to Israel apparently did not receive attention from the Israeli press comparable to the attention accorded to Marcuse's visit.
184 Typescript of an undated interview with Leo Löwenthal conducted by Emilio Galli Zugaro, p. 6, LLA.
185 Leo Löwenthal, "Ich will den Traum von der Utopie nicht aufgeben," *Die andere Erinnerung. Gespräche mit jüdischen Wissenschaftlern im Exil*, ed. Hajo Funke (Frankfurt am Main: Fischer Taschenbuch Verlag, 1989), p. 169.
186 Löwenthal, "Ich will den Traum von der Utopie nicht aufgeben," p. 170. In another interview, similarly, Lowenthal contrasted the composition of Israel in the mid-1980s with the composition of the Jewish population of Palestine in the early 1920s, underscoring that in the days during which he had still been a Zionist, the influence and the significance of Jews of European origin had been very large, and concluding that a "land of non-Europeans" had emerged from what had been a "European colony of idealists" [Typescript of an undated interview with Leo Löwenthal conducted by Emilio Galli Zugaro, p. 7, LLA].

187 Löwenthal, "Ich will den Traum von der Utopie nicht aufgeben," p. 171.
188 *Ibid.*, pp. 172–173.
189 *Ibid.*, p. 174.
190 *Ibid.*, p. 173.
191 *Ibid.*, p. 175.
192 Herlinde Koelbl, *Jüdische Portraits. Photographien und Interviews* (Frankfurt am Main: S. Fischer, 1989), p. 177.
193 Löwenthal, "Ich will den Traum von der Utopie nicht aufgeben," p. 177.
194 Lowenthal, "In Memory of Walter Benjamin: The Integrity of the Intellectual," pp. 232–233.
195 Löwy, *Redemption and Utopia*, p. 70.
196 The differences among these thinkers on matters related to Israel notwithstanding, *none* of them was embraced by the Jewish State in that country's formative decades. Moshe Zuckermann has compellingly analyzed the "non-reception" of the Critical Theorists in Israel, and has pointed to ways in which Critical Theory and Zionist ideology are incommensurable [Moshe Zuckermann, "Kritische Theorie in Israel – Analyse einer Nichtrezeption," *Theodor W. Adorno – Philosoph des beschädigten Lebens*, ed. Moshe Zuckermann. Tagungsbände des Minerva Instituts für deutsche Geschichte Universität Tel Aviv, III (Göttingen: Wallstein Verlag, 2004), pp. 9–24].

Conclusion

1 Wiggershaus, *The Frankfurt School*, p. 18.
2 Deutscher, *The Non-Jewish Jew and other Essays*, p. 27.
3 *Ibid.*, pp. 26–27.
4 Gershom Scholem, "Reflections on Jewish Theology," *On Jews and Judaism in Crisis*, p. 287.
5 Jäger, *Adorno*, p. 123.

Bibliography

Unpublished Sources
Archival Collections

American Jewish Committee, New York
    Records of the Scientific Research Division
Columbia University, New York
    Norbert Guterman Papers
    P. F. Lazarsfeld Collection
Deutsches Literaturarchiv/Schiller-Nationalmuseum, Marbach am Neckar
    Siegfried Kracauer Nachlass
Erich-Fromm-Archiv, Tübingen
Harvard University
    Leo Lowenthal Papers
Hoover Institution on War, Revolution and Peace, Stanford, California
    Hede Massing Papers
    Joseph Freeman Papers
Jewish National and University Library, Jerusalem
    Gershom Scholem Archive
Leo Baeck Institute, Jerusalem
New York Public Library
    Erich Fromm Papers
Stadtarchiv, Frankfurt am Main
Stadt- und Universitätsbibliothek, Frankfurt am Main
    Herbert-Marcuse-Archiv
    Leo-Löwenthal-Archiv
    Max-Horkheimer-Archiv

Verein für Geschichte der Arbeiterbewegung, Vienna
  Adler Archiv
Wagner Archives, Tamiment Institute, New York
  Jewish Labor Committee Collection
YIVO Institute for Jewish Research, New York
  American Jewish Committee Collection
  Horace Kallen Collection
  Isaac Nachman Steinberg Collection

Essays, Papers, and Dissertations

Adunka, Evelyn. "*Das messianische Denken Adornos. Eine Studie zur jüdischen Philosophie und Identität in diesem Jahrhundert.*" Diplomarbeit. Universität Wien, 1988.

Brown, Jeremy. "*Max Horkheimer's Israel.*" Unpublished paper.

Miron, Guy. "*Leo Löwenthal and Erich Fromm during the Weimar Republic*" [in Hebrew]. Master's thesis. Hebrew University of Jerusalem, 1993.

Schoenhagen, Angelika. "*Frieda Fromm-Reichmann. Leben und Werk*" Med. Diss. Mainz, 1980.

Published Sources

Primary Sources

Achad ha'talmidim [Erich Fromm?]. "Rabbiner Nobel als Führer der Jugend." *Neue Jüdische Presse*, 20 (February 2, 1922), p. 3.

Ackerman, Nathan W. and Marie Jahoda. *Anti-Semitism and Emotional Disorder. A Psychoanalytic Interpretation.* Studies in Prejudice. Edited by Max Horkheimer and Samuel H. Flowerman. New York: Harper & Brothers, 1950.

Adorno, T[heodor] W. "Anti-Semitism and Fascist Propaganda." In *Anti-Semitism. A Social Disease.* Edited by Ernst Simmel. New York: International Universities Press, 1946, pp. 125–137.

  Critical Models. Interventions and Catchwords. Translated by Henry W. Pickford. New York: Columbia University Press, 1998.

  "The Curious Realist: On Siegfried Kracauer." *New German Critique*, 54 (Fall, 1991), pp. 159–176.

  "Fragmente über Wagner." *Zeitschrift für Sozialforschung*, VIII (1939–1940), pp. 1–49.

  "Freudian Theory and the Pattern of Fascist Propaganda." In *Critical Theory: The Essential Readings.* Edited by David Ingram and Julia Simon-Ingram. New York: Paragon House, 1991, pp. 84–102.

  In Search of Wagner. Translated by Rodney Livingstone. London, New York: Verso, 2005.

Letters to his Parents 1939–1951. Edited by Christoph Gödde and Henri Lonitz. Translated by Wieland Hoban. Malden, MA: Polity, 2006.

"Messages in a Bottle." *Mapping Ideology*. Edited by Slavoj Žižek. London: Verso, 1994, pp. 34–45.

Minima Moralia. Reflections from a Damaged Life. Translated by E. F. N. Jephcott. London: Verso, 1974.

Negative Dialectics. Translated by E. B. Ashton. New York: Continuum, 1973.

The Psychological Technique of Martin Luther Thomas' Radio Addresses. Stanford, CA: Stanford University Press, 2000.

Prisms. Cambridge, MA: MIT Press, 1981.

"Reply to Peter R. Hofstätter's Critique of *Group Experiment*." In Theodor W. Adorno, *Guilt and Defense. On the Legacies of National Socialism in Postwar Germany*. Edited by Jeffrey K. Olick and Andrew J. Perrin. Cambridge, MA: Harvard University Press, 2010, pp. 197–209.

"Scientific Experiences of a European Scholar in America." In *The Intellectual Migration. Europe and America, 1930–1960*. Edited by Donald Fleming and Bernard Bailyn. Cambridge, MA: The Belknap Press of Harvard University Press, 1969, pp. 338–370.

The Stars Down to Earth and other essays on the irrational in culture. Edited and with an introduction by Stephen Crook. London and New York: Routledge, 1994.

"Zur Bekämpfung des Antisemitismus heute." *Gesammelte Schriften*. Edited by Rolf Tiedemann. XX, part 1. Frankfurt am Main: Suhrkamp, 1986, pp. 360–383.

Adorno, Theodor W. and Walter Benjamin. *The Complete Correspondence 1928–1940*. Edited by Henri Lonitz. Translated by Nicholas Walker. Cambridge, MA: Harvard University Press, 1999.

Adorno, Theodor W. and Alban Berg. *Correspondence 1925–1935*. Edited by Henri Lonitz. Translated by Wieland Hoban. Cambridge: Polity, 2005.

Briefwechsel 1925–1935. Edited by Henri Lonitz. Briefe und Briefwechsel, II. Suhrkamp: Frankfurt am Main, 1997.

Adorno, Theodor W. and Max Horkheimer. *Briefwechsel*, I-IV. Edited by - Christoph Gödde and Henri Lonitz. Suhrkamp: Frankfurt am Main, 2003–2006.

Adorno, Theodor W. and Ernst Krenek. *Briefwechsel*. Suhrkamp: Frankfurt am Main, 1974.

Adorno, Theodor W. and Lotte Tobisch. *Der private Briefwechsel*. Edited by Bernhard Kraller and Heinz Steinert. [Graz]: Literaturverlag Droschl [2003].

Adorno, T[heodor] W., Else Frenkel-Brunswik, Daniel J. Levinson, R. Nevitt Sanford in collaboration with Betty Aron, Maria Hertz Levinson and William Morrow. *The Authoritarian Personality*. Studies in Prejudice. Edited by Max Horkheimer and Samuel H. Flowerman. New York: Harper & Brothers, 1950.

Alexander, Franz. Review of *Authoritarianism and the Individual* and *The Authoritarian Personality*. *Ethics*, LXI, 1 (October 1950), pp. 76–80.

Anderson, Kevin B. and Russell Rockwell, eds. *The Dunayevskaya-Marcuse-Fromm Correspondence, 1954–1978. Dialogues on Hegel, Marx, and Critical Theory*. Lanham, MD: Lexington Books, 2012.

Benjamin, Walter. *The Correspondence of Walter Benjamin 1910–1940*. Edited by Gershom Scholem and Theodor W. Adorno. Translated by Manfred R. Jacobson and Evelyn M. Jacobson. Chicago and London: The University of Chicago Press, 1994.
Illuminations. Edited and with an introduction by Hannah Arendt. New York: Schocken Books, 1969.
Reflections. Essays, Aphorisms, Autobiographical Writings. Edited and with an introduction by Peter Demetz. Translated by Edmund Jephcott. New York: Schocken Books, 1978.
Bettelheim, Bruno and Morris Janowitz. *Dynamics of Prejudice. A Psychological and Sociological Study of Veterans*. Studies in Prejudice. Edited by Max Horkheimer and Samuel H. Flowerman. New York: Harper & Brothers, 1950.
Bredemeier, Harry C. Review of *The Authoritarian Personality*. *The Public Opinion Quarterly*, XIV, 3 (Autumn 1950), pp. 571–574.
Brown, J. F. Review of *The Authoritarian Personality, Dynamics of Prejudice, Anti-Semitism and Emotional Disorder, Rehearsal for Destruction*, and *Prophets of Deceit*. *Annals of the American Academy of Political and Social Science*, CCLXX (July 1950), pp. 175–177.
Buber, Martin. *Briefwechsel aus sieben Jahrzehnten*. II. Heidelberg: Verlag Lambert Schneider, 1973.
Buber, Martin and Franz Rosenzweig. "The Bible in German: In Reply." *Scripture and Translation*. Translated by Lawrence Rosenwald with Everett Fox. Indiana Studies in Biblical Literature. Bloomington and Indianapolis: Indiana University Press, 1994, pp. 151–160.
Craig, Gordon A. Review of *Rehearsal for Destruction*. *The Public Opinion Quarterly*, XIV, 2 (Summer 1950), pp. 348–350.
de Grazia, Alfred. Review of *The Authoritarian Personality*. *The American Political Science Review*, XLIV, 4 (December 1950), pp. 1005–1006.
Eister, Allan W. Review of *The Authoritarian Personality, Dynamics of Prejudice, Anti-Semitism and Emotional Disorder, Rehearsal for Destruction*, and *Prophets of Deceit*. *Southwest Review*, XXXV (Autumn 1950), pp. 293–295.
Friedman, Lee M. Review of *Prophets of Deceit* and *Rehearsal for Destruction*. *American Jewish Historical Quarterly*, XL (1950), pp. 199–201.
Fromm, Erich. "Dr. I. N. Steinberg." *Freeland* (January–March, 1957), p. 4.
"Ein Memorandum in eigener Sache." In *Erich Fromm und die Frankfurter Schule. Akten des internationalen, interdisziplinären Symposions Stuttgart-Hohenheim, 31.5.–2.6.1991*. Edited by Michael Kessler and Rainer Funk. Tübingen: Francke Verlag, 1992, pp. 249–256.
"Für eine Kooperation von Israelis und Palästinensern." In Erich Fromm, *Ethik und Politik. Anworten auf aktuelle politische Fragen*. Edited by Rainer Funk. Schriften aus dem Nachlass, IV. Weinheim and Basel: Beltz, 1990, pp. 227–235.
"Di gezunte gezelshaft." *Oyfn shvel* (November – December, 1955), pp. 5–7.
"Jewish State and the Messianic Vision." *Freeland* (September–October, 1951), pp. 11–12.

Das jüdische Gesetz. Zur Soziologie des Diaspora-Judentums. Dissertation von 1922. Edited by Rainer Funk and Bernd Sahler. Schriften aus dem Nachlass, II. Weinheim and Basel: Beltz, 1989.

"Märtyrer und Helden." In *Ethik und Politik. Anworten auf aktuelle politische Fragen.* Edited by Rainer Funk. Schriften aus dem Nachlass, IV. Weinheim and Basel: Beltz, 1990, pp. 216-226.

"On the Mental Health of the Jewish People. A talk between Dr. Erich Fromm and Dr. I. N. Steinberg." *Freeland* (June–August, 1952), pp. 2-4.

"Religious Humanism and Politics." *Judaism*, XII, 2 (Spring 1963), pp. 223-224.

"Remarks on the Relations between Germans and Jews." *On Being Human.* New York: Continuum, 1994, pp. 105-110.

" 'The Sane Society'. Conversation on the new book by Erich Fromm, between Dr. I. Steinberg and Dr. Erich Fromm." *Freeland* (November–December, 1955), pp. 8-9.

"Some Biographical Notes." *In the Name of Life. Essays in Honor of Erich Fromm.* Edited by Bernard Landis and Edward S. Tauber. New York: Rinehart and Winston, 1971.

"V. J. St. Achduth, Frankfurt a. M." *Der Jüdische Student. Zeitschrift des Kartells Jüdischer Verbindungen*, XVI, 3 (May 1919), p. 107.

"Vegn dem gaystikn gezunt fun yidishn folk." *Oyfn shvel* (May–July, 1952), pp. 3-4.

"Vegn moralishe printsipn." *Oyfn shvel* (March 1952), p. 12.

The Working Class in Weimar Germany. A Psychological and Sociological Study. Edited by Wolfgang Bonss. Translated by Barbara Weinberger. Berg: Leamington Spa, 1984.

"Yidishe melukhe un moshiakh-vizie." *Oyfn shvel* (June 1950), pp. 6-8.

You Shall be as Gods. A Radical Interpretation of the Old Testament and Its Tradition. New York: Holt, Rinehart and Winston, 1966.

"Zur Tagung der Agudas-Jisroel-Jugendorganisation." *Der Jüdische Student. Zeitschrift des Kartells Jüdischer Verbindungen*, XV, 5/6 (November 1918), pp. 80-81.

Fromm, Erich, Fritz Goithein, Leo Löwenthal, Ernst Simon, Erich Michaelis. "Ein prinzipielles Wort zur Erziehungsfrage." *Jüdische Rundschau*, XXVII, 103/104 (December 29, 1922), pp. 675-676.

Fromm-Reichmann, Frieda. "Reminiscences of Europe." In *Psychoanalysis and Psychosis.* Edited by Ann-Louise S. Silver. Madison, CT: International Universities Press, 1989, pp. 469-481.

Glazer, Nathan. "The Authoritarian Personality in Profile. Report on A Major Study of Race Hatred." *Commentary*, IX, 6 (June 1950), pp. 573-583.

Grossman[n], H[enryk]. "Der bundizm in galitsien." *Der sotsial-demokrat. Organ fun di yudishe sotsial-demokratishe partay in galitsien*, III, 37 (September 13, 1907), pp. 2-3; 38 (September 20, 1907), pp. 1-2; 39 (September 27, 1907), pp. 2-3; 40 (October 4, 1907), pp. 2-3; 44 (November 8, 1907), pp. 1-2; 46 (November 22, 1907), pp. 1-2; 47 (November 29, 1907), pp. 1-2.

"Vegen unzere agitatsie un propaganda." *Der sotsial-demokrat. Organ fun di yudishe sotsial-demokratishe partay in galitsien*, II, 33 (August 24, 1906), pp. 2–3; 36 (September 14, 1906), pp. 2–3.

Haereticus [Leo Löwenthal]. "Die Lehren von China." *Jüdisches Wochenblatt*, II, 25 (June 26, 1925), p. 279.

Horkheimer, Max. *A Life in Letters. Selected Correspondence*. Edited by Manfred R. Jacobson and Evelyn M. Jacobson. Lincoln, NE, and London: University of Nebraska Press, 2007.

[Answer to a questionnaire] *The Classification of Jewish Immigrants and its Implications. A Survey of Opinion*. New York: Yiddish Scientific Institute – YIVO, 1945, pp. 64–66.

Dawn & Decline. Notes 1926–1931 and 1950–1969. Translated by Michael Shaw. New York: The Seabury Press, 1978.

"Dokumente – Stationen [Gespräch mit Otmar Hersche]." *Gesammelte Schriften*, VII. Edited by Gunzelin Schmid Noerr. Frankfurt am Main: Fischer Taschenbuch Verlag, 1985, pp. 317–344.

Eclipse of Reason. New York: Continuum, 1992.

"The German Jews." *Critique of Instrumental Reason: Lectures and Essays since the End of World War II*. Translated by Matthew J. O'Connell and others. New York: Continuum, 1994, pp. 101–118.

Gesammelte Schriften, 19 vols. Frankfurt am Main: Fischer Taschenbuch Verlag, 1985–1996.

"The Jews and Europe." In *Critical Theory and Society. A Reader*. Edited by Stephen Eric Bronner and Douglas MacKay Kellner. New York and London: Routledge, 1989, pp. 77–94.

"Die Juden und Europa." *Studies in Philosophy and Social Science*. VIII (1939), pp. 115–137.

"Nachwort." In *Porträts deutsch-jüdischer Geistesgeschichte*. Edited by Thilo Koch. Cologne: Verlag M. DuMont Schauberg, 1961, pp. 255–272.

"Sociological Background of the Psychoanalytic Approach." In *Anti-Semitism. A Social Disease*. Edited by Ernst Simmel. New York: International Universities Press, 1946, pp. 1–10.

"Sozialpsychologische Forschungen zum Problem des Autoritarismus, Nationalismus und Antisemitismus." In *Autoritarismus und Nationalismus – ein deutsches Problem? Bericht über eine Tagung veranstalt vom Institut für staatsbürgerliche Bildung Rheinland-Pfalz im Fridtjof-Nansen-Haus in Ingelheim geleitet von Prof. Dr. Karl Holzamer*. Politische Psychologie. Eine Schriftenreihe. Edited by Wanda von Baeyer-Katte, Gerhard Baumert, Walter Jacobsen, Theodor Scharmann, Heinz Wiesbrock. II. Frankfurt am Main: Europäische Verlagsanstalt, 1963, pp. 61–66.

"The State of Contemporary Social Philosophy and the Tasks of an Institute for Social Research." In *Critical Theory and Society. A Reader*. Edited by Stephen Eric Bronner and Douglas MacKay Kellner. New York and London: Routledge, 1989, pp. 25–36.

Traditionelle und kritische Theorie. Fünf Aufsätze. Frankfurt am Main: Fischer Taschenbuch Verlag, 1992.

Über die deutschen Juden. Germania Judaica. Kölner Bibliothek zur Geschichte des deutschen Judentums. Schriftenreihe, Heft III. Cologne: DuMont, 1961.

"Was wir 'Sinn' nennen, wird verschwinden." *Der Spiegel*, XXIV, 1/2 (January 5, 1970), pp. 79–84.

Horkheimer, Max and Theodor W. Adorno. *Dialectic of Enlightenment*. Translated by John Cumming. New York: Continuum, 1990.

Dialectic of Enlightenment. Philosophical Fragments. Edited by Gunzelin Schmid Noerr. Translated by Edmund Jephcott. Stanford, CA: Stanford University Press, 2002.

Philosophische Fragmente. Frankfurt am Main: Fischer Taschenbuch Verlag, 1988.

"Vorwort." In Paul W. Massing, *Vorgeschichte des politischen Antisemitismus*. Frankfurter Beiträge zur Soziologie, VIII. Frankfurt am Main: Europäische Verlagsanstalt, 1959, pp. v–viii.

Horkheimer, Max, Erich Fromm, and Herbert Marcuse et al., *Studien über Autorität und Familie*. Forschungsberichte aus dem Institut für Sozialforschung. Schriften des Instituts für Sozialforschung, V. Lüneburg: Dietrich zu Klampen Verlag, 1987.

Horkheimer, Max and Samuel H. Flowerman, "Foreword to Studies in Prejudice." In T. W. Adorno, Else Frenkel-Brunswik, Daniel J. Levinson, and R. Nevitt Sanford in collaboration with Betty Aron, Maria Hertz Levinson and William Morrow. *The Authoritarian Personality*. Studies in Prejudice. Edited by Max Horkheimer and Samuel H. Flowerman. New York: Harper & Brothers, 1950, pp. v–viii.

Jansen, Peter Erwin and Christian Schmidt, eds. *In steter Freundschaft: Leo Löwenthal – Siegfried Kracauer Briefwechsel 1921–1966*. Springe: zu Klampen Verlag, 2003.

Jansen, Peter Erwin, ed. *Das Utopische soll Funken schlagen … Zum hundertsten Geburtstag von Leo Löwenthal*. Frankfurt am Main: Vittorio Klostermann, 2000.

Jurczak, Chester A. Review of *Prophets of Deceit* and *Rehearsal for Destruction*. *The American Catholic Sociological Review*, XI, 1 (March 1950), pp. 50–51.

Koelbl, Herlinde. *Jüdische Portraits. Photographien und Interviews*. Frankfurt am Main: S. Fischer, 1989.

Kracauer, Siegfried. "The Bible in German." *The Mass Ornament. Weimar Essays.* Translated by Thomas Y. Levin. Cambridge, MA; London: Harvard University Press, 1995, pp. 189–203.

Landheer, Bart. Review of *Rehearsal for Destruction*. *American Sociological Review*, XV, 2 (April 1950), p. 319.

Lasswell, Harold D. "Personality, Prejudice, and Politics." *World Politics*, III, 3 (April 1951), pp. 399–407.

Lee, Alfred McClung. Review of *Prophets of Deceit*. *Public Opinion Quarterly*, XIV, 2 (Summer 1950), pp. 347–348.

Löwenthal, Leo. "Doktor Stieglitz." *Jüdisches Wochenblatt*, II, 28 (July 17, 1925), p. 308.

"Ein Heinrich Heine-Film." *Jüdisches Wochenblatt*, II, 24 (June 19, 1925), p. 267.

"Eine Dostojewsky-Biographie." *Jüdisches Wochenblatt*, II, 33 (August 21, 1925), p. 359.
"Einer von unsere Leut'." *Jüdisches Wochenblatt*, II, 28 (July 17, 1925), pp. 307–308.
"Die grosse Passion." *Jüdisches Wochenblatt*, II, 35 (September 4, 1925), p. 380.
"Ich will den Traum von der Utopie nicht aufgeben." In *Die andere Erinnerung. Gespräche mit jüdischen Wissenschaftlern im Exil*. Edited by Hajo Funke. Frankfurt am Main: Fischer Taschenbuch Verlag, 1989, pp. 168–185.
"'Die Jagd Gottes'." *Jüdisches Wochenblatt*, III, 4 (January 22, 1926), pp. 30–31.
"Judentum und deutscher Geist, I. Salomon Maimon." *Bayerische Israelitische Gemeindezeitung*, VI, 14 (July 15, 1930), pp. 217–219.
"Judentum und deutscher Geist, II. Sigmund Freud." *Bayerische Israelitische Gemeindezeitung*, VI, 19 (October 1, 1930), pp. 299–300.
"Judentum und deutscher Geist, III. Ferdinand Lassalle." *Bayerische Israelitische Gemeindezeitung*, VII, 16 (August 15, 1931), pp. 245–247.
"Judentum und deutscher Geist, IV. Karl Marx." *Bayerische Israelitische Gemeindezeitung*, VIII, 7 (April 1, 1932), pp. 98–99.
"Jüdische Erzähler." *Jüdisches Wochenblatt*, II, 27 (July 10, 1925), p. 300.
"Die jüdische Religionsphilosophie Hermann Cohens." *Frankfurter Israelitisches Gemeindeblatt*, VIII, 9 (May 1930), pp. 357–359.
"Das Konzessionsgesetz in Polen." *Jüdisches Wochenblatt*, II, 23 (June 12, 1925), p. 257.
"Die Lage der Juden in Polen." *Jüdisches Wochenblatt*, II, 26 (July 3, 1925), pp. 287–288.
Mitmachen wollte ich nie. Ein autobiographisches Gespräch mit Helmut Dubiel. Frankfurt am Main: Suhrkamp, 1980.
"Moses Mendelssohn und der deutsche Geist." *Frankfurter Israelitisches Gemeindeblatt*, VIII, 1 (September 1929), pp. 7–9.
"Philosophisches." *Jüdisches Wochenblatt*, II, 9 (February 27, 1925), p. 100.
"Potasch und Perlmutter." *Jüdisches Wochenblatt*, II, 25 (June 26, 1925), p. 277.
"Rabbiner Dr. N. A. Nobel, verschieden am 24. Januar 1922." *Der jüdische Student. Zeitschrift des kartells jüdischer Verbindungen*, XIX, 2 (March 1922), pp. 87–88.
"Rabbiner N. A. Nobel. Ein Prinzipielles Vorwort zu einem Nekrolog." *Jüdisches Wochenblatt*, II, 3 (January 16, 1925), p. 25.
"Tolstoi und die Judenfrage." *Frankfurter Israelitisches Gemeindeblatt*, VII, 11 (July 1929), pp. 381–383.
Untergang der Dämonologien. Studien über Judentum, Antisemitismus und faschistischen Geist. Leipzig: Reclam Verlag, 1990.
"Vorurteilsbilder. Antisemitismus unter amerikanischen Arbeitern." *Schriften*. Edited by Helmut Dubiel. III. Frankfurt am Main: Suhrkamp, 1982, pp. 175–237.
Lowenthal, Leo. "As I Remember Friedel." *New German Critique*, 54 (Fall 1991), pp. 5–17.

"I Never Wanted to Play Along: Interviews with Helmut Dubiel." In *An Unmastered Past. The Autobiographical Reflections of Leo Lowenthal*. Edited by Martin Jay. Berkeley, Los Angeles, and London: University of California Press, 1987, pp. 17–159.

"In Memory of Walter Benjamin: The Integrity of the Intellectual." In *An Unmastered Past. The Autobiographical Reflections of Leo Lowenthal*. Edited by Martin Jay. Berkeley, Los Angeles, and London: University of California Press, 1987, pp. 216–234.

"Introduction." *Critical Theory and Frankfurt Theorists. Lectures–Correspondence–Conversations*. Communication in Society, IV. New Brunswick, NJ, and Oxford: Transaction Publishers, 1989, pp. 3–4.

"Recollections of Theodor W. Adorno." In *An Unmastered Past. The Autobiographical Reflections of Leo Lowenthal*. Edited by Martin Jay. Berkeley, Los Angeles, and London: University of California Press, 1987, pp. 201–215.

Lowenthal, Leo and Norbert Guterman. *Prophets of Deceit. A Study of the Techniques of the American Agitator*. Studies in Prejudice. Edited by Max Horkheimer and Samuel H. Flowerman. New York: Harper & Brothers, 1949.

Löwenthal, Viktor. "Kindheit im orthodoxen Milieu." In *Frankfurter juedische Errinerungen. Ein Lesebuch zur Erforschung der Geschichte der Frankfurter Juden*. Edited by the Kommission zur Erforschung der Geschichte der Frankfurter Juden. Sigmaringen: Jan Thorbecke Verlag, 1997, pp. 38–50.

Mann, Thomas. "The Pre-Nazi Architects of Hitler's Atrocities." *The New York Times*, Book Review (December 11, 1949).

Mannfeld, Wiltrud. "Fragen an Herbert Marcuse. Ein Interview zu seiner Biographie." *Befreiung denken – Ein politischer Imperativ*. Edited by Peter-Erwin Jansen. 2nd edition. Offenbach: Verlag 2000 GmbH, 1990, pp. 33–45.

Marcuse, Herbert. *Das Ende der Utopie. Vorträge und Diskussionen in Berlin 1967*. Frankfurt am Main: Verlag Neue Kritik, 1980.

Gespräche mit Herbert Marcuse. Conversation participants: Herbert Marcuse, Jürgen Habermas, Tilman Spengler, Silvia Bovenschen, Marianne Schuller, Berthold Rothschild, Theo Pinkus, Erica Sherover, Heinz Lubasz, Alfred Schmidt, Ralf Dahrendorf, Karl Popper, Rudi Dutschke, and Hans Christoph Buch. Frankfurt am Main: Suhrkamp Verlag, 1978.

Heideggerian Marxism. Edited by Richard Wolin and John Abromeit. Lincoln, NE, and London: University of Nebraska Press, 2005.

"The Problem and the Hope." *New Outlook*. XI (July/August 1968), pp. 56–58.

Die Studentenbewegung und ihre Folgen. Edited by Peter-Erwin Jansen. Nachgelassene Schriften, IV. Springe: zu Klampen Verlag, 2004.

Massing, Paul W. *Rehearsal for Destruction. A Study of Political Anti-Semitism in Imperial Germany*. Studies in Prejudice. Edited by Max Horkheimer and Samuel H. Flowerman. New York: Harper & Brothers, 1949.

McWilliams, Carey. "The Native Fascist." *The New York Times*, Book Review (December 4, 1949).

Nadell, Melvin. Review of *Prophets of Deceit*. *Sociology and Social Research*, XXXV (1950), pp. 59–60.

Review of *Rehearsal for Destruction*. *Sociology and Social Research*, XXXV (1950), pp. 65–66.

Neumann, Franz. "Anti-Semitism: Spearhead of Universal Terror." In Franz Neumann, Herbert Marcuse and Otto Kirchheimer, *Secret Reports on Nazi Germany. The Frankfurt School Contribution to the War Effort*. Edited by Raffaele Laudani. Princeton, NJ, and Oxford: Princeton University Press, 2013, pp. 27–30.

"Protocol of the Conversation between the Philosopher Herbert Marcuse and Israel's Minister of Defense, Moshe Dayan, December 29, 1971," *Telos*. 158 (Spring 2012), pp. 185–191.

"Research Project on Anti-Semitism." *Studies in Philosophy and Social Science*. IX (1941), pp. 124–143.

Review of *Prophets of Deceit*. *American Sociological Review*, XV, 1 (February 1950), p. 161.

Rosenzweig, Franz. *Briefe*. Edited by Edith Rosenzweig, with the assistance of Ernst Simon. Berlin: Schocken Verlag, 1935.

Briefe und Tagebücher. Edited by Rachel Rosenzweig and Edith Rosenzweig-Scheinmann, with the assistance of Bernhard Casper. II. The Hague: Martinus Nijhoff, 1979.

Scholem, Betty and Gershom Scholem. *Mutter und Sohn im Briefwechsel*. Edited by Itta Sheletzky in association with Thomas Sparr. Munich: Verlag C. H. Beck, 1989.

Scholem, Gershom. *Briefe*. I. Edited by Itta Shedletzky. Munich: Verlag C. H. Beck, 1994.

Briefe. II. Edited by Thomas Sparr. Munich: Verlag C. H. Beck, 1995.

ed. *The Correspondence of Walter Benjamin and Gershom Scholem 1932–1940*. Translated by Gary Smith and Andre Lefevere. Introduction by Anson Rabinbach. Cambridge, MA: Harvard University Press, 1992.

Scholem, Gershom and Theodor W. Adorno, eds. *The Correspondence of Walter Benjamin 1910–1940*. Translated by Manfred R. Jacobson and Evelyn M. Jacobson. Chicago and London: The University of Chicago Press, 1994.

Shanahan, William O. "The Germans and Modern History." *The Review of Politics*, XIII, 2 (April 1951), pp. 245–251.

Simon, Ernst. "Dank an Freunde." In *Was der Mensch braucht. Anregungen für eine neue Kunst zu Leben*. Edited by Hans Jürgen Schultz. Stuttgart, Berlin: Kreuz Verlag, 1977, pp. 82–93.

"Ihud." In *Struggle for Tomorrow. Modern Political Ideologies of the Jewish People*. Edited by Basil Vlavianos and Feliks Gross. New York: Arts, Incorporated, 1954, pp. 100–108.

"Franz Rosenzweig und das jüdische Bildungsproblem." *Brücken. Gesammelte Aufsätze*. Heidelberg: Verlag Lambert Schneider, 1965, pp. 393–406.

"N. A. Nobel (1871–1922) als Prediger." *Brücken. Gesammelte Aufsätze*. Heidelberg: Verlag Lambert Schneider, 1965, pp. 375–380.

Sechzig Jahre gegen den Strom. Briefe von 1917–1984. Schriftenreihe wissenschaftlicher Abhandlungen des Leo-Baeck-Instituts, 59. Tübingen: J. C. B. Mohr (Paul Siebeck), 1998.

"Selbstdarstellung." In *Pädagogik in Selbstdarstellungen*, I. Edited by Ludwig J. Pongratz. Hamburg: Felix Meiner Verlag, 1975, pp. 272–333.

"Wie ich Zionist wurde." *Entscheidung zum Judentum. Essays und Vorträge*. Frankfurt am Main: Suhrkamp, 1979, pp. 26–32.

Sontag, Raymond J. Review of *Rehearsal for Destruction*. *Political Science Quarterly*, LXV, 4 (December 1950), pp. 600–602.

Strauss, Leo. "Response to Frankfurt's 'Word of Principle'." *The Early Writings, (1921–1932)*. Translated and edited by Michael Zank. Albany: State University of New York Press, 2002, pp. 64–75.

Usher, Roland G. Review of *Rehearsal for Destruction*. *The American Historical Review*, LVI, 1 (October 1950), pp. 105–106.

Weil, Felix. "Die Gründung des Instituts für Sozialforschung." *Frankfurter jüdische Errinerungen. Ein Lesebuch zur Erforschung der Geschichte der Frankfurter Juden*. Kommission zur Erforschung der Geschichte der Frankfurter Juden. Sigmaringen: Jan Thorbecke Verlag, 1997, pp. 144–153.

Wittfogel, K[arl] A. "The History of Prehistoric China." *Zeitschrift für Sozialforschung*, VIII (1939–1940), pp. 138–186.

Wrong, Dennis H. Review of *Prophets of Deceit*. *American Journal of Sociology*, LVI, 3 (November 1950), pp. 278–279.

Secondary Sources

Abromeit, John. "Herbert Marcuse's Critical Encounter with Martin Heidegger 1927–33." *Herbert Marcuse. A Critical Reader*. Edited by John Abromeit and W. Mark Cobb. New York and London: Routledge, 2004, pp. 131–151.

Max Horkheimer and the Foundations of the Frankfurt School. Cambridge: Cambridge University Press, 2011.

Adler-Rudel, Salomon. *Ostjuden in Deutschland 1880–1940. Zugleich eine Geschichte der Organisationen, die sie betreuten*. Schriftenreihe wissenschaftlicher Abhandlungen des Leo-Baeck-Instituts, 1. Tübingen: J. C. B. Mohr, 1959.

Adunka, Evelyn. "Die Frankfurter Schule und das Judentum." *Österreichisches Wissenschaftsforum*, II, 3/4 (1988), pp. 29–43.

Review of E. Fromm, *Das jüdische Gesetz*. *Mnemosyne*, 10, January 1991.

"Theodor W. Adornos jüdisches Erbe – zu seinem 20. Todestag." *Illustrierte Neue Welt*, August/September 1989, p. 8.

Ahrens, Erich. "Reminiscences of the Men of the Frankfurt Lehrhaus." *Leo Baeck Institute Year Book*, XIX (1974), pp. 245–253.

Altwicker, Norbert, "Loeb-Lectures. Gastvorlesungen über Geschichte, Philosophie und Religion des Judentums an der Universität Frankfurt am Main 1956–1967." In *Die Frankfurter Schule und Frankfurt. Eine Rückkehr nach Deutschland*. Edited by Monika Boll and Raphael Gross. [Göttingen]: Wallstein, [2009], pp.158–161.

Arato, Andrew and Eike Gebhardt, eds. *The Essential Frankfurt School Reader*. New York: Continuum, 1982.

Arendt, Hannah. "Walter Benjamin: 1892–1940." In: Walter Benjamin, *Illuminations*. Edited by Hannah Arendt. Translated by Harry Zohn. New York: Schocken Books, 1969, pp. 1–55.

Asch, Adolph. *Geschichte des K.C.* London: n.p., 1964.

Aschheim, Steven E. *Brothers and Strangers. The East European Jew in German and German Jewish Consciousness, 1800–1923*. Madison: The University of Wisconsin Press, 1982.

Culture and Catastrophe. German and Jewish Confrontations with National Socialism and Other Crises. Houndmills, Basingstoke, Hampshire: Macmillan, 1996.

In Times of Crisis. Essays on European Culture, Germans, and Jews. Madison: The University of Wisconsin Press, 2001.

Astour, Michael [Mikhel Astur]. *Geshikhte fun der frayland-lige un funem teritorialistishn gedank*. 2 vols. Buenos Aires: Frayland lige, 1967.

Avineri, Shlomo. "Prague Summer: The Altneuschul, Pan Am, and Herbert Marcuse." *Jewish Review of Books* (Fall 2010), pp. 50–51.

Bahr, Ehrhard. "The Anti-Semitism Studies of the Frankfurt School: The Failure of Critical Theory." In *Foundations of the Frankfurt School of Social Research*. Edited by Judith Marcus and Zoltán Tar. New Brunswick, NJ, and London: Transaction Books, 1984, pp. 311–321.

Bamberger, I. Nathan. "A Note on Erich Fromm's Rabbinic Roots." *Tradition*, XXIX, 3 (1995), pp. 52–54.

Barboza, Amalia, "Die 'jüdische Identität' der Frankfurter Schule." In *Die Frankfurter Schule und Frankfurt. Eine Rückkehr nach Deutschland*. Edited by Monika Boll and Raphael Gross. [Göttingen]: Wallstein, [2009], pp. 162–169.

Belke, Ingrid and Irina Renz. "Siegfried Kracauer 1889–1966." *Marbacher Magazin*, 47 (1988).

Ben-Natan, Asher. *Die Chuzpe zu leben. Stationen meines Lebens*. Düsseldorf: Droste, 2003.

Benhabib, Seyla. *Critique, Norm, and Utopia. A Study of the Foundations of Critical Theory*. New York: Columbia University Press, 1986.

"Translator's Introduction." In: Herbert Marcuse, *Hegel's Ontology and the Theory of Historicity*. Translated by Seyla Benhabib. Cambridge, MA; London: MIT Press, 1987, pp. ix–xl.

Benhabib, Seyla, Wolfgang Bonss, and John McCole, eds. *On Max Horkheimer. New Perspectives*. Cambridge, MA; London: MIT Press, 1993.

Benjamin, Andrew, ed. *The Problems of Modernity. Adorno and Benjamin*. Warwick Studies in Philosophy and Literature. London and New York: Routledge, 1989.

Berman. Russell. "Adorno's Politics." In *Adorno: A Critical Reader*. Edited by Nigel Gibson and Andrew Rubin. Malden, MA: Blackwell Publishers, 2002, pp. 110–131.

Blomert, Reinhard, "Thora und Therapie. Das vergessene Sanatorium." *Psychoanalyse im Widerspruch*, III, 8/92, pp. 39–49.

"Das vergessene Sanatorium." In *Jüdisches Leben in Heidelberg. Studien zu einer unterbrochenen Geschichte*. Edited by Norbert Giovannini,

Jo-Hannes Bauer, and Hans-Martin Mumm. Heidelberg: Wunderhorn, 1992, pp. 249–262.
Boll, Monika, "Konzeptionen des Judentums zwischen Säkularisierung und Marxismus: Hannah Arendt und Max Horkheimer." In *Affinität wider Willen? Hannah Arendt, Theodor W. Adorno und die Frankfurter Schule*. Edited by Liliane Weissberg. Jahrbuch zur Geschichte und Wirkung des Holocaust. Frankfurt am Main and New York: Campus Verlag, 2011, pp. 103–116.
Bonss, Wolfgang and Axel Honneth, eds. *Sozialforschung als Kritik. Zum sozialwissenschaftlichen Potential der Kritischen Theorie*. Frankfurt am Main: Suhrkamp, 1982.
Bottomore, Tom. *The Frankfurt School*. London and New York: Routledge, 1989.
Brenner, Michael. "A Tale of Two Families: Franz Rosenzweig, Gershom Scholem and the Generational Conflict Around Judaism." *Judaism*, 42, 1993, pp. 349–361.
  The Renaissance of Jewish Culture in Weimar Germany. New Haven, CT, and London: Yale University Press, 1996.
Brodersen, Momme. *Walter Benjamin. A Biography*. Translated by Malcolm R. Green and Ingrida Ligers. Edited by Martina Derviş. London and New York: Verso, 1996.
Bronner, Stephen. *Of Critical Theory and Its Theorists*. London: Basil Blackwell, 1994.
Bros, Y[ankef]. "Tsu der geshikhte fun der i.s.d.p. in galitsie." *Royter pinkes. Tsu der geshikhte fun der yidisher arbeter-bavegung un sotsialistisher shtremungen bay yidn*, II. Warsaw: Farlag kultur lige, 1924, pp. 22–48.
Brumlik, Micha. "Messianic Thinking in the Jewish Intelligentsia of the Twenties." *Yearbook of the International Erich Fromm Society*, II, 1991, pp. 20–31.
  "Theologie und Messianismus im Denken Adornos." In *Ende der Geschichte. Abschied von der Geschichtskonzeption der Moderne?* Edited by Hartmut Schröter and Sabine Gürtler. Münster: Edition liberación, 1986, pp. 36–52.
  "Verborgene Tradition und messianisches Licht. Arendt, Adorno und ihr Judentum." In *Arendt und Adorno*. Edited by Dirk Auer, Lars Rensmann and Julia Schulze Wessel. Frankfurt am Main: Suhrkamp, 2003, pp. 74–93.
Buck-Morss, Susan. *The Dialectics of Seeing. Walter Benjamin and the Arcades Project*. Cambridge, MA; London: MIT Press, 1989.
  The Origin of Negative Dialectics. Theodor W. Adorno, Walter Benjamin, and the Frankfurt Institute. New York: The Free Press, 1977.
Buckmiller, Michael. "Die 'Marxistische Arbeitswoche' 1923 und die Gründung des 'Instituts für Sozialforschung'." In *Grand Hotel Abgrund. Eine Photobiographie der Frankfurter Schule*. Edited by Willem van Reijen and Gunzelin Schmid Noerr. Hamburg: Junius, 1990, pp. 145–183.
Bühler, Michael. *Erziehung zur Tradition – Erziehung zum Widerstand. Ernst Simon und die jüdische Erwachsenenbildung in Deutschland*. Studien zu jüdischen Volk und christlicher Gemeinde. Berlin: Selbstverlag Institut Kirche und Judentum, 1986.

"Erziehung zu Tradition und geistigem Widerstehen. Das Freie Jüdische Lehrhaus als Schule der Umkehr ins Judentum." In *Das Freie Jüdische Lehrhaus – eine andere Frankfurter Schule*. Edited by Raimund Sesterhenn. Schriftenreihe der Katholische Akademie der Erzdioezese Freiburg. Munich, Zurich: Verlag Schnell und Steiner, 1987, pp. 12–32.

Burston, Daniel. *The Legacy of Erich Fromm*. Cambridge, MA; London: Harvard University Press, 1991.

Calhoun, Craig. *Critical Social Theory. Culture, History and the Challenge of Difference*. Oxford; Cambridge, MA: Blackwell, 1995.

Carlebach, Julius. *Karl Marx and the Radical Critique of Judaism*. The Littman Library of Jewish Civilization. London, Henley, and Boston: Routledge & Kegan Paul, 1978.

Charney, Mita. "Erich Fromm on the 'Jewish National Character'." *Freeland* (March–April, 1953), p. 11.

Claussen, Detlev. *Grenzen der Aufklärung. Die gesellschaftliche Genese des modernen Antisemitismus*. Frankfurt am Main: Fischer Taschenbuch Verlag, 1994.

Theodor W. Adorno. One Last Genius. Translated by Rodney Livingstone. Cambridge, MA; London: The Belknap Press of Harvard University Press, 2008.

Theodor W. Adorno. Ein letztes Genie. Frankfurt am Main: Fischer Taschenbuch Verlag, 2005.

Cohen, Margaret. *Profane Illumination. Walter Benjamin and the Paris of Surrealist Revolution*. Berkeley, Los Angeles, and London: University of California Press, 1995.

Cohen, Naomi W. *Not Free to Desist. A History of the American Jewish Committee 1906–1966*. Philadelphia: The Jewish Publication Society of America, 1972.

Connerton, Paul. *The Tragedy of Enlightenment. An Essay on the Frankfurt School*. Cambridge: Cambridge University Press, 1980.

Coser, Lewis A. *Refugee Scholars in America. Their Impact and Their Experiences*. New Haven, CT, and London: Yale University Press, 1984.

Cramer, Erich. *Hitlers Antisemitismus und die Frankfurter Schule. Kritische Faschismus-Theorie und geschichtliche Realität*. Düsseldorf: Droste, 1979.

Crasemann, Michael, Felicitas Gürsching, and Wolfgang Saalfeld, "Jüdische Schüler an der alten Wöhlerschule im Westend." *Wöhlerschule 88*. [Frankfurt am Main], [1988], pp. 40–41.

Deak, Istvan. *Weimar Germany's Left-Wing Intellectuals. A Political History of the Weltbühne and Its Circle*. Berkeley and Los Angeles: University of California Press, 1968.

Deutscher, Isaac. "The non-Jewish Jew." In *The Non-Jewish Jew and other Essays*. Edited by Tamara Deutscher. New York: Hill and Wang, 1968, pp. 25–41.

Diner, Dan. "Reason and the 'Other': Horkheimer's Reflections on Anti-Semitism and Mass Annihilation." In *On Max Horkheimer. New Perspectives*. Edited by Seyla Benhabib, Wolfgang Bonss, and John McCole. Cambridge, MA, and London: MIT Press, 1993, pp. 335–363.

"Von Universellem und Partikularem: Max Horkheimer." In *Kritische Theorie und Kultur*. Edited by Rainer Erd, Dietrich Hoss, Otto Jacobi and Peter Noller. Frankfurt am Main: Suhrkamp, 1989, pp. 270–281.
Dinnerstein, Leonard. *Antisemitism in America*. New York, Oxford: Oxford University Press, 1994.
  Uneasy at Home. Antisemitism and the American Jewish Experience. New York: Columbia University Press, 1987.
Dubiel, Helmut. "Mehr als ein Zeitzeuge...." In *Das Utopische soll Funken schlagen ... Zum hundertsten Geburtstag von Leo Löwenthal*. Edited by Peter-Erwin Jansen. Frankfurt am Main: Vittorio Klostermann, 2000, pp. 9–19.
  Theory and Politics. Studies in the Development of Critical Theory. Translated by Benjamin Gregg. Cambridge, MA; London: MIT Press, 1985.
  Ungewissheit und Politik. Frankfurt am Main: Suhrkamp, 1994.
Eagleton, Terry. *Walter Benjamin or Towards a Revolutionary Criticism*. London, New York: Verso, 1981.
Ehrlich, Ernst Ludwig. "Max Horkheimer – ein Leben 'um der Wahrheit willen'." *Israelitisches Wochenblatt*, LXXIII, 13 (July 13, 1973), p. 29.
  "Max Horkheimers Stellung zum Judentum." *Emuna*, VIII (1973), pp. 457–459.
Eiland, Howard and Michael W. Jennings. *Walter Benjamin. A Critical Life*. Cambridge, MA and London: The Belknap Press of Harvard University Press, 2014.
Eloni, Yehuda. "German Zionism and the Rise to Power of National Socialism." *Studies in Zionism*, VI, 2 (1985), pp. 247–262.
Engel, Ursula. "Das Heidelberger 'Thorapeutikum'." *PsA-Info*, 30, [Berlin] (1988), pp. 4–16.
  "Vom 'Thorapeutikum' nach Chestnut Lodge. Frieda Fromm-Reichmann (1889–1957)." In *Psychoanalyse in Frankfurt am Main: zerstörte Anfänge, Wiederannäherung, Entwicklungen*. Edited by Tomas Plänkers, Michael Laier, Hans-Heinrich Otto, Hans-Joachim Rothe, and Helmut Siefert. Tübingen: Edition Diskord, 1996, pp. 141–152.
Erd, Rainer, ed. *Reform und Resignation. Gespräche über Franz L. Neumann*. Frankfurt am Main: Suhrkamp, 1985.
Feenberg, Andrew. *Critical Theory of Technology*. New York and Oxford: Oxford University Press, 1991.
  Lukács, Marx and the Sources of Critical Theory. New York, Oxford: Oxford University Press, 1986.
Feenberg, Andrew and William Leiss, eds. "Introduction. The Critical Theory of Herbert Marcuse." *The Essential Marcuse. Selected Writings of Philosopher and Social Critic Herbert Marcuse*. Boston: Beacon Press, 2007, pp. vii–xliii.
Fleck, Christian. *Transatlantische Bereicherungen. Zur Erfindung der empirischen Sozialforschung*. Frankfurt am Main: Suhrkamp, 2007.
Fleming, Donald and Bernard Bailyn, eds. *The Intellectual Migration. Europe and America, 1930–1960*. Cambridge, MA: The Belknap Press of Harvard University Press, 1969.
Freimüller, Tobias. "Max Horkheimer und die jüdische Gemeinde Frankfurt am Main." In *Die Frankfurter Schule und Frankfurt. Eine Rückkehr nach*

Deutschland. Edited by Monika Boll and Raphael Gross. [Göttingen]: Wallstein, [2009], pp. 150–157.

Friedeberg, Ludwig von. "Die Rückkehr des Instituts für Sozialforschung." In *Die Frankfurter Schule und Frankfurt. Eine Rückkehr nach Deutschland*. Edited by Monika Boll and Raphael Gross ([Göttingen]: Wallstein, [2009]), pp. 40–46.

Friedenberg, Edgar Z. "Neo-Freudianism and Erich Fromm." *Commentary*, XXXIV (1962), pp. 305–313.

Friedman, George. *The Political Philosophy of the Frankfurt School*. Ithaca, NY, and London: Cornell University Press, 1981.

Funk, Rainer. *Erich Fromm. His Life and Ideas. An Illustrated Biography*. Translated by Ian Portman and Manuela Kunkel. New York and London: Continuum, 2000.

Erich Fromm mit Selbstzeugnissen und Bilddokumenten. Reinbek bei Hamburg: Rowohlt, 1983.

Erich Fromm: The Courage to Be Human. New York: Continuum, 1982.

"Von der jüdischen zur psychologischen Seelenlehre. Erich Fromms Weg von der einen über die andere Frankfurter Schule." In *Das Freie Jüdische Lehrhaus – eine andere Frankfurter Schule*. Edited by Raimund Sesterhenn. Schriftenreihe der Katholische Akademie der Erzdioezese Freiburg. Munich, Zurich: Verlag Schnell und Steiner, 1987, pp. 91–108.

Gay, Peter. *Freud, Jews and Other Germans. Masters and Victims in Modernist Culture*. Oxford: Oxford University Press, 1978.

Geyer, Carl-Friedrich. *Kritische Theorie. Max Horkheimer und Theodor W. Adorno*. Freiburg, Munich: Verlag Karl Alber, 1982.

Gilloch, Graeme and Jaeho Kang. "Below the Surface: Siegfried Kracauer's 'Testfilm' Project." *New Formations*, 61 (Summer 2007), pp. 149–160.

Glatzer, Nahum N. "The Frankfort Lehrhaus." *Leo Baeck Institute Year Book*, I (1956), pp. 105–122.

Goldschmidt, Hermann Levin. "Erich Fromm: Abscheid von einem der grossen Humanisten des Abendlandes." *Israelit. Wochenblatt*, March 28, 1980.

Grigat, Stephan. "Befreite Gesellschaft und Israel. Zum Verhältnis von Kritischer Theorie und Zionismus." *Feindaufklärung und Reeducation. Kritische Theorie gegen Postnazismus und Islamismus*. Edited by Stephan Grigat. Freiburg: ça ira-Verlag, 2006, pp. 115–129.

Groiser, David. "Jewish Law and Tradition in the Early Work of Erich Fromm." In *The Early Frankfurt School and Religion*. Edited by Margarete Kohlenbach and Raymond Geuss. Houndmills, Basingstoke, Hampshire: Palgrave Macmillan, 2005, pp. 128–144.

Gross, Walter. "The Zionist Students' Movement." *Leo Baeck Institute Year Book*, IV (1959), pp. 143–164.

Gumnior, Helmut and Rudolf Ringguth. *Max Horkheimer. Mit Selbstzeugnissen und Bilddokumenten*. Reinbek bei Hamburg: Rowohlt, 1973.

Habermas, Jürgen. "Remarks on the Development of Horkheimer's Work." In *On Max Horkheimer. New Perspectives*. Edited by Seyla Benhabib, Wolfgang Bonss, and John McCole. Cambridge, MA, and London: MIT Press, 1993, pp. 49–65.

Halley, Anne. "Theodor W. Adorno's Dream Transcripts." *Antioch Review*, LV, 1 (Winter 1997), pp. 57–74.
Hammer, Espen. *Adorno and the Political*. London and New York: Routledge, 2006.
Hammerstein, Notker. *Die Johann Wolfgang Goethe-Universität Frankfurt am Main. Von der Stiftungsuniversität zur staatlichen Hochschule*, I. Neuwied, Frankfurt am Main: Alfred Metzner Verlag, 1989.
Handelman, Susan A. *Fragments of Redemption. Jewish Thought and Literary Theory in Benjamin, Scholem, and Levinas*. Bloomington and Indianapolis: Indiana University Press, 1991.
Hartmann, Frank. *Max Horkheimers materialistischer Skeptizismus. Frühe Motive der Kritischen Theorie*. Frankfurt am Main, New York: Campus, 1990.
Haselberg, Peter von. "Wiesengrund-Adorno." In *Theodor W. Adorno*. Edited by Heinz Ludwig Arnold. 2nd edition. Munich: Edition Text + Kritik, 1983, pp. 7–21.
Held, David. *Introduction to Critical Theory. Horkheimer to Habermas*. Berkeley and Los Angeles: University of California Press, 1980.
Heller, Otto. *Der Untergang des Judentums Die Judenfrage. Ihre Kritik. Ihre Lösung durch den Sozialismus*. Vienna and Berlin: Verlag für Literatur und Politik, 1931.
Hellige, Hans Dieter. "Generationskonflikt, Selbsthass und die Entstehung antikapitalistischer Positionen im Judentum. Der Einfluss des Antisemitismus auf das Sozialverhalten jüdischer Kaufmanns- und Unternehmersöhne im Deutschen Kaiserreich und in der K.u.K.-Monarchie." *Geschichte und Gesellschaft*, V (1979), pp. 476–518.
Heuberger, Rachel. "Die entdeckung der jüdischen Wurzeln. Leo Löwenthal und der Frankfurter Rabbiner Nehemias Anton Nobel." In *Das Utopische soll Funken schlagen ... Zum hundertsten Geburtstag von Leo Löwenthal*. Edited by Peter-Erwin Jansen. Frankfurt am Main: Vittorio Klostermann, 2000, pp. 47–67.
  "Leo Löwenthal und Erich Fromm. Die 'jüdischen Juden' der Frankfurter Schule." In *Die Frankfurter Schule und Frankfurt. Eine Rückkehr nach Deutschland*. Edited by Monika Boll and Raphael Gross. [Göttingen]: Wallstein, [2009], pp. 114–121.
  "Orthodoxy versus Reform. The case of Rabbi Nehemiah Anton Nobel of Frankfurt a. Main." *Leo Baeck Institute Year Book*, XXXVII (1992), pp. 45–58.
  Rabbi Nehemiah Anton Nobel. The Jewish Renaissance in Frankfurt am Main. Schriftenreihe des Jüdischen Museums Frankfurt am Main, X. Frankfurt am Main: Societäts-Verlag, 2007.
Hohendahl, Peter Uwe. *Prismatic Thought. Theodor W. Adorno*. Lincoln, NE, and London: University of Nebraska Press, 1995.
Honigmann, Peter. "Der Heidelberger Talmudistenkreis um Salman Baruch Rabinkow. Aus Anlass von Rabinkows 50. Todestag am 28. Mai 1991." *Frankfurter Jüdische Nachrichten* (March/April 1991), pp. 38–39.
  "Jüdische Studenten zwischen Orthodoxie und moderner Wissenschaft. Der Heidelberger Talmudistenkreis um Salman Baruch Rabinkow." *Menora. Jahrbuch für deutsch-jüdische Geschichte* (1992), pp. 85–96.

"Öffentliche Spurenverwischung. Erich Fromms Frühschrift zur Soziologie des Diasporajudentums." *Frankfurter Allgemeine Zeitung* (October 2, 1989), p. 14.

Hughes, H. Stuart. *The Sea Change. The Migration of Social Thought, 1930–1965*. New York, Evanston, San Francisco and London: Harper & Row, 1975.

Hunt, Richard. *German Social Democracy 1918–1933*. Chicago: Quadrangle Books, 1970.

I. n. shteynberg. *Der mentsh. Zayn vort. Zayn oyftu. 1888–1957*. New York: Dr. i. n. shteynberg bukh-komitet, 1961.

Ingram, David. *Critical Theory and Philosophy*. New York: Paragon House, 1990.

Jacobs, Jack. "A Friend in Need: The Jewish Labor Committee and Refugees from the German-Speaking Lands." *YIVO Annual*, XXIII (1996), pp. 391–417.

On Socialists and "the Jewish Question" after Marx. New York and London: New York University Press, 1992.

"Written Out of History. Bundists in Vienna and the Varieties of Jewish Experience in the Austrian First Republic." In *Search of Jewish Community. Jewish Identities in Germany and Austria, 1918–1933*. Edited by Michael Brenner and Derek J. Penslar. Bloomington and Indianapolis: Indiana University Press, 1998, pp. 115–133.

Jäger, Lorenz. *Adorno. A Political Biography*. Translated by Stewart Spencer. New Haven, CT, and London: Yale University Press, 2004.

Jameson, Fredric. *Late Marxism. Adorno, or, The Persistence of the Dialectic*. London, New York: Verso, 1990.

Jansen, Peter-Erwin. "Marcuses Habilitationsverfahren – eine Odyssee." *Befreiung Denken – Ein Politischer Imperativ. Ein Materialenband zu einer politischen Arbeitstagung über Herbert Marcuse am 13 u. 14 Oktober 1989 in Frankfurt*. Edited by Peter-Erwin Jansen. 2nd ed. Offenbach/Main: Verlag 2000 GmbH, 1990, pp. 141–150.

ed., *Das Utopische soll Funken schlagen ... Zum hundertsten Geburtstag von Leo Löwenthal*. Frankfurt am Main: Vittorio Klostermann, 2000.

Jarvis, Simon. *Adorno. A Critical Introduction*. New York: Routledge, 1998.

Jay, Martin. *Adorno*. Cambridge, MA: Harvard University Press, 1984.

The Dialectical Imagination. A History of the Frankfurt School and the Institute of Social Research, 1923–1950. Boston and Toronto: Little, Brown and Company, 1973.

"The Extraterritorial Life of Siegfried Kracauer." *Permanent Exiles. Essays on the Intellectual Migration from Germany to America*. New York: Columbia University Press, 1986, pp. 152–197.

"Introduction to a Festschrift for Leo Lowenthal on his Eightieth Birthday." *Permanent Exiles. Essays on the Intellectual Migration from Germany to America*. New York: Columbia University Press, 1986, pp. 101–106.

Force Fields. Between Intellectual History and Cultural Critique. New York and London: Routledge, 1993.

"The Jews and the Frankfurt School: Critical Theory's Analysis of Anti-Semitism." *New German Critique*, 19 (Winter 1980), pp. 137–149.

Marxism & Totality. The Adventures of a Concept from Lukács to Habermas. Berkeley and Los Angeles: University of California Press, 1984.

"1920. The Free Jewish School is founded in Frankfurt am Main under the leadership of Franz Rosenzweig." In *Yale Companion to Jewish Writing and Thought in German Culture 1096–1996*. Edited by Sander L. Gilman and Jack Zipes. New Haven, CT, and London: Yale University Press, 1997, pp. 395–400.

"Politics of Translation: Siegfried Kracauer and Walter Benjamin on the Buber-Rosenzweig Bible." *Permanent Exiles. Essays on the Intellectual Migration from Germany to America*. New York: Columbia University Press, 1986, pp. 198–216.

Jenemann, David. *Adorno in America*. Minneapolis: University of Minnesota Press, 2007.

Judaken, Jonathan. "Between Philosemitism and Antisemitism: The Frankfurt School's Anti-Antisemitism." In *Antisemitism and Philosemitism in the Twentieth and Twenty-first Centuries. Representing Jews, Jewishness, and Modern Culture*. Edited by Phyllis Lassner and Lara Trubowitz. Newark, DE: University of Delaware Press, 2008, pp. 23–46.

"Blindness and Insight: The Conceptual Jew in Adorno and Arendt's Post-Holocaust Reflections on the Antisemitic Question." In *Arendt and Adorno. Political and Philosophical Investigations*. Edited by Lars Rensmann and Samir Gandesha. Stanford, CA: Stanford University Press, 2012, pp. 173–196.

Kātz, Barry. *Herbert Marcuse and the Art of Liberation. An Intellectual Biography*. London: Verso, 1982.

Kausch, Michael. *Erziehung und Unterhaltung. Leo Löwenthals Theorie der Massenkommunikation*. Göttingen: Sovec, 1985.

Kellner, Douglas. *Critical Theory, Marxism, and Modernity*. Baltimore: The Johns Hopkins University Press, 1989.

"The Frankfurt School Revisited: A Critique of Martin Jay's The Dialectical Imagination." In *The Frankfurt School. Critical Assessments*. Edited by Jay Bernstein. I. London and New York: Routledge, 1994, pp. 41–62.

Herbert Marcuse and the Crisis of Marxism. Berkeley and Los Angeles: University of California Press, 1984.

Kern-Ulmer, Brigitte. "Franz Rosenzweig's Jüdisches Lehrhaus in Frankfurt: A Model of Jewish Adult Education." *Judaism*, XXXIX, 2 (Spring, 1990), pp. 202–214.

Kisman, Yoysef. "Di yidishe sotsial-demokratishe bavegung in galitsie un bukovine." In *Di geshikhte fun bund*, III. Edited by G. Aronson, S. Dubnow-Erlich [Dubnov-erlikh], J. S. Hertz [I. Sh. Herts], E. Nowogrudski [Novogrudski], Kh. Sh. Kazdan, and E. Scherer [Sherer]. New York: Farlag unzer tsayt, 1966, pp. 337–482.

Kluke, Paul. *Die Stiftungsuniversität Frankfurt am Main, 1914–1932*. Frankfurt am Main: Waldemar Kramer, 1972.

Knapp, Gerhard P. *Theodor W. Adorno*. Berlin: Colloquium Verlag, 1980.

Koch, Gertrud. *Kracauer zur Einführung*. Hamburg: Junius, 1996.

Koch, Richard. "Das Freie Jüdische Lehrhaus in Frankfurt am Main." *Der Jude*, VII (1923), pp. 116–120.

Kocyba, Hermann. "Volk und Gesetz. Über Erich Fromms Dissertation." *Babylon*, 7 (1990), pp. 116–124.
Kraushaar, Wolfgang, ed. *Frankfurter Schule und Studentenbewegung. Von der Flaschenpost zum Molotowcocktail 1946 bis 1995*. 3 vols. Hamburg: Rogner & Bernhard bei Zweitausendeins, 1998.
Künzli, Arnold. *Aufklärung und Dialektik*. Freiburg: Verlag Rombach, 1971.
Kuhn, Rick. *Henryk Grossman and the Recovery of Marxism*. Urbana and Chicago: University of Illinois Press, 2007.
  "Organizing Yiddish-Speaking Workers in Pre-World War I Galicia: The Jewish Social Democratic Party." In *Yiddish Language and Culture. Then and Now*. Edited by Leonard Jay Greenspoon. Studies in Jewish Civilization, IX. Omaha, NE: Creighton University Press, 1998, pp. 37–63.
Kundnani, Hans. *Utopia or Auschwitz. Germany's 1968 Generation and the Holocaust*. New York: Columbia University Press, 2009.
Landis, Bernard and Edward S. Tauber, eds. *In the Name of Life. Essays in Honor of Erich Fromm*. New York, Chicago, San Francisco: Holt, Rinehart and Winston, 1971.
Laudani, Raffaele. "Introduction." In Franz Neumann, Herbert Marcuse and Otto Kirchheimer, *Secret Reports on Nazi Germany. The Frankfurt School Contribution to the War Effort*. Edited by Raffaele Laudani. Princeton, NJ, and Oxford: Princeton University Press, 2013, pp. 1–23.
Ld. "Die Frankfurter Juden in Zahlen und Bildern." *Frankfurter Israelitisches Gemeindeblatt*, IX, 10 (June 1931), pp. 317–319.
Lenhardt, Christian. "The Wanderings of Enlightenment." *On Critical Theory*. Edited by John O'Neill. Lanham, MD: University Press of America, 1989, pp. 34–57.
Lesch, Martina and Walter Lesch. "Verbindungen zu einer anderen Frankfurter Schule. Zu Kracauers Auseinandersetzung mit Bubers und Rosenzweigs Bibelübersetzung." In *Siegfried Kracauer. Neuen Interpretationen. Akten des internationalen, interdisziplinären Kracauer-Symposions Weingarten, 2.-4. März 1989. Akademie der Diözese Rottenburg-Stuttgart*. Edited by Michael Kessler and Thomas Y. Levin. Tübingen: Stauffenburg Verlag, 1990, pp. 171–193.
Levin, Thomas Y. *Siegfried Kracauer. Eine Bibliographie seiner Schriften*. Marbach am Neckar: Deutsche Schillergesellschaft, 1989.
Lipshires, Sidney. *Herbert Marcuse: From Marx to Freud and Beyond*. Cambridge, MA: Schenkman Publishing Company, Inc., 1974.
Löwy, Michael. "Messianisme et nature dans la culture juive romantique. Erich Fromm et Walter Benjamin." In *Religion et écologie*. Edited by Danièle Hervieu-Léger. Paris: Les éditions du cerf, 1993, pp. 127–133.
  On Changing the World. Essays in Political Philosophy, From Karl Marx to Walter Benjamin. Atlantic Highlands, NJ, and London: Humanities Press, 1993.
  Redemption and Utopia. Jewish Libertarian Thought in Central Europe. A Study in Elective Affinity. Translated by Hope Heaney. Stanford, CA: Stanford University Press, 1992.
Lundgren, Svante. *Fight Against Idols. Erich Fromm on Religion, Judaism and the Bible*. Frankfurt am Main: Peter Lang, 1998.

McCole, John. *Walter Benjamin and the Antinomies of Tradition.* Ithaca, NY, and London: Cornell University Press, 1993.
Maier, Joseph. "Jüdisches Erbe aus deutschem Geist." In *Max Horkheimer heute: Werk und Wirkung.* Edited by Alfred Schmidt and Norbert Altwicker. Frankfurt am Main: Fischer Taschenbuch Verlag, 1986, pp. 146–162.
Malina, Peter. Review of E. Fromm, *Das jüdische Gesetz. Aschkenas,* 1/92.
Mannfeld, Wiltrud. "Fragen an Herbert Marcuse zu seiner Biographie." In *Befreiung Denken – Ein Politischer Imperativ. Ein Materialenband zu einer politischen Arbeitstagung über Herbert Marcuse am 13 u. 14 Oktober 1989 in Frankfurt.* Edited by Peter-Erwin Jansen. 2nd ed. Offenbach/Main: Verlag 2000 GmbH, 1990, pp. 33–45.
Marcus, Judith and Zoltán Tar. "The Judaic Elements in the Teachings of the Frankfurt School." *Leo Baeck Institute Year Book,* XXXI (1986), pp. 339–353.
Marcuse, Peter. "Herbert Marcuse's 'Identity'." In *Herbert Marcuse. A Critical Reader.* Edited by John Abromeit and W. Mark Cobb. New York and London: Routledge, 2004, pp. 249–252.
Maurer, Trude. *Ostjuden in Deutschland 1918–1933.* Hamburger Beiträge zur Geschichte der deutschen Juden, XII. Hamburg: Hans Christians Verlag, 1986.
Mayer, Eugen E. "Nehemiah Anton Nobel." In *Guardians of Our Heritage (1724–1953).* Edited by Leo Jung. New York: Bloch Publishing Company, 1958, pp. 565–580.
Mendes-Flohr, Paul. "'The Stronger and the Better Jews': Jewish Theological Responses to Political Messianism in the Weimar Republic." *Studies in Contemporary Jewry. An Annual,* VII, Jews and Messianism in the Modern Era: Metaphor and Meaning. Edited by Jonathan Frankel. New York and Oxford: Published for the Institute of Contemporary Jewry, The Hebrew University of Jerusalem, by Oxford University Press, 1991, pp. 159–185.
Migdal, Ulrike. *Die Frühgeschichte des Frankfurter Instituts für Sozialforschung.* Campus Forschung, CCVII. Frankfurt am Main, London: Campus Verlag, 1981.
Miner, Robert. "'Politics As Opposed to Tradition': The Presence of Nietzsche and Spinoza in the 'Zionist Essays' of Leo Strauss." *Interpretation. A Journal of Political Philosophy,* XXXVII, 2 (Winter 2010), pp. 203–226.
Morgan, David W. *The Socialist Left and the German Revolution. A History of the German Independent Social Democratic Party, 1917–1922.* Ithaca, NY, and London: Cornell University Press, 1975.
Mosse, George L. *German Jews beyond Judaism.* Bloomington: Indiana University Press; Cincinnati: Hebrew Union College Press, 1985.
   Germans and Jews. The Right, the Left and the Search for a "Third Force" in Pre-Nazi Germany. New York: Grosset & Dunlap, 1971.
Mosse, Werner E. "German Jews: Citizens of the Republic." *Die Juden im nationalsozialistischen Deutschland. The Jews in Nazi Germany. 1933–1943.* Edited by Arnold Paucker with Sylvia Gilchrist and Barbara Suchy. Schriftenreihe wissenschaftlicher Abhandlungen des Leo Baeck Instituts, 45. Tübingen: J. C. B. Mohr [Paul Siebeck], 1986, pp. 45–54.
Müller, Hartmut. "Der Lebensweg Frieda Fromm-Reichmanns." *PsA-Info,* 30, (1988), pp. 1–3.

Müller-Doohm, Stefan. *Adorno. A Biography*. Translated by Rodney Livingstone. Malden, MA: Polity, 2005.
Niewyk, Donald L. *The Jews in Weimar Germany*. Baton Rouge and London: Louisiana State University Press, 1980.
Noerr, Gunzelin Schmid. "Die Archive der 'Frankfurter Schule' und das Alexander-Mitscherlich-Archiv der Stadt- und Universitätsbibliothek Frankfurt am Main." In *Psychoanalyse in Frankfurt am Main: zerstörte Anfänge, Wiederannäherung, Entwicklungen*. Edited by Tomas Plänkers, Michael Laier, Hans-Heinrich Otto, Hans-Joachim Rothe, and Helmut Siefert. Tübingen: Edition diskord, 1996, pp. 766–769.
Gesten aus Begriffen. Konstellationen der Kritischen Theorie. Frankfurt am Main: Fischer Taschenbuch Verlag, 1997.
Offe, Claus. *Reflections on America. Tocqueville, Weber and Adorno in the United States*. Translated by Patrick Camiller. Cambridge: Polity, 2005.
O'Neill, John, ed. *On Critical Theory*. Lanham, MD: University Press of America, 1989.
Paier, Dietmar. "Einleitung." In Else Frenkel-Brunswik, *Studien zur autoritären Persönlichkeit. Ausgewählte Schriften*. Edited by Dietmar Paier. Graz and Vienna: Verlag Nausner & Nausner, 1996), pp. 7–70.
Petuchowski, Jakob J. "Erich Fromm's Midrash on Love. The Sacred and the Secular Forms." *Commentary*, XXII (1956), pp. 543–549.
Pfeiffer-Belli, Erich. "Frankfurt um 1900 und danach." In *Adorno in Frankfurt. Ein Kaleidoskop mit Texten und Bildern*. Edited by Wolfram Schütte. Frankfurt am Main: Suhrkamp Verlag, 2003, pp. 21–29.
Plug, Jan. "Idiosyncrasies: Of Anti-Semitism." In *Language Without Soil. Adorno and Late Philosophical Modernity*. Edited by Gerhard Richter. New York: Fordham University Press, 2010, pp. 52–75.
Poppel, Stephen N. *Zionism in Germany, 1897–1933*. Philadelphia: Jewish Publication Society of America, 1977.
Pulzer, Peter. "Jewish Participation in Wilhelmine Politics." In *Jews and Germans from 1860 to 1933: The Problematic Symbiosis*. Edited by David Bronsen. Reihe Siegen, IX. Heidelberg: Carl Winter Universitätsverlag, 1979, pp. 78–99.
Rabi, Yaakov. "Marcuse, the Non-Jewish Jew, in Israel." *Israel Horizons*, XX, 1–2 (January–February, 1972), pp. 12–17.
Rabinbach, Anson. "Between Apocalypse and Enlightenment. Benjamin, Bloch, and Modern German-Jewish Messianism." *In the Shadow of Catastrophe. German Intellectuals between Apocalypse and Enlightenment*. Berkeley, Los Angeles, and London: University of California Press, 1997, pp. 27–65.
"The Cunning of Unreason: Mimesis and the Construction of Anti-Semitism in Horkheimer and Adorno's *Dialectic of Enlightenment*." *In the Shadow of Catastrophe. German Intellectuals between Apocalypse and Enlightenment*. Berkeley, Los Angeles, and London: University of California Press, 1997, pp. 166–198.
"The Frankfurt School and the 'Jewish Question,' 1940–1970." *Against the Grain. Jewish Intellectuals in Hard Times*. Edited by Ezra Mendelsohn, Stefani Hoffman, and Richard I. Cohen. New York, Oxford: Berghahn, 2014, pp. 255–276.

"Israel, die Diaspora und das Bilderverbot in der Kritischen Theorie." In *Die Frankfurter Schule und Frankfurt. Eine Rückkehr nach Deutschland.* Edited by Monika Boll and Raphael Gross. [Göttingen]: Wallstein, [2009], pp. 252–263.

"'Why Were the Jews Sacrificed?' The Place of Antisemitism in Adorno and Horkheimer's *Dialectic of Enlightenment.*" In *Adorno. A Critical Reader.* Edited by Nigel Gibson and Andrew Rubin. Malden, MA: Blackwell Publishers Inc., 2002, pp. 132–149.

Raulet, Gérard. "Secularisation, Myth, Anti-Semitism: Adorno and Horkheimer's *Dialectic of Enlightenment* and Cassirer's *Philosophy of Symbolic Forms.*" In *The Early Frankfurt School and Religion.* Edited by Margarete Kohlenbach and Raymond Geuss. Houndmills, Basingstoke, Hampshire: Palgrave Macmillan, 2005, pp. 171–189.

Reemtsma, Jan Philipp. "Nicht Kösteins Paradox. Zur *Dialektik der Aufklärung.*" In *Jüdische Denker im 20. Jahrhundert.* Edited by Hanna Lehming. Hamburg: E.B.-Verlag, 1997, pp. 29–45.

Reichmann, Eva G. "Max Horkheimer the Jew. Critical Theory and Beyond." *Leo Baeck Institute Year Book,* XIX (1974), pp. 181–195.

Reijen, Willem van. *Adorno: An Introduction.* Translated by Dieter Engelbrecht. Philadelphia: Pennbridge Books, 1992.

Reijen, Willem van and Jan Brensen, "The Disappearance of Class History in 'Dialectic of Enlightenment'. A Commentary on the Textual Variants (1947 and 1944)." In Max Horkheimer and Theodor W. Adorno, *Dialectic of Enlightenment. Philosophical Fragments.* Edited by Gunzelin Schmid Noerr. Translated by Edmund Jephcott. Stanford, CA: Stanford University Press, 2002, pp. 248–252.

Reijan, Willem van and Gunzelin Schmid Noerr, eds. *Grand Hotel Abgrund. Eine Photobiographie der Frankfurter Schule.* Hamburg: Junius, 1990.

Reinharz, Jehuda. "The Lehrhaus in Frankfurt am Main: A Renaissance in Jewish Adult Education." *The Yavneh Review. A Student Journal of Jewish Studies,* VII (1969), pp. 7–29.

Rensmann, Lars. *Kritische Theorie über den Antisemitismus. Studien zu Struktur, Erklärungspotential und Aktualität.* Edition Philosophie und Sozialwissenschaften 42. Berlin and Hamburg: Argument Verlag, 1998.

"Returning from Forced Exile: Some Observations on Theodor W. Adorno's and Hannah Arendt's Experience of Postwar Germany and Their Political Theories of Totalitarianism." *Leo Baeck Institute Year Book,* XLIX (2004), pp. 171–193.

Reyzen, Zalmen. *Leksikon fun der yidisher literatur, prese un filologie.* I. Vilna: Farlag fun b. kletskin, 1926.

Richarz, Monika, ed. *Jüdisches Leben in Deutschland,* III. Selbstzeugnisse zur Sozialgeschichte, 1918–1945. Stuttgart: DVA, 1982.

Rolnik, Eran J. *Freud in Zion. Psychoanalysis and the Making of Modern Jewish Identity.* The History of Psychoanalysis Series. London: Karnac, 2012.

Rose, Gillian. *The Melancholy Science. An Introduction to the Thought of Theodor W. Adorno.* New York: Columbia University Press, 1978.

Rosen, Zvi. "Critical Theory and Jewish Humanism as the Fundamentals of Judaism in the Thought of Max Horkheimer." [In Hebrew, title translated] *Machbarot le-Machshava Sotsialistit*, 12 (September 1988), pp. 41–9.
Max Horkheimer. Munich: C. H. Beck, 1995.
"Über die gesellschaftliche Rolle des Judaismus bei Max Horkheimer." In *Kritische Theorie und Religion*. Edited by Matthias Lutz-Bachmann. Religion in der Moderne. Würzburg: Echter, 1997, pp. 23–57.
Salzberger, Georg. *Leben und Lehre*. Edited by Albert H. Friedlander. Frankfurt am Main: Waldemar Kramer, 1982.
Samelson, Franz. "Authoritarianism from Berlin to Berkeley: On Social Psychology and History." *Journal of Social Issues*, XLII, 1 (1986), pp. 191–208.
Schacter, Jacob J., ed. "Reminiscences of Shlomo Barukh Rabinkow." In *Sages and Saints*. Edited by Leo Jung. Hoboken, NJ: Ktav Publishing House, Inc., 1987, pp. 93–132.
Scheible, Hartmut. *Theodor W. Adorno. Mit Selbstzeugnissen und Bilddokumenten*. Reinbek bei Hamburg: Rowohlt, 1989.
Schivelbusch, Wolfgang. *Intellektuellendämmerung. Zur Lage der Frankfurter Intelligenz in den zwanziger Jahre*. Frankfurt am Main: Insel Verlag, 1982.
Schmidt, Alfred and Norbert Altwicker, eds. *Max Horkheimer heute: Werk und Wirkung*. Frankfurt am Main: Fischer Taschenbuch Verlag, 1986.
Schmidt, James. "The 'Eclipse of Reason' and the End of the Frankfurt School in America." *New German Critique*, XXXIV, 1 (Winter 2007), pp. 47–76.
"Genocide and the Limits of Enlightenment: Horkheimer and Adorno Revisited." In *Enlightenment and Genocide, Contradictions of Modernity*. Edited by James Kaye and Bo Stråth. Philosophy and Politics, 5. Brussels: P.I.E.–Peter Lang, 2000, pp. 81–102.
"Language, Mythology, and Enlightenment: Historical Notes on Horkheimer and Adorno's Dialectic of Enlightenment." *Social Research*, LXV, 4 (Winter 1998), pp. 807–838.
Scholem, Gershom. *From Berlin to Jerusalem. Memories of My Youth*. Translated by Harry Zohn. New York: Schocken Books, 1980.
On Jews and Judaism in Crisis. Selected Essays. Edited by Werner J. Dannhauser. New York: Schocken Books, 1976.
"On the Social Psychology of the Jews in Germany: 1900 – 1933." In *Jews and Germans from 1860 to 1933: The Problematic Symbiosis*. Edited by David Bronsen. Reihe Siegen, IX. Heidelberg: Carl Winter Universitätsverlag, 1979, pp. 9–32.
"…und alles ist Kabbala." *Gershom Scholem im Gespräch mit Jörg Drews*. 2nd edition. Munich: Edition text + kritik, 1998.
Walter Benjamin. The Story of a Friendship. Translated by Harry Zohn. New York: Schocken Books, 1981.
Schoolman, Morton. *The Imaginary Witness. The Critical Theory of Herbert Marcuse*. New York: New York University Press, 1984.
Schroyer, Trent. *The Critique of Domination. The Origins and Development of Critical Theory*. Boston: Beacon Press, 1975.
Schultz, Hans Jürgen, ed. *Mein Judentum*. Stuttgart, Berlin: Kreuz Verlag, 1978.

"Der Mensch ist noch nicht das, was er werden kann." *Bulletin des Leo Baeck Instituts*, 68, (1984), pp. 23–40.

Schütte, Wolfram, ed. *Adorno in Frankfurt. Ein Kaleidoskop mit Texten und Bildern*. Frankfurt am Main: Suhrkamp Verlag, 2003.

Schwarzschild, Steven S. "Adorno and Schoenberg as Jews. Between Kant and Hegel." *Leo Baeck Institute Year Book*, XXXV, (1990), pp. 443–478.

"Remembering Erich Fromm." *The Jewish Spectator* (Fall 1980), pp. 29–33.

Seymour, David. "Adorno and Horkheimer: Enlightenment and Antisemitism." *Journal of Jewish Studies*, LI, 2 (Autumn, 2000), pp. 297–312.

Shapira, Jochack. "Fromm and Judaism." *Incontro con Erich Fromm. Atti del Simposio Internazionale su Erich Fromm: "Dalla necrofilia alla biofilia: linee per una psicoanalisi umanistica." Firenze, novembre 1986 – Palazzo Vecchio*. Firenze: Edizioni medicea, 1988, pp. 223–235.

Shulman, V[iktor]. "25 yor. Tsum yobiley fun der yidisher s. d. partay in galitsie ("galitsianer bund") 1-ter may 1905–30." *Naye folkstsaytung* (April 30, 1930), p. 5.

Slater, Phil. *Origin and Significance of the Frankfurt School. A Marxist Perspective*. London, Henley, and Boston: Routledge & Kegan Paul, 1977.

Smith, Gary, ed.,. *Benjamin. Philosophy, Aesthetics, History*. Chicago and London: The University of Chicago Press, 1989.

Söllner, Alfons. *Neumann zur Einführung*. Hannover: Soak-Verlag, 1982.

Spier, Selmar. *Vor 1914. Erinnerungen an Frankfurt geschrieben in Israel*. Frankfurt am Main: Verlag Waldemar Kramer, 1961.

Steinberg, Isaak N. "Territorialism." In *Struggle for Tomorrow. Modern Political Ideologies of the Jewish People*. Edited by Basil Vlavianos and Feliks Gross. New York: Arts, Incorporated, 1954, pp. 112–129.

Stirk, Peter M. R. *Max Horkheimer: A New Interpretation*. Hemel Hempstead: Harvester Wheatsheaf; Lanham, MD: Barnes & Noble Books, 1992.

Synnott, Marcia Graham. "Anti-Semitism and American Universities: Did Quotas Follow the Jews?" In *Anti-Semitism in American History*. Edited by David A. Gerber. Urbana and Chicago: University of Illinois Press, 1986, pp. 233–271.

Tar, Zoltán. *The Frankfurt School. The Critical Theories of Max Horkheimer and Theodor W. Adorno*. New York: Schocken Books, 1985.

Tarr, Zoltan and Judith Marcus, "Erich Fromm und das Judentum." In *Erich Fromm und die Frankfurter Schule. Akten des internationalen, interdisziplinären Symposions Stuttgart-Hohenheim, 31.5. – 2.6.1991*. Edited by Michael Kessler and Rainer Funk. Tübingen: Francke Verlag, 1992, pp. 211–220.

Tauber, Zvi. *Befreiung und das "Absurde." Studien zur Emanzipation des Menschen bei Herbert Marcuse*. Schriftenreihe des Instituts für Deutsche Geschichte Universität Tel Aviv, XV. Gerlingen: Bleicher Verlag, 1994.

"Herbert Marcuse: Auschwitz und My Lai?" In *Zivilisationsbruch. Denken nach Auschwitz*. Edited by Dan Diner. Frankfurt am Main: Fischer, 1988, pp. 88–98.

Tawil, Raymonda Hawa. *My Home, My Prison*. New York: Holt, Rinehart and Winston, 1979.

Tiedemann, Rolf. "Introduction: 'Not the First Philosophy, but a Last One': Notes on Adorno's Thought." In Theodor W. Adorno, *Can One Live after Auschwitz? A Philosophical Reader*. Edited by Rolf Tiedemann. Translated by Rodney Livingstone and others. Stanford, CA: Stanford University Press, 2003, pp. xi–xxvii.

Toury, J[acob]. *Die politischen Orientierungen der Juden in Deutschland. Von Jena bis Weimar*. Schriftenreihe wissenschaftlicher Abhandlungen des Leo Baeck Instituts, XV. Tübingen: J. C. B. Mohr, 1966.

Traverso, Enzo. *The Marxists and the Jewish Question. The History of a Debate (1843–1943)*. Translated by Bernard Gibbons. Atlantic Highlands, NJ: Humanities Press, 1990.

Türcke, Christoph and Gerhard Bolte. *Einführung in die Kritische Theorie*. Darmstadt: Primus Verlag, 1997.

Udovitch, Abraham L. "Foreword." In S. D. Goitein, *A Mediterranean Society. The Jewish Communities of the Arab World as Portrayed in the Documents of the Cairo Geniza*, V. The Individual: Portrait of a Mediterranean Personality of the High Middle Ages as Reflected in the Cairo Geniza. Berkeley, Los, Angeles, and London: University of California Press, 1988, pp. ix–xviii.

Über Theodor W. Adorno. With articles by Kurt Oppens, Hans Kudszus, Jürgen Habermas, Bernard Willms, Hermann Schweppenhäuser und Ulrich Sonnemann. Frankfurt am Main: Suhrkamp Verlag, 1968.

Ulmen, G. L. *The Science of Society. Toward an Understanding of the Life and Work of Karl August Wittfogel*. The Hague, Paris, and New York: Mouton Publishers, 1978.

Veauthier, F. Werner. "'Jüdisches' im Denken der Frankfurter Schule." In *Juden in Deutschland. Lebenswelten und Einzelschicksale. Ringvorlesung der Philosophischen Fakultät der Universität des Saarlandes im Wintersemester 1988/89*. Edited by Reinhard Schneider. Annales Universitatis Saraviensis Philosophische Fakultät, I. St. Ingbert: Röhrig Universitätsverlag, 1994, pp. 271–307.

Volkmann, Michael. *Eine andere Frankfurter Schul'. Das Freie Jüdische Lehrhaus 1920–1927*. Prophezey Schriften im TVT, 2. Edited by Beate Schröder. Tübingen: TVT-Medienverlag, 1994.

Volkov, Shulamit. "The Dynamics of Dissimilation. *Ostjuden* and German Jews." In *The Jewish Response to German Culture. From the Enlightenment to the Second World War*. Edited by Jehuda Reinharz and Walter Schatzberg. Hanover, NH, and London: University Press of New England, 1985, pp. 195–211.

Weisberger, Adam and Gerda Lederer. "Horkheimer and Adorno." *Midstream* (August/September 1994), pp. 19–23.

Wertheimer, Jack. *Unwelcome Strangers. East European Jews in Imperial Germany*. New York and Oxford: Oxford Univesity Press, 1987.

Wessel, Julia Schulze and Lars Rensmann."The Paralysis of Judgment. Arendt and Adorno on Antisemitism and the Modern Condition." In *Arendt and Adorno. Political and Philosophical Investigations*. Edited by Lars Rensmann and Samir Gandesha. Stanford, CA: Stanford University Press, 2012, pp. 197–225.

"Radikalisierung oder 'Verschwinden' der Judenfeindschaft? Arendts und Adornos Theorien zum modernen Antisemitismus." In *Arendt und Adorno*.

Edited by Dirk Auer, Lars Rensmann, Julia Schulze Wessel. Frankfurt am Main: Suhrkamp, 2003, pp. 97–129.
Wheatland, Thomas. *The Frankfurt School in Exile*. Minneapolis and London: University of Minnesota Press, 2009.
Wheeler, Brett R. "Antisemitism as Distorted Politics: Adorno on the Public Sphere." *Jewish Social Studies*, VII, 2 (Winter 2001), pp. 114–148.
Wiggershaus, Rolf. *The Frankfurt School. Its History, Theories, and Political Significance*. Translated by Michael Robertson. Cambridge, MA: MIT Press, 1994.
Theodor W. Adorno. Munich: C. H. Beck, 1987.
Wilcock, Evelyn. "Negative Identity: Mixed German Jewish Descent as a Factor in the Reception of Theodor Adorno." *New German Critique*, 81 (Fall, 2000), pp. 169–187.
Wilson, Ross. *Theodor Adorno*. London and New York: Routledge, 2007.
Wolfsberg, Oskar. *Nehamia Anton Nobel, 1871–1922, Versuch einer Würdigung*. Frankfurt am Main: J. Kaufmann Verlag, 1929.
Wolin, Richard. *The Frankfurt School Revisited and Other Essays on Politics and Society*. New York and London: Routledge, 2006.
Heidegger's Children. Hannah Arendt, Karl Löwith, Hans Jonas, and Herbert Marcuse. Princeton, NJ and Oxford: Princeton University Press, 2001.
"Introduction. What Is Heideggerian Marxism?" In Herbert Marcuse, *Heideggerian Marxism*. Edited by Richard Wolin and John Abromeit. Lincoln, NE and London: University of Nebraska Press, 2005, pp. xi–xxx.
"Reflections on Jewish Secular Messianism." *Studies in Contemporary Jewry. An Annual*, VII. Jews and Messianism in the Modern Era: Metaphor and Meaning. Edited by Jonathan Frankel. New York and Oxford: Published for the Institute of Contemporary Jewry, The Hebrew University of Jerusalem, by Oxford University Press, 1991, pp. 186–196.
The Terms of Cultural Criticism. The Frankfurt School, Existentialism, Poststructuralism. New York: Columbia University Press, 1992.
Walter Benjamin. An Aesthetic of Redemption. Berkeley, Los Angeles, and London: University of California Press, 1994.
Worrell, Mark P. "Joseph Freeman and the Frankfurt School." *Rethinking Marxism*, XXI, 4 (October 2009), pp. 498–513.
"The Other Frankfurt School." *Fast Capitalism*, 2.1 (2006), www.fastcapitalism.org
Ziege, Eva-Maria. *Antisemitismus und Gesellschaftstheorie. Die Frankfurter Schule im amerikanischen Exil*. Frankfurt am Main: Suhrkamp, 2009.
"Arendt, Adorno und die Anfänge der Antisemitismusforschung." In *Affinität wider Willen? Hannah Arendt, Theodor W. Adorno und die Frankfurter Schule*. Edited by Liliane Weissberg. Jahrbuch zur Geschichte und Wirkung des Holocaust. Frankfurt am Main and New York: Campus Verlag, 2011, pp. 85–102.
Zuckermann, Moshe. "Kritische Theorie in Israel – Analyse einer Nichtrezeption." *Theodor W. Adorno – Philosoph des beschädigten Lebens*. Edited by Moshe Zuckermann. Tagungsbände des Minerva Instituts für deutsche Geschichte Universität Tel Aviv, III. Göttingen: Wallstein Verlag, 2004, pp. 9–24.

Index

Achduth (Unity), chapter of the KJV, 33–34
Achduth (Unity), Orthodox Jewish organization, 27
Ackerman, Nathan A., 107
Adler, Victor, 38–39
Adorno, Margarete (Karplus), 49–50, 55
Adorno, Maria. *See* Wiesengrund, Maria (Adorno)
Adorno, Theodor, .1, 24, 52, 155
  See also The Authoritarian Personality
  on antisemitism, 53–65, 107–109, 202, 220–221
  antisemitism project, of the Institute for Social Research and, 59, 188–189
  Benjamin as influence on, 61
  family background, 54
  feelings about Israel, 225–226
  in Institute of Social Research, 57–58
  Judaism and, 55, 108
  Kracauer, S., and, 54–55
  Minima Moralia, 108
  The Psychological Technique of Martin Luther Thomas' Radio Addresses, 97
  religious background, 54
  response to "The Jews and Europe," 51–52
Agudas-Jisroel (Union of Israel), 33
AJC. *See* American Jewish Committee
Alexander, Franz, 92–93
The American Catholic Sociological Review, 100
American Historical Review, 105

American Jewish Committee (AJC), 66–68
  Committee on Scientific Research in, 85–87
  Department for Scientific Research in, 84
  Horkheimer, Max, and, 199–200
  Institute of Social Research and, 66–67, 82–84, 197
  response to antisemitism, 68
American Jewish Historical Quarterly, 101
American Journal of Sociology, 101
American Nationalist Confederation, 62–63
American Sociological Review, 102, 105
The American Zionist, 115–116
Amit, Daniel, 213
antisemitism, 154. *See also* antisemitism project, of the Institute of Social Research; *The Authoritarian Personality*
  Adorno, T., on, 53–65, 107–109, 202, 220–221
  AJC response to, 68
  as anti-democratic, 69
  in colleges and universities, 62
  Critical Theory and, 44, 201–202
  in *Dämmerung*, 11
  Department for Scientific Research study on, 84–87
  in *Dialectic of Enlightenment*, 74–75, 78–79
  Dreyfus Affair and, 57
  economic influences on, 74
  as emotional release, 76
  fascism and, 44–45, 58–59, 75

258

foundations of, in objective social conditions, 106–107, 206
Freud on origins of, 202
for Fromm, E., 130
German American Bund and, 63
in German military, 10
global expansion of, 135
global impact of, 108
of Heidegger, 114, 208–209
Holocaust and, 57
Horkheimer, M., assessments of, 9–12, 44–47
in housing, 62
Institute of Social Research studies, 3, 60
internalized, 227–228
"The Jews and Europe" and, 58
liberalism and, 60, 75
for Lowenthal, L., 14, 31, 63, 74
Marcuse, H., on, 69
towards Marcuse, H., 113–115
from Marxist perspective, 44–45
mimesis and, 77–78
National Socialism and, 44–45
in Nazi Germany, as factor for national integration, 65
in Nazi Germany, as influence on foreign policy, 59
nomadism and, 66
non-totalitarian, 70
organizations, in U.S., 62–63
as phenomenon of German class culture, 65
political, 71
in postwar Europe, 134–135
psychological roots of, 73, 76, 203
in *The Psychological Technique of Martin Luther Thomas' Radio Addresses*, 97
rationality of, 71
in *Rehearsal for Destruction. A Study of Political Anti-Semitism in Imperial Germany*, 103–104
religious origins of, 77
spearhead theory of, 69
totalitarian, 70, 106–107
in U.S., 62–64, 78–82
of Wagner, 53–54
during Weimar Republic, 9–12
Anti-Semitism and Emotional Disorder (Ackerman and Jahoda), 88, 107
antisemitism project, of the Institute of Social Research, 58, 66–74
for Adorno, 59, 188–189
AJC and, 66–68
initial proposal for, 187
internal conflicts over, 65–66
"The Jews and Europe" as foundation of, 58
labor study's relationship to, 78–82, 194–197
methodological principles and assumptions of, 70
motivations for, 64–65
Rosenblum support of, 69
Arbeiterfürsorgeamt der jüdischen Organisationen Deutschlands (Workers' Welfare Agency of the Jewish Organizations of Germany), 23
Arendt, Hannah, 13, 52, 208–209
The Art of Loving (Fromm, E.), 32, 130–131
Aschheim, Steven E., 176
Assall, Paul, 144
assimilation, of German Jews
CV and, 17, 26–27
Germanness and, 16
Austrian Social Democratic Workers' Party, 38
The Authoritarian Personality, 79, 82, 84, 88–93
Alexander, review of, 92–93
authors of, 200–201
Bredemeier, review of, 92
Brown, J. F., review of, 91
Bunzel, review of, 91
critical response to, 91–93, 101
de Grazia, review of, 91
Eister, review of, 91–92
foundational arguments in, 88
Glazer, review of, 92
Hyman, review of, 93
Sheatsley, review of, 93
Avineri, Shlomo, 117, 211, 213

Baader, Franz von, 23
Bamberger, Seligmann Bär, 33
Bayerische Israelitische Gemeindezeitung, 31
Beeri, Eliezer, 120
Begin, Menachem, 122
Behemoth (Neumann, F.), 68
Beit-Hallahmi, Benjamin, 88

Index

Ben-David, Arye, 143
Benjamin, Walter, 61, 155
 Adorno, T., influenced by, 61
 financial difficulties of, 48–49
 Institute of Social Research and, 48
 interest in Judaism, 49
 Lowenthal, L., relationship with, 180–181
 as refugee, 51
 response to "The Jews and Europe," 48–51
 Scholem, G., and, 50–51
 suicide of, 180
Ben-Natan, Asher, 220–221
Benziman, Uzi, 121–122
Beratungsstelle für ostjüdische Flüchtlinge (Advisory Board for East European Jewish Refugees), 23
Berg, Alban, 56
Bettelheim, Bruno, 107
Bildung (self-cultivation), 41
Blau-Weiss. *See* Jüdischer Wanderbund Blau-Weiss
Bloch, Ernst, 138–139
B'nai, B'rith, 8, 112
Bredemeier, Harry C., 92
Brown, J. F., 101
Brown, Jeremy, 142
Buber, Martin, 16, 21, 25, 123–124
 Fromm, E., and 126, 131, 173
 Kracauer, S., and, 54
 Lowenthal, L., and, 166
 translation of Book of Genesis, 25–27
Bunzel, Joseph H., 91

Carlebach, Julius, 10
Centralverein deutscher Staatsbürger jüdischen Glaubens (CV), 17
 Lowenthal, L., and, 19
chasidism, 34
Cohen, Arthur A., 120
Cohen, Hermann, 14–15, 30
 Fromm, E., influenced by, 32
 Germanness for, 16
 Lowenthal, L. influenced by, 14–15
 Marburg school and, 14
 rejection of Zionism, 15
Commentary, 92
Committee on Scientific Research, of AJC, 85–87

Communist Party of Germany, 102
Communist Party of Israel, 120
Communist Party of Poland, 39
Contemporary Jewish Record, 68
Coughlin, Charles, 63, 97–98
Craig, Gordon, 105
Critical Theory
 antisemitism and, 44, 201–202
 development of, 1
 fascism and, 75
 Institute of Social Research and, 2
 Jewish messianism and, 141–142, 147
 Jewish origins of, 141, 150–151
 Judaism and, 227–228
 key tenets of, 90
 Marxism and, 65
 origins of, 1–2
 societal insights through, 151
CV. *See* Centralverein deutscher Staatsbürger jüdischen Glaubens

Dämmerung (Horkheimer, Max), 11
Darmstadter, Karl D., 127, 215
Dayan, Moshe, 120
de Grazia, Alfred, 91
Deak, Istvan, 41
Defenders of the Christian Faith, 62–63
democracy, antisemitism and, 69
"The Demonic: Outline of a Negative Philosophy of History" (Lowenthal L.), 22
Department for Scientific Research, 84–87
Der Spiegel, 141–142
Deutscher, Isaac, 117, 149
Dialectic of Enlightenment (Horkheimer, Max and Adorno, T.), 54, 60–61, 74
 antisemitism in, 74–75, 78–79
 "Elements of Anti-Semitism" in, 74–78, 93–94, 193–194
 mimesis in, 77–78
 Prophets of Deceit and, 99
 proposed sequels to, 110
Dialectical Imagination (Jay), 215–216
Diner, Dan, 3, 46
Doctor Faustus (Mann), 104
Dreyfus Affair, 57
Dubiel, Helmut, 1, 27
Duker, Abraham, 188
Dynamics of Prejudice (Bettelheim and Janowitz), 88

Index

Eastern European Jews, 23–24, 67, 112, 182–183
Ebbinghaus, Julius, 137
Eclipse of Reason (Horkheimer, Max), 75–76, 97
  Guterman's role in, 95
Ehrmann, Henry, 211
Einstein, Albert, 16
Eisner, Kurt, 15
Eister, Allan W., 91–92
"Elements of Anti-Semitism." *See Dialectic of Enlightenment*
Escape from Freedom (Fromm, E.), 32
"Essay on Liberation, An" (Marcuse, H.), 115, 119

Fascism. *See also The Authoritarian Personality*
  antisemitism and, 44–45, 58–59, 75
  Critical Theory and, 75
  in "The Jews and Europe," 46–47
  propaganda for, 72–73
  in *Prophets of Deceit*, 97–98
The Fascist Personality, 88. *See also The Authoritarian Personality*
Ferdinand Lassalle Verein, ŻPSD and, 39
Feuchtwanger, Ludwig, 31–32
Flowerman, Samuel H., 86
Frankfurt am Main, 21
  antisemitism in, 55–57
  Horkheimer, Max, and, 132–133
  Jewish communities in, 21
Frankfurt School. *See also* Critical Theory; Institute of Social Research
  academic history of, 1
  internal conflicts within, 150–151
  Marxism and, 41
  relocation to Switzerland, 43–44
Frankfurter Zeitung, 25–26
Freeland, 124
Freeland League, 124–126
Freie Jüdische Lehrhaus
  (Free Jewish House of Learning), 24–25, 54–55
  Fromm, E., and, 24–25
  Kracauer, S., and, 24–25
  Lowenthal, L., and, 24–25
  Rosenzweig, F., and, 24
  Scholem, G., and, 24
  Simon, E., and, 24
Frenkel-Brunswick, Else, 200–201

Freud, Sigmund, 30
  for Lowenthal, L., 30–31
  on origins of antisemitism, 202
Friedenberg, Edgar, 131
Fromm, Erich, 1–3, 13, 20, 32–37
  anti-Zionist stance of, 129
  The Art of Loving, 32, 130–131
  Cohen as influence on, 32
  correspondence with Darmstadter, 127, 215
  early religious background, 32, 129–130
  Escape from Freedom, 32
  Freeland League and, 124–126
  Ginsburg and, 22
  in Institute of Social Research, 35
  on Israel as Jewish state, 123–132
  on Jewish nationalism, 172
  Judaism for, 131
  in KJV, 33–34
  on Nazi antisemitism, 130
  relationship with Horkheimer, Max, 207, 213
  The Sane Society, 32
  in Switzerland, 177
  Talmudic study of, 35–36, 217
  You Shall be as Gods, 36–37
  in Zionist organizations, 32–33
Fromm, Naphtali, 33
Fromm, Seligmann Pinchas, 33
Funke, Hajo, 145

Gay, Peter, 23
General Jewish Workers' Bund, 38
German American Bund, 63
German Nationalist People's Party, 45
Germanness
  for Cohen, H., 16
  Jewishness and, 16
  for Löwenthal, V., 17
Germany. *See also* Frankfurt am Main; Nazi Germany; Weimar Republic
  class culture in, antisemitism as result of, 65
  Communist Party in, 102
  Zionist movements in, German Jewish response to, 16–17
Gesellschaft für jüdische Volksbildung in Frankfurt am Main (Society for Jewish Adult Education in Frankfurt), 33
Ginsburg, Golde. *See* Lowenthal (Ginsburg), Golde

Glazer, Nathan, 92
Goldburg, Robert E., 116
Goldmann, Nahum, 118–119, 126
Graeber, Isacque, 68
"Gregor" (Horkheimer, Max), 10
Grossmann, Henryk, 2–3, 37–40, 65, 156
  early political involvement of, 37–38
  move to Vienna, 39
  in PPSD, 37–38
  in ŻPSD, 37–39
Grünberg, Carl, 2–3, 37, 40
Gumnior, Helmut, 141
Gumpertz, Fritz, 36
Gumperz, Julian, 2–3
Gurland, Arkady, 65, 70, 79
Guterman, Norbert, 94–102.
  See also *Prophets of Deceit*
  academic career, 95
  Eclipse of Reason and, 95
Guttmann, Heinrich, 138

Haaretz, 121
Haereticus (Lowenthal, L.), 27
Heidegger, Martin, 114–115
  antisemitism of, 114, 208–209
  declaration of Nazi support, 114, 209
  relationship with Marcuse, H., 209
Heller, Otto, 46
Herz, Otto, 109
Herzl, Theodor, 138
  Jewish National Fund and, 139
Hildesheimer, Esriel, 20
Hirsch, Katharina von, 47, 58
Holocaust, antisemitism and, 57
Horkheimer, Babette (Lauchheimer), 8
Horkheimer, Max, 1–3, 7–12, 42, 83
  See also *Dialectic of Enlightenment*; "The Jews and Europe"
  in AJC, 199–200
  assessments of antisemitism, 9–12, 44–47
  critique of German refugees, 45
  Dämmerung 11
  early religious background, 7–8
  Eclipse of Reason, 75–76, 95, 97
  "Egoism and the Freedom Movement," 97
  estrangement from family, 9
  exile in Switzerland, 43
  exile in U.S., 12, 44
  fear of postwar antisemitism, 134–135
  in Frankfurt am Main, 132–133
  "Gregor," 10
  as influence on Lowenthal, L., 64, 146–147
  Institute of Social Research and, 2
  interest in Judaism, 133–134, 227
  on Israel, 132–142
  "Jochai," 10
  Marxism for, 10–11, 44
  Nobel and, 162
  Notizen, 136
  Pollock friendship with, 8–9
  Prophets of Deceit and, 95–96
  relationship with Fromm, E., 207, 213
  relationship with Marcuse, H., 207
  return to Germany, 207
  Zeitschrift für Sozialforschung and, 95
  Zionism and, 136–137, 139–141
Horkheimer, Moses, 8–9
Horkheimer, Rose Christine (Riekher), 9
Horovitz, Jakob, 35
Horovitz, Markus, 35
Howe, Irving, 98
Huberman, Bronisław, 56
Hughes, H. Stuart, 117
Husserl, Edmund, 114
Hyman, Herbert H., 93

Ichud, 125
Independent Social Democratic Party of Germany (USPD), 15–16
Institute of Psychoanalysis, Frankfurt am Main, 35
Institute of Social Research, 2–3.
  See also antisemitism project, by Institute of Social Research; *specific members*
  Adorno, T., and, 57–58
  AJC and, 82–84, 197
  antisemitism studies by, 3, 60
  Benjamin, relationship with, 48
  closing of, under Nazi regime, 43
  creation of, 2, 149
  Critical Theory and, 2
  in early days of Nazi Germany, 43
  financial health of, 57–58
  Fromm, E., and, 35
  Grossmann and, 2–3
  Grünberg and, 2–3
  Gumperz and, 2–3
  Gurland and, 65
  Guterman and, 95

Horkheimer, Max, and, 2
Kirchheimer and, 155
Kracauer, S., relationship with, 155
Lowenthal, L., and, 31–32, 52
Marcuse, H., and, 43–44
Massing and, 3
move to Switzerland, 43–44
Neumann, F., and, 155
non-Jewish members of, 42
Pollock and, 2–4
reestablishment of, 135–136
Sternheim and, 48
Studien über Autorität und Familie, 109–110
Weil, F., and, 3
Wittfogel and, 155
internalized antisemitism, 227–228
Israel
Adorno, T., and, 225–226
Critical Theory and, 111–112
Freeland League and, 124–126
Fromm, E., and, 123–132
Horkheimer, Max, and, 132–142
immigration to, 119–120
independence declaration of, 123–124
Lowenthal, L., and, 142–147
Marcuse, H., and, 117–123
members of Frankfurt School and, emotional connection to, 111–112
Six-Day War, 131–132, 138, 143

Jahoda, Marie, 107
James True Associates, 62–63
Janowitz, Morris, 107
Jaspers, Karl, 22
Jay, Martin, 1, 3, 9, 25, 110, 135–136, 213
Dialectical Imagination, 215–216
on Horkheimer, Max, 10–11
Jewish diaspora, 73–74, 146
Jewish Labor Committee (JLC), 78–80
Jewish messianism, 141–142, 147
Jewish National Fund. *See* Keren Kajemeth Leisrael
Jewish Social Democratic Party in Galicia (ŻPSD), 37–39
Jewish Social Studies, 101
Jewish Theological Seminary, 188
Jewishness
Adorno, T., relationship to, 55, 108
Benjamin relationship to, 49

Bildung, relationship to, for German Jews, 41
Fromm, E., relationship to, 32, 131
German Jews, relationship to, 40
Germanness and, 16
Grossmann, relationship to, 175
Horkheimer, Max, relationship to, 8, 52
Lowenthal, L., relationship to, 14, 20, 144–146
Marcuse, H., 112–113, 116–117, 122
Pollock, relationship to, 9, 40–41
in Weimar Republic, 41
"The Jews and Europe" (Horkheimer, Max), 44–47
Adorno, T., response to, 51–52
Benjamin response to, 48–51
as foundation for antisemitism project, 58
Hirsch, response to, 47
Kracauer, S., response to, 48
Lang, response to, 48
Mayer, response to, 48
Scholem, G., response to, 51
Sternheim, response to, 48
JLC. *See* Jewish Labor Committee
"Jochai" (Horkheimer, Max), 10
Jonas, Hans, 208–209
Judaism. *See also* Jewishness; Orthodox Judaism; Reform Judaism
Critical Theory and, 141, 150–151, 227–228
Fromm, E., relationship to, 131
Horkheimer, Max, relationship to, 133–134, 227
messianism and, 141–142, 147
renunciation of, 11
Judaken, Jonathan, 78
Jüdische Gemeinde Frankfurt am Main (Jewish Community of Frankfurt), 133
Jüdische Rundschau, 18
Jüdischer Wanderbund Blau-Weiss (Jewish Hiking Association Blue-White), 18, 34
Jüdisches Wochenblatt, 27
Scholem, S., criticism of, 167
Jurczak, Chester, 100

Karpf, Maurice, 136
Karplus, Margarete. *See* Adorno, Margarete (Karplus)
Kartell jüdischer Verbindungen (KJV), 16–19, 33–34
Kātz, Barry, 113–114

Keren Hajessod Vereinigte Israel Aktion (Foundation Fund – United Israel Action), 139
Keren Kajemeth Leisrael (Jewish National Fund), 139–140
Kinkel, Walter, 14–15
Kirchheimer, Otto, 71–72, 155
KJV. *See* Kartell jüdischer Verbindungen
Knights of the White Camellia, 62–63
Koelbl, Herlinde, 146
Korsch, Karl, 41
Kosygin, Aleksei N., 115
Kracauer, Isidor, 166
Kracauer, Siegfried, 21, 25, 155, 166
   Adorno, T., and, 54–55
   Buber and, 54
   critique of Buber/Rosenzweig translation, 25–27
   at Freie Jüdische Lehrhaus, 54–55
   Horkheimer, Max, and, 31
   on "The Jews and Europe," 48
   Lowenthal, L., and, 25–27, 30
   Nobel and, 54
   Rosenzweig, F., and, 54
   in U.S., 85
Krause, Ludwig, 35
Krenek, Ernst, 56
Kuhn, Rick, 39

labor study, of antisemitism, 78–82, 194–195
   publishing strategy for, 196–197
Landauer, Gustav, 15
Lang, Olga, 48
Laski, Harold, 63–64
Lassalle, Ferdinand, 30
Lasswell, Harold, 102
Lazarsfeld, Paul, 81–82
League of National German Jews, 45
Lee, Alfred McClung, 100–101
"Die Lehren von China" (Lowenthal, L.), 27–28
Lehrer, Leibush, 101
Lehrhaus. *See* Freie Jüdische Lehrhaus
Lerner, Michael, 116–117, 211
Leviné, Eugen, 174
Levinson, Daniel J., 200–201
Levy, Harry, 27
Lewis, Theodore N., 116
liberalism, antisemitism and, 60, 75
Lichtheim, George, 52

Lind, Robert, 68–69
Löwenthal, Golde (Ginsburg), 22–23, 27
   Fromm, E., and, 22
   in *Jüdisches Wochenblatt*, 27
   marriage to Lowenthal, L., 22–23
   Reichmann, F., and, 29
Löwenthal, Mendel, 12
Löwenthal, Rosie, 163
Löwenthal, Victor, 12–13, 24, 113
   Germanness of, 17
   rejection of Zionism, 19
   response to son's marriage, 22–23
Löwith, Karl, 208–209
Löwy, Michael, 147
Lowenthal, Leo, .2–3, 7, 12–14, 70
   See also Prophets of Deceit
   academic influences on, 14–15
   on antisemitism, 14, 31, 63, 74
   Aschheim and, 176
   on Benjamin, 180–181
   Buber and, 166
   Cohen as influence on, 14–15
   CV and, 19
   "The Demonic: Outline of a Negative Philosophy of History," 22
   early religious background, 12–13
   at Freie Jüdische Lehrhaus, 24–25
   on Freud, 30–31
   Horkheimer, Max, as influence on, 64, 146–147
   Institute of Social Research and, 31–32, 52
   Israel and, 142–147
   on Jewishness for Adorno, T., 109
   in KJV, 16–19
   "Die Lehren von China," 27–28
   marriage to Ginsburg, 22–23
   on Marx, 30
   move from Orthodox Judaism, 30
   Nobel as influence on, 20–21
   relationship with Reichmann, F., 29
   relationship with Rosenzweig, F., 25
   on U.S. antisemitism, 63, 191–192
   in USPD, 15–16
Lukács, Georg, 41
Lustiger, Arno, 138
Luxemburg, Rosa, 149–150
Lynd, Robert, 68–69

MacIver, Robert, 70
Magnes, Judah, 123–124

Maimon, Salomon, 30
Malik, Charles, 126
Mann, Thomas, 104–105
Marburg school, 14
Marcus, Judith, 37
Marcuse, Carl, 112–113
Marcuse, Gertrud (Kreslowsky), 112–113
Marcuse, Herbert, 1, 64, 113–115, 155
   antisemitism towards, 113–115
   censure of, 115–116
   critique of Israeli policies, 118–119
   early religious background, 112
   Essay on Liberation, An, 119
   on function of antisemitism, 69
   in Israel, 119–121, 213
   on Israel as Jewish state, 119–121
   Jewishness for, 112–113, 116–117, 122
   move to Switzerland, 43–44
   on nature of antisemitism, 209–210
   One-Dimensional Man, 119
   relationship with Heidegger, 209
   relationship with Horkheimer, Max, 207
   Scholem, G., and, 115
   secularism of, 117
   Zionism, attitude towards, 117–123
Marcuse, Peter, 112, 117
Marx, Karl, 30, 51–52, 149–150
Marxism
   Critical Theory and, 65
   Frankfurt School and, 41
   for Horkheimer, Max, 10–11, 44
Marxistische Arbeitswoche (Marxist Work Week), 47
Massing, Paul, .3, 65, 70–71, 102–107
   See also Rehearsal for Destruction. A Study of Political Anti-Semitism in Imperial Germany
   in Communist Party of Germany, 102
   in concentration camp, 103
Mayer, Hans, 48
McGovern, George, 127
McWilliams, Carey, 100
McWilliams, Joseph E., 97–98
Mead, Margaret, 84
Mendelssohn, Moses, 30
Mendes-Flohr, Paul, 229
Merriam, Charles, 58
Merton, Robert, 84
mimesis
   antisemitism and, 77–78
   in *Prophets of Deceit*, 99

Minima Moralia (Adorno, T.), 108
Mosse, George, 41
Myrdal, Gunnar, 85

National Socialism. *See* Nazism
National Union for Social Justice, 62–63
Natorp, Paul, 14–15
Naumann, Max, 45
Nazism, 44–47
   antisemitism and, 59, 65
   Heidegger support of, 114, 209
   Reichsjugend movement and, 56
   underestimation of threat, by German Jews, 43
Neumann, Franz, 59, 67–68, 70, 117, 155, 184
   Behemoth, 68
Neumann, Yeshi, 211
New York Times, 100, 104–105
Nobel, Nehemiah Anton, 20–21
   Buber and, 21
   as conservative rabbi, 161
   Fromm, E., and, 20, 32
   Horkheimer, Max, and, 162
   Kracauer, S., and, 21, 54
   Lowenthal, L., and, 20
   Rosenzweig, F., and, 21
   Simon, E., and, 21
   Zionism for, 20
nomadism, antisemitism and, 66
non-Jewish Jews, 117, 150
non-totalitarian antisemitism, 70

Office of Strategic Services (OSS), 187
"On the Jewish Question" (Marx), 51–52
One-Dimensional Man (Marcuse, H.), 119
Orthodox Judaism, 30
Oz, Amoz, 120

Petuchowski, Jakob J., 130–131
Phelps, George Allison, 97–98
Piani, Janguido, 122
Polish Social Democratic Party (PPSD), 37–38
political antisemitism, 71
Political Science Quarterly, 105–106
Pollock, Friedrich, 2–3, 40–41, 139
   friendship with Horkheimer, M., 8–9
   indifference towards Judaism, 9
   on Jewishness, 40–41
Portraits of German Jewish Intellectual History (Koch), 41–42

Postęp (Progress), 37
PPSD. *See* Polish Social Democratic Party
Princeton Radio Research Project, 57
Prophets of Deceit (Lowenthal, L. and
    Guterman), 94–102
  Adorno, T., and, 96, 100–102
  Brown, review of, 101
  Dialectic of Enlightenment and, 99
  fascist agitation as subject in, 97–98
  Friedman (*American Jewish Historical
    Quarterly*), review of, 101
  Horkheimer, Max, involvement in,
    95–96
  introduction in, 96–97
  Jews as subject in, 98–99
  Jurczak, review of, 100
  Lasswell, review of, 102
  Lee, review of, 100–101
  Lehrer, review of, 101
  McWilliams, C., review of, 100
  mimesis in, 99
  Nadell (*Sociology and Social Research*),
    review of, 101–102
  responses to early drafts, 95–96
  source material for, 97–98
  Wrong, review of, 101
Proskauer, Joseph M., 190
*The Psychological Technique of Martin
    Luther Thomas' Radio Addresses*
    (Adorno, T.), 97
Public Opinion Quarterly, 100–101, 105

Rabinbach, Anson, 3, 60–61
Rabinkow, Salman Baruch, 36, 124
rationality, antisemitism and, 71, 75–76
Redemption and Utopia (Löwy), 147
Reform Judaism, development of, 34
*Rehearsal for Destruction. A Study of
    Political Anti-Semitism in Imperial
    Germany* (Massing), 103–107
  Craig, review of, 105
  forward to (Horkheimer, Max and
    T. Adorno), 106
  historical focus of, 103–104
  Landheer (*American Sociological
    Review*), review of, 105
  Mann, review of, 104
  Nadell (*Sociology and Social Research*),
    review of, 105
  Shanahan, review of, 106
  Sontag, review of, 105–106

  study of antisemitism in, 103–104
  Usher, review of, 105
Reichmann, Adolph, 28
Reichmann, Eva, 133
Reichmann, Frieda, 27–30
  Fromm, E., and, 29–30, 32–33
  Judaism of, 29
  Kracauer, S., and, 169
  Lowenthal family and, 29
  psychoanalytic technique of, 169–170
  Simon, E., and, 29
Reichsjugend movement, 56
Rengstorf, Karl Heinrich, 138–139
Rensmann, Lars, 3
The Review of Politics, 106
Richter, Hans, 85
Riekher, Rose Christine. *See* Horkheimer,
    Rose Christine (Riekher)
Riezler, Kurt, 114
Roman Catholicism, Jews converting to, 11
Rosen, Zvi, 9
Rosenblum, David, 68–69
Rosenzweig, Adele, 163
Rosenzweig, Franz, 20–21, 55
  Buber and, 25
  Freie Jüdische Lehrhaus and, 24–25
  Fromm, E., and, 33–34
  Kracauer, S., and, 25–26, 54
  Lowenthal, L., and, 25
  Salzberger and, 32–33
  Star of Redemption, 55
  translation of Book of Genesis, 25–27
Rosenzweig, Georg, 20

Sadat, Anwar, 122
Salzberger, Georg, 32–33
The Sane Society (Fromm, E.), 32
Sanford, R. Nevitt, 200–201
Savio, Mario, 211
Schaff, Adam, 131–132
Schmidt, James, 100
Scholem, Arthur, 20
Scholem, Betty, 163
Scholem, Gershom, 13, 17, 20, 28, 31, 42,
    150
  Adorno, T., and, 52, 225–226
  Benjamin and, 50–51
  Fromm, E., and, 24–25, 29–30
  Horkheimer, Max, and, 50–51
  "The Jews and Europe," reaction
    to, 51

Index

Lichtheim, criticized by, 52
Lowenthal, L., and, 29–30
Marcuse, H., and, 115
Simon, E., and, 21, 30
Schwarzkopf, Chetwood T., 115
Schwarzschild, Steven S., 131
SDS. *See* Sozialististischer Deutscher Studentenbund
self-cultivation. *See* Bildung
Shanahan, William O., 106
Sheatsley, Paul B., 93
Sherman, Charles B., 79
Sherover, Erica, 211
Silver Legion, 62–63
Simmel, Ernst, 72, 123
Simon, Ernst, 14, 21, 27, 29–30, 143, 159
Simon, Toni (Rapaport), 169
Simonsohn, Berthold, 138–139
Six-Day War, 131–132, 138, 143
Slawson, John, 87, 136, 199–200, 203
Smith, Gerald L. K., 97–98
Sneh, Moshe, 120
Social Democratic Party of Germany (SPD), 15
Sociology and Social Research, 101–102, 105
Sontag, Raymond J., 105–106
Der sotsial-demokrat, 39
Sozialististischer Deutscher Studentenbund (SDS) (Association of German Socialist Students), 117, 220–221
SPD. *See* Socialist Democratic Party of Germany
spearhead theory, of antisemitism, 69
Spier, Selmar, 171
Star of Redemption (Rosenzweig, F.), 55
state capitalism, 45–46
Steinberg, Isaac Nachman, 124–126
Sternheim, Andries, 48
Street Journal, 118–119
Students for a Democratic Society, 117
Studien über Autorität und Familie (Horkheimer, Max, Fromm, E., Marcuse, H., et al.), 109–110
Stuttgarter Neues Tageblatt, 56

Talmud, 35–36, 217
Tar, Zoltán, 37
"Theses on the Philosophy of History" (Benjamin), 61
Thomas, Norman, 126
Tiedemann, Rolf, 60
Torah-peuticum, 34–35
totalitarian antisemitism, 70, 106–107

United Israel Action, 139
United States (U.S.). *See also* American Jewish Committee
 antisemitism in, 62–64, 78–82
 exile to, for members of Institute of Social Research, 12, 44
 labor study, of antisemitism in, 78–82, 194–195
 Lowenthal, L., on antisemitism in, 63, 191–192
University of Frankfurt, 2.
 See also Frankfurt School
Usher, Roland, 105
USPD. *See* Independent Socialist Democratic Party

Van Leer Foundation, 119–120, 143
Vienna, 39
 Grossmann in, 39
 Huberman lauded in, 56

Wagner, Richard, 53–54
Waldman, Morris, 203
Weber, Max, 15
Weil, Felix J., 2, 13, 31, 41, 47, 82, 154
Weil, Hermann, 2, 154
Weimar Republic
 antisemitism in, 9–12
 Communism among Jews in, 19
 Jewishness in, 41
 Marxism in, 41
 Zionism in, 16–19
Wheatland, Thomas, 1, 187
Wiesengrund, Maria (Adorno), 54
Wiesengrund, Oscar, 24, 54, 59, 113
Wiggerhaus, Rolf, 1
Wittfogel, Karl August, 3, 48, 155–156
WIZO. *See* Women's International Zionist Organization
Wolff, Georg, 141
Wolin, Richard, 109–110
Women's International Zionist Organization (WIZO), 139
Wrong, Dennis, 101

Yiddish Scientific Institute (YIVO), 225–226
You Shall be as Gods (Fromm, E.), 36–37
Younker, Ira M., 87

Zedtwitz, Joachim von, 228
Zeitschrift für Sozialforschung, 95, 97
Zionism. *See also* Israel
  Fromm, E., and, 32–33, 129
  Horkheimer, Max, and, 136–137, 139–141
  Lowenthal, L., and, 15–19
  Marcuse, H., and, 117–123
  Nobel and, 20
  rejection of, by Cohen, H., 15
  rejection of, by Lowenthal, V., 19
  WIZO, 139
Zionist movements. *See also* Israel
  German Jewish response to, 16–17
  in Weimar Republic, 16–19
  WIZO, 139
ŻPSD. *See* Jewish Social Democratic Party in Galicia

Printed in Great Britain
by Amazon